Understanding and Treating

Dissociative Identity Disorder

RELATIONAL PERSPECTIVES BOOK SERIES

Volume 49

RELATIONAL PERSPECTIVES BOOK SERIES

LEWIS ARON & ADRIENNE HARRIS
Series Editors

The Relational Perspectives Book Series (RPBS) publishes books that grow out of or contribute to the relational tradition in contemporary psychoanalysis. The term "relational psychoanalysis" was first used by Greenberg and Mitchell (1983) to bridge the traditions of interpersonal relations, as developed within interpersonal psychoanalysis and object relations, as developed within contemporary British theory. But, under the seminal work of the late Stephen Mitchell, the term "relational psychoanalysis" grew and began to accrue to itself many other influences and developments. Various tributaries—interpersonal psychoanalysis, object relations theory, self psychology, empirical infancy research, and elements of contemporary Freudian and Kleinian thought—flow into this tradition, which understands relational configurations between self and others, both real and fantasied, as the primary subject of psychoanalytic investigation.

We refer to the relational tradition, rather than to a relational school, to highlight that we are identifying a trend, a tendency within contemporary psychoanalysis, not a more formally organized or coherent school or system of beliefs. Our use of the term 'relational' signifies a dimension of theory and practice that has become salient across the wide spectrum of contemporary psychoanalysis. Now under the editorial supervision of Lewis Aron and Adrienne Harris, the Relational Perspectives Book Series originated in 1990 under the editorial eye of the late Stephen A. Mitchell. Mitchell was the most prolific and influential of the originators of the relational tradition. He was committed to dialogue among psychoanalysts and he abhorred the authoritarianism that dictated adherence to a rigid set of beliefs or technical restrictions. He championed open discussion, comparative and integrative approaches, and he promoted new voices across the generations.

Included in the Relational Perspectives Book Series are authors and works that come from within the relational tradition, extend and develop the tradition, as well as works that critique relational approaches or compare and contrast it with alternative points of view. The series includes our most distinguished senior psychoanalysts along with younger contributors who bring fresh vision.

RELATIONAL PERSPECTIVES BOOK SERIES

LEWIS ARON & ADRIENNE HARRIS
Series Editors

RELATIONAL PERSPECTIVES BOOK SERIES

LEWIS ARON & ADRIENNE HARRIS
Series Editors

Understanding and Treating
Dissociative
Identity Disorder

A Relational Approach

Elizabeth F. Howell

Routledge
Taylor & Francis Group
New York   London

Routledge
Taylor & Francis Group
711 Third Avenue
New York, NY 10017

Routledge
Taylor & Francis Group
27 Church Road
Hove, East Sussex BN3 2FA

© 2011 by Taylor and Francis Group, LLC
Routledge is an imprint of Taylor & Francis Group, an Informa business

Printed in the United States of America on acid-free paper

International Standard Book Number: 978-0-415-99496-5 (Hardback) 978-0-415-99497-2 (Paperback)

Library of Congress Cataloging-in-Publication Data

Howell, Elizabeth F., 1946-
    Understanding and treating dissociative identity disorder : a relational
approach / Elizabeth Howell.
        p. cm. -- (Relational perspectives ; 49)
    ISBN 978-0-415-99496-5 (hardcover : alk. paper) -- ISBN 978-0-415-99497-2
(pbk. : alk. paper) -- ISBN 978-0-203-88826-1 (e-book)
    1. Dissociative disorders--Diagnosis. 2. Dissociative disorders--Treatment. 3.
Dissociation (Psychology) I. Title.

RC553.D5H693 2011
616.85'23--dc22   2010041387

Visit the Taylor & Francis Web site at
http://www.taylorandfrancis.com

and the Routledge Web site at
http://www.routledgementalhealth.com

With gratitude to my patients for their generous permission to share about their lives and treatment and for what they have taught me.

Contents

A Personal Note

If this book were a piece of music, the hauntingly beautiful, melancholy, and soul-searing thematic melody to Tchaikovsky's 1876 ballet, *Swan Lake*, might be its preface. When I recently watched a performance of this ballet, it suddenly dawned on me that the premise of the folk myth the ballet dramatizes is child sexual abuse: An evil predator has captured young maidens and turned them into swans. The melody evokes the isolation from humanity and the longing for human form and human interaction as well as the horror of being trapped in one's deprivation and pain. This is what child abuse does: It deprives people of their human birthright to exist comfortably in their bodies, in their minds, and in interaction with other humans.

It is not possible to help people with dissociative identity disorder (DID) to improve their lives significantly without acknowledging in the deepest way the horrors of child abuse. The majority of persons suffering from the extremes of bouncing from one reality to another, often without control and often without knowing it, come by this affliction as a result of early, prolonged, and repeated child sexual abuse, usually at the hands of someone who is supposed to love them and has the role of a protector. And, many who have severe posttraumatic stress disorder (PTSD) and dissociative problems that do not rise to the level of DID have suffered this same kind of abuse that betrays their trust and fractures their ability to orient in the world.

This topic is especially meaningful to me since I have a brother and a sister whose early deaths were indirect results of child sexual abuse. My brother, Kit, who died of lung cancer at age 43, was an endearingly pretty boy who was abused by a school teacher, a man much admired on the faculty. My sister, Gwynneth, died at age 57 from an autoimmune disorder and other complications. She was abused throughout her adolescence by our father. I was lucky enough to have certain family dynamics in my favor that protected me from overt sexual abuse. But, I had to watch it happening to my sister and could do nothing about it.

Preface

One of my patients told me that for as long as she could remember, she had always used "the 'we' of me" when referring to herself in her own mind. She never really thought much about what this meant; it was just one of those things. As far as she remembers, she did not hear voices as a child or overtly switch identity states (to her knowledge or to the observation of others). Even though she did derive substantial benefit from several decades of psychotherapy, she still did not know that she had dissociated identities. All she knew was that she had struggled for many years to overcome an extraordinarily difficult childhood. When her dissociated identities began to emerge in psychotherapy with me, her conscious life transformed. Although in many ways profoundly more painful, her world was now much richer, even if more complicated, with so many "people" in it who had much to say to her, to each other, and to me. The phrase she had always used to describe herself—"the 'we' of me"—now made sense.

This is the case with many who are dealing with dissociative identity disorder (DID). They have lived confusing, often crisis-ridden, terrifying, and quite routinely painful—even if sometimes outwardly successful—lives. Frequently, they had no idea of what was really the matter with them until some revelatory crisis took place. Some, for example, have broken down when their own child or a young relative reached the age at which they had been abused. This triggering event caused them to be flooded with unbearable memories that had been previously dissociated. One such person, before her breakdown, would openly speak without affect of how her brother-in-law had continuously raped her as a child. She proudly thought she was strong to have withstood such duress. It is true that she, or at least her defenses, *were* strong up to a point—the point at which her biological child became the age at which her own brutal childhood abuse began. For other people, the trigger for breakdown is different. Those who have used addictions to quell and mask unbearable feelings of horror and pain, terrifying memories, and internal voices may find that achieving sobriety unleashes the voices, the nightmares, and the undeniable presence of the dissociated parts of themselves. If they are lucky enough to be in therapy with someone who can recognize these shifts, the dissociated parts can be welcomed into the treatment.

One highly dissociative patient of mine vigorously debunked the idea of DID and spent a good deal of time talking around his pain until a crisis plunged him into such despair that when he called me, it was undeniable for both of us that a dissociated part of him I had never met before was present. At that point, I was able to address that dissociated part of him, and from then on, we could talk much more openly. It was a "terrible" relief for him: His biggest fear had come true, but at least he no longer had to fear it. Now, the others who had been there all along had a chance to become known.

In my experience as a DID therapist and a frequent consultant to therapists with dissociative patients, it makes all the difference in the life of a person with DID to have a therapist who can recognize their dissociated parts and work with them. Unfortunately, there are many patients with DID who have sought therapy and, although somewhat improved, were nonetheless left feeling hollow in comparison to what could have been or what did occur later when they were able to get the proper treatment.

What, then, are the obstacles to being understood that face people who have severe dissociative disorders who are receiving help from the mental health profession? One of the obstacles is the paucity of accurate professional, as well as public, knowledge about DID. Ironically, the personality organization of highly dissociative individuals mirrors the dissociative organization of our culture.

Our culture has dissociated dissociativity. Profound aggressor/victim themes and psychodynamics, along with narcissistic, sadistic, or psychopathic coloring, run deep in our culture while simultaneously being denied. Victims are often blamed and shamed. One of the most shaming aspects of DID may be that this extremely painful and disorganizing problem of living is so often viewed as not existing. Until recently, abnormal psychology and psychiatric textbooks routinely informed their readers that multiple personality disorder (MPD), now termed DID, is an extremely rare presentation, if it exists at all. The existence of dissociative parts is often disbelieved, and therapists who listen to these aspects of their clients are often accused of reifying (i.e., making real something that is not) a delusional multiplicity.

The pervasiveness of professional resistance to the acknowledgment of DID is sometimes remarkable. To illustrate, I was recently told by two different colleagues of two almost identical series of events having to do with the hospitalization in two different hospitals of two different patients with DID: Both patients were hospitalized for suicidal behavior, and both had told the hospital staff that they had DID. In both cases, the hospital staff immediately contradicted the patients, telling them that they did not have DID because it does not exist. In one case, the therapist was pointedly informed by the attending doctor that DID does not exist because he had never seen it. Then, something changed: In both cases, the patients began to floridly switch, demonstrably proving the existence of DID to the staffs and supporting proper diagnosis of the patients. In one case, the patient (who was educated about her condition) was able to instruct some of the staff about DID and its symptomatology. As a result, staff members were able to recognize and understand her switches when they occurred. However, the continued similarity in the trajectory of events for the two patients was rather chilling. Having finally understood that DID exists and that its symptoms can be witnessed, the administration and staff next requested of these vulnerable, suicidal patients that they consent to being filmed. Fortunately, both patients refused.

Despite the frequent denial of the existence of DID, current epidemiological research sets the prevalence of DID at 1.1% to 3% of the general population (International Society for the Study of Trauma and Dissociation [ISST-D], in press). This puts the prevalence of DID as at least equal to or higher than schizophrenia, which is at about 0.5% to 1.5% (American Psychiatric Association, 2000, p. 308). According to Foote and Park (2008), "A fair amount of data suggests that DID is encountered worldwide and may not be rarer than schizophrenia" (p. 221). A recent large scale study of a representative sample of 628 women in Turkey by Sar, Akyuz, and Dogan (2006) found that 18.3 had a lifetime diagnosis of a dissociative disorder. Of these, 8.3% had DDNOS and 1.1 had DID.

Prevalence among patient populations is even higher. Foote, Smolin, Kaplan, Legatt, and Lipschitz (2006) found that 29% of an outpatient group had a dissociative disorder. Of these 10% had dissociative amnesia, 9% had Dissociative Disorder Not Otherwise Specified (DDNOS), 6% had Dissociative Identity Disorder (DID), and 5% had depersonalization disorder. Interestingly, only 5% of this group of 82 patients had a dissociative diagnosis recorded in their charts. Brand, Classen, Lanius, Loewenstein, McNary, Pain, and Putnam (2009), collapsing the results of many studies, report prevalence rates of dissociative disorders among outpatients that range from 12 to 38%. Sar, Koyuncu, Ozturk, Yargic, Kundakci, Yazici, et al. (2007) found that 37.9% of patients presenting to the psychiatric emergency room had a dissociative disorder.

DID is usually the outcome of chronic and severe childhood trauma, which can include physical and sexual abuse, extreme and recurrent terror, repeated medical trauma, and extreme neglect. Pathological dissociation generally results from being psychically overwhelmed by trauma. In a recent study, Brand, Classen, Lanius et al. (2009) found that 86% of their sample of patients with dissociative disorders reported having suffered childhood sexual abuse and 79% reported physical abuse. However, the traumatic experiences that may result in dissociative disorders do not always stem from sexual, physical, or emotional abuse. Disorganized attachment which often underlies the dissociative structure of dissociative disorders (discussed more fully in Chapter 5) may result from overwhelming experiences in the infant's interpersonal environment that are not caused by parental maltreatment. Parental illness, depression, or problematic attachment styles may be psychically overwhelming and lead to disorganized attachment. In addition, medical trauma may be dissociogenic. For example, some dissociative patients have reported histories of chronic medical problems and hospitalizations that involved severe pain and unavoidable separations from well-meaning parents. Medical trauma may involve both the chronic and severe pain of certain diseases and conditions as well as painful procedures intended to remediate these medical conditions. Some dissociative adult patients have reported the trauma of being left alone to suffer their pain as children in the hospital. Such children may be additionally confused by the fact that their parents are either hurting them, as part of necessary medical interventions or allowing others to hurt them (Na'ama Yehuda, personal communication, 2010).

Despite the fact that child abuse is frighteningly common and that stories about the abduction and sadistic sexual torture of little children are often in the news, the denial of child abuse remains rampant in our society. Estimates of prevalence of contact (i.e., physical rather than verbal) sexual abuse of girls below the age of 18 average at about 25%. One study (Amodeo, Griffin, Fassler, Clay, & Ellis, 2006) placed the prevalence rate of child sexual abuse at 27.9%. A Canadian study (Hébert, Tourigny, Cyr, McDuff, & Joly, 2009) revealed a prevalence rate of 22.1% for women and 9.7% for men. Another large study, encompassing over 15,000 interviews with young adults (Hussey, Chang, & Kotch, 2006), found that 28.4% of the respondents reported experiencing physical assault from a parent or adult caregiver, and 4.5% reported contact sexual abuse perpetrated by a parent or adult caregiver before the beginning of the sixth grade. These numbers are consistent with those of earlier reports on abuse prevalence. A study of 900 women (Russell, 1986) found a rate of 38%, and Gartner (1999) estimated a sexual abuse rate of approximately 17% for boys.

Attitudes about dissociative disorders seem to be highly connected to both knowing and not knowing about child sexual abuse. Of course, perpetrators want to remain hidden. And understandably, most of us would rather avoid identifying with either the perpetrator or the victim. To acknowledge that this kind of trauma could happen to us or to those we love can be utterly terrifying. For many, denying the existence of such abuse reduces the anxiety of dealing with the reality that it does exist.

DID is a prototype for the dissociative structure of the mind. I am in agreement with Bromberg (1998, 2006) that this mental structure characterizes us all. Taking into account the inevitability of trauma, especially relational trauma, and the fact that dissociation is a common aspect of trauma, how could it be otherwise? Many of today's clinicians are increasingly appreciative of a multiple-self view of the personality and the dissociative structure of the human mind. From this perspective, none of us is a singular unit, but rather a highly organized aggregation of self-states that are internally dissociated to varying degrees and in varying ways. In this way, work with people with DID ("multiples") may serve to inform us of new approaches for providing "good psychotherapy" for people who are not multiples.

Acknowledgments

I am immensely grateful for the help and contributions to this book of generous friends and colleagues. First of all, thanks to Cheryl Seaman, an artist as well as specialist in DID, for her evocative and on-target book cover illustration. Special thanks to Marg Hainer and Na'ama Yehuda, who independently spent hours on hours reading over and making suggestions for many of the chapters, including different versions of the same chapters. I am grateful to Rich Chefetz and the Shielagh Shusta-Hochberg for their generosity in carefully reading and fully and helpfully commenting on several major chapters. Many thanks to Giovanni Liotti, who carefully read and commented on Chapter 5. Deep appreciation is given to John O'Neil for his reading of Chapter 2 and his many astute observations and to Kelly Forrest for her reading of and comments on the attachment chapter and for her sharing with me access to her own work. I wish to give special thanks to my daughter Alicia Murray, a psychiatrist, for her extremely helpful—and last minute—reading of an earlier version of the chapter on neuroscience. My gratitude is extended to Bethany Brand for her reading and comments on the chapter on diagnostic assessment and access to her work, to Karen Hopenwasser for her helpful reading and comments on the section on dissociative attunements, to Sheldon Itzkowitz for his reading of and suggestions about Chapter 10, and to Cleonie White for her helpful comments on the neuroscience chapter. (Of course, any mistakes are mine.) Very importantly, I want to thank Philip Bromberg for the theoretical inspiration that he has continuously given. I also want to express my appreciation to Richard Kluft for the pioneering work he has done in the field of dissociative disorders giving to the mental health world conceptual and technical tools for understanding and treating dissociative disorders.

I cannot say enough to thank my editor, Lewis Aron, for his astute reading and suggestions for the book and his encouragement. He has a wonderful eye for spotting what needs to be clarified, what is missing, and what kinds of reorganizations might be helpful. I also want to express my appreciation to Kristopher Spring, editor, and Marsha Hecht, project editor, for their capable help and support.

Finally, I want to thank my fiancé, Patrick Flanagan, for the many, many tireless, but really, tiring hours he spent copyediting and for helpful comments about organization and style. I also thank him for making room in his life in the last year for this book, along with me.

The generosity of all of these people is a wonderful gift.

Introduction

Despite the significant prevalence of dissociative disorders—rates ranging from 12–38% for dissociative disorders in outpatients (Brand, Classen, Lanius, et al., 2009), as high as 18% for dissociative disorders in the general population (Sar, et al., 2006), and a prevalence rate of 1.1—3% for DID in the general population (ISST-D Guidelines, in press), professional education has not usually included training in the treatment of dissociative disorders. Because of this paucity of training, clinicians are often at a loss regarding how to recognize, diagnose, and work with their highly dissociative patients. All too frequently, when clinicians do recognize that a patient has a serious dissociative disorder, they fear that they will be unable to acquire the skills necessary to treat dissociation and that they must refer their patient elsewhere. A therapeutic relationship may thus be unnecessarily broken.

Working with highly dissociative patients, however, is not necessarily as daunting as it might first seem. Although the conceptual language about the organization of dissociated self-states and knowledge about working with these dissociated self-states need to be learned, it is not difficult to do so. This knowledge transcends theoretical orientation, adding to the clinician's understanding of the human mind. Once therapists have worked with their first correctly diagnosed DID patient, the picture can become much clearer. Prior to having the nature of their problems understood, highly dissociative patients may simply seem to be extremely "difficult" patients, persons who are full of contradictions, unexplainable extremes of emotions, and inclinations to self-destruction. Yet, when it becomes apparent that the contradictory statements, extreme emotional states, and self-destructive behaviors are coming from different dissociated parts of the person, the overall presentation becomes less confusing and the prognosis far more hopeful.

A recent naturalistic study of the reports of 280 patients with dissociative disorders and their therapists indicates that the prognosis for people with dissociative disorders—when treated by a clinician who is knowledgeable about such treatment—is good. Patients in the later stages of treatment engage in less self-injury and have fewer hospitalizations; they report less distress and lower posttraumatic and dissociative symptoms; and their functioning is more adaptive overall than in those patients who are in initial stages of treatment (Brand et al., 2009). Although clearly it is challenging, work with highly dissociative patients is also some of the most rewarding psychotherapeutic work that one can do. Although treating DID does require specialized knowledge, this knowledge becomes general knowledge useful in understanding almost every patient a clinician sees—"the dissociative mind" is increasingly understood to characterize us all.

DID IS FREQUENTLY MISDIAGNOSED AS SOMETHING ELSE

Because DID has erroneously been thought to be rare (because highly dissociative people tend to present polysymptomatically and because the disorder is so often hidden), assessing and treating clinicians have often missed the diagnosis. As a result, patients have often been given other diagnoses that remain in their charts while the underlying highly dissociative structure of their personality continues to be missed. Research has showed that people with DID spend from 5 to nearly 12 years in the mental health system before receiving a correct diagnosis (as cited in ISST-D, in press). People with DID have often been previously misdiagnosed as schizophrenic, schizoaffective, bipolar, or borderline. Many never recover from the effects of these misdiagnoses. What is worse, their real issue—DID—is less likely to be addressed, with the result that they may never receive the treatment they need. Instead, patients often have received inappropriate medications, and they may have received unnecessary electroconvulsive shock therapy.

DID IS OFTEN HIDDEN

Although it is not rare, DID is often hidden. In contrast to the flamboyant and dramatic switches portrayed by Sally Field in the movie *Sybil* (Petrie, 1976), switches of identity states can often be subtle or even invisible to an observer. Kluft (2009) observed that only about 6% of those with DID exhibit obvious switching in an ongoing way. Another reason for DID to have been thought to rare is that, to the extent that they are aware of their extreme dissociativity, many highly dissociative people work to hide it. Often, they are afraid that they will be considered crazy and will be put away if they are found out. Simply put, it is not socially adaptive to show one's fragmented personality. In addition, many with DID are not aware of this fragmentation. All they know is that their lives are chaotic and hard to manage: They may often be overwhelmed by intense affects like terror, black despair, or fury that seem to come out of nowhere; they may lose huge chunks of time and not know what they did or thought; they may be unaware of their behavior and therefore be unable to explain it to others; they may find themselves in strange places with no explanation of how they got there. Although as adults they look like grown-ups, when switched into a child identity they often feel like and can appear like helpless children (e.g., speaking in a childlike voice) and may be unable to negotiate important interpersonal matters with others. Their fragmentation may not be recognized until attentive emotional intimacy with another human being, often a therapist, allows it to be known.

WHAT IS DID?

The person with DID essentially lives with various simultaneously active and subjectively autonomous strands of experience that are rigidly and profoundly separated from each other in important ways, such as in memory, characteristic affects, behavior, self-image, body image, and thinking styles. These different segments of experiencing have their own sense of separate identity—their own sense of an "I"—including a sense of personal autobiographical memory; they may have different names. Putnam (1989) described these different identities as "highly discrete states of consciousness organized around a prevailing affect, sense of self (including body image), with a limited repertoire of behaviors and a set of state dependent memories" (p. 103). This division of the self into different dissociated subjectivities puts people with DID at a loss regarding how to understand or explain their experience, and it often makes their lives difficult to manage.

The term *dissociative identity disorder,* currently used in the *Diagnostic and Statistical Manual of Mental Disorders, Fourth Edition* (*DSM-IV*; American Psychiatric Association [APA], 1994) and its text revision (*DSM-IV-TR*; APA, 2000), is an improvement over the previous term *multiple personality disorder* (MPD), which was used in the third edition (*DSM-III*; APA, 1980). MPD was, as a term, misleading in its suggestion that there were literally separate personalities, rather than interrelated though differentially dissociated parts with separate subjectivities that are all facets of one person. The dissociative parts are not separate persons—they are part of one person. Even though individuals with DID may experience their dissociated identities as different persons, even as having separate bodies, it is important that clinicians (while understanding and empathizing with their patients' subjective reality) not reify a delusional sense of separateness but help the patient understand that dissociated identities are all part of who they are.

The extent to which these separate strands of experience (involving a sense of self-in-relationship, certain dominant affects, a sense of history, subjectivity, and relative sovereignty) are linked with or dissociated from other aspects of mental life varies among patients. Different dissociative parts may or may not have knowledge of the affects, behaviors, histories, motives, and thoughts of other parts. How coconscious patients are also varies—that is, the extent to which they have knowledge of and are privy to the thoughts, history, and affairs of the other parts varies. Often, the part of the self that is in executive control is unaware of the thoughts and activities of other parts (often called *one-way amnesia*). However, this is a tricky topic to try to make clear. For example, coconsciousness may be minimal before beginning psychotherapy for DID but tends to increase considerably in the course of appropriate psychotherapeutic work. Although parts other than the part who is most often in executive control (often called the "host") are more likely to know of each other and of the host, this is not always the case and is not always the same for different parts of the same patient. Some parts may be unknown by many of the others. The dissociative structure of each patient is different.

SWITCHING

The phenomenon generally considered most characteristic of DID is *switching*: Different internal identities can be prone to suddenly taking executive charge, in effect pushing the identity that had previously been in charge, out of charge. This generally results in amnesia on the part of the identity that had been pushed aside for the events that occurred while the other identity was in control. Switching is also known as *full dissociation* (Dell, 2009c).

Clearly, switching is a problem when people do not remember portions of their activities and thoughts. To compensate for this lack of memory, people with DID will often try to fill in the blanks with something they think makes sense given the context, especially in social situations. However, because their compensatory version of events may not match what did happen, and because their behavior may have been different in different identity states, persons with DID may be accused of lying and may indeed come to feel that they are liars. Amnesia can be even worse when people do not know they have amnesia—or that they have dissociated identities—for them, life is and feels even more chaotic.

The current diagnosis in *DSM-IV-TR* (APA, 2000) places the primary emphasis on the phenomenon of switching and provides the following diagnostic criteria for dissociative identity disorder (300.14):

A. The presence of two or more distinct identities or personality states (each with its own relatively enduring pattern of perceiving, relating to, and thinking about the environment and self).

B. At least two of these identities or personality states recurrently take control of the person's behavior.

C. Inability to recall important personal information that is too extensive to be explained by ordinary forgetfulness.

D. The disturbance is not due to the direct physiological effects of a substance (e.g., blackouts or chaotic behavior during Alcohol Intoxication) or a general medical condition (e.g., complex partial seizures). Note: In children, the symptoms are not attributable to imaginary playmates or other fantasy play. (p. 529)[1]

THERE IS NOT ONLY FULL DISSOCIATION BUT ALSO PARTIAL DISSOCIATION

Full dissociation (i.e., switching) is not the only problem in DID. Switching, when an identity state has disappeared from consciousness and another has taken its place, can indeed be quite a problem. However, there is a larger set of problems that has to do with the influence of dissociative parts who are "beneath the surface" on the part that is in executive control at a given time. Such partial dissociation (Dell, 2006b, 2009a, 2009c, 2009d) includes the following phenomena: intrusive visual images; auditory experiences (including hearing voices in the head); olfactory experiences; somatic experiences; unbidden, unsettling, and unexplainable thoughts and emotions; experiences of "made" volitional acts, impulses, and thoughts; and the withdrawal of perceptions, thoughts, and emotions.

In cases of made volitional acts, parts of the body—a hand, an arm, or a leg—may not be in the person's control and can seem to have a life of its own. For example, a person may feel that her hand, not herself, performed a certain motion. In addition to experiences being intruded into consciousness, aspects of experiences may also be withdrawn: Vision, hearing, bodily sensations, emotions, and thoughts may be "taken away" either in part or in whole from the person's experience (or from the experience of the identity that is in executive control). Withdrawn experiences may include "hysterical" symptoms such as functional blindness or can manifest as partial blindness for certain things, as in negative hallucinations (something or someone who is there is not perceived). For example, one of my patients reports that when she goes into the grocery store, she does not see any other people. (Seeing the other people would make her overwhelmingly anxious.) Such intrusions and withdrawals, especially when constant, can have the potential to make a person's life chaotic indeed. There are occasions when intrusions or withdrawals may be visible or known to others—as in the case of a paralysis or a reported hallucination—but for the most part these experiences remain unknown and contribute to private turmoil or agony (Dell & O'Neil, 2009).

This last aspect of DID—partial dissociation—has often been misunderstood as schizophrenia. Dell (2001, 2002, 2006b), Kluft (1987a), Putnam (1997), and Ross (1989) have outlined the ways in which dissociative disturbances have often been misunderstood as indications of psychosis or schizophrenia. Kluft reported that patients with DID endorse 8 of the 11 first-rank Schneiderian symptoms (Schneider, 1959, as cited in Kluft, 1987a) that are considered pathognomonic of schizophrenia. These symptoms are voices arguing, voices commenting on one's action, influences playing on the body, thought withdrawal, thought insertion, made impulses, made feelings, and made volitional acts. In DID, rather than as indications of schizophrenia, the hallucinated voices and the made actions are understood as due to the activities of a dissociative identity. The psychotic person is more likely to attach a delusional explanation, such as "The CIA has implanted a chip in my brain." In contrast, the person with DID, although probably unaware of the source, often knows that these experiences are not normal and does not seek to explain them in a delusional way (Dell, 2009c). In addition, the person with DID—as opposed to someone who is psychotic—often has the ability to be in two states of mind at once: While the person experiences the self as having the "crazy" thought, the person is able to hold the tension and know that it is just that, a crazy thought. Of course, this knowledge that one is having thoughts that others would consider crazy only tends to contribute to the highly dissociative person's fear or belief that he or she is crazy!

DID IS CONFUSING TO EVERYONE

The phenomena of full and partial dissociation are highly confusing to the person with DID as well as to those who notice them. Unlike someone who suffers primarily from depression or anxiety and who can label the problem, the person with DID generally suffers from amnesia about the very symptoms experienced and often cannot specifically identify the problem. For the person with DID, the sense of self, of continuity of being, of identity, is highly discontinuous. As noted in *DSM-IV-TR* (APA, 2000), "the essential feature of the Dissociative Disorders is a disruption in the usually integrated functions of consciousness, memory, identity, or perception" (p. 519).

This emphasis on disturbance in identity is an important one. Because there is more than one identity, our linguistic descriptions often imply, but do not state, differences in the perspectives of the different identities. Understanding DID can be complicated, and it is hard to escape the considerable awkwardness that ensues when we try to speak and write of such things as consciousness, disruptions of consciousness, intrusions into consciousness, even amnesia. Especially as when we speak this way, we are often speaking from the perspective with which we, as "singletons," think. For instance, consider the amnesia requirement of Criterion C: "Inability to recall important personal information that is too extensive to be explained by ordinary forgetfulness" (APA, 2000, p. 529). One might ask, "Who (which part) fails to recall?" "Whose consciousness?" or "Whose thinking has been disrupted?" These questions are especially relevant when the host, the part of the self that usually presents to the world, is a collection of several parts who pinch hit for each other or when the host is primarily a shell who faces the world while other parts "fill in" as needed. From the perspective of dissociative parts who want to be in executive control but who are not currently "out," their bids for time to be in control of the body or for attention are not intrusions. However, the part that is in executive control most of the time may experience these bids as intrusions and disruptions, and an observer may classify them as such. The perspective one takes—part or whole, looking out or looking in—makes all the difference.

MULTIPLE SELF-STATES AND DISSOCIATED IDENTITY STATES

When we speak of partial dissociation as an important aspect of DID, it is important to note that partial dissociation is not specific to DID or even to dissociative disorders. It also characterizes posttraumatic stress disorder (PTSD): The flashbacks and intrusions so characteristic of PTSD are examples of partial dissociation. In addition, partial dissociation can be an aspect of everyday life for most people. The self of all of us is not a unity but consists of multiple self-states that emerge and alternate in accordance with which self-state is in the forefront of consciousness at a given time. Current research in neurobiology, cognitive psychology, and developmental psychology indicates that the brain, the mind, and the self are normally multiple (Dennett, 1991; Erdelyi, 1994; Gazzaniga, 1985; Kirmayer, 1994; Siegel, 1999). Neurobiologists increasingly understand the brain as organized into neural systems that to some degree function independently of one another (LeDoux, 2002). Such parallel and multitrack processing help to explain dissociative phenomena on a neurological level. Furthermore, as Siegel (1999) maintained, "the idea of a unitary, continuous 'self' is actually an illusion our minds attempt to create. . . . We have multiple and varied 'selves,' which are needed to carry out the many and diverse activities of our lives" (p. 231).

Yes, we all have multiple self-states. For all of us, our mental life is characterized by constant changes in self-state to match the current context. Much of the time, most of us are aware (although less often than we think) of the matches of self-state to context, and we remember both (or we think we do). For example, we may wear a "therapist hat" while in the office, have a caregiving orientation when in contact with our children, and respond in a different way, involving early attachment system internal working models, when speaking to our parents. What is important for psychological health is the degree of dissociation between self-states or, to put it more positively, the degree to which we experience our multiple self-states as contextually interrelated and part of what comprises the sum of who we are. Or, as Philip Bromberg (1998) has put it, health is the ability to "stand in the spaces between realities without losing any of them" (p. 186).

CONTEXTUALIZATION

As humans, we adapt to the varying contexts of our lives. However, we may not always be aware of the extent to which our lives are bound by context. For example, when I go to my gym, I have to recite a certain eight-digit number to get in. When I stand in front of the admission desk, I remember this number, but only then. If someone were to ask me my number anywhere else in the building or outside of it, I would not be able to recite it. This is a mild version of what DID is like. My point is not that I have a "gym self," but that my memory for how to get in to the gym has to be triggered. Away from the front desk, I have no conscious memory of that number. Although this may mean that my gym self is in great need of support and integration with the rest of me, the point here is that there is a piece of memory that has to do with my internal world that is not usually available to me. To access it, I have to deliberately and physically trigger it.

Although this is not representative of a dissociative disorder (a dissociative experience alone does not constitute a dissociative disorder), I am called to access a memory that is related to only a specific context. A person with DID has more and larger modules of self-contained experiences that are not easily accessible to consciousness, but the basic organization of context dependency is the same. In infancy, behavior is organized as a set of discrete behavioral states, such as states of sleep and waking, eating, elimination, and so on. These behavioral states become linked over time and grouped together in sequences (Putnam, 1997). Psychological trauma impedes this linkage; as a result, individuals who have been severely neglected or highly traumatized in childhood have not had the interpersonal attention, support, and encouragement necessary to interconnect their self-states and the varying contexts of their lives.

THERAPIST TRAINING FOR DID

Therapists who work with dissociative patients should have solid skills and knowledge in general psychotherapy, such as in assessment, boundary management, ethics, transference and countertransference, general therapeutic skill, as well as concern and empathy. Although working with highly dissociative people does require solid therapeutic skills, a specialized understanding of the highly dissociative mind is also necessary. Specific theoretical and technical approaches may vary, but those that result in facilitating psychic health derive from an understanding of the psychic structure underlying DID.

The first step needs to be arriving at a correct diagnosis. It is important to remember that DID is a problem of hiddenness. Therapists treating patients with DID should be aware of the signs of switching from one identity state to another as well as the signs of intrusions or partial dissociation. Untrained clinicians may be unaware of the switching in the session and assume that they are meeting with only one identity state throughout. This deprives them of important information. For instance, if the patient cannot remember or make sense of what was said in the session, this may well not be due to resistance or anxiety as we might normally understand them but could be due to dissociation. When it is understood that different dissociative identities not privy to the experience of other identities may have been present, the behavior of the patient makes more sense. As clinicians, we strive to be alert to when the patient's experience has radically changed either through a switch or through partial dissociation. Working with highly dissociative people requires familiarity with trauma treatment as well as the ability to deal with traumatic transferences and to tolerate strong emotional pressures in the consulting room.

The ISST-D has a training program for clinicians for work with dissociative disorders. Training information may be found at http://www.isst-d.org under Training and Conferences.

ORGANIZATION OF THIS BOOK

In the chapters that follow, I explain the nature of dissociation and dissociative disorders and how I work psychotherapeutically with people who are highly dissociative. I use examples from my practice liberally to illustrate various principles.

Chapter 1 introduces three of my patients who have generously given me permission to use descriptions of their lives and their psychotherapy in an ongoing way in this book. Their stories serve as anchoring points for understanding what the experience of having DID is like and for understanding ways to work with DID psychotherapeutically.

Chapter 2 explores the topic of the dynamic unconscious and the dissociative structure of mind. The interrelationships of dissociation, relationality, and multiplicity are examined, and finally the historical context of the waxing and waning of recognition of dissociative processes and dissociative problems is explicated.

Chapter 3 examines the organization of the personality system in DID, the "We of Me." This includes the most commonly active dissociative identities and how they are organized in relationship to each other, trance logic, the closed system, and the third reality as described by Kluft (2000). It also explains different conceptual schemes for understanding the organization of dissociated parts of the self.

Chapter 4 describes how DID is a trauma disorder. It also explains why trauma is best defined as "that which causes dissociation." It explains the meaning of complex trauma, relational trauma, and the proposed working diagnosis, disorders of extreme stress not otherwise specified (DESNOS).

Chapter 5 covers the development of DID as understood both through the trauma model and in terms of disorganized attachment. The self does not begin as a unity. Consequently, the dissociative fragmented self is not so much a "shattered self" as one in which early attachment dilemmas dictated disorganized attachment while the early interpersonal environment did not facilitate integration.

Chapter 6 covers some neurobiological correlates of the structure and psychodynamics of dissociated self-states.

Chapter 7 addresses understanding the organization of dissociated self-states under the rubric of the Karpman triangle of victim, persecutor, and rescuer. It also covers the creativity of creating self-states and the importance of contextualization within the self in healing.

Chapter 8 covers assessment and diagnosis. It addresses the importance of assessing both switching and intrusions in DID. Face-to-face interviews as well as screening and assessment instruments are discussed.

Chapter 9 deals with a frequently covered topic in trauma treatment: phase-oriented treatment. Important topics are avoiding retraumatiztion, stabilization, grounding, and so on, as part of Phase 1. It also covers what I call "the central conflict," which concerns the tendencies of some dissociated parts to want to tell about the traumas while other parts do not want to be bothered with their feelings and are afraid of being destabilized. This chapter also covers the topic of abreaction, which is viewed as an interpersonal and integrative activity.

Chapter 10 covers facilitating coconsciousness and coparticipation in the treatment. Many different kinds of problems and solutions, with illustrations from my practice, are presented.

Chapter 11 deals with working with persecutory alters and understanding how they have come into being. This chapter includes an extensive case vignette.

Chapter 12 includes multiple dimensions of coconstruction in the therapeutic relationship, including multiple transferences and countertransferences, traumatic and erotic transferences, and issues of boundary management that stem from disorganized attachment. It also includes the topics of projective identification and dissociative attunements.

Chapter 13 covers dreams in DID and in trauma, including how they are both very different from and also similar to more ordinary dreams. Some of the important differences are spelled out, including how the same dream may be dreamt from different perspectives by different dissociative identities. It includes two vignettes about the use of dreams in therapy with DID patients.

Chapter 14 discusses the topic of suicidality, which is a significant risk for those with DID. The complicated meaning of suicidality is covered, including the many ways that what looks suicidal from the outside may be construed by parts of the system. For example, some parts may be homicidal toward other parts, engaging in activity that from the outside looks suicidal. Although this is delusional because the physical death of the body includes all parts and the behavior is not intended to be suicidal to the part that is out, the danger of lethality is just as high.

Chapter 15 covers the dissociative structure of the mind across diagnoses, including the topic of comorbidity. I examine a case of "psychosis" that was in fact about somatoform and dissociatively held memories. The psychosis was resolved when the dissociated material was pulled together in a story. I also examine the particular way in which I think that borderline personality disorder is dissociation based. Finally, I suggest that the universality of some archaic superego problems stems from dissociation and cuts across diagnostic levels.

In this book there are many excerpts from sessions that are intended to illustrate various principles. Obviously, I have my own particular style in the way I work and interact, just as everyone has their own style; so these excerpts are not meant to be prescriptive. Everyone working with DID will develop their own style.

Secondly, for the reader unfamiliar with DID, the switching, the various cast of characters who come forth in one body, and the trance logic may seem strange, perhaps even too strange to initially take in. Trance logic could be described as a waking dream logic, in which the ordinary rules of logic do not apply. To some degree, we all operate with trance logic— and to say so is not pejorative. We accept and value trance logic in art and some religious ceremonies. Or, for example, a person in mourning may expect the dead person to enter the room. In the personifications of the inner world of DID, thinking is more concrete, contributing to the trance logic. Instead of "I feel so sad I can hardly stand it," The Sad One appears, newly in central command of the body.

Despite this patina of strangeness, when you think about the psychic system and its psychodynamics, this basic structure of multiple self-states is universal, although its elaboration varies with the person. Perhaps it is like talking about quarks when the prevailing theory is atoms: The intricacy of the structure that characterizes us all is simply more manifest in DID. Once you accept this proposition—not so difficult when it is before you, the experience is comprehensible and compelling.

NOTE

1. The proposed fifth edition of the *DSM* (DSM5), slated for publication in 2013, modifies these criteria for DID.

Part I

Understanding Dissociative Identity Disorder

Chapter 1

The Lives and Psychotherapy of Three People With DID

INTRODUCTION

I have enormous respect and admiration for the courage, endurance, and capacity to love that these individuals with dissociative identity disorder (DID) have, and I am grateful to them for their consent for me to use incidents from their lives as they reported them to me and from their treatment to illustrate what it is like for a person to have DID and what it is like for a therapist to work with a person who has DID. Although identifying information has been changed, these are not composites. Before I begin to tell of their stories, I want to remind the reader that life can be stranger than fiction. These are horrifying stories. I refer to work with three patients (Janice, Dennis, and Margaret) at various points throughout this book. The work with them is not the only discussion of case examples, but these individuals offer anchoring cases.

JANICE

Janice is a 43-year-old woman, recently remarried, who has two teenage daughters. Although an accomplished painter, she is just beginning to show her work. An extremely caring person who is kind and sensitive to the feelings of others, she generally presents as upbeat, cheerful, optimistic, and highly energetic. Yet, there have been many times when she has privately experienced overwhelming depression and suicidality. Especially as a child, Janice got through life by pleasing others. She developed a pleasing face and a funny face, among others—faces that hid her immense grief. Luckily, she is extremely intelligent, and this helped her to figure out and adaptively adjust to many unbearably difficult situations as she was growing up.

Janice came into treatment with me almost 4 years ago to work on her newly discovered DID. She has been in therapy with a number of different therapists for most of her adult life, but her DID was never diagnosed until a recent 2-month hospitalization in a trauma program. During this time, she did much work on herself. She did time lines of her history, drawings, and some of her alters were identified. In our early work, her awareness that she has DID emerged gradually, like an increasingly flickering light-bulb that finally comes on. This began with an examination of her need to rescue stray, needy, damaged people, people who could in fact sometimes be dangerous. When the rescuer part was contacted, a very sad child of about 6 emerged who described the most recent rescue operation in detail, as well as others. She finally admitted with great sadness and pain that she rescued others because she could not rescue Janice. The enormous sadness of this part was partially communicated to Janice. She was amazed to know about this part of herself and to know the sadness of this part. Following this session, other parts emerged, each time with Janice experiencing some of their sadness, an experience often upsetting and sometimes overwhelming to her. As a result, this initial work with parts was carefully titrated. She recently reported that she realized that she had always thought of herself as The "We" of Me, but that she had never before now put together its meaning.

All Janice remembers about the development of her multiplicity is that by the time she was in middle childhood, she would privately refer to herself as The We of Me. Janice's "we" is a polyfragmented multiple. She has at least a hundred parts, many of them for particular purposes or roles, existing in many clusters and layers, parts behind other parts. Most of the parts do not have names, although I recognize many of them by their behavior. There is a little 4-year-old who speaks with a lisp and with a 4-year-old's language structure. There are many young children who go by "Janey," some adolescent ones, and several adult ones. Of those who have specific names, there is Tomboy, who is a cheerful, enthusiastic, happy tomboy companion to her father. There is The Little Girl in the Torn Dirty Slip, who was sexually abused and has always felt tortured and ashamed. There is The Mother, who takes care of her children when Janice, as the host, is too exhausted. There is The Driver, who takes care of safe driving when other parts have become too upset. There is The One Who Knows How to Get Things Done. There is The Sexy One. Then, there are many prison guards and gatekeepers who have functioned to keep parts with overwhelmingly scary, shameful, angry, and painful memories and feelings locked up, and there is a hierarchy among these guards and gatekeepers. There is the seemingly suicidal, but actually internally homicidal, Ereshkigal, who wants to kill the host, Janice. Then, there are The Suicides, who become activated when things begin to feel hopeless. They have provided hope to the system with their prospective solution of ending pain by ending life. However, in our work together, they have continued to expand the realm of their subjectivity to include connections with other parts. They have also gained awareness that as an adult Janice has much more power than she did as a child, that in current reality, pain is not forever, and that if she did murder herself, her children would suffer immeasurably. (See Chapter 14 for more discussion of suicidality.) Then, there are many other parts who come and go. In response to my asking their identity, they often say, "Oh, I'm just one of them."

Janice is a middle child in a family of four, with two older brothers and a younger sister. She grew up as a kind of real-life Cinderella, but without the unqualified happy ending. From her infancy until she was about 5, she was sickly: As a baby and young child, she could not hold food down and frequently had a fever, facts of life that made her mother angry. If Janice had a temperature in the morning before kindergarten and first grade, the school would not take her. Janice described how this infuriated her mother because it interfered with her daily bridge game. When it was finally discovered that she was allergic to milk, Janice began to thrive physically.

Janice remembers that she was frequently punished, but she rarely understood the reasons for her punishments. Her mother often spanked her with a hairbrush on many parts of her body, including her chest and back, arms, and hands as well as her butt. When Janice tried to defend herself by putting her hands in front of her chest or behind her back, her mother would strike her hands with the brush.

Janice's mother did not intervene when her father heaped strange and sometimes violent punishments on her. Although he also spanked her with a belt, his most notable punishment was his placing her in a certain chair, where she would have to sit and listen to him excoriate her verbally for what he saw as her misdeeds and inadequacies. There were many times when she was forced to sit in this chair for hours while he stood over her telling her what a terrible person she was. In particular, he would demand that she repeat after him that she was "a liar, a thief, and a cheater." Janice knows the phrase by heart by virtue of being forced to repeat it so many times. Despite this maltreatment, Janice also found ways to please her father. This included singing songs to him while still a child, such as "I'm a little teapot, short and stout; sock to me baby, let it all hang out." She recalled that her father and his friends thought it was hilarious.

Janice soon learned to keep her mouth shut and put on a happy face. She developed the art of servicing the different members of her family in different ways. For her father, she was hostess and maid for his many cocktail parties. She also developed an alter, Tomboy, who was her father's sidekick in his hunting expeditions with his cronies. Tomboy knew just when to get down when the rifles would go off. Unlike other children and her siblings, Janice had to be home from school by 4 p.m. to attend to household chores. Janice brought tea to her mother on a tray every day when she came home from school. She also massaged her mother's back often because her mother was frequently bedridden with what she described as back pain. By the time she was a young adolescent, Janice cooked many family meals. She poignantly remembers baking her father's birthday cake when she was about 10 years old—only to have him become furious with her because the candles on the cake had melted by the time she was able to carry the cake to him. She made a birthday party for her sister, also only to be rebuffed. On her mother's instruction, she sewed her sister's wedding dress and two bridesmaid's gowns. In contrast to the way she treated Janice's siblings, whom she showered with expensive clothing, Janice's mother refused to buy all but the bare necessities for Janice. (It should be borne in mind that Janice's desperate need to please—as well as her ability to do so—might have contributed to the way that her family came to rely on her.)

Considering that Janice's parents seem to have had a great need to control her and to keep her at home, it seems strange that she seemed as a young child to be wandering around a great deal on her own, with no one noticing. When Janice was about 5, some friends of one of her brothers enticed her into the basement of an abandoned house. This was her "torture room." They would force her to lie down. Then, they would fill her vagina with muddy sand. Next, they would place a board on her and walk on her pelvis. They told her that they would kill her if she told, and she never did. Her mother never seemed to be curious about her frequent urinary tract infections. Even today, since she has remembered these times, she has tortured herself with wondering why she went back, and the complete answer to this is still not clear. Most likely, she was terrified to refuse, and possibly, even though it was bad attention, it was some attention. In addition, her body was aroused—just as are the bodies of children who voluntarily engage in sex play. Because of the terror and shame, these awful experiences were dissociated as The Little Girl in the Torn Dirty Slip until recently. There was so much shame about these instances that The Little Girl in the Torn Dirty Slip was isolated, "locked up," by other parts, who believed that she was dirty and bad and should not be allowed to come out. Gradually, in therapy this part found the courage (and was allowed out by the rest of the system) to come out and to talk about these harrowing times, including the physical pain, terror, and shame. It is because she came out to talk to me that this paragraph could be written in a coherent narrative sequence. Before that, it was a bad feeling that would come over her, but it was also what she called a "butterfly" memory. She would at times have a fleeting memory of this or other harrowing times, but then it would disappear, and all she would remember is the image of a butterfly.

As a child, she would often wander into the woods for long periods of time, often taking off her clothes, and dancing around, pretending that she was a fairy. On one occasion, two wild boars came by. She quickly climbed a tree and was completely still and quiet in utter terror for a long time. As soon as they left, she ran home. She told no one because she did not want anyone to know that she had been out, and she did not want the privilege taken away from her. In her later, early adult years, she often traveled in third-world countries, alone, in third-class transport and not wearing a bra. Now, in the present, she remembers the driver looking at her breasts and realizes that she could have been raped, killed, and disappeared. She has had many close calls in her life and has, indeed, cheated death many times. For example, she was attacked by a widely feared and dangerous rapist and was raped and nearly murdered in her apartment.

Janice's parents did not want to be disturbed after Janice's bedtime. Because she was so terrified of her parents and of disturbing them, and because she symbolized them as monsters at the doorway of her bedroom who would kill her if she exited, she was afraid to get up from bed and go to the bathroom at night. As a result, she often wet the bed. This continued until she was 8 years old. Her mother's solution to this was to refuse to wash the sheets, to make Janice sleep in them, and when she did have them washed, to hang them out in the yard for everyone to see and to know that Janice had again wet the bed. Furthering this humiliation, her brothers would then ride their bikes through the neighborhood, informing the neighbors that Janice had wet the bed. Needless to say, Janice's sister followed suit and treated her in the same humiliating manner as did her parents.

Despite continuous, flagrant, serious maltreatment, Janice focused her life on pleasing her mother, and this most likely did establish the kind of inverted caretaking bond that her mother apparently needed as well as palliate her mother's ire at her. She became a little soldier (or many such) with respect to herself, containing her pain, fury, terror, and longings. Not surprisingly, Janice attempted to hang herself with her mother's stockings when she was 8 years old.

Odd attitudes about sexuality were enacted by both of her parents and an uncle and aunt toward the child, Janice. When she was 12, Janice had sewed her own Easter dress, but before she could wear it to church, she remembers that her mother suddenly flew into a rage and ripped out the hem, insisting that Janice had made it an inch shorter than what she thought she had marked. Her father often told her, but not her sister, that girls and women could only be wives, secretaries, or prostitutes. However, neither she nor any of her parts have reported physical incest with her father.

By the time Janice was a preadolescent and an adolescent, she began to spend summer months and many weekends with some friends of her parents, whom she addressed as uncle and aunt. The "uncle" was, in fact, her father's boss. Until she was in the postpartum period of the birth of her first child, she had always remembered these times as idyllic. These people were kind to her, did things with her, and showered positive attention on her. In contrast to how she was treated at home, they thought well of her and praised her. They did not demand that she perform such chores as cooking and sewing. She idealized them and thought of them as her saviors.

While she was recuperating from the birth of her first child, she was plunged into severe depression by the onset of a different sort of memories of the time she spent with the uncle and aunt. She became largely unable to function or to paint for about 13 years. She remembered that the uncle would come into her room at night and fondle her. In addition, to "Uncle's" nightly fondlings, she remembered sudden gushings of vaginal blood that alarmed no one. Both the uncle and his wife stated to Janice that she should support herself through college by prostitution, with no embarrassment or reflection on what they were saying. The uncle planned to continue his sexual exploitation of her beyond her childhood by suggesting to her that she should support herself through college by going to the environs of the Alaska pipeline and setting up shop as a prostitute. He told her that he would help her get set up in this work, and that he would visit her. At the time, it did not occur to her that this might be objectionable. It was not until her mid-20s that Janice began to feel weird about having sex with him and stopped it. She did not formulate the experience: She did not think about or remember any precursors to this behavior. It was just something she did.

In the home of her nuclear family, there also were strange issues with sexuality and control in which it seemed that Janice was the recipient of much projection about sexuality. She was also frequently "locked up," confined to her room for long periods of time or to the home for months at a time in the summer, as if she were promiscuous, which she was not.

About a year ago, Janice received some elucidating information: The situation of her birth was highly unusual. Janice's mother was having an affair about 9 to 12 months before her birth and mistakenly believed that Janice was the biological offspring of the man with whom she had been consorting. When Janice was a baby, her mother told her father of the affair. It is only recently that Janice recovered this memory from her mother, on a special trip that she had arranged both to comfort and to become closer to her mother. This information was the explanatory key that had been missing from so much of her story of brutal sadistic abuse and extreme exploitation on the part of her parents and her "uncle." Since her sister and brothers had not been treated as she was, it was always curious to her (and to me) why she had been singled out for such treatment. The pattern of triangulation (in Murray Bowen's terms; both parents made her a scapegoat to protect the harmony of their own relationship) had always been apparent, but there had been no obvious explanation regarding why. For instance, while her siblings were sent to college by her parents, Janice put herself through college. The implication that she was a "whore" that was attributed to her in late childhood and adolescence becomes her parents' projection regarding her mother's extra-marital affair. Following her mother's revelation, Janice requested genetic testing. This testing revealed that her father was indeed her biological father.

DENNIS

Dennis, who has DID, is a personable, extremely intelligent, 32-year-old man. He works in finance and owns a motorcycle repair shop on the side. Clearly, he is a man of many talents. Yet, he suffers an inner chaos and immense psychic pain. He finds some surcease from his suffering in focused work and in the joy of being in the presence of true friends. He came into treatment with me after finding my earlier publications on the Internet. At that time, he stated that he was aware that he had some dissociative problems and was interested in dissociation but did not "believe in" DID. We have been working together for about 3 years, but not continuously, as he has had to take some breaks for financial reasons. Much of this work has been painful for him as some horrifying memories have come back to him in the process.

Dennis endures painful conflicts around his right and ability to make a living, his right to have enough food to eat, and life versus death. He has experienced a horrifying history. Over the time of our work together, a number of his parts have shared their thoughts and feelings and let me into their worlds. Since then, he has regained some important memories, and his parts have become more collaborative with each other; as a result, his life has made more sense to him and is somewhat less difficult.

Dennis is the only child of two artists, a father who was chronically and dangerously drug addicted, often on crack and speed, and a mother desperately trying to cope with the situation as well as with personal troubles and extremely physically debilitating rheumatoid arthritis. Unfortunately, there was no one available in an extended family willing and able to help. Dennis reports that when he was a baby his mother often had to leave the apartment and spend nights walking around to escape his father's violence (and he does have an iconic memory of being in a carriage outside in the snow, looking up at his mother). When he was 3, he was placed in day care in someone's home so that his mother could work. Unfortunately, the sons of the woman who ran the day care center forced him and some of the other children to perform fellatio on them in the bathroom. He was unable to tell his mother because even at 3 years of age, he felt too alone and afraid of upsetting her fragile equilibrium.

When he was young, Dennis began to see images of a beautiful young girl with long dark hair, an alter named Sophia. He felt that she was nurturing to him, and he took great comfort in her presence. At first, he experienced her as literally outside himself. Somewhat later, he interpreted her as a poltergeist. Then, she became an imaginary companion. Later, she went back inside (in his subjective experience), where she grew up alongside him. When he was young, she was almost always a source of solace. When he became an adult, some competition for ownership and control of the body began to emerge.

As the abuse, violence, and terror in his household continued, his mother was eventually able to escape with her son to another state, where she thought her dangerous husband would be unable to find them. They lived in relative peace for a few years until the father did find them, when Dennis was 7 years old. When Dennis's mother discovered that his father knew their whereabouts, she was certain that she and her son were in grave danger, and that the father may be intending to kill her and perhaps both of them. The father did appear and stated that he wished to take Dennis away with him to California. Dennis's mother knew not only that if she refused him things could get dangerous but also that Dennis's life would be in jeopardy if he went with his father. Dennis, consciously knowing little of the father whom he had not seen for so many years, on hearing that the father was nearby, wished that he could go with his father. After the mother refused his father's request to take Dennis away with him, the father came by the next day, "out of his mind" high on speed and with a gun. The mother, who had prepared herself for this eventuality, had put Dennis to bed and told him not to come out of his bedroom. A friend had given her a gun, and she shot Dennis's father on the stairs as he was coming to kill her. Despite having been put to bed, Dennis did leave his room and witness the event. He has only recently become aware that he saw the shooting, having previously only remembered loud sounds from that night. Throughout his childhood and adolescence he had frequent episodes of unexplained hysterical blindness, probably related to his amnesia for witnessing this event.

Following the shooting, Dennis disappeared into the woods for 3 days, hiding in trees, at times motionless. When he emerged, he was both more divided and much more psychologically distressed as well as internally oppressed. Dennis has never recovered from this tragedy. Even though he was a child, this tragedy was an adult-onset trauma (in which the self collapses as well as divides) for him. This adult onset-type trauma is partly about the intimate knowledge of death (Boulanger, 2007). A common problem of those who have confronted or barely escaped their own death or have been suddenly confronted with horrors of the death or murder of someone close to them is the belief that they are dead. This amounts to a strong, dark shadow of death in life cast continuously over existence. It creates a posttraumatic reduction of thinking to psychic equivalency (in which one's thoughts are the exact equivalents of external events) such that the capacity to think about one's feelings and thoughts is vastly diminished or even wiped out. Since subjectivity has collapsed, so has intersubjectivity. In this sense, the self actually has died for the symbolic universe on which selfhood depends has been destroyed. Even today, Dennis frequently has zombie dreams.

Thereafter, Dennis suffered from both adult-onset trauma and the childhood-onset trauma that result in the dissociative divisions of selfhood. As a young child, he had extremely high blood pressure and was often ill. The doctors could not figure out what was wrong with him.

Following her husband's death, Dennis's mother moved the two of them to another state. As a single mother seriously physically disabled because of rheumatoid arthritis, she was not always able to find work, and they were extremely poor. She had raised him alone, emotionally and financially. Neither her family nor her deceased husband's family had been available to help. When he was a child, his mother had been almost his only emotional contact. She loved him, cared for him, and did the best she could in mothering him, but she was limited psychologically as well as physically. Her own work skills were limited by her physical disability, and there were many times that the two of them were completely without food. At these times, it would be up to Dennis to find ways to obtain food by raiding the homes of people nearby who were away. He would also siphon the gas from others' cars when they were away, even sometimes when they were not. He felt terrible about doing these things, but they were simply necessary. To illustrate the severity of the deprivation that he and his mother experienced, when his mother was able to acquire and keep work and when the paychecks came in, she would buy food, and they would gorge until they were sick. Not surprisingly, Dennis currently becomes extremely anxious about having enough money to eat.

In their new location, by the time Dennis was 8, a new trauma began. His mother, trying to compensate for his lack of a father, located the Big Brother charity. Unfortunately, the two men assigned to him were sadistic pedophiles who took him into the woods, tied him up and raped him—repeatedly—for about 2 years. He would often get a terrible stomachache before it was time for him to go with them, but he was unable to tell his mother of the abuse and terror that he was enduring alone. He was again afraid of upsetting her. He was afraid that she would kill these men if she knew, and that then his mother would be taken away from him.

Despite all the trauma that he endured, Dennis kept his mind. He was a brilliant child who spent most of his time in the library. He was so intelligent that on more than one occasion a teacher would accuse him of plagiarism on a paper that he had written because the teacher could not imagine that someone his age would be capable of writing it.

He completed high school and managed to get through college despite the fact that he was switching frequently, although in his "host" presentation he was unaware of this. As Sophia became more and more frequently out, that part sought to take over Dennis's body, and plans for a sex change operation were begun with a psychologist and a physician who specialized in this process. As Dennis consumed massive amounts of female hormones, he became increasingly suicidal. He was hospitalized on multiple occasions and eventually received shock treatments.

When he was released from the hospital, he began to try to recoup his losses. Although he was not aware at the time that the sex change process had been initiated because he had DID, he did realize that it would not work for him to change his sex.

Soon after this event, he began psychotherapy with me.

MARGARET

Margaret is a 35-year-old woman, married with two children, who is employed as a university professor of literature. She is well groomed, attractive, and well put together. Margaret is a remarkable woman: loving and well loved, highly intelligent, energetic, highly sensitive, psychologically astute, multitalented with a strong work ethic. Mercilessly persecuted as a child, she still, but increasingly less so, suffers conflicts about her right to exist for herself and not solely as an object of use for others. Under stress, she has had some periods of amnesia as well as minifugues, not remembering how she got to a destination. In her childhood and adolescence, a great portion of her life was about managing continued survival, a project that often became exhausting and that led to profound states of depersonalization and derealization. Since almost no one was interested in her feelings, it is understandable that she has rageful and murderous self-states who give her a lot of trouble, at times contributing to suicidality.

The oldest of three girls, she reports that she was torturously abused throughout her childhood by her mother, her father, her stepfather, and her stepfather's son. On many occasions, she was raped, beaten almost to a pulp, tied up, or left for dead. On two occasions, her father attempted to murder her. Her mother was brutally cruel to her. As an adolescent, she often was on her own, sleeping in alleys, sometimes wishing that her heart would just stop and that death would wipe out her misery. She has also had an adult near-death experience following childbirth.

There was one saving grace. She had a beloved grandfather, who loved her and whom she adored. She spent some happy times in the summer with him until he died when she was 11 years old, and her memories of those times are positive and comforting.

Her mother would rarely feed her children, although she would leave milk and cereal for them on the bottom shelf of the refrigerator so that they could feed themselves when they were young. Margaret raised the youngest child from babyhood until Margaret left home at 15. While Margaret's mother was frequently physically abusive to her, for instance, slamming her against the wall if she thought Margaret was in her way, her constant verbal humiliations were far worse: She would call Margaret a "fat cow" and other similar derogatory appellations (Margaret was not overweight). Margaret fared worse in her mother's treatment than her younger sister did because her mother identified with her sister, and rejected her, saying that she looked like her father. Margaret remembers that on one occasion, when she was a young adolescent, her mother sent her off overnight with a strange man. She was lucky to have survived for the man took her to a motel room where he and other men raped her. However, in other ways, the mother's household was an equal opportunity reign of terror: On one occasion, her mother deliberately killed the children's pet cats by running over them with her automobile.

Probably the worst aspect of the way Margaret's mother treated her was that she was a blaming bystander for the physical and sexual abuse of her children by her husbands. Since she was a little girl, Margaret's father had abused her sexually, sometimes in sadistic ways, such as tying her up and leaving her alone, still tied up, for hours after he was done. Her father, a tortured and torturing soul who was also an alcoholic, tried to murder her on more than one occasion, once by drowning when she was a young child and once by trying to shoot her with a gun. Fortunately, Margaret was able to run away, and she was savvy enough to grab and run away with the bullets so that he could not use the gun to kill her. Her father was also physically abusive and could fly into a rage on a dime, with little or no warning. On one occasion, he knocked out Margaret's front teeth as well as bruising and bloodying many parts of her body. Her mother's response, rather than anger at her husband or protectiveness toward Margaret, was anger at Margaret that she would now have to get the blood out of the blouse. On another occasion, her father threw her out of his moving car and then tried to run over her.

Margaret's mother left her father for her stepfather when Margaret was a young adolescent. The stepfather's rapes and sexual abuse were even more sadistic than her father's. One on occasion, he announced that he was going to take her to get an abortion because he said he knew that she had been sexually promiscuous with boys. He first took her to a hotel room, where he raped her. Then, he took her to a seedy place, where a dilation and curettage (D & C, often used for early-term abortions) was performed. Following this, he delivered her to her place of work, instructing her to tell her employer that she would need to sit, rather than stand, that afternoon. This situation was odd since the stepfather had had a vasectomy, and he also knew that Margaret was not having sex with boys. Margaret today surmises that his purpose was blackmail—that if she were ever to complain about his rapes of her, that he would be able to blame her for alleged "promiscuity" instead, presenting himself as "the good guy" who took her to get an abortion.

When Margaret was 11, on the occasion of the funeral of her beloved grandfather, she was brutally raped and severely beaten by the teenage son of her stepfather. She had to find a way to bury her bloody clothes so that her mother would not punish her further.

When Margaret was physically able at age 15 to leave home, she did. She found a job at a department store, taking herself to school for classes, and sleeping in the store after hours. When she was unable to sleep in the store, she would sleep in alleyways. The temperature at night was often cold, and she many times wished that she would just die in her sleep. Eventually, she was able to buy herself a car. She would sleep in her car when the nights were freezing. She remembers that her mother would send messages to her, via her sister at school, to come home, and eventually she did go home— where, of course, the rapes recommenced. Finally, Margaret told a school counselor whom she felt she could trust about the rapes and about her intention simply to leave town. Not anticipating the extent of Margaret's mother's response, the counselor reported Margaret's visit to Margaret's mother whose response was to have Margaret arrested in the process of her attempted getaway and to have her hospitalized for 3 months on the basis of her being supposedly mentally disturbed. (The purpose was to protect the mother's reputation; i.e., the mother was not negligent or abusive and Margaret was crazy.)

Some of these events reported here Margaret has always known. But, some of the events of her life, perhaps the worst ones, were deeply dissociated, and she has become conscious of them from piecemeal recollections and through the communications of dissociated identities when they were ready to do so. Through our work, as Margaret has pieced more and more of the shards of her life together, she more and more feels that "she has a story." Her life makes more sense to her. The major task of Margaret's early life was survival. For her, unlike Janice, pleasing her parents was not an option: They could not be pleased. Neither was it safe for her to express any sort of angry feelings. Luckily, she was able to internalize the good experiences she had with her grandfather. To her credit, she was able to establish good relationships with some teachers, by whom she felt somewhat emotionally supported. But on the whole, Margaret was starkly alone, her survival up to her alone, and the ambivalent conflicts regarding whether she wanted to survive also hers alone. She has a tremendous capacity to connect meaningfully with other people, which she has used as an adult, but that capacity was seldom met with adequate environmental opportunity when she was growing up.

While Margaret made two suicide attempts in her early adult life and has been suicidal at some times in our work, there have been no actual attempts during this time. While much healing has occurred, more remains to be done. There is at least one murderous and furious, but extremely pained, self-state who exists alone and needs more communication with me and with Margaret. There are other raging self-states as well, who need more communication. On an interpersonal level, Margaret is improving in her ability to support herself in the accurate acknowledgment of angry feelings. There is a remarkable beauty to her courage and her ability to love.

Chapter 2

The Dynamic Unconscious and the Dissociative Structure of the Mind

> The longer we have been occupied with these phenomena, the more we have become convinced that *the splitting of consciousness which is so striking in the well-known classical cases under the form of* "double conscience" [the French term is "dual consciousness"] *is present to a rudimentary degree in every hysteria, and that a tendency to such a dissociation, and with it the emergence of abnormal states of consciousness (which we shall bring together under the term "hypnoid") is the basic phenomenon of this neurosis.*
>
> Freud (Breuer & Freud, 1893–1895a, p. 12; italics in original)

Today, but only just recently in historical time, dissociation, relationality, and multiplicity have become part of mainstream models of the psyche. We are in a position now to revise and enrich the way we understand the dynamic unconscious from the standpoint of knowledge of the dissociative structure of the mind. In this chapter, I examine the interrelationships of multiplicity, relationality, trauma, dissociation, and repression and the effect of all of these on the way we understand the dynamic unconscious.

Current understandings and meanings are well rooted in past ones. To that end, in the second part of this chapter, I provide a somewhat brief history of the trajectory of how dissociation has been understood in the mental health culture. Dissociation is like the Cheshire Cat in Lewis Carroll's *Alice in Wonderland*: Now you see it, now you don't—it is irrepressible and keeps popping up. Thus, I examine the social and historical context from which our understanding of dissociative identity disorder (DID) has emerged.

RELATIONALITY, MULTIPLICITY, TRAUMA, AND DISSOCIATION

Many have said that with the advent of relational theory, psychoanalysis has undergone a sea change. But, it is the amalgamation of this model with other emergent viewpoints that makes for such a profound shift in the way we understand the mind. Together with awareness of multiplicity, trauma, and dissociation, this change is even more profound. Our concept of the unconscious undergoes a radical revision to include a tightly woven system of interrelated dissociated self-states; our concept of psychic structuring emphasizes dissociation and the effects of trauma, as well as internalizations of relationships, well beyond the classical id/ego/superego structural model; our understanding of therapeutic action shifts to include and perhaps even to emphasize bearing witness, including affective responsiveness and affective honesty, especially with trauma patients, but to others as well. The relational unconscious, which involves communication between interacting unconscious minds, takes on more texture and complexity when we consider the various dissociated self-states that comprise the individual unconscious.

Relational Theory

Relational theory, which puts the emphasis on relationship, pulls together the intellectual work of many clinicians and is influenced by different social movements. As Bromberg (2009b) described it:

> Relational psychoanalysis is now a central piece of the psychoanalytic landscape, most notably in the United States and increasingly so internationally.... The school of Relational psychoanalysis was not born of a single seminal theorist or homogeneous group of theorists from which it then evolved, diverged, or remained loyal, and it is thereby not subject to evaluation by its degree of deviation from orthodoxy. Freud, Klein, Ferenczi, Fairbairn, Winnicott, Sullivan, and Kohut are all important parental figures but none carries parental authority. The range of theory, moreover, is extremely diverse because the value accorded a given concept or system of concepts derived from any given figure is more clinically than theoretically determined. The term "relational"...was selected...[because] [i]t clearly and concisely represented the core viewpoint...that the human mind, its normal development, its pathology, and the process of its therapeutic growth are relationally configured and it assured that the term be not so conceptually specific that it would convey adherence to one given set of ideas. (pp. 347–348)

The relational orientation thus bridges the intrapsychic and the interpersonal, internal object relations with external interpersonal ones. However, it not only bridges but also synthesizes these for the intrapsychic and the interpersonal are closely interrelated, each influencing the other (Aron, 1996). Increasingly, we understand problems in living as the result of failed relationships, usually with attachment figures of early life. Recognition of the importance of attachment comes with the relational model. Human beings are innately wired for attachment and relationality

(Bowlby, 1969/1982). But, along with attachment comes the capacity for shame (Lewis, 1981). While shame has its prosocial purposes, too much of it can be traumatic, bringing about dissociation (Bromberg, 1998). Thus a key explanatory model for what causes these failed relationships to become continuous problems in living is dissociation.

Relationality, multiplicity, and traumatic dissociation all come together to frame a different way of understanding the human mind. We see the impact of ways the person was traumatized, the shame the person felt about that, and how the person has defensively responded to anxiety and shame. While acknowledging the importance of conflict, relational theory in its focus goes beyond drive and defense as well as beyond simply maladaptive behavior. It addresses the conflict between differing and opposing relational aspects and configurations of the self, for example, the shamed self versus other parts of the self that may operate more adaptively and with less conscious pain. Stephen Mitchell's (1993) observation about the importance of being able to experience the conflict between multiple versions of the self was prescient:

> One of the great benefits of the analytic process is that the more the analysand can tolerate experiencing multiple versions of himself, the stronger, more resilient and durable he experiences himself to be. Conversely, the more the analysand can find continuities across his various experiences, the more he can tolerate the identity confusion entailing by containing multiple versions of self. (p. 116)

If Sigmund Freud would have been able to see and work with the idea that dissociation could be used defensively (O'Neil, 2009), that is, that the dissociative structure of the mind, as well as autohypnosis, are defensively relied on, we might have a different psychodynamic grounding today. The concept of conflict in the relational psychodynamics among dissociated self-states—as was adumbrated in the work of Pierre Janet (1907, 1925) in his descriptions of phobias of memories and parts of the self that hold traumatic memories—might have been passed on to us clearly. Dissociative disorders might have been accepted all along, rather than seemingly banished into the ether, only to return to people's awareness more recently from the same unconscious cultural place of banishment. And, if Freud (1896/1962) had stayed with his first theory of hysteria, his so-called seduction theory, in which he connected child sexual abuse to hysteria, our current psychology might be different. But, the upshot is that both the dissociative structure of mind and the reality of child abuse had to be largely rediscovered.

The dissociative model of the mind was already in the zeitgeist when Freud began to write. Multiple personality was well recognized, even a fascination, among a sizable group of clinicians at that time. Theorists and clinicians were writing about "double consciousness," as was the early Freud. Freud continued to write about how real relationships affect psychodynamics, notably in *Mourning and Melancholia* (1917/1959a). His description of how the shadow of the object falls on the ego in situations of psychic loss that are infused with hate not only adumbrated his later descriptions of the superego but also set the stage for later articulations of internalized object relations.

Yet, aside from his clinical cases, much of his later writing moved away from explicitly interpersonal concerns—and away from direct attention to dissociation. In the work that followed, Freud exposed "the belief in ... conscious thought as an ultimate datum of human experience" (Fromm, 1980, p. 134). His popularization and descriptions of the operations of the unconscious gave us a way to understand interior life in a way that had not been previously possible. Freud's emphasis on unconscious determinism, unconscious defense, sexuality, aggression, fantasy, dreams, and our roles in the creations of our problems, along with his provision of a psychoanalytic method for relieving human suffering, as a partial list, provided a way of thinking about the mind that resonated with people's wish for self-understanding.

Many find certain aspects of Freud's theories objectionable, for example, his sexism, but he also gave us the tools to understand sexism. From Freud's work, we inherit, in the archeological idiom that he so loved, a multilayered tradition of acceptance of trauma and denial of trauma, attention to the child's conflicts around sexuality and aggression in the theory of the Oedipus complex, but in a theory that was itself embedded in the recognition of trauma.[1]

In accordance with Freud's turning aside from exogamous trauma and dissociation, explicit theories and approaches involving human interpersonal relationships were developed separately by such people as Karen Horney, Harry Stack Sullivan, Clara Thompson, Steven Mitchell, Judith Herman, Philip Bromberg, Heinz Kohut, Jessica Benjamin, Lewis Aron, Donnel Stern, Jody Davies, Mary-Gail Frawley-O'Dea, Robert Stolorow, Adrienne Harris, and Jean Baker Miller and her cohorts at the Stone Center, among others. Sullivan's interpersonal theory of human development emphasized each person's history of interpersonal relationships with significant real others, and he described the organization of self in terms of the internalizations of the interactive patterns of these relationships. Mitchell (1991, 1993, 2000) not only articulated the concept of the multiple self, emphasizing the embeddedness of humans in human relationships, but also noted the dynamic struggle between needs for intimacy and closeness along with corresponding needs for differentiation and separateness.

The women's movement, which explicated relational trauma such as rape as both personal and political, required a relational posture, one that acknowledged trauma. Then, the end of the Vietnam War, with masses of traumatized soldiers returning home, made the importance of trauma unmistakable. This created a space for some women's problems such as rape, battering, and child sexual abuse to be recognized as traumatic. Trauma and relationality, as joined ideas, became a natural outflow of the confluence of these two movements in time. But, once these influences dialectically fed each other, enabling a consolidation of the relational turn, trauma was rerecognized as implicit, such that dissociation became implicit in relationality as well. Judith Herman (1992) powerfully articulated a relational approach to posttraumatic and dissociative problems in living. Davies and Frawley (1994) incorporated trauma theory and dissociation into their relational psychoanalytic theory, with its emphasis on various transference-countertransference positions. But, it is Bromberg who articulated in most depth and in most specificity the effects of relational trauma on the human mind.

Relationality, Trauma, and Dissociation

Relationality puts the emphasis on relationships, including the interconnectedness of selves to other selves as well as parts of the self to each other. But, it also serves as an explanatory platform for understanding disconnection of selves and parts of selves. As Lewis Aron noted (1996), "Relational theory is . . . anchored in the idea that it is relationships (internal and external, real and imagined) that are central" (p. 18). The idea that relationships are central applies both to the genesis of problems and to the mode of treating them. It acknowledges that people are who they are largely because of their relationships and how they have represented these intrapsychically, and that in the therapeutic relationship, the therapist is part of the relationship that is coconstructed rather than some objective outside party who does not influence the interactions.

This shift from a one-person psychology to a two-person psychology allows for the awareness that a substantial portion of psychological problems is likely to be exogenous (external) in origin rather than endogenous (internal). As such, a two-person psychology allows for the rerecognition of the reality of trauma. In a one-person model, the credo of unconscious psychic determinism too often foreclosed awareness that there is a world beyond our own unconscious intentions and orchestrations. In contrast, the relational psychoanalytic approach allows for the recognition that trauma, in and of itself, not just as a result of inner conflicts and instinctual pressures, arouses overwhelming and intolerable affects—and thus the inevitability of dissociation.

Although psychoanalysis traces its origins to the treatment of trauma and dissociation (Breuer & Freud, 1893–1895a,b), until the last few decades the trauma/dissociation field and that of psychoanalysis have existed by and large separately from one another. This was in part because Freud's views on instinctual drives and infantile development for the most part left out exogamous trauma and blamed the child as the guilty one for having incestuous wishes (Betcher & Pollack, 1993; Devereux, 1953; Fromm, 1980; Pines, 1989; Rachman, 1997; Ross, 1982; Stolorow & Atwood, 1979).

And, partly as a consequence of this omission, trauma theories have relied on learning theory and cognitive psychology rather than psychoanalysis for their theoretical foundations.

Multiplicity and Dissociative Multiplicity

Multiplicity is implicit in both a relational and a dissociative model of mind. The capacity for multiplicity is involved in social interactions and fostered the survival of human groups (Slavin & Kreigman, 1992). None of us could enact different roles, such as mother, father, daughter, son, student, teacher, victim, rescuer, persecutor, and so on without the capacity for multiplicity. People's minds are patterned into a multitude of organizations in accordance with experiences, feelings, thoughts, and fantasies about significant others. And, this patterning reflects different aspects of many people in many relationships. Thus, psychic representations of these relationships are multiple and various. As Mitchell (1991) noted, "because we learn to become a person through interactions with different others and through different interactions with the same other, our experience of self is discontinuous, composed of different configurations, different selves with different others" (p. 128). Building on these concepts but adding the influence of dissociation, Bromberg (2009a) wrote:

> Today, increased attention is being paid to the normal multiplicity of states of consciousness. This is evoking a conceptual shift toward a view of the mind as a configuration of discontinuous, shifting states of consciousness. These states are understood to have varying degrees of access to perception and cognition because many domains of dissociated self-experience have only weak or nonexistent links to the experience of "I" as a communicable entity. (p. 638)

Thus, it is not only that we have multiple self-states, in accordance with roles, context, evoked affect, and so on but also that, as a result of experiences that were traumatic, many of these ways of being we have are separated, dissociated from each other. The inevitability of trauma, especially some relational trauma, along with the psychic splits it occasions, requires a construct of psychic structure that encompasses dissociation. A construct of psychic structuring based on relationships, then, must include dissociation. Trauma is ubiquitous and affects us all to varying degrees. In Chapter 4, I show how the presence of trauma implies the presence of dissociation. Especially as trauma becomes a more dominant discourse, more and more practitioners in the field are aware of "the dissociative structure of the mind" (Bromberg, 1998, p. 8). From this perspective, none of us is a unity but rather a highly organized aggregation of self-states that may be barely, mildly, or highly dissociated.

Although the topics of multiplicity and dissociation come from different sources, together they are aptly relevant to a discussion of dissociated self-states and DID. In double-bind situations of contradictory attachment, such as child abuse by a parent or caregiver or in traumatic bonding, dissociative multiplicity allows the child's attachment to and love of caretakers, both vital to survival and psychological well-being, to endure relatively undisturbed despite experiences such as abandonment or abuse that might otherwise be psychologically ruinous. An implicit recognition of the importance of dissociative multiplicity and how too much problematic dissociation can interfere with personal cohesion is embedded in our language: We regularly say things such as, "pull yourself together," "he is coming unglued," "she was beside herself," "don't fall apart," and so on.

In dissociative problems in living, the mutuality of relationships, between people as well as within the organization of the self, has largely collapsed or is missing. The person can only rely on the self and thus creates a relatively closed system of the personality to compensate for the missing mutuality. A closed system, dominated by defensive dissociation, precludes intersubjectivity—the mutual recognition of separate, self-reflective, and agentic selves. The closed system also impedes intersubjectivity between self-states, what I call interstate intersubjectivity. This is the awareness of the contextual interdependence and interrelatedness of parts of the self that comprise personal depth. The closed system is evidence of the lack of an adequate internalization of an empathic other who could be influenced as well as be influential. It is this route *in* from a standpoint outside the self that facilitates the linkage of parts of the self. To address the deficits of the closed system, mutuality in the psychotherapeutic relationship is paramount. Aron's (1996) statement that "relational analysts share an emphasis on mutuality and reciprocity in the psychoanalytic relationship" (p. 123) is especially apt for trauma and for dissociative patients.

When we begin to talk about the dissociative multiplicity that characterizes those with DID, and to some extent all of us, we have an intricately multilevel structure in which there are internal relationships (intrapersonal) as well as external ones (interpersonal) that mirror and repeat in important ways the problems in the early relationships. There is a correspondence and reciprocal relationship between the intrapsychic and the interpersonal. The psychodynamics among the parts replay the patterns and motivations that existed between key figures in the early interpersonal environment and the child. This means that we will likely find both intrapersonal and interpersonal repetitions of dominant/submissive, annihilating/annihilated, and sadistic/masochistic patterns that characterized interpersonal relationships of the early environment, usually either the family or other kinds of total environments such as day care or both. The dissociated parts of the personality are in powerful and passionate dynamic interaction.

THE CONSTRUCT OF THE UNCONSCIOUS

Probably the most fundamental concept to psychoanalysis and psychodynamic psychotherapy, of whatever persuasion, is the unconscious. Freud's popularization of the construct of the unconscious made it possible for ordinary people, not just philosophers, to think about and understand their actions, thoughts, and motivations with much more complexity and expansiveness. The repressed unconscious is considered a unity, the contents of which were formed by the agency or will, albeit unconscious, of the person. There is a feeling of power about the repressed unconscious. In contrast, the dissociated unconscious consists of many autonomous subcenters of consciousness that are not necessarily a product of a person's agency. They are more likely the result of a person's having been psychologically overwhelmed.

As we consider dissociative multiplicity, our understanding of unconscious life undergoes a radical revision to include a tightly woven system of interrelated dissociated self-states. Dissociative multiplicity allows us to ask whether the unconscious as a unitary construct that is solely repression based is the best explanatory model. It also allows us to question the idea of conscious and unconscious as separate realms that at best interact (Bromberg, 2006). Bromberg's contrasting view of mental life is "as a nonlinear, self-organizing repatterning of self-state configurations that produce shifting representations of 'me'" (p. 3). Bromberg (1993) articulated an expansion of the construct of the unconscious:

> What we call the unconscious might usefully include the suspension or deterioration of linkages between self-states, preventing certain aspects of self—along with their respective constellations of affects, memories, values, and cognitive capacities—from achieving access to the personality within the same state of consciousness. (p. 182)

Indeed, we have in DID the most striking example of making the unconscious conscious. This lies in the intercommunication of dissociated identity states and the integration of their memories and affects, after which the person has much more access to what had been part of the dissociated unconscious.

Repression

As we think about the unconscious, we usually invoke the concept of repression. The usefulness of also invoking dissociation has just been discussed. How are repression and dissociation defined? The word *repression* refers to a willful exclusion of information from consciousness; the "essence of repression lies simply in turning something away, and keeping it at a distance, from the conscious" (Freud, 1915/1959b, p. 147). It involves pushing out of consciousness both unpleasant and unwanted memories and any wishes that conflict with internalized prohibitions. With respect to the latter, repression could be said to involve will acting on wishes.

One important issue is that repression is usually understood to be an unconscious process, initially as well as throughout. There is a logical problem with the specification that repression is solely an unconscious process, though, because this requires knowing and not knowing at the same time: Repression can ultimately require an infinite series of inner homunculi to do the repressing (Erdelyi, 1994; Kihlstrom, 1984; Stern, 1997). The repressing part of the ego must repress that it is repressing and so on. Potential solutions might allow that repression could initially be conscious (Erdelyi, 1994) as well as the invocation of dissociation as explanatory process. (For further discussion of this matter, see Howell, 2005, pp. 144–151.)

What Is Dissociation?

Because the word *dissociation* is used so variously, especially as it pertains to different theoretical perspectives, people are often confused regarding what it really means. In the most general sense, dissociation refers to the separation of realms of experience that would normally be connected. As Putnam (1989) says, views about dissociation "converge around the idea that dissociation represents a failure of integration of ideas, information, affects, and experience" (p. 19). However, the word refers to many kinds of phenomena, processes, and conditions:

- Dissociation refers to dissociative structure in which self-states are kept rigidly segmented. A spatial metaphor for dissociative structure is vertical splitting (Hilgard, 1977; Kohut, 1971), but it also refers to processes, such as spacing out, psychic numbing, and even experiencing oneself as floating above one's body.
- Dissociation is both adaptive and maladaptive, both verb and noun, both cause and effect (Spiegel, 1990b; Tarnopolsky, 2003).
- Dissociation is both a psychologically defensive response, protecting against painful affects and memories, and an organismic and automatic response to immediate danger (Van der Hart, Nijenhuis, & Steele, 2006).
- Dissociation can be understood as taxonic, that is, as describing a certain type of individual or, alternatively, as existing on a continuum—describing all of us, varying in degrees (Putnam, 1997).
- Dissociation is both occurrent (in evidence or in process) and dispositional (a capability that can be tapped) (Braude, 1995, 2009).

Thus, there are multiple views of the etiology and nature of dissociation. Yet, when dissociation is so many things, there is the potential for conceptual confusion—the word can be used so loosely that it begins to lose its meaning.

To my way of thinking, the simplest organization of these multiple meanings is in terms of, first, the dissociative structure of mind and, second, the dissociative processes. Dissociative structure is exemplified in Fairbairn's endopsychic model as well as in Van der Hart, Nijenhuis, and Steele's (2006) theory of the structural dissociation of the personality, which expands on Janet's (1907, 1925) early thoughts. It also includes Sullivan's (1933) "not me" and Bromberg's (1998, 2006) descriptions of dissociated self-states. And, it includes Bucci's (1997, 2002, 2003) cognitive-psychoanalytic model of dissociation that involves the lack of sufficient referential process to link symbolic and subsymbolic aspects of experience. In addition, dissociative structure may include unformulated experience (Stern, 1997), especially inasmuch as one dissociative part of the person is unformulated by another (Howell, 2005). Finally, dissociative structure is manifested in identity confusion, identity alterations, and both macro- and microamnesias.

Dissociative process refers to activity such as going into trance as well as depersonalization and derealization. It also includes Sullivan's selective inattention: As a result of unbearable anxiety arising from interactions with caregivers, certain kinds of experiences may become part of "not-me." Dissociative processes may contribute to the dissociative structure. Stern (1997) partially relied on the concept of selective inattention to develop his model of unformulated experience. Here, keeping the experience unformulated into meaningful constructs does not have to imply a dissociated self-state. However, the existence of unformulated experience may lead to dissociative structure. For example, Mary and Jane are separate dissociated identity states. As Mary begins to learn about Jane's experience through integrative processes, Jane's experience becomes more and more formulated to Mary.

John O'Neil (2009) uses the term "dissociative multiplicity" to make the distinction between dissociation that does not imply multiplicity (such as trance states, selective inattention, some forms of depersonalization) from dissociation that does imply multiplicity (such as multiple dissociated self-states). O'Neil's distinction of dissociation of function versus multiplicity largely parallels my distinction between dissociative process and structure.

Repression and Dissociation

Repression is only active and motivated. In contrast, dissociation is both an automatic, psychologically passive, and an active motivated defense. Repressed "materials are experienced as once familiar, rediscovered aspects of mental life . . . [which] have been previously experienced, psychologically digested, encoded, and then forgotten" (Davies & Frawley, 1994, p. 66). In contrast, dissociation occurs when the person is unable to integrate or synthesize experience, and dissociated material is generally organized in such a way that one realm of experience requires the exclusion of another. However, probably the most important difference is that dissociation is occasioned by experience that is unassimilable, often unbearable, whereas repression is a defense that deals with the unpleasant.

Bromberg (2006) describes how defensive dissociation involves unbearable conflict between different versions of "me":

> Repression defines a process that is designed to avoid disavowed mental content that may lead to unpleasant intrapsychic conflict. Dissociation shows its signature not by disavowing aspects of mental *contents* per se, but through the patient's alienation from aspects of *self* that are inconsistent with his experience of "me" at a given moment. It functions because conflict is *unbearable* to the mind, not because it is *unpleasant*. (p. 7; emphasis in original)

Some differences between repression and dissociation are outlined:

- Repression is both motivated and defensive. In contrast, dissociation often is, but does not have to be motivated or psychologically defensive. For example, dissociation can arise automatically in the moment of trauma or nondefensively in response to hypnosis.
- Repression refers to formulated experience, and dissociation as a process often implies unformulated experience (Stern, 1997).
- Repression usually refers to a piece of information that was accessible at one time but not at another, whereas dissociation refers to states and systems of states that are often mutually exclusive (Spiegel, 1994). They exist side by side. For example, "My father is a wonderful man" is fiercely believed by one self-state, while another suffers from the memories of abuse. The metaphor for repression is *horizontal splitting*, and that for dissociation is *vertical splitting* (Hilgard, 1977; Kohut, 1971).
- In contrast to repressed memories, which are assumed to have been willfully (albeit, supposedly unconsciously) forgotten and are therefore at least somewhat independent of context, dissociated experience is especially vulnerable to being elicited by context (adapted from Howell, 2005, p. 147).

Dissociation and Repression Interact

Does the unconscious then pertain to repressed or dissociated material? I think that its contributors include both dissociation and repression, often in interaction and put into effect one by the other. I think that the dissociative model is the best place to start, but room should be allowed for the operation of repression. For example, a model that includes different interacting autonomous centers of unconscious activity, which themselves have repressive capabilities and actions, might be more comprehensive than either the strictly repression-based or dissociation-based model.

As O'Neil (2009) observes, dissociated identities (alters) in people with DID have the capacity for repression: "In general...a given alter has its own Id, Ego, and Superego" (p. 113). Repression and dissociation also often potentiate each other (Dell, 2009b).

Psychoanalysis traces its origins to the study of dissociative unconscious processes involving double consciousness and multiplicity. Double consciousness implies dual centers of conscious. (Because the centers are dissociated, their respective mental activity is unconscious, each to the other.) However, Freud discontinued writing in this way, adopting instead his construct of the (unitary) unconscious. In their observations of the double consciousness of hysteria, Breuer and Freud (1893–1895a) stated, "The basis and the *sine qua non* of hysteria is the existence of hypnoid states" (p. 12). In "The Preliminary Communication," Freud both endorsed hypnoid hysteria (dissociation) and then later, in his own chapter on the psychotherapy of hysteria, renounced it, advocating for the active defensive activity of repression. He wrote: "I have never in my own experience met with a genuine hypnoid hysteria. Any that I took in hand turned into defense hysteria" (Breuer & Freud, 1893–1895, p. 286). As O'Neil (2009) noted, Freud's "inaugural category mistake" was "of assuming that the hypnoid state could not be the result of active defense" (p. 319).

But, here we are getting ahead of ourselves. We return to Freud shortly. Now, the immediate question is, "What has happened with dissociation?"

DID AS THE CHESHIRE CAT: A HISTORICAL VIEW

Trance, Hypnosis, Demons, and DID

Dissociative capacity is part of our human DNA, probably developed in the service of survival (Dell, 2009b). This capacity has the potential for both adaptive and maladaptive utilization. Throughout the world and long before people thought in terms of categories of mental disorders (e.g., psychosis, neurosis, schizophrenia, bipolar, depression, etc.), human cultures have valued the human capacity to enter into dissociative trance. Positive manifestations of trance have been a part of the religious ceremonies of many communities and have been exhibited in various rituals and healing ceremonies as well as in personal mystical and religious experiences of intense absorption, ecstasy, and transformation (Cardeña, 2001; Ellenberger, 1970; Hilgard, 1994; James, 1902/1958; Levine, 1997). Dissociative trance is also essential for the work of shamans, healers across cultures and throughout history, who have used it as a way to heal the afflictions of others and to prepare the body to be entered by spirits (Randal, Geekie, Lambrecht, & Taitima, 2008, p. 340). Interestingly, the shaman is not so much possessed by the spirits but rather summons and takes possession of them.

One particular kind of dissociative trance that has been documented throughout history is possession trance. This includes both benign spirit possession and demon possession (Cardeña, 2001; Hilgard, 1977; Levine, 1997). Currently, at least 50% of our 488 non-Western cultures "have a structured belief in Spirit Possession as a valued and valid aspect of self" (Hegeman, 2010, p. 99). In many cultures, possession trance provides socially accepted ways for the powerless to exert some power and influence. For example, Lewis-Fernandez (1994) described how possession by the spirit of a deceased relative allowed a powerless new bride some respect and control over her life. The spirit instructed the in-laws to provide the daughter-in-law with better care. Because the in-laws respected and feared the spirit, the possession syndrome also allowed the daughter-in-law greater control over her life.

Spirit possession—especially demon possession—can tell a story symbolically and express important conflicts. Somer (2004) documented the occurrence of trance possession in 16th-century Near Eastern Judaism, in which a *dybbuk*, the spirit of a deceased person, clung to the possessed person. Interestingly, records of the exorcisms indicated that the spirits in these cases were male, and they often entered the possessed person's body through the vagina and the rectum, suggestive of sexual intercourse. According to Somer (2004), "by allowing individuals to communicate about their forbidden secrets and inner conflicts through a 'non-me' agent, the dybbuk may have enabled ventilation and some processing of otherwise inexpressible traumatic and/or guilt-promoting experiences" (pp. 142–143).

Somer (2004) further noted that the phenomenology of these possession experiences is similar to that of DID. Similarly, as Ellenberger (1970) speculated, "instances of multiple personality may have existed long ago, but remained unnoticed" (p. 127). And, Kluft (1994) maintained that "DID is the contemporary and demystified form of an anthropological commonplace" (p. 2). As in demon possession, people with DID often have parts named Devil, Satan, or Lucifer. As in demon possession, demon parts in DID refer to the host in the third person and often in contemptuous terms, for example, calling the host a wimp, an idiot, and so on.

In Western culture, before the Enlightenment, the remedy or treatment for demonic possession was exorcism by priests. (Of course, this practice is still present, but much less so.) The process by which the dissociative symptoms of demon possession came under the purview of science and became understood as mental health problems first took a route through the study of hypnosis (Dell, 2009b) and only secondarily through the route of understanding the effects of trauma. Hypnosis offered the first approach to understanding the division of the personality, and it was understood that these parts of the person preexisted the application of the hypnosis.

The Study of Dissociative Trances Began With Hypnosis

Anton Mesmer (after whom *mesmerism* took its name) offered the first challenge to exorcism as a cure for demon possession in the late 1770s. His *magnetism*, a secular form of hypnotism that he considered "scientific," began a process by which the treatment of emotional distress was liberated from the domination of the church. Mesmer's magnetic approach elicited altered states of consciousness and evidence of dissociation; indeed, according to a fascinating account by Middleton, Dorahy, and Moskowitz (2008), "accounts of individuals switching between identity states and demonstrating amnesia between states or switching into fugue states, had always been part of the literature associated with mesmerism" (p. 10).

In Mesmer's magnetic healing, practitioners called *animal magnetists* would make magnetic passes with their hands, and the patient would go into a sort of hysterical crisis, which would then result in relief or improvement of the patient's symptoms. Among his followers was the Marquis de Puységur, who in the late 1700s discovered what he called artificial somnambulism. In one case, instead of developing a crisis, the patient appeared to go into a deep sleep in which he spoke, but about which he had amnesia on awakening. Because of the similarity to sleepwalking, about which people have amnesia, or natural somnambulism, it was called artificial somnambulism (Dell, 2009d, p. 714; Van der Hart & Dorahy, 2009).

Thus, while convulsive hysterical crises had been described by doctors and philosophers of ancient Greece, as well as in the Middle Ages and the Renaissance (Janet, 1907), these crises could now be linked to the dual consciousness of somnambulism. Increasingly, the dissociative symptoms that had formerly been seen as signs of demonic possession were understood as secular, personal problems. By the late 1700s, what we now understand as DID was described as a particular disorder. In 1791, the mesmerist Gmelin published an 87-page report on the dramatic switching of identity states of a young woman (cited in Middleton, Dorahy, & Moskowitz, 2008). Following Gmelin's report and others like it, many cases of dual and multiple personalities were reported and published during the 1800s in both Europe and the United States. The most influential of these early cases was that of Mary Reynolds (1785–1854) in the United States. At the age of 26, she suffered a series of fits, which left her deaf and blind for several weeks. This was followed by the emergence of a young child state and eventually a more energetic and cheerful new Mary, but the switches went on for 18 years. Her changes in state were accompanied by amnesia (Carlson, 1986).

Following the discovery of evidence of a double consciousness and multiple personality, the topic was the subject of considerable study and thought. Especially in France, there were notable contributions to the study of the division of consciousness (*dédoublement*) in the early to late 1800s. In 1888, Jules Janet, an uncle to Pierre Janet, used the model of double consciousness in a way that was a precursor to the idea of multiple personalities (Van der Hart & Dorahy, 2009).

In addition to double personality, before and during the 19th century there was considerable interest in the spontaneous occurrences of trances, state-specific memory, and autohypnotic trance speaking in France as well as England. Frederick Myers (1887) proposed the existence of a supraliminal self and a subliminal self in psychic structure. In England, the Society for Psychical Research was an important organization that studied such events. In the late 1800s, this organization hailed members such as William James and Pierre Janet—and even Sigmund Freud as a corresponding member (Alvarado, 2002).

Hysteria and Double Consciousness

By the mid-1800s, clinicians were beginning to link the phenomenon of double consciousness, or the splitting of consciousness, that occurred in hypnosis with hysteria (Van der Hart & Dorahy, 2009). Generally, the central problem for people with hysteria was dissociation. The people who studied dissociation in the 19th century were a motley group, including magnetizers, philosophers, and physicians, among others. The topics studied, although wide ranging, cohered closely around hypnosis, autohypnosis, and double consciousness:

> In addition to somnambulism, dissociative phenomena of interest included possession phenomena, automatic writing, talking tables, mediumship, and various manifestations of hysteria. Multiple personality disorder, which was regarded as the most complex form of hysteria, received special attention. (Van der Hart & Dorahy, 2009, p. 9)

However, hysteria covered a range of problems in living (primarily in women), including what we would now call dissociative disorders, somatoform disorders, borderline personality disorder (BPD), posttraumatic stress disorder (PTSD), and reactive psychosis. Hysteria was commonly used as a diagnostic medical term from the 1700s until its elimination from the *DSM* in the late 1900s.

Charcot Finds the Link

It was Jean Martin Charcot, a renowned neurologist based at the Salpêtrière Clinic in France and teacher to Freud, and others who began to make the link among dissociation, trauma, and hysteria. His understanding of neurology and his dramatic demonstrations of the dissociative nature of hysteria "brought about ... a synthesis between the traditions of hypnosis and official psychiatry, at the same time elevating hypnosis to a level worthy of scientific investigation" (Middleton et al., 2008, p. 11). Charcot linked hysterical symptoms with subconscious ideas that had been split off from consciousness, but he believed that the basic cause of hysteria was constitutional weakness (Dell, 2009b; Van der Hart & Dorahy, 2009). Freud was greatly influenced by Charcot, whose work he translated, as a result of which some of Charcot's work appeared in German before it appeared in French (Dell, 2009b). Freud even named his son, Martin, after Charcot.

Janet's Giant Step

It was Charcot's student at Salpêtrière, the eminent Pierre Janet, who explicitly linked hysteria to traumatic antecedents. His descriptions of that linkage were astute, precise, and prolific. Despite his large body of published work, it should be noted that Janet worked within the French tradition of scientific investigation that advocated careful observation, not grand theory building (Dell, 2009a, 2009d). Starting in his 1889 doctoral thesis, Janet wrote of the influence of trauma on hysteria and was the first to use the concepts of trauma and dissociation to explain the many symptoms of hysteria (Nijenhuis & Van der Hart, 1999; Van der Kolk & Van der Hart, 1989). He observed that "vehement emotions" evoked by trauma can prevent the integration of traumatic memories, to the extent that frightening or novel experiences may not be integrated into the existing cognitive schemata. As a result, aspects of these experiences became separated from ordinary consciousness, operating subconsciously and autonomously (Janet, 1907, 1919, 1925). "Fixed ideas" (idées fixes), which are volatile thoughts or images that have become subconscious, are formed around memories of vehement affect organizing "cognitive, affective and visceral elements of the trauma while simultaneously keeping them out of conscious awareness" (Van der Kolk & Van der Hart, 1989, p. 1532). Because these fixed ideas become isolated from personal consciousness and one's will, they are vulnerable to being triggered by emotions and ideas (Van der Hart & Friedman, 1989; Van der Kolk & Van der Hart, 1989). Consequently, they powerfully organize symptoms, intruding into consciousness as behavior, emotions, and thoughts. Janet's word to describe this process, by which aspects of experience were separated and stored subconsciously, was désagrégation, which meant dissociation.

Importantly, the frightening or overwhelming event does not disappear but remains active as a fixed idea that becomes a subconscious center around which other aspects of psychological experience may cohere. As Janet (1907) stated, "Things happen as if an idea, a partial system of thoughts, emancipated itself, became independent and developed itself on its own account" (p. 42). Importantly, Janet emphasized that fixed ideas belong to a mental system that is not subject to conscious will: "The power of such ideas depends upon their isolation. They grow, they install themselves in the field of thought like a parasite, and the subject cannot check their development by any effort on his part... because they exist by themselves in a second field of thought detached from the first" (1925, p. 600).

Awareness of Dissociation Spreads to America: William James and Morton Prince

Many of Janet's concepts and ideas (e.g., his descriptions of what we now call PTSD and more recently somatoform disorders) have had considerable influence on and have been assimilated into the psychological and mental health literature (Van der Hart et al., 2006). In particular, one of Janet's students was Jean Piaget, who relied heavily on Janet's ideas about assimilation and accommodation (Ellenberger, 1970).

Janet, an eminent scholar and sought-after clinician, was well known in his time and had many followers in America as well as in Europe (Van der Hart & Friedman, 1989; Van der Kolk & Van der Hart, 1989). In the early 1900s, William James and Morton Prince, among others, were fascinated by Janet's ideas and wrote prolifically about dissociation and multiple personality disorder (MPD). James, who was also influenced by Frederick Myers's idea of the subliminal self, wrote of dissociation in *Principles of Psychology* (1890/1950). Morton Prince (1906/1969) published the well-known multiple personality case of Miss Beauchamp, as well as other works on dissociation and multiple personality. Boris Sidis published *Multiple Personality: An Experimental Investigation Into the Nature of Human Individuality* (1904), which he dedicated to James.

Dissociation in Europe: Jung and Bleuler

Janet's ideas about dissociation directly influenced those of Carl Jung, whose concept of "complex," which he described in terms of dissociation, had a similar meaning to Janet's concept of fixed ideas (Ellenberger, 1970; Moskowitz, Read, Farrelly, Rudegeair, & Williams, 2009). Similar to Janet's description of fixed ideas, Jung described complexes as "affectively-charged clusters of ideas accompanied by somatic interventions" (Moskowitz et al., 2009, p. 522). Again similar to Janet, Jung (1907/1960) emphasized the relative autonomy of complexes: "Today we can take it as moderately certain that complexes are in fact 'splinter psyches.' The etiology of their origin is frequently a so-called trauma, an emotional shock, or some such thing, that splits off a bit of the psyche" (p. 98).

Jung's term *complex* was also adopted by Eugen Bleuler, his close associate at the Burgholzi Hospital (Moskowitz et al., 2009). In his book *Dementia Praecox* (1911/1950), in which he introduced the term *schizophrenia*, Bleuler, like Jung, emphasized the importance of dissociation, stating that "different psychic complexes ... dominate the personality for a time" (p. 9) and observing that "the patient appears to be split into as many different persons or personalities as they have complexes" (p. 361).

Freud also incorporated Jung's term *complex* into his own writing and terminology, although he changed the meaning by draining it of assumptions of autonomy (Moskowitz, 2008). For instance, the term he coined, *Oedipus complex*, describes a conflict of a unified person's desires and internalized prohibitions rather than a subconscious part of the self that has its own autonomy.

Sigmund Freud

As we know, psychoanalysis began with the study of dissociation; of course, it would have, given its historical context. Freud and his early colleague, coauthor of *Studies on Hysteria* (1893–1895a,b) Josef Breuer, utilized concepts of dissociation that were current, involving double consciousness, somnambulism, splitting of consciousness, and so on. According to Ellenberger and Janet, Breuer and Freud adopted some of Janet's ideas and terms. Janet (as cited in Ellenberger, 1970) claimed priority for the discovery of fixed ideas and cathartic therapy, and by 1914, Janet expressed the conviction that Freud took many of his ideas, renamed them, and called them his own. In *Psychological Healing* (1925), Janet stated that he introduced the term *subconscious*, after which Freud wrote of *the unconscious*; he also claimed that after he wrote of *psychological analysis*, Freud coined *psychoanalysis*. Ellenberger (1970) also noted that Janet's concept, *the function of reality*, was renamed as *the reality principle*, and cited his agreement with Regis and Hesnard's statement that, "The methods and concepts of Freud were modeled after those of Janet, of whom he seems to have inspired himself constantly—until the paths of the two diverged" (pp. 539–540).

The dissociative nature of hysteria is clearly described in *Studies on Hysteria* (Breuer & Freud, 1893–1895a,b). Breuer's patient, Anna O. (Bertha Pappenheim), described therein with her switching of languages and her amnesia for occurrences in other states, probably had DID—as did some of Freud's patients described in the same book (Ross, 1989).

In the "Preliminary Communication" to *Studies on Hysteria* (1893–1895a), Breuer and Freud emphasized *hypnoid states*, a term that Breuer adopted from Charcot (Breger, 2000), which in turn Charcot had adapted from the French expression for somnambulistic states (Van der Hart & Dorahy, 2009). Indeed, Breuer and Freud stated that the existence of hypnoid states was "the basis and the *sine qua non* of hysteria" (1893–1895a, p. 12; italics in original).

They went on to connect these hypnoid states with traumatic memories that have not been associatively linked with other thoughts, and that are "found to belong to the ideational content of hypnoid states of consciousness with restricted association" (p. 15). These ideas are associated among themselves and form a "more or less highly organized rudiment of a second consciousness, a *condition seconde*" (p. 15; italics in original).

In the "Preliminary Communication" to *Studies on Hysteria* (1893–1895a), Breuer and Freud explicitly linked hysteria with splitting of consciousness, and dissociation:

> *The longer we have been occupied with these phenomena, the more we have become convinced that the splitting of consciousness which is so striking in the well-known classical cases under the form of* "double conscience" [footnote: the French term "dual consciousness"] *is present to a rudimentary degree in every hysteria, and that a tendency to such a dissociation, and with it the emergence of abnormal states of consciousness (which we shall bring together under the term "hypnoid") is the basic phenomenon of this neurosis.* In these views we concur with Binet and the two Janets. (p. 12; italics in original)

Despite these statements, Freud soon dismissed hypnoid hysteria, even in *Studies on Hysteria* (1893–1895b), in favor of *defense hysteria*, saying that every case of seeming hypnoid hysteria that he had seen had turned into defense hysteria. Thus, while dissociation was the crucible for the birth of psychoanalysis, this period in which it was explicitly studied came to be called the *prepsychoanalytic period* by Freud and his followers.

O'Neil (2009) views this as unfortunate, noting that Breuer's hypnoid hysteria was the "first psychoanalytic example of a state of mind" (p. 317), and that Freud made a category mistake in dismissing it. O'Neil cogently asks: "Why can the rationale for dissociation not be defense? The auto-hypnotic nature of hypnoid states was clear from the beginning to all concerned. Why was Freud unable to conceive of such an act of autohypnosis as unconsciously motivated or intended?" (p. 308). Following from an earlier discussion, in which he contrasted Pythagorean splitting (which consists of a number of polar opposites, such as "good/bad, light/dark" and so on) and the orthogonal grid of Empedocles (which would enable one to think of good and dark, for example), O'Neil says,

> Freud was trapped in his own Pythagorean table of opposites. One side of the table would be bad, Janet, Breuer, heredity, degeneracy, trauma splitting of consciousness, hypnoid hysteria, dissociation. The other side would be good, Freud, drive, defense, repression, conversion. He was unable to advance an Empedoclean grid which would have allowed for the defensive dissociative induction of hypnoid states, a

move which would have allowed him to distinguish dissociation from repression, without dismissing it, and forego the subsequent general psychoanalytic marginalization and abandonment of that significant patient population represented by a number of cases in his own *Studies on Hysteria* (Breuer & Freud, 1895). And so the latter is not only the primal book of psychoanalysis, but also the primal book of the psychoanalytic misinterpretation of major posttraumatic pathology. (p. 308)

Another step that many have regarded as unfortunate was Freud's abandonment of his so-called seduction theory, which was his first theory of the etiology of hysteria. In 1896, Freud presented "The Aetiology of Hysteria" (1896/1962), which described his theory of hysteria that linked the symptoms of hysteria with child sexual abuse. In this article, Freud stated that he had discovered that in each of 18 cases of hysteria, 2 of them corroborated, there were "one or more occurrences of premature sexual experience" (p. 203). In this work, he claimed that he had found the cause of hysteria, of which he and Breuer had earlier only found the mechanisms. He likened his discovery to finding the *caput Nili*—the source of the Nile—of neuropathology (p. 203). (The discovery of the source of the Nile River in Africa was the most important discovery of the 19th century, according to Janet, 1925.)

Freud (1896/1962) clearly felt strongly about this issue of the sexual abuse of children, arguing that:

> The idea of these infantile sexual scenes is very repellent to the feelings of a sexually normal individual; they include all the abuses known to debauched and impotent persons, among whom the buccal cavity and the rectum are misused for sexual purposes...on the one hand, the adult...who is armed with complete authority and the right to punish, and can exchange one role for the other to the uninhibited satisfaction of his moods, and on the other hand, the child, who in his helplessness is at the mercy of this arbitrary will, who is prematurely aroused to every kind of sensibility and exposed to every sort of disappointment, and whose performance of the sexual activities assigned to him is often interrupted by his imperfect control of his natural needs—all these grotesque and yet tragic consequences reveal themselves as stamped upon the later development of the individual and of his neurosis, in countless permanent effects which deserve to be traced in the greatest detail. (pp. 214–225)

However, Freud did not think that his presentation was received well, writing to Fliess soon afterward that Krafft-Ebing, who chaired the meeting, had called it a "scientific fairy tale," and that the "donkeys gave it an icy reception" (p. 189).

As we know, soon after, in 1897, Freud supplanted his seduction theory with his theory of infantile sexuality and the Oedipus complex. Reversing his former stance about the reality of child abuse that he felt had not been accepted, he posited that most often patients' memories of sexual abuse were instead wishful manifestations of oedipal desire. It was these desires rather than sexual traumas that were repressed. (Freud never denied that child sexual abuse does occur and is pathogenic.)

Among Freud's officially stated reasons for his change of mind was that if all of these hysterics had histories of child sexual abuse, this would mean that an unbelievable percentage of the adult population would be abusers. This logic is fallacious for there is not a one-to-one correspondence between number of child abusers and victims; most pedophiles and child abusers have more than one victim. Indeed, some have thousands (Salter, 2003). Freud also pointed to the fact that when he informed his patients of his discovery that they had been abused, they fled treatment, which he took as an indication that he had been wrong. He also noted the difficulty of determining the veracity of the unconscious. Whatever all the reasons may have been, his view of the child's dilemma soon changed significantly (Breger, 2000; Brothers, 1995; Davies & Frawley, 1994; Gay, 1988; Kupersmid, 1993; Masson, 1986; Matari, 1998; Tabin, 1993).

Breger (2000), Brothers (1995), Kupersmid (1993), and Masson (1984) suggested that Freud's internal conflicts, as opposed to the officially presented version of theoretical views, led to his abandonment of the seduction theory. In the year and a half between his presentation of "Aetiology of Hysteria" (1896/1962) and his abandonment of the seduction theory, Freud's father died, and recognition of his father's abuse of his siblings may have influenced his retraction. In 1896 and 1897, he wrote letters to his friend Robert Fleiss; he "baldly asserted that his father had sexually abused several of his siblings and was responsible for their neuroses" (Masson, 1985, p. 231, as quoted in Brothers, 1995, p. 8). Regardless of the reasons, the upshot was that Freud's new theoretical focus deemphasized dissociation and the traumatic roots of hysteria in child sexual abuse.[1]

Despite the fact that his official dissociation period was short-lived, Freud's future work did describe dissociative phenomena without emphasis that this was the case. In *The Dissociative Mind* (Howell, 2005), I outlined four different models, or ways of thinking about dissociation (Dissociationisms 1, 2, 3, and 4), which Freud adopted in the course of his work:

- *Dissociationism 1* was the splitting of consciousness that he and Breuer espoused in the "Preliminary Communication" (1893–1895a). This has to do with hypnoid states, in which the phenomenon is one of doubling or multiplication, by which one becomes more than one. This was similar to Janetian dissociation and was more of Breuer's position than Freud's in the course of *Studies on Hysteria* (1893–1895a,b). Here one *becomes* two.

- *Dissociationism 2,* also present in the "Preliminary Communication," was the beginning of Freud's concept of repression. It was about how "one *makes* two," that is, how people can make some matters unconscious, dividing the mind into conscious and unconscious parts. This process has to do with things

> all of a distressing nature, calculated to arouse the affects of shame, of self-reproach, and of psychical pain, and the feeling of being harmed; they were all of a kind that one would prefer not to have experienced and would rather forget.... [This incompatible idea] provoked on the part of the ego a repelling force of which the purpose was a defense against this incompatible idea [which was]...forced out of consciousness and out of memory. (Breuer & Freud, 1893–1895b, p. 269)

The person repressing memories or wishes acts as a unity, at least with respect to the material being repressed, and a structural dissociation is created. Part of experience, whether it is a memory or a wish, is no longer accessible.

- *Dissociationism 3* had to do with the split between the ego and the superego, which was adumbrated in *Mourning and Melancholia* (1917/1959a) and in *Group Psychology and Analysis of the Ego* (1921/1955) and outlined in *The Ego and the Id* (1923/1961a): "This modification of the ego retains its special position; it confronts the other contents of the ego as an ego ideal or super-ego" (p. 34).
- *Dissociationism 4* concerns, "The Splitting of the Ego in the Process of Defence" (Freud, 1938/1961b), in which he describes how two contradictory views of reality can exist in the mind simultaneously without an experience of conflict or resolution. He seemed to be addressing the effects of trauma in this article, but he never finished it.

Back to Bleuler: Schizophrenia Incorporates and Overshadows Hysteria and Multiple Personality Disorder

Shortly after Freud abandoned his seduction theory, Bleuler changed the term *dementia praecox*, which had been Kraepelin's term, to *schizophrenia*, describing the new disorder, schizophrenia, as dissociation based, a move that would ironically have the ultimate effect of overshadowing dissociative processes in mental disorders. In *Dementia Praecox or the Group of Schizpophrenias*, Bleuler (1911/1950) introduced *schizophrenia*, drawn from the Greek, meaning "split mind." He chose this term to replace the earlier term, *dementia praecox*, which he considered less exact on the basis that the disorder was not necessarily early (praecox) or dementia (Moskowitz, 2008). What Bleuler wanted to emphasize about schizophrenia was that "the 'splitting' of the different psychic functions is one of its most important characteristics" (p. 8). Clearly, many of Bleuler's patients had what today we would describe as DID and dissociative disorder not otherwise specified (DDNOS), Example 1, as described in *DSM-IV-TR*.

As previously noted, Bleuler and Jung were close collaborators, and Bleuler adopted use of Jung's term, *complex*, which was so similar to Janet's fixed ideas. Fixed ideas and dissociation were the hallmarks of hysteria, and now we have dissociation also as the hallmark of schizophrenia. Thus, as Moskowitz et al. (2009) observed, in the fruits of these collaborations between Jung and Bleuler, we have the beginning of a nosological problem: Dissociation was the hallmark now of both hysteria and schizophrenia. Another confound is that hysteria and MPD were understood to be neuroses with traumatic origins, while Bleuler believed that schizophrenia was biologically based (Moskowitz et al., 2009).

With Bleuler's (1911/1950) emphasis on the importance of dissociation in schizophrenia, dissociative disorders also came to be largely subsumed under the category of schizophrenia. Writers such as Harold Searles and R. D. Laing, who wrote on schizophrenia in the 1950s and 1960s, described many cases of schizophrenia as involving overt switching of identity states—clearly cases of DID. And even today, many people understand schizophrenia as *split mind* and confuse it with DID, which in fact it once included.

In the late 1800s and early 1900s, many clinicians, both in Europe and in the United States, were interested in dissociation and dissociative disorders. For the first decade or so of the 20th century, MPD, now termed DID, was accepted and familiar. However, by the mid-1900s there was little explicit interest in dissociation, and with a few exceptions, dissociation and MPD became rarely discussed. After around the 1920s and until recently, dissociation, along with the topic of child sexual abuse, had been largely dissociated—if not banished—in psychoanalysis. Like dissociated content itself, the topic of dissociation did not go away but kept popping up, sometimes using different terms, but the clinical descriptions were similar. Jung wrote of dissociative problems using his term *complexes*. Other theorists such as Fairbairn and Ferenczi also wrote of dissociation, but most predominantly used the word *splitting* rather than dissociation.

Much as he valued Freud's work, Fairbairn (1944/1952a) felt that theory needed to go back to hysteria for an adequate understanding of the mind. Fairbairn's thinking was also influenced by Janet's view of the causal role of dissociation in hysteria. Instead, however, of pursuing this line of thinking, the theory Fairbairn developed emphasized the psychic structural consequences of problematic attachments. Notably, Fairbairn believed that dissociative and the schizoid personality organization was normative.

Fairbairn worked with sexually abused children and acknowledged the importance of child abuse as a contribution to schizoid disorders. He wrote of MPD (1931/1952b), although he did not emphasize it in the articulation of his theory.

In his famous "Confusion of Tongues" paper, Ferenczi (1932/1949) emphatically pointed to the problem of adults' sexual exploitation of children and its disastrous effects on their emotional lives. In this, as well as in earlier papers and his *Clinical Diary* (Dupont, 1988), he clearly spelled out dissociative responses to abuse and the clear structuring of the personality into dissociated parts, stating, "There is neither shock nor fright without some splitting of the personality" (1932/1949, p. 229). He added that each of the fragments behaves like "a separate personality yet does not know, even of the existence of the others" (p. 229). Like Fairbairn, Ferenczi also viewed dissociation as normative, and according to Bromberg (2009):

> Ferenczi pioneered the contemporary analytic view that regressive reliving of early traumatic experiences in the analytic transference is to some degree curative in itself because it encourages active mastery of the traumatic "past" through use of the here-and-now analytic relationship. (p. 638)

Although the issue is complicated—Aron and Harris (1993) emphasized that it was primarily Ferenczi's unorthodox experiments with clinical technique rather than his views about the disastrous results of childhood sexual trauma that disturbed Freud—Ferenczi was "diagnostically" slandered (Breger, 2000) by Freud and Ernest Jones, who viewed him as demented, a view contradicted by the reports of others that his mind was sound (Rachman, 1997). However, the fact that everyone saw what happened to him after expressing his views must have been important implicit professional instruction.

So, what happened to cause the sudden decrease in explicit attention to dissociation in the early 20th century? One thing that happened was that, from about 1910 to 1925, interest in dissociation was displaced by psychoanalysis (Dell, 2009b). Concurrent with this was the encapsulation of dissociation within the new diagnosis of schizophrenia. With respect to social forces in the United States, Hilgard (1977) noted that three things led to the decrease of the popularity of thinking about dissociation. First, there was the rise of psychoanalysis with its focus on incestuous wishes; next came the rise of behaviorism, which eschewed anything unconscious or subconscious; finally, a third development had to do with academia, where thinking about dissociation had also been current. Some academics, notably Clark Hull (Dell, 2009d), espoused the noninterference theory, which held that there was no influence between dissociated parts of the mind. Had these academics been clinicians, the incorrectness of this stance probably would have been obvious. The position was correctly attacked by other scientists, but the unfortunate result was that the theory of non-interference then became a refutation of dissociation theory itself, and as a result, "dissociation theory went out of favor without effective criticism" (Hilgard, 1977, p. 12).

However, dissociative symptoms did not just go away, but reemerged under different names.

Back to Hysteria: Shell Shock

The symptoms of hysteria, the woman's disease, returned in grand force in soldiers during World War I, but it was called *shell shock*. Again, after the Vietnam War, with so many psychologically damaged veterans returning home, it became impossible to ignore the effect of trauma and traumatic dissociation. PTSD became an official psychiatric diagnosis, replacing earlier terms such as *shell shock* and *battle fatigue*. Soon, with the advent of the women's movement, it was noticed that not only soldiers were traumatized but also women and girls by rape and child sexual abuse, with severe dissociative consequences. Furthermore, these occurrences were not "out of the ordinary" (Brown, 1991). Soon, child sexual abuse, along with its dissociative consequences, became more thinkable almost a century after Freud's abandonment of the seduction theory.

Dissociation Today

Today, there is a resurgence of interest in the dissociative mind and how it operates. Although relational psychoanalysts are in the forefront, the idea of dissociation and multiple self-states currently influences much of the field of psychotherapy. The current explosion in relational psychoanalysis concerning dissociative processes has included writers such as Bromberg, Chefetz, Davies, Frawley-O'Dea, Frankel, Grand, Harris, Hegeman, Howell, Itzkowitz, Mitchell, Pizer, Reis, Schwartz, and D. B. Stern. However, Bromberg has been the figure in the forefront as the first current writer to publish prolifically about the universality of the dissociative mind. Oddly, however, with a few exceptions, this interest in multiple self-states and dissociation has not included much published writing about DID per se.

I think that, in large measure, DID has been considered rare because of our need to believe that child abuse is rare. Since DID often results from severe, chronic, early child abuse, staying unaware of the former leads to the obfuscation of the latter. As Hegeman (2010) stated, "Disbelief is the universal Western affective countertransference, both to abuse and shifts in identity" (p. 99). The idea that DID is rare serves not only to shield from public consciousness the ugly and painful realities of a high prevalence of child abuse but also to shield perpetrators themselves. Just as Freud's social environment was one in which child sexual abuse was common, so is ours. Just as Freud may have understandably feared professional shame for his beliefs and observations, current clinicians face the same dilemma.

Dissociative problems in living have never disappeared among the people suffering from them. Starting in the late 1700s, clinicians were beginning to describe, name, and treat dissociated people. For about a century, interest and knowledge continued to develop in Europe and in the United States. Since the early 1900s, it waned again for almost another century. Now again, interest in dissociation and dissociative disorders is reemerging both among clinicians and in the public. Although this reemergence comes from a confluence of sources, such as increased awareness of the impact of psychological trauma, awareness of the importance of dissociative disorders in the mental health field can be attributed in large measure to the work of certain pioneers, who had the insight and courage to recognize and name DID. Most notable among these is the psychoanalyst Richard Kluft, who has written prolifically and convincingly about DID. His work in many ways brings psychoanalysis back to its origins, and he provides an insight-oriented, somewhat modified psychoanalytic approach to the treatment of DID. He has given clinicians a roadmap for treating DID. Frank Putnam, in addition to his clinical contributions, such as the still unsurpassed text, *The Diagnosis and Treatment of Multiple Personality Disorder* (1989), has contributed research on the impact of early trauma and dissociation, including his Discrete Behavioral States (DBS) model (1997), providing a basis of knowledge that might have otherwise been unavailable. Colin Ross has also written prolifically as well as conducted invaluable research on DID. In addition to Kluft, Putnam, and Ross, other early towering figures in the treatment of DID include Catherine Fine, Philip Coons, Elizabeth Bowman, David Spiegel, Onno van der Hart, Jim Chu, Richard Loewenstein, Bessel van der Kolk, Paul Dell, and Richard Chefetz. This list is by no means exhaustive, and other towering clinician/writers such as Ellert Nijenhuis, Kathy Steele, Steve Gold, and Bethany Brand have more recently enriched and broadened the field with their contributions.[2]

In addition to Kluft's more traditional psychoanalytic orientation, some relational psychoanalysts, notably Philip Bromberg, are also unearthing and using the early "pre-psychoanalytic" constructs of psychoanalysis concerning the centrality of dissociation not only in application to explicit dissociative disorders, but also in application to more ordinary problems in living. Steve Mitchell, the early pioneer in relational psychoanalysis, wrote presciently and illuminatingly about dissociation and multiple self-states. This relational perspective that encompasses dissociation and multiplicity is greatly enriched by drawing explicitly on the dissociative mind of DID. *What is most important, in my view, is that working with DID and understanding this basic dissociative structure of the mind, makes it possible for the clinician to understand the universal dissociative structure of the mind,*

*including minds that would not be formally diagnosed as having a disso-
ciative disorder.* Reasoning backwards, how could it be otherwise? Trauma
is universal; so is dissociation.

This premise that the dissociative mind of DID is the "touchstone," as
Bromberg (1993) has noted, for understanding other problems in living,
profoundly affects our understanding of general therapeutic action and
efficacy. With respect to extrapolating from work with DID to more usual
constructs of therapeutic action, an important avenue to therapeutic change
is to let other self-states have a voice and not to privilege the powerful over
the less powerful, or the more attractive, i.e., superficially more adaptive,
self-states over the less attractive ones, i.e., those that are more painful,
emotionally intense, and/or more discordant with cultural and/or gender
norms. It is important that the fears and desires of the more pain-ridden
self-states not be denied. This then leads to the importance of encouraging inner dialogue—and eventually mutual acceptance among dissociated
self-states.

So, DID is not so unusual in its structure at all, but is the kernel behind
many other manifestations of psychic life, maladaptive as well as adaptive.

NOTES

1. As I noted in *The Dissociative Mind* (Howell, 2005), Freud's reconstruction of
   the myth of Oedipus retained the traumatic roots of the story:

   > Even though his new theory seemed on the surface to move away from
   > themes of child abuse, it was, in fact, embedded in these. In his formulation
   > of his new oedipal theory, Freud focused only on the part of the story about
   > the embattled tragic hero who marries his mother, and he "forgot" (in a way
   > that could be understood as Bartettian reconstruction; see Erdelyi, 1985,
   > 1990, 2001), the beginning framework of the Oedipus story, which had to
   > do with sexual abuse and pederasty (Devereux, 1953; Fromm, 1980; Ross,
   > 1982; Pines, 1989; Betcher & Pollack, 1993; Brothers, 1995). The reason
   > for the curse, which was Oedipus's fate, was that prior to his ascension to
   > the throne, his father, King Laius, had abducted and raped the teenage son
   > of the king Polybus, the ruler of a neighboring kingdom. Polybus's retalia-
   > tory curse was the one we all know: Laius's own son would murder him
   > and marry Laius's wife, his mother. To avoid the curse, Laius instructed
   > that his infant son be abandoned to die with a stake pierced through his
   > ankles (hence the name *Oedipus* meaning "swollen foot"). Oedipus was
   > rescued and brought up as the son of a neighboring king. He left home to
   > avoid the curse prophesied by the Delphic Oracle (Ross, 1982), but met
   > his fate anyway when he quarreled with and slew another traveler, who,
   > unbeknownst to him, was Laius, his real father. Thus, Freud's most famous
   > myth was framed in themes of child abuse, both pederasty and infanticide;
   > but he only focused on the tragic adult struggles that were the outcomes of

these early circumstances—as if these meanings could be segregated from their earlier history. (p. 72)

2. Partly because of the efforts of Kluft and Ross, we have the new Showtime series, *The United States of Tara* (Cody & Kaplow, 2009), which has DID as its topic and follows the fictional life of a woman with DID.

Chapter 3

"The We of Me"
Personality Organization in DID

> Due to a simple arithmetical mistake: [People] have failed to notice that
> two or three or seventeen selves per body is really not more metaphysi-
> cally extravagant than one self per body.
>
> Dennett (1991, p. 419)

Janice, introduced in Chapter 1, refers to herself in her mind as the "We of
Me" and has done so, even though she did not know that she had dissociative identity disorder (DID), for as long as she can remember. Her phrasing
is extraordinarily apt for others with DID as well. This chapter addresses
the personality organization of that We of Me.

In psychodynamic psychotherapy with a person with DID, just as in less
overtly dissociative or less severe problems in living, the clinician works
with the psychodynamic system of the patient. But in DID, these psychodynamically interacting parts have their own separate centers of subjectivity,
identity, autonomy, and sense of personal history. What are the different
parts like? How did they develop? What are their functions? How do the
different parts of the system operate together? What are their interrelationships? How is the organization of self-states structured? Did this organization work in some way in the family of origin? If so, how? What are the
sources and patterns of antagonism and harmony in the system?

Persons with DID generally experience their different dissociated parts
as different "people." They do this even when at the same time they consciously acknowledge that their different identities are all part of the same
person. It is also common for clinicians, especially those new to DID, to
on some level subjectively experience different presentations as different
"persons," especially when there are significant differences in voice tone,
inflection, posture, facial expression, attitude, use of language, and so on.
The clinician must tread a fine line with respect to honoring the patient's
subjective experience but also always be clear that, even though experien-
tially different, all of the parts participate in one overall personality system,
as well as sharing one body. The different identities are highly interrelated
parts of a system that comprises the total person.

The basic organization of the self-states in DID includes those who mostly operate on the surface and interact with the world, as well as parts less frequently interacting with the outside world, such as those who hold traumatic experiences. Parts may be differentiated, among other things, by function and affect state. Enmity, aversion, and opposition to the affect states of other parts contribute to the continuing separation of parts. For example, some parts may hold memories of terror, others of fury. The parts who maintain functionality in the everyday world most often do not want to be affected by the terror or the fury held by other parts because these affects are likely to be destabilizing. They are destabilizing with respect to the continuity of effective functioning in the workaday world and because the traumatic memories held by other parts are often close to unbearable in themselves. Accessing these can also be an assault on the sense of continuing selfhood.

There is often antagonism between parts, with different parts holding different kinds of memories and having opposing views about how best to manage unmanageable feelings, as well as how to get on with the business of daily living. One of the reasons there is such antagonism is that it was not possible early on for the horrible dissociated experiences to be welcomed into dialogue with an affectionate and accepting other person, and this could not be internalized. Thus, the functional parts are the only ones accepted and recognized by other people. The parts holding the terrible memories are exiled and treated as "not-me" (Chefetz & Bromberg, 2004).

In the internal world of the person with DID, a common pattern roughly conforms to the Karpman drama triangle (1968), composed of parts who are the suffering victims, the perpetrators, and the rescuers. Victim parts are often suffering children, and their identities have to do with the relationships with the abusers, corresponding to certain affective and cognitive understandings of these relationships, as well as the age of the child at the time of traumatization. Abuser parts often represent internalizations of the early persecutors. Rescuer parts are frequently framed around significant positive, real persons in the patient's life, and they may also be framed around restitutive fantasies. The interrelationships among the parts also repeat the kinds of relationships that the patient experienced and witnessed in childhood.

A common organization in females with DID is of a somewhat drained, nonconfrontational, and submissive part who is most often in executive control, along with dissociative rageful and terrified parts, child parts, and so on, who are not usually "out front." Such an organization may well have worked in the family of origin, protecting the child from knowledge, affects, and behaviors that would have been dangerous or too disorganizing. As a result, though, these DID patients often feel chronically victimized and chronically disempowered. Although cultural gender patterns often allow more conscious aggression for males with DID, this is not always the case. And there are females whose host is not drained and depressed: they may be angry, compulsively optimistic, or openly guarded, for example. The important thing to bear in mind is that the part out front most of the time is not the whole person—there are other identities dissociated from this one.

The number of parts in a DID system usually ranges in the teens. In some cases, it is only a few, and there are also *polyfragmented* multiples who have many, many parts—perhaps close to a hundred or more parts. Many people with DID have parts with names, but this is not always the case. For some, the parts do not have names but perform functions or hold emotions. And, some people may have different parts with names and other parts who do not have names.

Dissociative identities exist in a *third reality* (Kluft, 1998, 2000), an inner world that is visualized, heard, felt, and experienced as real. This third reality is often characterized by trance logic. In trance logic, ideas and relationships of ideas about things in reality are not subject to the rules of normal logic. Because they are kept in separate "compartments," contradictory beliefs and ideas can exist together; they do not have to make sense. In this way, the internal world contains many subjectivities that experience themselves as separate people. There is a pseudodelusional sense of separateness and independence (Kluft, 1998). Trance logic is characteristic of dreams and hypnosis. Because of this freedom from logical critique, identities existing in a person's third reality may seem fantastical. However, they are experienced as just as real as are the religious convictions and experiences of some, which might be seen as "fantastical" from a strictly logical point of view.

Dissociated parts of the person often have different physical images of themselves and of each other. For instance, Dennis, introduced in Chapter 1, has a female part who has comforted him since childhood. He describes her as having beautiful black hair. In his third reality (Kluft, 1998), she was visualized exactly this way and experienced as real.

Corresponding to the trance logic, different dissociated parts often have different psychophysiological organizations, such as different allergies, taste preferences, handedness, eyesight and glasses prescriptions, and responses to medications. The organization of self-states is often imagined in three-dimensional space. The parts are often layered behind one another, with those representing deeper trauma behind deeper layers of identity states (Kluft, 1993, 2000, 2009). Frequently, they are grouped or clustered together (Fine, 1993), for example, with child parts of approximately the same age together. Or, parts may be contained within another part. For instance, in drawing the parts in her system, one of my patients drew a picture of a very fat woman who was fat because she had within her three other identities.

How do we understand and define these dissociated parts or alters? As Kluft (2000) noted, "Alters may be understood as rather desperate efforts to disavow and mitigate the impact of overwhelming life events" (p. 267). In 1988, Kluft provided a more precise definition of the word *alter*:

> A disaggregate self-state ... is the mental address of a relatively stable and enduring pattern of selective mobilization of mental contents and functions, which may be behaviorally enacted with noteworthy role-taking and role-playing dimensions, and sensitive to intrapsychic, interpersonal, and environmental stimuli. It is organized in and associated with a relatively stable (but order effect dependent) pattern of neuropsychophysiological activation, and has crucial psychodynamic contents. It functions both as a recipient, processor, and storage center for perceptions, experiences, and the processing of such in connection with past events and thoughts, and/or present and anticipated ones as well. It has a sense of its own identity and ideation, and a capacity for initiating thought processes and actions. (p. 51)

Among the most commonly encountered parts, or alters, are (a) the part who is in executive control most of the time (i.e., the host); (b) child parts; (c) abuser or persecutor parts, including parts modeled after the abusers; (d) differently gendered parts; (e) seductive parts; (f) protector, rescuer, or soother parts; and (g) a manager. There are also commonly adolescent parts; angry and terrified parts of different ages; homicidal and suicidal parts; parts named Satan, Lucifer, Devil, Demon, and such; parts named No One; mute parts; dead parts; extremely functional and efficient parts; parts who know a language or a skill that others do not know; gatekeeper parts who keep other traumatized parts from emerging; parts who have various other functions such as The One Who Watches and Remembers; and sometimes animal parts. There are also often parts who are really just fragments with one isolated function, such as The One Who Cooks, The One Who Cleans, and so on. Parts may change in the way they function and in their positions in the system over time.

THE PART IN EXECUTIVE CONTROL MOST OF THE TIME

The part of the self who is in executive control most of the time is generally called *the host*. I prefer not to use the term *host* because of the inference that the person is possessed and that exorcism is the cure and because of the association of host with parasites. In addition, the association of host at a dinner party or for houseguests suggests that this part of the person is hosting the other parts. The term also conjures up images of pods from science fiction stories and films. The advantage of the term is that it is one word, and for this reason, using it is sometimes the best way to be clear. Therefore,

I frequently use other phrases, such as *the usually presenting part*, *the part who appears most of the time*, or *the part in executive control most of the time*, but when necessary, I use *host*. Kluft (1984) has described the host as "the one who has executive control of the body the greatest percentage of the time during a given time" (p. 23). This part of the person usually goes by the name that the patient goes by, the name used socially in the world. This part is the one out front and actually often functions as a kind of shell, a *front*. In accordance with gender, among other things, the presentation of the host may vary.

Especially in women, the part in executive control most of the time is likely to be compliant, depressed, depleted, and masochistic. In many cases, though, this part may be energetic, idealizing, or cheery, while other parts hold grief, terror, rage, and depression. (Of course, these are not the only structured patterns; there are many variations and combinations.) What is constant is that the experience of the part or parts who function and interact in the world most of the time has been protectively separated from those of other encapsulated parts who hold powerful emotions such as rage and terror, as well as memories that would be too destabilizing for the functioning of the person if the host were conscious of them. Thus, the more depressed, depleted, and masochistic front parts have in their personality system other parts who hold, for example, rage, anger, terror, pain, and agency. The energetic front parts are likely to serve in a counteracting way to the dissociated very depressed and hopeless, and sometimes dead, parts.

Different parts can take over as host at different periods in a person's life. They may or may not have coconsciousness with the preceding usually presenting part. One of my patients described how she suddenly "came to" in class one day when she was about 8 years old, having forgotten everything she learned the previous year but feeling more in contact with her self of prior years. Another described how, as an adult, an alter different from the usual host acted as host for a period over 1 year. Interestingly, this was contextually bound: She was living in a different location than her usual domicile.

It is frequently noted that the usually presenting part is not the original personality. Actually, this part could not be the original personality because no one has an original personality. A person's sense of self and identity is built up and synthesized over time (Putnam, 1997). Furthermore, the usually presenting part is, by definition, a part in relation to and in relationship with other parts in the total organization of the personality. People do not start out in life unified but developmentally accomplish the joining and harmonious functioning of different behavioral and mental states (Putnam, 1997). However, those people who develop DID are likely to have received much less help from their parents or caregivers in identifying, linking, and accepting their emotions and thoughts, such that the internal working models that they developed of relationships are more likely to be contradictory and segregated.

The part most often in executive control is not necessarily only one part and may be comprised of various look-alike versions who may or may not have coconsciousness with each other, and who take over for each other when one of them gets too tired or is unable to deal with the current situation. In some cases, no one individual host is in executive control most of the time because there are so many of them who have ever so slightly different important roles to play in daily life. Janice, introduced in Chapter 1, is often anxious when she thinks about her identity because there are so many of them who take control when needed—so many "hosts" who fill in for each other—and she does not know who she is. This is a terrifying thought to her. Much of the time when she wakes up in the morning, she does not know who she is. It takes the wearing on of the day, with a pattern of different self-states being triggered by different activities and demands, for her to begin to feel comfortable in an organization of self.

Another patient discovered that the part of her that most often presented in the world was primarily a shell that in its own cumbersome way did conduct transactions with the world but had little vitality or consistent ongoing perceptions. She described how, when in this self-state, she could recognize and catalogue events: She would deliberately pull up in her mind many visual flashes of past situations and events, and then she would register current situations by referencing them according to the many different visual flashes of other similar events of other times. This patient even drew diagrams in which the outer layers, depicting the surface of interaction with the world, bore the patient's given name, while more articulated parts were on the inside. As she became more integrated, a more vital part of her who had grown up in the psychotherapy from a young child to an adolescent, decided to take over the role of controlling executive functioning most of the time. This part, who had originally had a different name in the system, decided to take the patient's given name, the name that the previous host had used.

CHILD PARTS

Most people with DID have at least several child parts. Child parts tend to hold most of the abuse memories. As a result, they are often exiled in the system (Schwartz, 1997) and avoided (Van der Hart et al., 2006) by other parts in the system, including the host, who do not want to be bothered with their painful feelings. Although it may seem odd to say this, one should keep in mind that child alters are not real children. Even while speaking in childlike ways, child alters often understand abstract concepts and long words. As Shusta-Hochberg (2004) noted: "It is important to remember that the patient is an adult, despite the childlike ego-states. These parts are not actual children" (p. 16). This is in agreement with Ross's (1997) statement that "child alters are not packets of childness retained in a surrounding sea of adult psyche. They are stylized packets of adult psyche" (p. 147). The ages of child parts often correspond to ages at which they were abused, yet they may also be younger or older. Some may mature and become older in the treatment, as well as in life, and some may stay the same age.

A child part's identity often corresponds to particular kinds of relationships with the abuser. Different interpretations of and responses to traumatization may be expressed by parts who have different memories of traumatic experiences and attitudes toward the abuser. For instance, one incestuously abused adolescent part has great affection for her perpetrator parent and speaks about the relationship in accepting, even caring, ways, while another part the same age hates him. Often, there may be twins, in which one child part is compliant and eager to please, and another child part is The Evil One. Some child parts hold memories of terror and pain. Some may be mute, expressing how they have learned that they may not tell anyone, and some may only be able to whisper, indicating their terror of being heard or noticed. Behind some traumatized parts, there are often more traumatized others. Some parts have the job of performing sexually. Other enraged ones may appear to have identified with the abuser and may behave in ways that are destructive to the body. Others do not themselves hold traumatic memories and may be able to enjoy things they actually did as children, such as play with toys or watch cartoons. Defensive reliance on child parts who only play can be a problem for an adult who needs to be engaged in a world of other adults. For instance, Josephine managed to escape from awareness and memory of her mother's physical abuse when she was young by playing and being "happy." Now, when things upset her, she frequently reverts to being a playful child, rather than dealing with the difficult situation.

RESCUER, SOOTHER, AND PROTECTOR PARTS

Rescuer, soother, and protector parts all have different manifestations. These parts may be overtly protective, as in a caretaking part, often modeled on a real person. Or, they may be invented. *Soother* parts are often modeled after an adult figure, such as a protective and caring grandparent who was a source of protection and solace for the patient when she was a child. For instance, there may be a part named after a loving babysitter or a benign grandparent.

In many cases, however, there was no such model, and personified hope was created in a new part. One patient, who had been brutally abused, isolated, and often exposed to severe neglect, described how she would make protectors and friends of the rocks and bushes and believed they would care for her. A part may be an invented kindly mother figure and may be named after an important valued attribute, such as Hope or Faith, or even after a physical thing, such as a hard beautiful rock. For instance, a patient had a part named Diamond who watched over her. Diamond had been through the earth's compression and could now withstand all manner of stresses. Diamond could not be hurt and could therefore be relied on as a soother/protector. As Ferenczi (1931) wrote, "The man abandoned by all gods...now splits off from himself a part which in the form of a helpful, loving, often motherly, minder commiserates with the tormented remainder of the self, nurses him and decides for him...so to speak a guardian angel. This angel sees the suffering or murdered child from the outside" (p. 237).

Protector parts may also be *fighters*. Their job is to protect the patient from external danger. One of my female patients described how when a menacing person came into the subway car, a strong male part came out who was ready to fight. Protector parts may also have had the original function of anticipation of or identification with the abuser. To preemptively protect the child so that the child may anticipate the abuse rather than be surprised by it, protector parts become persecutors modeled on the abusers. Thus, parts who were protectors when the person was a young child may become persecutors in time, holding anger and rage and meting out punishments to other parts of the self.

ABUSER PARTS ARE COMMON

Abuser parts generally hold rage and contempt for the most frequently presenting part as well as other parts. They are often responsible for self-injury and may at times be homicidal toward the host or other parts. Often, they are angry adolescents—or angry children—bent on feeling powerful. Unfortunately, this can be accomplished without difficulty in the third reality (Kluft, 1998) of the internal system, and these parts may torture or abuse little child parts in the system who cannot fight back, or they may abuse the host or other parts. These abuser parts are often named Satan, Devil, Lucifer, or Demon. Sometimes, they have more esoteric names, such as those of mythological figures or of powerful gods or goddesses of different cultures. Usually, these parts can become engaged in the treatment such that they become important allies. As this occurs, they bring much more agency and energy into the person's conscious life.

Although this may not be initially apparent, most of the time the angry parts and those modeled after the abuser all function protectively at the deepest level. These parts live in the past, and they are protecting the person from behaving in ways that would have been dangerous in the past. For example, Janice, introduced in Chapter 1, has a part called Ereshkigal, named after the Sumerian goddess of destruction. She believed herself to be all powerful. She wanted to kill the host, whom she believed to be "wimpy" and not deserving of life. I was able to engage with her by intuiting her protective function: "I bet you were very much able to make her behave perfectly in that family of hers. She should be very appreciative for all the help you gave her. I think she really needed your help." Her first response was, "Yes. I was pretty good at that. But she is still just a piece of crap and deserved everything that she got." But soon afterward, she was able to appear protectively in situations when the patient was the object of someone else's aggression. In time, the patient was able to recognize simply that she was angry without Ereshkigal's appearance.

There are, however, some cases in which psychopathic parts are not protective but wish only for their own power (Blizard, 1997; Bryant, Kessler, & Shirar, 1996; Rosenfeld, 1971). Working with these parts is much more difficult. Curtis (1997) reported on a patient with whom he had been working who had a psychopathic part who committed a serious crime. Since the whole of him was not psychopathic, he reported this to his therapist and then turned himself in to the police.

DIFFERENTLY GENDERED PARTS

Many people with DID have differently gendered parts. These are often highly stereotyped, not only as gender tends to be but also in accordance with the fact that young children rely more heavily on stereotypes than do adults (Bem, 1983). Some of my female patients have male parts who are strong and can be aggressive. These parts appear when there is a perceived physical danger. Their presence is a protective comfort, and it can also be a physical asset, coming in handy when needed, for these parts can be extraordinarily strong, much stronger than the host. For instance, one of my patients who was going door to door as part of her work, felt threatened at one point. A male alter emerged who then frightened the threatening person at the door. Male parts may also represent identifications with male abusers. Often male parts are more psychologically protective against the stereotyped perception of female vulnerability. They may believe that if they are boys, then they cannot be raped as girls are. In addition, the gender of some male parts derives from the physical circumstance that they were anally raped.

Male patients with DID may also have female parts. Similarly to male parts of biological females, these parts have various functions. They may represent the experience of being raped and demeaned by the abuser, who called the patient "sissy" and "girl." Or, female-identified parts in male persons may be identifications with a female abuser. Or, female parts may serve a different function altogether: As stereotypically nurturing females, they may provide internal comfort to a distraught and traumatized little boy.

MANAGERS

Managers usually have extensive knowledge of events and of the system. They are often available to explain to the therapist the internal systemic dilemmas that are not otherwise evident. Generally, they are fairly empty of affect. Another term for managers has been *internal self-helpers* (Putnam, 1989). However, in my experience, so-called managers and internal self-helpers may have agendas of their own, which may not be best for the well-being of the person-as-whole. I remember meeting one self-identified manager/helper who had all the characteristics of knowledge and minimal affect; however, it turned out what she really represented was a defense against interaction in the world with other people. She had minimal affect because that was her defensive style, not because she was a manager or internal self-helper.

PSYCHOTIC PARTS AND DEAD PARTS

At times, people with DID have parts who are psychotic. This does not mean that the whole person is psychotic, but that only a part of her is. As such, when a person with DID presents with psychotic behavior, it is important to assess whether there is a psychotic part. Another possibility is that the seemingly psychotic behavior is not psychotic at all but is the result of flashbacks of experiences that have not been labeled or contextualized. As a result, the patient cannot explain the bizarre behavior, which from the outside may appear psychotic (Moskowitz et al., 2009).

The topic of dead parts shares commonalities with psychosis. Some persons with DID have endured such horrific abuse that they believed they were about to die and that they did die. These dead parts have then been locked away, only to reemerge when the person experiences extraordinary stress that brings into question the viability of existence. For instance, Margaret, introduced in Chapter 1, began to talk about how she was sure she smelled like rotting flesh and how she thought she was dead and others around her just did not notice. She wondered how long it would take others to realize she was dead. Further exploration revealed that as a child she had nearly frozen to death, in addition to earlier near-death experiences. This part of her experience was too much for her to endure and could not be assimilated. There was no one around who could help her to assimilate her experience and to recognize that she had lived through it. Although Margaret managed to survive, the experience of nearly dying and believing she had died became locked away in her inner world as a dead part.

ANIMAL IDENTITIES

Some people with DID have animal parts. While in animal identity states, they may exhibit animal-like behaviors, such as growling, scratching, or running on all fours (Goodwin & Attias, 1999; Putnam, 1989). They may also hear animal calls inside the head (Goodwin & Attias, 1999) or have visual flashbacks involving animal identities. Other clinical cues that may indicate the presence of animal identities include excessive fear of animals, excessive involvement with a pet, and cruelty to animals (Hendriksen, McCartney, & Goodwin, 1990).

Children often identify with animals and experience them as peers and friends. Abused children may develop animal parts they experience as protectors, peers, or both in an environment where there was no protection. Or, the patient may have identified through loss with a beloved pet that was lost, innocently killed, or murdered to terrify the child, to demonstrate the abuser's omnipotence, or to enforce silence.

Sometimes, parts named after the cat family (leopard, cougar, tiger) may serve as protector states that are allowed to express the emotion the host cannot. One of my patients would begin growling and switch into Tiger when she became upset. On the other hand, the presence of cat-family parts, or other animal parts, may be more serious and indicate the possibility of dangerous violence—something that should be assessed.

Animal identities may also be self-representations that are consistent with the abuser's treatment and labeling of the child. For example, the child may have been treated like an animal. Dog parts are not infrequent identifications. A part named Dog may represent how the patient was treated like a dog and forced to bark like a dog by her abusers (Bryant et al., 1992). Or, the child may have been forced into sexual behaviors with animals, leading to a view of the self as an animal or as bestial and inhuman. Hendriksen et al. (1990) described a patient who was forced by her parents to eat out of a dog bowl and to act like a dog. Her father then involved the family dog in acts of bestiality in his abuse of her. Any reference to sex made her feel as if she "turned into a dog," and she did indeed then act like a dog. Further, as Hendriksen et al. (1990) stated:

> Working with animal alters is helpful in addressing the extreme guilt resulting from participation in acts felt to be inhuman. Because of the victim's induction as a co-participant in animal torture, the issue of responsibility has become even more muddled than in other incest situations. The animal is often chosen for victimization because it is the child's pet. From the patient's point of view, their pet was victimized because they loved it. Therefore, the child's love itself is contaminated and potentially lethal. This, together with the victim's extreme guilt about the seriousness of the infraction, leads to self-esteem deficits at the level of not experiencing oneself as a member of the human race. Work with the animal alter can be a pathway to self-forgiveness for the victim. As therapist and patient begin to understand the animal alter and its violent propensities as a natural consequence of sadistic

abuse, the patient's underlying sense of beastliness becomes accessible to treatment. (p. 221)

Animal parts may also express evaluations of one's own experience metaphorically. My patient Anna experiences herself at times as a fish and as different kinds of snakes. This probably derives from the fact that she grew up in a coastal village where many people fished for a living. Sometimes, she awakens from sleep, feeling that she is wriggling like a fish, and is unable to use her arms and legs for a few minutes. Perhaps the brutal way she was treated, often with her arms and legs pinned down, made her feel like a "beast of prey," and she understood this feeling in terms of something with which she was more familiar—as if she were one of the fish that were so much a part of her home environment. The expectation of ruthless domination is reflected in her dyadic animal identity constructions: Sometimes, she is afraid to go into the bathroom because she sees in there a big fish and a little fish. The little fish is no longer flapping around but is now half-dead. During the time of her abuse and imprisonment as a household and sexual slave, she also felt half-dead, with no strength or energy. She also switches into snake identities, even though she was not familiar with snakes where she grew up. One of these is a cobra identity that she experiences as a protector. Sometimes in the sessions, when she switches to this identity, her face and chest puff up, almost as one would imagine a cobra. She also hallucinates snakes that represent her abuser, specifically the penis. Indeed, she has at times hallucinated her abuser as a 6-foot-long snake in bed with her. During the time of Anna's abuse in a strange land far away from her home, there was no human being—other than another little girl at school, when she was allowed to go—to whom she could turn for empathic understanding or help.

Animal identifications in children and in adult patients without DID also occur. Goodwin and Attias (1999) comment on the meaning of insects for Kafka and note that in Freud's famous case of the Rat Man, the patient was tormented by the fear that a rat would eat into his anus. As Freud (1909) noted, "He could truly be said to find 'a living likeness of himself in the rat'" (p. 216, cited in Goodwin & Attias, 1999, p. 257).

DIFFERENT CONCEPTUAL SCHEMES FOR UNDERSTANDING THE ORGANIZATION OF PARTS OF THE SELF

A number of schemes have been introduced that DID therapists have found helpful in understanding the organization of dissociative parts. As mentioned, one such is the Karpman (1968) drama triangle, which consists of the victim, the abuser, and rescuer. Although not specifically addressing

DID, Davies and Frawley (1994) described the internal psychodynamics between an adult persona who takes care of daily functioning in the world and the child personae, who are less adjusted, more demanding, and protest against the constraints imposed by the adult self. The child and adult selves feel betrayed and abandoned each by the other.

Davies and Frawley (1994) introduced a useful scheme for understanding transference and countertransference positions in trauma work as well as typical associated self states. This includes four matrices encompassing eight relational positions. These matrices, as described by the authors, include the following:

- the uninvolved nonabusing parent and the neglected child;
- the sadistic abuser and the helpless, impotently enraged victim;
- the omnipotent rescuer and the entitled child who demands to be rescued;
- the seducer and the seduced. (pp. 167–185)

More recently, Frawley-O'Dea (1999) added a fifth matrix to the original four: the certain believer and the chronic doubter.

Several authors in the field of dissociation have offered useful conceptual schemes for the organization of dissociated parts. Frankel and O'Hearn's (1996) ghetto model describes roles of antibonding alters who perform much like the *kapos* in concentration camps. His model of antibonding parts has much in common with Fairbairn's (1944/1952, 1951) description of the antilibidinal ego.

Richard Schwartz (1997) introduced his internal family systems model, in which he outlined the roles of exiles, managers, and firefighters. The *exiles* are usually child parts who hold painful memories along with fear, neediness, and shame. Because these memories and feelings, when conscious, make the person vulnerable, the parts who hold them are banished. The *managers* have the job of running the person's life. (They are distinguished from the internal managers of the system previously described.) Managers may have different characteristics, such as being controlling, perfectionistic, risk avoidant, or caretaking of others, but they all have the job of keeping the exiles exiled to keep the feelings they hold out of consciousness. There are times, however, when the exiles will be triggered by life circumstances despite all of the manager's best efforts. When the exiles threaten to break out and flood the person with their feelings, another group of parts, the *firefighters*, emerge to put out the fire of these feelings (Schwartz, 1997). The firefighters are often substance-using or self-harming parts whose purpose is to put out the internal fire of emotions associated with memories of traumatization. This scheme is close to the experience of many with DID, and for those who have addictions, it helps to give them a conceptual handle on their compulsions for extinguishing pain.

INNER ANTAGONISMS: THE THEORY OF THE STRUCTURAL DISSOCIATION OF THE PERSONALITY

What these models have in common is antagonism between parts, with different parts holding different kinds of memories and having opposing views about how to conduct a life and how to manage unmanageable feelings. A comprehensive theory that explains this antagonism between the different parts of the personality is Van der Hart et al.'s (2006) *Structural Dissociation and the Treatment of Chronic Traumatization*. This theory is synthesized from a number of different sources, including Janet's initial observation that dissociation results from trauma and that the effects of this affect the person's behavior and thoughts subconsciously; Putnam's (1997) discrete behavioral states (DBS) model; evolutionary theories of animal defense; the thinking of Charles Myers (1940), a World War I physician/psychologist; neurodevelopmental theories; and knowledge regarding psychobiological action systems.

These last are innate, self-organizing behavioral systems. Under the impact of trauma, especially chronic trauma, two types of psychobiological action systems—the ones devoted to daily life and the ones devoted to defense—become segregated and divided against each other (Van der Hart, Nijenhuis, Steele, & Brown, 2004).

Van der Hart et al. (2006) noted the remarkable correspondences between these two sets of psychobiological action systems, having to do with daily life and defense, and the parts of the personality that Charles Myers (1940) observed in posttrauma patients: the emotional personality and the apparently normal personality. Van der Hart et al. (2006) corrected this terminology to the emotional part (EP) of the personality and the apparently normal part (ANP) of the personality. According to the theory of the structural dissociation of the personality, as a result of trauma, the EP remains fixated in the traumatic experiences, which it often reenacts. It is focused on a narrow range of cues that were relevant to the trauma. This leaves a constricted ANP to conduct the daily business of life. To do so, the ANP must avoid the affect and information held by the EP. It is important to recognize that this aspect of the personality is only *apparently* normal; it is not the same as the personality before the trauma. It is much more constricted and is subject to intrusions of the EP, including nightmares, dreams, somnambulism, intrusive thoughts, flashbacks, and somatoform symptoms.

The ANP is vigilantly avoidant of the information and affect held by the EP. Indeed, it is likely to be partially or totally amnestic for the trauma. It is phobic of the memory of the trauma, of cognitions, emotions, as well sensory memories encoded in the body having to do with the trauma. The topics of trauma may be passively avoided or actively suppressed. In either case, over time, the avoidance is likely to become automatic. Because of the vigilance and constriction required by such avoidance, this aspect of the self, only apparently normal, does indeed differ substantially from the premorbid presentation.

The most important point about the ANP and the EP is that they are dissociated, as separate dissociative parts of the personality. Even though the ANP may often appear to have a larger scope and greater functionality, once there is an EP, the ANP can only be a part of the personality. It is not correct to say that the EP is dissociated from the ANP as if the ANP is whole and unaffected except for those intrusive troublemakers, the EPs (Van der Hart et al., 2006).

The action systems that correspond to the ANP and the EP are, respectively: (a) action systems devoted to carrying on daily life, such as those concerning reproduction, childrearing, attachment, sociability, exploration, and play; and (b) defensive action systems and subsystems devoted to the survival of the individual in conditions of threat. These last defensive action systems and subsystems of the EP include hypervigilance, fight, flight, freeze, and total submission. The freeze state is accompanied by analgesia; the total submission state is accompanied by anesthesia. Related to defense is a subsystem of recuperation, in which pain perception is reinstated, and wound care begins (Nijenhuis, 1999; Nijenhuis, Van der Hart, Kruger, & Steele, 2004; Van der Hart, Nijenhuis, & Steele, 2006). Thus, the EP is fixated in the action system of defense, such as hypervigilance, fight, fright, freeze, and total submission.

Van der Hart et al. (2006) emphasized that persons with DID are beset with what the authors called *tertiary structural dissociation*, which they contrasted with *primary* and *secondary* structural dissociation. Primary structural dissociation involves one EP and one ANP. An example of primary structural dissociation is simple posttraumatic stress disorder (PTSD). Here, the ANP tends to be detached and numb, characterized by partial or complete amnesia of the trauma, whereas the EP is usually limited in scope but is *hypermnestic*, reexperiencing the trauma (Van der Hart et al., 2004). Secondary structural dissociation involves one ANP and more than one EP. Examples of secondary structural dissociation are complex PTSD and dissociative disorder not otherwise specified (DDNOS). Secondary structural dissociation is characterized by dividedness of two or more defensive subsystems. For example, there may be different EPs who are devoted to flight, fight, freeze, total submission, and so on (Van der Hart et al., 2004). In tertiary structural dissociation, there are two or more ANPs as well as two or more EPs. There may be different ANPs who perform aspects of daily living, such as work in the workplace, childrearing, and playing.

For example, my patient Anna, who has DID and was frequently raped and used as a prostitute by her caretakers, at times wakes up from sleep as if fighting someone off with her flailing arms and legs. This activity, over which she has no control, is the intrusion of an EP of her personality. When she began treatment, Anna had florid DID and intrusive and reenactive PTSD symptoms but lacked coherent memories of the causes of many of her symptoms. In treatment, she has been recapturing and piecing together memories of her early adolescence by means of flashbacks and somatic reenactments. Sometimes, these relived traumatic experiences have taken hours or even days to unwind—like an unstoppable film, from beginning to end. She has been, in effect, spellbound to watch and participate in, again, the horrors that have already happened. However, unwelcome as they have been, many of these memories have now become narrative memories. Horrible as they were to experience, she now has the memory, a memory that is autobiographical, because she was truly "there," as she was not in the first experiencing, in the reexperiencing. These lengthy flashbacks can be understood as the intrusions of different EPs. Like many of the victims of child sexual abuse, Anna did not initially remember these events as narrative memory but initially experienced them as flashbacks, dissociated visual imagery, and somatic, motor reenactments.

THE CLOSED SYSTEM, THE SELF-CARE SYSTEM, AND THE THIRD REALITY

The organization of self-states in highly dissociative people is a partially closed system, which has elements in common with the self-care system and the third reality (Kluft, 1998). An open system allows interaction with the outside and transformation of the individual through interactive interchange with others. It assumes interaction with, and influence from, the outside. A whole is more than the aggregate of its parts because it is in constant interaction with, and thus continually transformed by, the environment. Fairbairn (1958) contrasted the closed system of internal objects and the parts of the self that are attached to them, to an open system that allows for interaction with the outside. He noted:

> A real relationship with an external object is a relationship in an open system; but, insofar as the inner world assumes the form of a closed system, a relationship with an external object is only possible in terms of transference, viz., on condition that the external object is treated as an object within the closed system of inner reality. (p. 381)

Fairbairn (1958) described how the terror of psychic disintegration contributes to the maintenance of the closed system of internal objects. Fairbairn's model of endopsychic structure, involving the interdynamics of exciting object, the rejecting object, the libidinal ego, and the antilibidinal ego (or internal saboteur) describes some of the alters we see in DID. Alters who bond with the good ("exciting") aspects of perpetrators are much like libidinal egos, and contemptuously abusing, rejecting alters are very much like internal saboteurs, responsive to and modeled after rejecting objects. "Fairbairn saw that psychic structure is the personification of failed experiences with objects" (Grotstein, 2000, p. 177).

Under conditions of abuse, neglect, or gross insensitivity, an inordinate degree of self-sufficiency is required of the young child. Because this is generally too much to muster, the child may invent an omnipotent protector, helper, or inner caretaker (Beahrs, 1982; Bliss, 1986). In such a situation, self-care is provided by parts of the self, not by the outside interpersonal world. Kalsched (1996) described the *self-care system* as a way for a child to manage traumatic attachments and as a way to provide from within the self a supplement to the scarce supplies available in the interpersonal environment. The threat of "unthinkable" agonies and the terror of going mad activate the self-care system, which not only restores missing aspects of the needed attachment relationships as aspects of the self but also uses such quasi-delusional methods as perceptually "blanking out" threatening figures. The self-care system generates a sense of psychic stability by creating illusory sources of protection and comfort, and it provides an effective and often lifesaving coping strategy in a frightening or abusive interpersonal environment. The self-care system generates a sense of psychic stability by creating the illusion of sources of protection and comfort. It gives a particular meaning to "pulling yourself up by your bootstraps."

The closed self-care system has some elements in common with the *third reality*, described by Kluft (1998). The third reality can be an immense internal world with, for instance, castles, dungeons, fields, and so on (Oxnam, 2005). In the creation of this world, there can be much playful creativity. Unless there can be some real connection of inside parts with the outside world, the inside cannot grow because it remains more of a closed system. As long as these parts remain segregated from each other, contradictions in their beliefs, wishes, and motivations will not be experienced as problematic or conflictual. Inviting the parts into interaction with the therapist and to share their third reality with the therapist is, then, integrative. The therapist operates as a relational bridge (Bromberg, 1998) for self-states to share more aspects of their segregated experience with each other.

Chapter 4

DID Is a Trauma Disorder

The basic problem for a traumatized individual becomes his own self-cure.

Bromberg (1994, p. 538)

Dissociative identity disorder (DID) is an outcome of psychological trauma that was early, chronic, and severe. A history of sexual, physical, or emotional abuse has been found in the vast majority of people with DID. In this sense, it is a chronic trauma disorder (Ross, 1989). In 1986, Putnam et al. found in their study of 100 subjects that 85–95% of the respondents reported a history of sexual or physical abuse. In later studies, Ross (1997) found that 88.5 to 96% of patients with DID in three large studies reported a history of sexual or physical abuse. Anderson and Alexander (1996) found that, as opposed to adult female incest survivors without DID, those with DID reported significantly more severe and earlier sexual abuse as well as more physical abuse. Brand, Classen, McNary, and Zaveri (2009) found that, in a sample of patients with dissociative disorders, 86% and 79% had suffered sexual and physical abuse, respectively.

Psychological trauma and dissociation are inextricably linked. Trauma, especially psychological trauma that is early, severe, and chronic, has a profound effect on personality development. This effect is much more complicated than the arrest of a particular phase of development. A typical understanding of child development in the last century was that it involved the mastery of developmentally relevant tasks, whether we call these psychosexual stages, psychosocial stages, stages of interdependence, or the developmental epochs of infancy, childhood, preadolescence, and adolescence. Far beyond arrest of a particular phase of development, trauma in childhood changes brain structure, increases stress hormones, affects the endocrine system, numbs the self, makes the world unsafe, interferes with attachments, and causes the dissociation of certain areas of experience from consciousness—as well as other detrimental effects. All of these are interdependent to varying degrees and, depending on other life events and circumstances, may become compounded. What is the meaning of the relationship between trauma and dissociation? In what ways is problematic dissociation linked with trauma?

WHAT IS PSYCHOLOGICAL TRAUMA?
OBJECTIVE VERSUS SUBJECTIVE TRAUMA

A central dilemma that is often discussed in the trauma field concerns the distinction between so-called objective trauma (sometimes called massive trauma) and subjective trauma. A condition for the diagnosis of posttraumatic stress disorder (PTSD) in the the fourth edition of the *Diagnostic and Statistical Manual of Mental Disorders* (*DSM-IV-TR*; American Psychiatric Association [APA], 1994) is that the "person experienced, witnessed, or was confronted with an event or events that involved actual or threatened death or serious injury, or a threat to the physical integrity of self or others" (p. 467). However, not everyone who has been subjected to what can be viewed as objective or massive trauma—as specified in *DSM-IV*—actually develops PTSD. Not only that, but various kinds and severities of traumatic events affect different people in different ways. As a result, many trauma experts prefer to define as traumatic that which is overwhelming to the individual or to the individual's defenses rather than what may be viewed as an *objective* trauma. Others dispute this approach, noting that without an objective measure of trauma, anything that is merely upsetting might be described as traumatic. In such a case, the word *trauma* may be so diluted that it loses its meaning. One result of this dilemma is that the current connotations of the word include both these meanings: *Trauma* may refer both to an objectively catastrophic event and to something that feels subjectively upsetting. This dual meaning creates confusion. Some (e.g., Shapiro, 2001) have dealt with this dilemma pragmatically by dividing traumatic events into Big "T" (big trauma) versus small "t" (small trauma) ones. Although useful in a practical way, in the sense that it gives us a basic language for talking about the dimensions and expected impact of a traumatic event, this distinction does not address the objective-versus-subjective dilemma.

How, then, do we resolve these confusions and contradictions in definition? One useful approach lies in a description of the specific effects of the traumatizing event on the person. For example, as Spiegel (1990a) explained:

> Trauma can be understood as the experience of being made into an object; the victim of someone else's rage, of nature's indifference, or of one's own physical and psychological limitations. Along with the pain and fear associated with rape, combat trauma, or natural disaster comes a marginally bearable sense of helplessness, a realization that one's own will and wishes become irrelevant to the course of events, leaving either a view of the self that is damaged; contaminated by the humiliation, pain, and fear that the event imposed; or a fragmented sense of self. (p. 251)

In the same vein of thought, Herman (1992) noted, "At the moment of trauma the victim is rendered helpless by overwhelming force" (p. 33). Horowitz (1976) also emphasized the individual's helplessness in the face of trauma and pointed to the importance of the degree to which the traumatic event could be assimilated into the person's cognitive framework. Unbearably intense affect overwhelms the person's ability to organize information and even to think. As a result, the traumatic events or circumstances cannot be assimilated or taken in. The neurobiological result is the sensorimotor, rather than narrative, registration of the unendurable experience. This lack of assimilation results in vulnerability to flashbacks as well as a deficit in narrative memory with regard to the event.

This deficit in memory has been compared to "an irreversible negative— a photographic negative that cannot produce a positive image.... Within the shape of the trauma, there is only a negative, a blackness that cannot be cognized" (Raine, 1999, p. 114). In the language of Jacques Lacan, this is the Real, the traumatic, the unknowable. As Boulanger (2007) explained, "The Real is the unsymbolizable and unbridgeable gap at the heart of traumatic experience. The Real is ineffable; by definition it can neither be captured nor be given meaning" (p. 55). In verbal terms, trauma is itself unknowable and unrepresentable. One could say that trauma punctures the psyche, and that hole or lack is in of itself unknowable, unsymbolizable— we can only infer it in terms of its aftereffects. It is unformulated, and importantly, it is dissociated.

Following from the descriptions of the authors just mentioned, one can see how the most fundamental effect of trauma is dissociation. Accordingly, we might best define *trauma* as "the event(s) that cause dissociation" (Howell, 2005, p. ix). People vary so much in their resilience to so-called objectively traumatizing events that it does not make sense to speak of trauma as defined by objective trauma. It also does not make sense to classify as traumatic that which is merely upsetting. We cannot *quantify* trauma, but we can *define it conceptually* in terms of its effects on individuals.

Thinking of *trauma* as the events that cause dissociation makes irrelevant the confusing discussions about objective trauma (which does not necessarily result in posttraumatic stress to all who are exposed to it) versus subjective trauma (which may run the risk of categorizing anything merely distressing as traumatic). It also supersedes the question regarding whether the event is a big T or a small t trauma. Defining trauma as an event that causes dissociation focuses on the "fault lines" or "fissures" in the mind rather than on the external event. If an event is so overwhelming that it cannot be assimilated, it cannot be linked with other experience, resulting in gaps in memory and experience. This is a description of dissociation. As a result of the trauma, there is a change in the structure of the person's psyche. There is now a structural dissociation: Parts of experience have become structurally separated from other aspects of experience.

Although this definition suggests that the concept of trauma requires dissociation, the reverse is not true. Dissociation, which is a more inclusive concept, refers to many kinds of phenomena, processes, conditions, and abilities, such as absorption and hypnosis, as well as posttraumatic responses. The statement is not tautological because trauma does not define dissociation. What requires emphasizing is that *trauma implies dissociation*.[1]

DISSOCIATION AS A RESPONSE TO TRAUMA

Dissociation Is Initially Adaptive

Problematic or maladaptive dissociation is often a rigidified outcome of repeated psychological trauma. However, dissociation is often initially adaptive, protecting the traumatized person from unbearable knowledge, preserving sanity, and even fostering survival. In a general sense, *dissociation* refers to a separation of experiences, feelings, memories, and so forth that would normally be connected. The capacity for dissociation is an aspect of human nature that can be of great value. For instance, by use of dissociation, psychological trauma that might otherwise completely overwhelm a young child and lead to a breakdown of functioning can be encapsulated in subconscious parts of the mind, allowing the child to continue functioning in the day-to-day world. The capacity for dissociation can be soothing in times of unbearable stress. For example, many highly dissociative patients report that they have found ways to voluntarily "disappear" from traumatic experiences by going into a trance state, becoming lost in the wallpaper, or mentally going into a mouse hole in the wall.

Dissociative ability serves as a means to survival in life-threatening circumstances as an aspect of biological endowment. People may use dissociation to trance out, go into neutral gear (Terr, 1994), develop psychic numbness (Lifton & Markusen, 1990), mentally float to the ceiling or sky, and so on. Such responses are commonly reported by victims of rape, near drowning, serious automobile accidents, building collapses, natural disasters, and wartime disasters, to name a few. At such times, dissociation allows people to separate themselves from the experience of the trauma. As Van der Kolk (1996b) noted, "During a traumatic experience, dissociation allows a person to observe the event as a spectator, experience no, or only limited, pain or distress; and to be protected from awareness of the full impact of what has happened" (p. 192).

Dell (2009b) has synthesized and reformulated much of what is known about the kind of dissociation that often occurs in such extreme circumstances and has marshaled an impressive array of research documenting the phylogenetic roots of what he called "evolution-prepared survival-oriented dissociation" (p. 764). He noted in particular that the response to near-lethal falling likely has the longest phylogenetic history—that is, that adaptive, survival-oriented responses are likely to have evolved by natural selection. He suggested that life-threatening falls represent the prototypical danger for humans in the physical world.

To further elucidate this point, Dell (2009d) cited and quoted from the research of Heim, an avid mountain climber who summarized reports of the experiences of dozens of mountain climbers who experienced potentially lethal falls but survived:

> There was no anxiety, no trace of despair, no pain; but rather calm seriousness, profound acceptance, and a dominant mental quickness and sense of surety. Mental activity became enormous, rising to a hundred-fold velocity or intensity. The relationships of events and their probable outcomes were overviewed with objective clarity. No confusion entered at all. Time became greatly expanded. The individual acted with lightning-quickness in accord with accurate judgment of his situation. . . . Men who had fallen from great heights were unaware that their limbs had been broken until they attempted to stand. (Heim, 1892, as cited in Dell, 2009d, p. 761)

As Dell (2009b) noted, almost 95% of the victims Heim studied had similar experiences, and other investigators of near-fatal falls have reported similar instances of people feeling calm, detached, depersonalized. Dissociation helped the people who had near-fatal falls to manage the trauma of falling. In their research, Shilony and Grossman (1993, as cited in Dell, 2009b) in fact reported that those who failed to experience depersonalization during trauma reported significantly greater psychopathology.

Although depersonalization that occurs at the time of the trauma is normal and often beneficial, it is the persistence of depersonalization over time that becomes problematic.

Persistent and Automatic Dissociation Is Maladaptive

The value of the capacity for dissociation is inestimable. That said, if this dissociation is maintained for too long or becomes automatic, it then becomes maladaptive. If a person's way of life becomes organized around dissociative avoidance of any reminders of trauma, this also is problematic. The problem is that automatic dissociation does not work: Continuously avoided overwhelmingly painful experience cannot be integrated and will therefore intrude into the person's life.

An important issue in understanding dissociation and its potential to maladaptively impact one's life is whether the dissociation is or is not under voluntary control. For example, consider the phenomenon often called *highway hypnosis*, which is not hypnosis at all, by the way, but involves the ability to dual task: attend to one's thoughts and the road simultaneously when the road is a familiar one. Because we can do things that are familiar fairly automatically, we are often surprised on arrival at our destination that we do not remember all the turns and stops we made in the process. Highway hypnosis would be extremely dangerous, however, if we could not return attention to the road when necessary. Problematic dissociation is that way: Once it has been put on automatic, it is hard to stop. Intrusions cannot be controlled. Reality cannot be reattended to at will. Often, when triggered, highly dissociative people cannot control the switching between self-states. In all forms of problematic dissociation, too much of the disso-ciative behavior is involuntary.

Complex PTSD and Disorders of Extreme Stress Not Otherwise Specified

It is important to explore and understand the other ways in which dissocia-tion is part of the concept of trauma-related disorders. DID is considered to be a form of *complex PTSD* (Courtois, 1999, 2004; Ford & Courtois, 2009; Herman, 1992; Van der Kolk, 1996b). Although PTSD has now become a culturally accepted concept as well as a much-used diagnosis, it only partially describes the most predominant forms of posttraumatic problems as reflected in everyday living (Herman, 1992). The diagnosis of PTSD was originally developed in response to the symptoms displayed by large numbers of returning Vietnam veterans. Previously described as *battle fatigue* and *shell shock*, these symptoms included amnesia; somatoform and hysterical presentations such as contractures, tics, tremors, and stut-tering; as well as symptoms of intrusion, constriction, and numbing. An existing problem in the original formulation of PTSD in the third edition of the *DSM* (*DSM-III*; APA, 1980) was that to qualify as traumatic, an event had to be out of the ordinary. Indeed, a prime example was the horrors of war. Traumatologists Brown (1991) and Herman (1992) noticed, however, that in contradiction to the *DSM-III* requirement, many traumatic experi-ences occur with such frequency that they are not necessarily "out of the ordinary." In certain times and cultures, war is itself ordinary. In addition, posttraumatic symptoms characterized not only soldiers but also cut across a much larger swath of the population, characterizing people who had suf-fered chronic posttraumatic stress from such events as rape, battering, and childhood sexual abuse. These events are severe and expectably traumatiz-ing, and to many of the people who suffer from them, they are not neces-sarily out of the ordinary at all. By the time of *DSM-IV* (APA, 1994), the out-of-the-ordinary requirement was dropped.

In the late 1980s and the 1990s, and following the formulation of PTSD, the concept of psychological trauma was becoming more thinkable, and the atrocity of child abuse (especially child sexual abuse) was becoming less deniable. However, a conceptual model for peoples' posttraumatic responses to such events did not yet exist. Modeled as it is on the effects of exposure to single-incident traumas such as combat fatigue and disaster, the diagnosis of PTSD does not describe the effects of prolonged and repeated relational trauma and victimization that occurs early in life. There are important differences between childhood-onset trauma and adult-onset trauma (Boulanger, 2007). Trauma, especially psychological trauma that is early, severe, and chronic, has profound effects on development. It affects brain structure, the endocrine system, and stress hormones, as well as makes the world in general feel unsafe, and creates dissociative experiences. Indeed, Van der Kolk (2005) and others have proposed a new diagnosis of *developmental trauma disorder* for children with histories of complex trauma because of the awareness that the current diagnosis of PTSD is not developmentally sensitive.

Judith Herman (1992) coined the term *complex PTSD* because the criteria for PTSD alone do not adequately describe the kind of suffering and life problems characteristic of a great many chronically traumatized people. Complex PTSD originates in relational trauma: the often early, severe, and chronic traumatic mistreatment by family members or others entrusted with care of the child. As opposed to single-event trauma, complex relational trauma is likely to result in alternating dissociated self-states with contradictory, idealizing, and devaluing relational patterns. The symptom presentation involves damage to relationships and identity, a potential for revictimization, and emotional dysregulation. Both PTSD and complex PTSD affect the psychobiological systems, but in complex PTSD, these disruptions and deficits are more pervasive, chronic, and often more severe and more conducive to personality fragmentation than in simple PTSD. Complex PTSD includes DID as well as other trauma-based disorders, such as borderline personality disorder (BPD). Howell and Blizard (2009) have proposed *chronic relational trauma disorder* as a term and concept that encompasses both DID and BPD.

Complex PTSD was reformulated as a proposed new diagnosis, *disorders of extreme stress not otherwise specified* (DESNOS), by the working group (Luxenberg, Spinazzola, & Van der Kolk, 2001) for the *DSM-IV* (APA, 1994). This proposed diagnosis has focused on different problem areas that research found to be associated with this kind of trauma (Van der Kolk, 1996b). These areas include (a) affect dysregulation, including impulse control, self-destructive behavior, and dyscontrol of anger; (b) disturbances in attention or consciousness; (c) somatization; (d) alterations and disturbances in self-perception; (e) alterations and disturbances in relationships; and (f) alternations and disturbances in meaning systems.

Although it is not an official diagnosis, the DESNOS syndrome has been the subject of much research, and it has been proposed for inclusion in the DSM. Many clinicians find the concept of complex PTSD and the description of DESNOS extremely useful for their thinking and clinically attributable to their patient population.

The following lists Luxenberg et al.'s (2001) diagnostic criteria for the proposed DESNOS syndrome:

I. Alteration in Regulation of Affect and Impulses
    A. Affect Regulation
    B. Modulation of Anger
    C. Self-Destructive
    D. Suicidal Preoccupation
    E. Difficulty Modulating Sexual Involvement
    F. Excessive Risk-Taking
II. Alterations in Attention or Consciousness (A or B required):
    A. Amnesia
    B. Transient Dissociative Episodes and Depersonalization
III. Alterations in Self-Perception (Two of A–F required):
    A. Ineffectiveness
    B. Permanent Damage
    C. Guilt and Responsibility
    D. Shame
    E. Nobody Can Understand
    F. Minimizing
IV. Alterations in Relations with Others (One of A–C required):
    A. Inability to Trust
    B. Revictimization
    C. Victimizing Others
V. Somatization (Two of A–E required):
    A. Digestive System
    B. Chronic Pain
    C. Cardiopulmonary Symptoms
    D. Conversion Symptoms
    E. Sexual Symptoms
VI. Alterations in Systems of Meaning (A or B required):
    A. Despair and Hopelessness
    B. Loss of Previously Sustaining Beliefs (p. 375)

Note the many times the word *alterations* is used in the criteria for DESNOS. This highlights how important psychological fragmentation and lack of self-coherence are in this syndrome. One way to understand such alternations—although not specifically stated here—is as a change or a switch of self-state. As noted, these criteria are not specific to DID but apply to other trauma-based disorders, such as BPD (Howell, 2002a), as well. What needs emphasizing here is that DID falls within the domain of trauma-based disorders, and that dissociation in some manifestations is an integral aspect of trauma-based disorders.

The Dissociative Nature of PTSD

Many clinicians and researchers view PTSD as a dissociative disorder and believe that it should be included in the *DSM* under the category of dissociative disorders rather than under anxiety disorders (Brett, 1996; Chu, 1998; Van der Hart et al., 2006). Indeed, "many writers argue that dissociation is central to the development and maintenance of PTSD, and that dissociative symptoms are important to both the diagnosis and conceptualization of PTSD.... Dissociation has repeatedly been found to be related to the severity of chronic PTSD" (Waelde, Silvern, Carlson, Fairbank, & Kletter, 2009, p. 449). Not only are dissociation scores of people with PTSD higher than those without PTSD (Bremmer et al., 1992), but also a recent meta-analysis by Ozer, Best, Lipsey, and Weiss (2003) found that peritraumatic dissociation (i.e., dissociation that occurs at the time of, or immediately after, the stressful event) was the most predictive of PTSD when measured along with variables such as prior trauma exposure and current stressors. Briere, Scott, and Weathers (2005) have clarified this finding: By distinguishing between acute dissociation at the time of the trauma and persisting dissociation afterward, they found that the greater risk for PTSD lies in dissociation that persists over time.

Onno van der Hart and his colleagues (Nijenhuis et al., 2004; Van der Hart, 2000; Van der Hart, Van Dijke, Van Son, & Steele, 2000) elegantly formulated an explanation of how PTSD is dissociative. They emphasized that the alternations between intrusions and numbing in the PTSD construct are in themselves manifestations of dissociation:

> [T]raumatic intrusions are positive dissociative phenomena, and complex traumatic re-experiences are also dissociative. It follows that all phenomena that are manifestations of trauma re-experiences (reactivated traumatic memories), such as flashbacks, should be seen as positive dissociative symptoms. To the extent that this theoretical position can be accepted by students of trauma, they cannot but consider the re-experiencing phenomena in PTSD, such as "recurrent and intrusive recollections of the event, including images, thoughts, and perceptions" (APA, 1994, p. 428) as positive dissociative phenomena. The same is true of Acute Stress Disorder (ASD). (Van der Hart et al., 2000, p. 51)

In their landmark article, "Trauma-Related Dissociation: Conceptual Clarity, Lost and Found," Van der Hart et al. (2004) noted that intrusion, which is a key diagnostic feature of PTSD in the *DSM-IV* (APA, 1994), should be understood as dissociative: "Intrusions imply a lack of integration of the part(s) of the personality that remain fixated in traumatic events, thus a lack of integration of the personality. Positive dissociative symptoms, including intrusions, are common in trauma-related disorders" (p. 908).

Similarly, Ginzburg, Butler, Saltzman, and Koopman (2009) stated that, "PTSD hyperarousal symptoms (i.e., hypervigilance, exaggerated startle, sleep disturbance, concentration difficulties, and anger) may be viewed as manifestations of dissociative processes. Hyperarousal symptoms may reflect the anxiety attached to the dissociated fixed ideas" (p. 462).

The positions of Nijenhuis et al. (2004) and Ginzburg et al. (2009) are accepted by many (myself included), but that is not to say that those in the PTSD field and the dissociative disorders field are always in agreement in how research is interpreted. The dissociative nature of PTSD is a controversial topic, with some researchers and theorists taking the position that PTSD does not necessarily inherently involve dissociation but may instead have dissociative subtypes (see Waelde et al., 2009, for a discussion on dissociative subtypes). These theorists concentrate more on the hyperarousal aspects of PTSD, such as elevated heart rate and blood pressure. For example, David Spiegel, in his electronic "Expert Commentary: *Dissociation and ASD and PTSD—DSM-V Considerations*" (featured in the Members' Clinical Corner, International Society for the Study of Trauma and Dissociation in January 2009) noted that many of those working in the PTSD field have focused not so much on the dissociative aspects of PTSD but more on anxiety and arousal, and in particular

on a model of hyperactivation of the noradrenergic system, both peripherally and in the brain (e.g., in the locus coeruleus). Irritability, increased heart rate and blood pressure associated with trauma reminders, flashbacks, and nightmares have been key symptoms targeted for treatments such as exposure, cognitive restructuring, and coping skills training.

Whether PTSD is inherently dissociative or has dissociative subtypes, and how much of a role dissociation plays in PTSD, remains a sometimes highly controversial issue among traumatologists. To some degree, it can even seem as if the field itself is dissociated into a split awareness about the realities of trauma and its impact.

PROFESSIONAL CONFUSION ABOUT THE EFFECTS OF TRAUMA AND DISSOCIATION ON PROBLEMS IN LIVING

Partly because the phenomenon of dissociation has been so "dissociated" within the mental health field, the *DSM* itself is full of inconsistencies with regard to the influence of dissociation and the definitions of its impact. For example, Van der Hart et al. (2006) have observed that in the *DSM-IV* (APA, 1994), intrusive PTSD symptoms are called *dissociative flashback episodes*, while flashbacks of acute stress disorder (ASD) are not considered dissociative. Even though the numbing and avoidance symptoms of ASD are considered dissociative, the same symptoms are not identified as dissociative in PTSD. Adding to the commentary on the inconsistencies and confusions about trauma disorders and dissociative disorders, Colin Ross, in his electronic "Expert Commentary: *How the Dissociative Structural Model Integrates DID and PTSD, Plus a Wide Range of Comorbidity*" (featured in the Members' Clinical Corner, International Society for the Study of Trauma and Dissociation in May 2009), observed that "the structure and rules of the DSM result in many people meeting criteria for numerous different disorders. This is routinely the case in DID and PTSD." In addressing the presence of dissociative features in many disorders, Ross added:

> When the intrusion is a physiological sensation, in *DSM-IV-TR* language we call that *somatization*. When the intrusion is an impulse to pluck hairs out of your head, or a sudden intrusion of a rage state, we call that an *impulse control disorder*. However when the intrusion is an impulse to wash your hands repeatedly, we call the impulse a *compulsion* and diagnosis OCD. The intruding affect is anxiety rather than rage. When a flashback episode intrudes, we call it a *dissociative flashback episode* and diagnose an anxiety disorder. When the intrusion is an auditory hallucination, we call that *psychosis* according to *DSM-IV-TR*. When the same symptom occurs in DID, we call it a *dissociative symptom*.
>
> Similarly, when traumatic affect is withdrawn from the apparently normal part (ANP) of a Vietnam veteran, we call that *numbing* and make it a symptom of PTSD. If the same symptom occurs in someone with BPD, we call it *emptiness*, but if the diagnosis is schizophrenia, we call it a *negative symptom of schizophrenia*. When a man perceives a threatened abandonment by his wife, flies into a rage, and beats her to control her and maintain his insecure attachment to her, we call this *intermittent explosive disorder*. The original trauma was failure of secure attachment by his primary female attachment figure in childhood, and the trigger in the present causes a reaction far out of proportion to the realistic threat in the present. The intruding affect is rage, but the underlying affect is fear and annihilation anxiety.
>
> When the trigger in the present is a news helicopter flying overhead, the original trauma was combat in Vietnam, and the intruding affect is fear, we call this a "dissociative flashback episode" and diagnose PTSD.

It would seem simpler and far clearer to note the underlying importance of trauma and dissociation in many disorders that are otherwise classified. And yet, as Luxenberg et al. (2001) explained:

Trauma-related disorders, including dissociative disorders, continue to be grossly underdiagnosed. This underrecognition can be best understood in light of the multiplicity of symptoms with which these patients present that may not be readily recognized as being related to their traumatic experiences. (p. 377)

NOTE

1. In a field such as the trauma and dissociation field, it is important to be precise as much as we can. One common problem is that the words *trauma* and *abuse* are often—although incorrectly—used interchangeably. Abuse, however painful and horrible, is not necessarily affectively or cognitively overwhelming of itself. Unfortunately, too many studies and reviews on the topic fail to make this distinction and end up observing that since the documented or recalled abuse did not correlate highly with dissociation, this means that traumatic events do not necessarily imply dissociation. Trauma may be conflated with abuse, and then when a person does not respond posttraumatically, it is erroneously concluded that trauma did not result in dissociation. An individual can endure terrible circumstances, even life-threatening events, but they are not necessarily perceived or experienced as traumatic to that person. Many variables may be at stake, including past history of trauma, overall resilience, and the social context, to name a few. For example, if one has the opportunity and ability to communicate emotions about the event to another person who is responsive and caring, it may link the traumatic event with one's ongoing life experience and with interpersonal connection, thus lessening the extent to which the experience is overwhelming and making it more tolerable. This does not mean that abuse is not bad. Abuse is terrible and unacceptable, but it *does not always result in trauma*. When it does, in my view the *effect of that trauma is dissociation*.

Chapter 5

Dissociated Self-States, Trauma, and Disorganized Attachment

[T]he essential experience of trauma [is] an unraveling of the relationship between self and nurturing other, the very fabric of psychic life.

Laub and Auerhahn (1993, p. 287)

Attachment theory, which assumes a two-person or even a multiperson psychology (Cortina & Marrone, 2004; Cortina & Liotti, 2010), has been a contributor to relational psychodynamic theory. This is especially true for a relational psychodynamic theory that encompasses dissociative processes.

This chapter explains why a trauma theory is not enough to understand the origin and persistence of dissociated self-states—and why the theory and knowledge base must include attachment, specifically disorganized attachment (DA). The chapter includes key aspects of attachment theory as well as functions of the attachment behavioral system, internal working models (IWMs), and attachment classifications, along with an emphasis on DA. The links between DA, incompatible, segregated IWMs, and dissociated self-states are described.

DISORGANIZED ATTACHMENT PREDICTS LATER DISSOCIATION BETTER THAN DOES DOCUMENTED TRAUMA

The high correlations between dissociative disorder diagnoses and antecedent child abuse, notably physical and sexual abuse, are well known. However, careful studies (Carlson, 1998; Lyons-Ruth, 2003, 2006; Ogawa, Sroufe, Weinfield, Carlson, & Egeland, 1997) have revealed that, statistically, DA is a better predictor of later dissociation than is discernable and known abuse or specific instances of childhood trauma. Why should this be? Certainly, the kinds of family environments in which abuse occurs are also characterized by emotional abuse and neglect. Poor psychological integration follows from family environments characterized by combinations of abuse, trauma, deprivation, and neglect (Allen, 2001) and from attachment dilemmas, particularly DA. In this sense, the antecedents of dissociative identity disorder (DID) stem not only from trauma (Gold, 2000) but also from other factors, such as severe neglect and attachment dilemmas in the context of early environments (Liotti, 1999).

It is not only the "traumatic event" in isolation but also the context of the event that makes something traumatic. It can make all the difference if a traumatized child can tell a sympathetic caregiving figure what happened and receive support. The child is then not alone with the trauma and is given the opportunity to connect the terrifying moment with a comforting one and reassure herself of general safety and of the reality of her perceptions. On the other hand for example, if the child is told he or his loved ones will die if he reveals what happened, then the child ends up bearing the terror in isolation. The child's affective state may be so unbearable that it rises to the level of the traumatic and cannot be managed in awareness. A child may be sexually and physically abused by his or her father only to be disbelieved and rejected by his or her mother. In many cases, the latter may be more unbearable than the former. Add to that the reality that the mother who permits abuse of a child may be the same mother who was highly misattuned, unresponsive, or neglectful when that child was a baby; these qualities can well contribute to DA. With such a parent, there may be hidden trauma as well: Parental behaviors that are highly neglectful or grossly misattuned can be traumatizing to an infant even if they might not be traumatizing to an older child or to an adult (Howell, 2008).

Clearly, there are difficulties in predicting which situations will end up being traumatic as well as determining which ones will be labeled so, but what is it about DA that predicts dissociative disorders? This chapter addresses the meaning of the findings that show DA as the best predictor of later dissociation.

THE TRAUMA MODEL OF DID

A prototypical example of the trauma/abuse model of DID is that of a little girl who is "on the ceiling" watching another little girl below as she is raped by her father (Ross, 1989). A traumatically abused and terrified child may well deal with overwhelming affect and pain by distancing herself from this experience to such a degree that she disidentifies with the experience and becomes an observer (rather than an experiencer) of the event. In this depersonalized state, she then *pseudodelusionally* (Kluft, 1984) views this as happening to another child. This "other child" then "holds" the affects and memories that are unbearable to the little girl watching from above. This separation protects the child from being continually overwhelmed and safeguards the ability to function.

But now, there are at least two little girls—the conscious little girl who is up on the ceiling watching another little girl suffering and the little girl who is suffering, experiencing the rape. The first little girl may go to school the next day knowing nothing of the one who was raped by her father. Thus, parts of the self who in effect hold some terrible information and unbearable emotions are not known by other parts who must go on living, go to school, to work, and so on. In psychological trauma, particularly at the hands of a person on whom one is dependent, dissociation allows a sequestering of the traumatic experience so that it allows the traumatized individual to continue functioning in a double-bind relationship (Spiegel, 1986), often without having to notice the inherent contradictions.

A child who is subject to sexual abuse in the home may "forget" the night's events during the day and use all her resources to "be like a normal person" during the day. In her stunning book, *Miss America by Day* (2003), Marilyn Van Derbur, who was Miss America in 1958, described how she was both a "day child" and a "night child." The day child knew nothing of the night child until she became older and began psychotherapy. This dynamic by which the victim bonds with the idealized aspects of the abuser while tuning out the abusive aspects along with the terror has also been called *traumatic bonding* (Dutton & Painter, 1981). Often applied to battered spouses or to those with Stockholm syndrome, it also characterizes victims of child abuse.

In cognitive psychological terms, Jennifer Freyd (1996) has described this sort of situation leading to dissociation as *betrayal trauma*. An aspect of betrayal trauma theory is *betrayal blindness*, in which mechanisms of trust and distrust become confused. Here, the capacity to dissociate may be life preserving for such a child might not be able to go on living were she aware of continual abuse in this way. Some children who are too aware of their situation and for whom dissociation was not adequate do attempt suicide. Others just wish that they could die. In psychoanalytic terms, Ferenczi (1949) and Fairbairn (1952) have also articulated forms of dissociative adaptations to attachment dilemmas. Dissociation can literally save the child from the intolerable.

A Previously Whole Personality Is Not Shattered

So far, we are discussing two dissociated identities: the one who knows and suffers and the one who stays connected in an idealizing way with the caregiver. One might think of the little child on the ceiling as *splitting off* the identity of the child below, but that is not exactly what happens, at least not usually on a one-time basis. In a one-time event that is overwhelming and inconsistent with already existing reasonably good attachment and in which there are no precursors for a differently personified identity, such as DA, the traumatized person would more likely develop posttraumatic stress disorder (PTSD), including anxiety or depersonalization symptoms, but not dissociated identity states. This would be in contrast to the chronic abuse cases, in which there are early and continuous attachment dilemmas.

So, in this prototypical model of the little child on the ceiling, we need to consider (a) how trauma impedes the linking of self-states (since a familial environment that is abusive or neglectful fails to facilitate the child's ability to link and integrate experiences) and (b) as a result of early traumatic attachment dilemmas, how the child had to develop contradictory, segregated models of attachment that involve alternating activation of the attachment system with the fear system, otherwise known as DA. In essence the substrate for the separation of the little girl on the ceiling and the other little girl whom she watches being raped (as well as possibly additional parts who are needed in other times and other ways) is already there in the child's inner world. This ongoing separation was "called forth" by the impossible dilemma of the rape by the caretaker.

The Nonfacilitative Environment and Trauma Impede the Normal Linking of Experience: Putnam's Discrete Behavioral States Model

Rather than resulting from a "shattering" of a previously intact and unified identity, the formation of day and night children (and other internal identities) stems not only from trauma but also from "a developmental failure of consolidation and integration of discrete states of consciousness" (Putnam, 1997, p. 176). Putnam's discrete behavioral states (DBS) model of the personality emphasizes that rather than starting out as a unity, the human personality must become integrated over time. Psychological trauma and neglect impede the process of integration. In his DBS model, Putnam (1997) describes how mental states, or states of consciousness, are the building blocks of human behavior and consciousness. For example, behavioral states, such as deep sleep, rapid-eye-movement (REM) sleep, and awakening, which were discrete in infancy, become linked over time in sequences. Infants go through orderly transitions, or *switches*, that involve discontinuous jumps from one state to another, for example, from sleep to wakefulness to fussiness to crying. While at first these are clearly biological states involving such biological activity as eating and elimination, they begin to succeed each other in orderly sequences so that the transitions between them become regularly linked. The linking of affective/biological states occurs similarly. As these linkages become more complex, the child gains greater control and ability to self-regulate.

One of the important effects of trauma and neglect is that the expected linking of associative pathways among states is impeded. For example, states of terror are not linked with other states of mind. This is particularly likely in a neglectful environment in which the parents or caregivers cannot or will not attune to or help label the child's emotions to help them to connect these emotional states to other emotional states. This is in contrast to ways that more helpful caregivers assist in emotion regulation, such as downregulating overarousal, minimizing negative affect, and assisting a child to transition from negative to positive states (Tronick, 1989) as well as promoting integration by facilitating the child's reflective functioning, for example, letting the child know that she is in the caregiver's mind in an empathic way (Fonagy, Gergely, Jurist, & Target, 2002). Trauma also interrupts metacognitive, self-observing, self-reflective functions, which can facilitate the integration of states. As a result of trauma, the child is then left with overwhelming affect without context and without soothing, resulting in disjointed, out-of-context states.

Originally, behavioral/mental states are not linked. It is in the course of development, in a facilitative interpersonal environment, that they become linked.

RELATIONAL TRAUMA, ATTACHMENT, AND DISSOCIATION

Relational trauma is profoundly about attachment. As Laub and Auerhahn (1993) so cogently said, "The essential experience of trauma [is] an unraveling of the relationship between self and nurturing other, the very fabric of psychic life" (p. 287). When it comes to dissociated self-states, even though the trauma/dissociation field and the field of attachment studies developed separately and use somewhat different languages, incompatible segregated IWMs and dissociated self-states describe basically the same phenomena.

Bowlby's Relational Attachment Theory

John Bowlby's (1969/1983) first revolutionary insight concerned the evolutionary survival benefits of attachment, thus grounding attachment behavior in the science of ethology. It became a scientific underpinning for the relational theories of human development and of psychotherapy and, among others, of Fairbairn, Guntrip, and Winnicott. Bowlby's second major contribution was his concept of IWMs, which involves expectations regarding the availability of the attachment figure, the mental representations of the self and the attachment figure, and the affects about them. Bowlby proposed that difficult attachment conditions could foster the development of multiple, segregated IWMs. Inconsistent and segregated IWMs are especially characteristic of a later-identified attachment style, DA. Both segregated IWM and DA have direct relevance to our understanding of dissociated self-states. Specifically, it appears that the segregated IWMs of DA are the precursors and substrates for a great portion of dissociated self-states.

Bowlby (1969/1983) was proposing a new instinct theory (Bretherton, 1992)—a theory of an evolutionary origin and biological basis for attachment behavior—when he presented ethological and observational evidence that infant primates, including humans, are hardwired for attachment in the service of survival. Based on his study and observations, he postulated that proximity to the mother provided protection against predators. Inasmuch as it increased the chances of survival, physical closeness was understood to be the goal of the attachment system. This theory contradicted the then-prominent Hullian learning theory, which classified attachment behavior as a secondary drive, derivative only of the primary drive of hunger. Attachment theory also contradicted Freudian dual-instinct theory. As a result, Bowlby's assertion of the primacy and the reality of attachment relationships—beginning with the mother—was not immediately accepted into psychoanalysis. So much so that Bowlby, asserting the importance of the real interpersonal environment as opposed to an exclusionary emphasis on fantasies, once stood up at a psychoanalytic meeting, emphatically insisting to the audience, "But, there *is* such a thing as a *bad* mother" (Mitchell, 2000, p. 84; italics in text).

Bowlby came to understand attachment, which was often indicated by infant behaviors such as clinging, crying, and following, as a behavioral system. A behavioral system is a motivational system that is not secondarily derivative of more primary drives, but a primary one by its own right. The attachment system is not the only behavioral system but is one among others, such as those that control mating, feeding, fear, exploration, caregiving or parenting, and dominance (Bretherton, 1992). Behavioral systems may operate sequentially, and they may also activate or inhibit each other. For example, the attachment system and the fear system work in tandem, and fear often activates the attachment system. The exploratory system is activated and enhanced by the attachment system; conversely, the infant's exploratory behavior is inhibited in the absence of the attachment figure. Notably, the attachment system is regarded as

> preemptive when aroused, since it mobilizes responses to fear or threat. In that sense, the quality of regulation of fearful affect available in attachment relationships is foundational to the developing child's freedom to turn attention away from issues of threat and security toward other developmental achievements, such as exploration, learning and play. (Lyons-Ruth, 2003, p. 885)

Importantly, the attachment system does not operate only in infancy. Attachment is intrinsic to emotional security, and the need for it pertains to us throughout the life cycle. As Bowlby (1984), now famously, said, "All of us, from the cradle to the grave, are happiest when life is organized as a series of excursions, long or short, from the secure base provided by our attachment figures" (p. 11).

Current attachment theorists have further developed Bowlby's initial observation about the importance of proximity to the caregiver by identifying additional functions of attachment, such as the infant's reduced anxiety and enhanced feeling of security (Fonagy, 2001). Most important, attachment helps regulate affect. Lyons-Ruth (2001, 2003) further articulates Hesse and Main's (1999) observation concerning the importance of the attachment figure as a solution to fear and stresses that the attachment system modulates psychological fear and distress. She views the attachment system as analogous to the immune system: Just as the biological immune system modulates physical disease, so does the infant's attachment to the caregiver modulate and reduce fearful affect. This emphasis on reduction of fearful arousal is a large departure from libidinal and aggressive drives as motivational systems. Instead, attachment theory "regrounds clinical theory in the developmental dynamics of fear" (Lyons-Ruth, 2001, p. 40). However, she more recently specified that regulation of fearful arousal is not only dependent on such parental behaviors as soothing but also depends on positively toned intersubjective exchanges between infant and caretaker that contribute to the infant's felt security: "Therefore, there is now a convergence of developmental, behavioral, biological, and evolutionary arguments for enlarging our model of the attachment motivational system to include positive components of the infant–caregiver relationship, components that also serve to down-regulate fearful arousal in early life" (Lyons-Ruth, 2006, p. 601).

Internal Working Models

As Bowlby's thinking evolved, it became less behavioral and more focused on mental processing. Although his first revolutionary insight concerned the survival benefits of attachment, an equally important concept in Bowlby's attachment theory is that of IWMs, which organize the child's cognitions, affects, and expectations about attachment relationships. IWMs appraise and predict attachment emotions of self and others. As such, they guide attachment behavior. They generalize from past experience with the attachment figure (Bowlby, 1973) in a way that is similar to Daniel Stern's (1985) conceptualization of representations of interactions that are being generalized (RIGs). They are "superordinate structures that combine numerous schemas 'of being with.' ... They regulate the child's behavior with the attachment figure" (Fonagy et al., 1995, p. 235).

Bowlby (1973, 1980) noted that babies and children develop multiple IWMs that may be unintegrated and contradictory. Bowlby addressed defense against the child's interpersonal attachment dilemmas (such as unavailable, intermittently available, or intrusive caretakers) in terms of what he called "defensive exclusion." Here, the child may either deactivate attachment or disconnect her perceptions and emotions, a style that allows the child to stay attached but to disconnect observations and feelings that are contradictory to her attachment.

The IWMs in infancy are aspects of implicit memory. Initially, they operate subsymbolically. As the child grows older, the IWMs become more explicit and may become verbally coded as part of autobiographical memory. These IWMs represent unconscious procedural knowledge of being with another person that reflect implicit models of relationships and are often adaptations to the parents' inadequacies, inconsistencies, and defenses (Lyons-Ruth, 1999, 2001). When these implicit procedural ways of being with another are contradictory—for example, "Mother is safe and protective, and I am safe" versus "Mother is dangerous, and I am endangered and terrified"—or when implicit procedural knowledge contradicts seemingly clear explicit information (e.g., a physically violent parent insists that there has never been abuse), the contradictions can set the stage for conflicting and segregated IWMs.

Segregated and incompatible IWMs can be the precursors for milder dissociative disorders as well as ordinary problems in living. One IWM may become dominant in its way of regulating emotions and interpersonal perceptions, while others may become segregated from ordinary experience as aspects of not-me (Sullivan, 1953). This may be the case in avoidant or resistant attachment. For example, a person we will call Sarah, who is primarily characterized as having a preoccupied attachment (corresponding to resistant attachment of childhood), would often find herself in relationships in which others cannot see her needs, realities, and contributions as valid. In spite of that, she keeps trying to get these people's positive attention, mostly unsuccessfully and only on occasion successfully. As a result, she has frequently been extremely distressed. In therapy, she has become more aware of a main cause of her distress (her own expectations) as well as the fact of her distress and the accompanying feeling of the injustice of it. This IWM became more linked with the rest of her ongoing consciousness; as a result, she has learned to increasingly assert herself. She was risking disconnection—but fortunately without that outcome, thus redefining the attachment parameters of her relationships. In addition, she has been increasingly able to extricate herself from interpersonal situations that were intractably similar to her early attachment dilemmas, with the result that she is now in more relationships in which she feels valued and noticed. Her problematic IWM is still there, but because she has worked with her feelings about it and linked it with her ongoing experience, it no longer defines her life as it had in the past. She has become aware of it, understands it, and has learned to apply new models that support healthier relationships.

In a general sense, a child who is put in situations in which only the subjectivity of the caregiver matters is unable to express thoughts and feelings that conflict with those required by the caregiver and therefore may keep contradictory implicit knowledge segregated from the acceptable "factual" view. The child might have a split-off knowledge about her own needs while simultaneously convincing herself that her needs are what her caregivers need from her. Here, the distinction between implicit, procedural memory and explicit, declarative memory is especially relevant. Procedural memory pertains to things like "how to ride a bike" or "how to interact with Mommy." Certain procedural memories, which may not be conscious, may exist in contradiction to conscious declarative memory, which may contain autobiographical episodes of memory (called episodic) or informational propositions about the self and others (called semantic). Although procedural memory is not lost or changed, declarative memory changes with experience. Thus, a person may have certain kinds of relational procedural "knowledge" that is enacted. This knowledge may not be consciously known. Indeed, early schemata that contributed to DA are encoded in implicit memory and "are too complex and intrinsically contradictory to be later synthesized in a unitary, cohesive structure of explicit semantic memory. In this sense the IWM of early [disorganized] attachment is intrinsically dissociative" (Liotti, 2004, p. 479). For example, the person may have been told that the abusing parent was a wonderful person, or that parent may have represented him- or herself to the world as such. This sets up at least two conflicting IWMs and ways of relating to the world, which, especially if there is amnesia for abuse, may be extremely confusing to the person. If there is no collaborative relationship within which to work out these contradictions, these patterns remain deeply segregated systems of attachment.

These incompatible, segregated IWMs can be understood as dissociated self-states. There is a striking similarity between the concept of segregated, incompatible working models and that of dissociated self-states. Indeed, inasmuch as IWMs involve an expectation of a particular kind of relationship that involves the person, expectations of the other, and affects about these expectations, one could say that IWMs are self-states, and that segregated, incompatible IWMs are dissociated self-states (see Forrest's 2001 work, which provides a neuroscience view and focus on these expectancies as the important cross-temporal contingencies that infants must learn to mediate if they are to cohere an integrated self).

Attachment and Attachment Classifications

Mary Ainsworth and her colleagues (Ainsworth, Blehar, Waters, & Wall, 1978) began a classification of infant attachment to the mother by means of a procedure called the strange situation. This involved the mother leaving her baby (aged 12 to 18 months) in an unfamiliar situation for a few minutes and then returning twice; an observation and coding were made of the baby's style of response to both being left and to being reunited. Ainsworth et al. described three types of attachment: secure attachment and two insecure attachment types—anxious avoidant and anxious resistant. A little over half of the babies studied were found to be secure. Next in frequency was avoidant attachment, followed by resistant attachment.

Babies who were securely attached cried and showed other signs of being upset by the mother's absence, but they were quickly comforted when the mother returned. Avoidantly attached babies did not show behavioral distress in the mother's absence and actively avoided contact with her when she returned. A smaller third group of infants was classified as anxious resistant. These babies were distressed in the mother's absence, but they were not comforted by her return. Rather, they continued to be distressed and resisted being comforted. (This group has also been called anxious ambivalent.)

Securely attached babies develop IWMs that are coherent and consistent. The self is regarded as lovable, and others are regarded as trustworthy and available. In contrast, insecure attachment classifications are also coherent, but they are more problematic. They are coherent because they comprise an organized pattern of attachment that includes contradictory conscious and unconscious components. This organized pattern works as a defensive system that is adaptive to the early interpersonal environment and operates as a form of self-regulation and affect regulation.

Wallin (2007) understood these insecure patterns to involve two or more contradictory working models. With regard to the avoidant/dismissing classification, he wrote:

> These "minimizing" or "deactivating" strategies are woven through the contradictory models—conscious and unconscious—that shape the inner and interpersonal experiences of avoidant/dismissing individuals. One model is consciously embraced and involves the sense that the self is good, strong and complete, while others are untrustworthy, needy, and inadequate. The second model which is unconscious and feared, entails a disturbing sense that the self is flawed, dependent, and helpless, while others are likely in response to be rejecting, controlling and punitive. Deactivating strategies support the first model as a defense against the second (Mikulincer & Shaver, 2003). More specifically, these strategies promote distance, control, and self-reliance (the essence of the conscious model) while inhibiting emotional experience that might activate the attachment system (as it is dispiritingly represented in the unconscious model). (pp. 90–91)

This defensive organization works as a response to an intrusive, misattuned, rejecting and/or distant mother. It works to tamp down emotional yearning for attachment. The parasympathetic nervous system can be activated to cut down on experienced emotional reactivity, even though physiological measures indicate that the distress has been felt. Avoidantly attached children may also be thought of as repressing the affects of attachment (Liotti, 1999). Later in life, avoidantly attached children may idealize the parents (Liotti, 1992), thus contributing to the contradictions in the IWM. In short, in avoidant or dismissing attachment style, deactivation of attachment and devaluation are used as defenses—although idealization is also used defensively. Here, the experienced reactivity of the self is over-regulated (Wallin, 2007).

In contrast, there is the anxious resistant attachment classification (or corresponding adult "preoccupied" classification). These children

> were understood to inhabit a representational world shaped by multiple, unintegrated working models. These models were thought to be the outcome of contradictory experiences with unpredictable attachment figures....Presumably closeness was associated with favorable experiences that generated the model of a distressed self in interaction with a sometimes responsive other—while abandonment was linked to problematic experience that resulted in a model of an autonomous self in interaction with an unresponsive other (Mikulincer & Shaver, 2003). (Wallin, 2007, pp. 92–93)

This overall organization views the self as close and connected to the other, but the self is stressed, and the other is unpredictable. Here, there is hyperactivation of the sympathetic nervous system. Emotions are turned on, and the person is consciously aware of them. Resistantly attached children may also be thought of as denying one side of an ambivalent attitude (Liotti, 1999). This attachment style is often adaptive to an interpersonal environment in which the caregiver is unreliably responsive.

Liotti (personal communication, December 2010) notes that securely attached infants expect "well," while avoidant ones expect to be rejected, and resistant ones do not know what to expect. It should be noted here that these categories are in a certain sense oversimplifications: Not everyone fits into such neat categories; and, additionally, a child can have different attachment styles with different attachment figures. However, what is important to remember is that the secure, avoidant, and resistant strategies are all identifiable organized patterns. They are not all necessarily happy ones (especially with respect to the insecure strategies), but they represent a purposeful pattern that has developed that enables the child to stay attached and to self-regulate in the best possible way given the interpersonal environment to which they have adapted.

It is only in later years into attachment research that a fourth attachment pattern, called *disorganized/disoriented*, was identified (Main & Solomon, 1986, 1990). (The corresponding adult attachment style is called unresolved.) Disorganized attachment (DA), which affects about 15% of infants (Van Ijzendoorn et al., 1999, as cited in Liotti & Gumley, 2008), is associated with maltreatment or gross insensitivity on the part of the caretaker. When the child faces the dilemma of both seeking safety from and fearing the caretaker at the same time, the child's attachment strategies are likely to become disorganized. As a consequence, multiple, segregated, incompatible working models of attachment may develop. These "multiple and dissociated mental structures...control the child's actions. These structures may be related to incoherent, simultaneous representations of the self and the attachment figure" (Liotti, 1995, p. 348).

In the strange situation, babies with disorganized attachment (DA) will do such things as run in circles, run toward and then run away from the caregiver, have a facial expression in which one side is eager to greet and another is terrified, or even just collapse in a heap. On videotape, they appear to simultaneously approach and withdraw or to do both things in quick succession (Jacobvitz, 2000; Lyons-Ruth, 2003). The attachment system is activated, but the fear system is also activated in what is a repetitive approach–avoidance conflict. The infant approaches the attachment figure, governed by the attachment system, but then retreats as the fear system takes over. This may become a positive-feedback loop, intensifying the distress. "Caught in this loop, the child will experience such an overwhelming flow of contradictory affects as to exceed his or her capacities for a coherent, or even an ambivalent, organization of behavior and attention. Therefore, his or her attachment behavior will become disorganized and disoriented" (Liotti, 1999, p. 764). Neither approach nor avoidance works as a means of self-organization or as a way to alleviate fear. As a result, disorganized children have a collapse of their defensive or coping strategy. As babies and young children, they have not been able to find a way of regulating affect. Although this disorganization is classified as a kind of an attachment style, one could argue that it is less an attachment style than it is an unresolved conflict about the viability of attachment.

Liotti (2011) puts it this way:

> Being exposed to frequent interactions with a helplessly frightened, hostile and frightening, or confused caregiver, infants are caught in a relational trap, created by the dynamics of two inborn motivational systems, the attachment system and the defense (fight-flight) system. The attachment and the defense systems normally operate in harmony (i.e., flight from the source of fear to find refuge in proximity to the attachment figure). They, however, clash in such a type of infant-caregiver interaction where the caregiver is at the same time the source and the solution of the infant's fear ("fright without solution": Main & Hesse, 1990, p. 163). The consequence of the simultaneous activation of the defense and the attachment system is the "failure to terminate attachment interactions,

due to the fact that fear is in itself a powerful activator of the attachment system. (Solomon & George, 1999, p. 385)

This pattern of DA is predicted by maltreatment and neglect (Carlson, 1998) and has been found to occur in about 80% of maltreated infants (Carlson, Cicchetti, Barnett, & Braunwald, 1989). Maltreatment and severe neglect, however, are not the only path to DA. About 15% of the infants of low-risk families, in which the infants did not appear to have been abused, are also disorganized (Liotti, 1999; Lyons-Ruth, 2003). What then precipitates the DA in this group?

Hesse and Main (1999) hypothesized that frightening or frightened (FR) parental behavior could lead to disorganized attachmenmt (DA) in the absence of overt maltreatment. With reference to the first, they described some of the mothers of these "low-risk" disorganized infants: Offering none of the metasignals of play, these mothers teased their babies by spontaneously entering into predatory, animal-like behavior—growling, hissing, baring their teeth, stalking their infants on all fours, in one case mock mauling the baby, with fingers extended like claws. The authors explained as follows:

> [F]rightening parental figures put their offspring in an irresolvable and disorganizing paradox in which impulses to approach the parent as the infant's "haven of safety" will inevitably conflict with impulses to flee from the parent as a source of alarm. Here, we argue that conditions of this kind place the infant in a situation involving *fright without solution* [emphasis added], resulting in a collapse of behavioral and attentional strategies. (p. 484)

From studies such as these, we learn that infants are particularly sensitive to instances when they are presented with conflicting needs (such as approaching or fleeing), even if these instances are not perceived by the parent as traumatizing or maltreating. The parents might have been meaning to play with the infant, but they were not attuned to the child's experience, affect, or needs, resulting in the infant experiencing fright without solution. Repeated exposure to such experiences might well result in DA even when the parent is not abusive but is sufficiently out of tune with the infant and the infant's needs.

The Intergenerational Transmission of Attachment Style and the Adult Attachment Interview

The scary and misattuned mothers who hissed at their babies and crawled on all fours described by Hesse and Main (1999) were not overtly abusive and were not consciously intending to harm their children. It is likely that they were transmitting unresolved trauma from their own histories. Because of their own unresolved traumas, they tended to reenact their disconnected procedural relational models of how to do things with another (inconsistent and segregated IWM), resulting in serious misattunement and varying degrees of neglect. Hesse and Main (1999) documented a correspondence between the attachment styles of the infant and those of the mothers. Secure, autonomous parents tended to have secure babies; dismissing parents, avoidant babies; and preoccupied parents, anxious, resistant babies. In addition, behavior of parents classified as unresolved/disorganized corresponded to that of their disorganized infants. (However, the unresolved category will also be given a secondary category, and if the second category is secure, then there is less likelihood of having an infant with DA.) The authors coded the parents' attachment classifications using the Adult Attachment Interview (AAI), an interview developed by Main and her colleagues in which respondents are asked to describe and evaluate some of their own early attachment experiences. Rather than life history, coherence and collaborativeness of discourse are key criteria for coding these interviews. The parents' ability or lack of ability to speak coherently and collaboratively, while describing their own life events and early attachment experiences in the context of an interview that activates the attachment system, predict their infant's attachment style, suggesting a source of intergenerational transmission. The ability to think about and describe personal experience in a coherent way and to empathically think about what others are thinking fosters the child's emotional development. The lack of opportunity for narration of self-experience with important figures (the very narration that secure attachment allows) is detrimental to the development of integrating capabilities. Thus, a parent's unresolved trauma—as can become manifest in brief moments during the AAI—would be expected to affect the coherence and collaborativeness of their discourse. Liotti (2004) noted that parents with unresolved traumatic memories are likely to have their attachment system activated along with their caregiving system when they engage in caring for their own children. The activation of the attachment system arouses strong emotions, including fear and anger, and these emotions are likely to show even as they attempt to soothe their babies. Although they are not overtly maltreating their babies, such parents may be unwittingly frightening them.

Main's development of the AAI connected the related themes of trauma, IWMs, DA, and coherence of narrativity. The AAI, in a sense, scores unresolved trauma—although it should be noted that the coding of the unresolved classification does not depend on the veridicality of the reports of trauma. Unresolved trauma leads to dissociated mental structures, whether we call these structures self-states or an IWM. Not surprisingly, the parents of dissociative patients are more likely than others to have experienced a major loss around the time of the patient/subject's birth. Liotti,

Intreccialagli, and Cecere (1991), cited in Liotti (2006), found that a large portion (62%) of parents of 46 patients with dissociative disorders had suffered a serious loss either 2 years before or 2 years after the birth of the baby. In contrast, only 16% of parents of psychiatric patients without dissociative disorders had suffered such a loss.

Fright Without a Solution

The concept of *fright without a solution* (Hesse & Main, 1999) describes the prototypical dilemma of the child who develops DA. However, this may be more complicated than directly frightening or frightened parental behavior. Noting that she and her colleagues had found that "*absence* of caregiver responses will also lead to infant disorganization," Lyons-Ruth (2006) suggests that "the more general caregiving mechanism related to disorganization may be the lack of effective caregiver regulation of fearful arousal, rather than explicit fear of the caregiver herself" (p. 610). In the course of a 19-year longitudinal study, Lyons-Ruth and her colleagues (Lyons-Ruth, 2001, 2003, 2006) found that overall disrupted attachment was highly associated with DA: "Both in our own work and in the work of three additional laboratories, these disrupted affective communication processes at 12 to 18 months of age are related to the extent of the infant's disorganized attachment behavior" (Lyons-Ruth, 2006, p. 606). Lyons-Ruth and her colleagues (Lyons-Ruth, 2006) examined five broad forms of disrupted parental affective communication with the infant: withdrawal, negative-intrusive responses, role-confused responses, disoriented responses, and affective communication errors. The last included the mother's failure to respond to the infant's affective signals and giving simultaneous conflicting cues to the infant—for example, a mother laughing at her baby's distress while picking up the baby.

Although the developmental pathway from DA to DID is not clear, DA has been linked to the development of dissociative symptoms (Carlson, 1998; Liotti 1992, 2004, 2006; Lyons-Ruth, 2001; Ogawa et al., 1997). In fact, DA was noted as a better predictor for dissociative experiences than documentations of abuse. In a longitudinal, prospective study extending from infancy to late adolescence, Ogawa et al. (1997) found that DA and proneness to dissociation were significantly related. In longitudinal studies involving disorganized infants, Lyons-Ruth (2003, 2006) found that contrary to expectation, maltreatment and trauma per se did not predict later dissociative symptoms. Instead, "maternal disrupted communication at 18 months made a strong contribution to the prediction of dissociative symptoms at age 19" (p. 610). The researchers found no prediction from factors of poverty, single parenthood, early history of maltreatment, or the mother's dissociative symptomology up to age 7. None of these predicted the incidence of dissociative symptoms in the adolescent at 19 (Lyons-Ruth, 2006).

What then in unrepaired maternal disrupted behavior is traumatic? As previously noted, neglectful or grossly misattuned maternal behavior that would not be traumatizing to an older child or an adult might well be so for an infant. This may lead to DA. As Liotti (2011) observes:

> The interaction between a frightened/frightening, helpless or abdicating caregiver and a disorganized infant experiencing fright without solution is an extreme example of emotional misattunement, that is, of threatened failure in the intrinsic intersubjectivity of human experience (Stern, 1985, 2004). Instead of preserving secure intersubjectivity, the infants' experience is alike to feeling utterly alienated from one's own primary relatedness, that is, to feeling alone while being in the perceptual (as opposed to communicational and affectional) presence of another person. This experience may be understood as a type of early relational trauma, that exerts an adverse influence on the development of the stress-coping system in the infant's brain. (Schore, 2009, pp. 385–386)

Is Disorganized Attachment Inherently a Dissociative Process?

Disorganized infants exhibit trancelike and disconnected behaviors (Jacobvitz, 2000; Lyons-Ruth, 2003). They often exhibit stilled behavior and appear to be staring into space. Many of the behaviors displayed by infants with DA are phenotypic of dissociation (Main & Morgan, 1996), and Liotti (1992, 1995, 1999) has proposed that DA may be considered a prototype for dissociative disorders.

The disorganized infants who are caught in *fright without a solution* have highly conflicting and segregated IWMs that, by the nature of the interpersonal situation in which the attachment figure is traumatizing, dangerous, or feared, cannot be linked. Therefore, these working models are dissociated.

Disorganized Attachment: Hypnoid States in Babies

One may understand DA as the result of early trauma—trauma in the sense of something that exceeds the integrative capacity of the infant or young child's consciousness—and that these early contradictory IWMs in DA are the result of dissociative processes (Liotti, 2006). Based on observations that these babies, like dissociative adults, go into trancelike behaviors, one could also say that these traumatized babies exhibit hypnoid states.

Liotti (2006) suggests that the emotionally shifting, frightening, or violent interpersonal environment to which these disorganized infants are subject simply cannot be assimilated and organized for use by the infant in any coherent fashion: "The simultaneous emotional perception of self and the caregiver in DA could exceed the integrative power of consciousness in this developmental period" (p. 58). Referring to Bower's (1971) early work, which found that, in contrast to younger infants, those over 20 weeks old responded with alarm when presented with multiple perceptual images of the mother, Liotti (2006) infers that this means that the infants' integrative powers have increased by 20 weeks: Because the older infants expect continuity, they are alarmed at the lack of it. Liotti (2006) notes that this is significant because this is the same period that the attachment bond is developing. Second, he suggests that this unintegratable confusion puts the infant into an altered state, a trance—as can happen with adults (i.e., with confusional techniques in Ericksonian hypnosis).

In other words, with regard to DA, the *basic substrates* that may later develop into dissociated parts of the self *are already there*—in infancy. These substrates probably also set the stage for developing self-hypnotic abilities of the person with a dissociative disorder.

Dissociative Disorders May Develop From Disorganized Attachment

Liotti (1992) has proposed that the development of DID depends on an earlier development of DA in which the baby has many disconnected, contradictory IWMs, and that it is only this, in combination with severe and repeated trauma, that yields DID. He has developed a compelling model by which DA may develop into either less-serious problems in living or full-blown dissociative disorders, depending on whether later events in the child's life are mitigating (allowing an opportunity for synthesis of dissociated structures) or further traumatizing (which would prevent such synthesis).

A child who had reparative stabilizing attachment experiences subsequent to early experiences yielding the DA might be prone to dissociative experiences such as daydreaming and may have a high score on the Dissociative Experience Scale (DES) (see Chapter 8 on Assessment) but would otherwise be relatively unimpaired. A child who had fewer reparative experiences but had not experienced serious trauma and maltreatment might develop a mild dissociative disorder. But, a child with DA who was subsequently subjected to serious abuse would be likely to develop DID.

How then would this come about? Following Edelman (1989), Liotti (1992) suggests a process by which DID may develop and by which the switch process occurs. Edelman's (2004) theory of consciousness assumes that information is processed in a parallel distributed way with respect to a primary form of consciousness (PC) that is shared by humans and certain other higher-developed mammals. "Primary consciousness is the state of being mentally aware of things in the world, of having mental images in the present" (Edelman, 2004, p. 9). This develops from an ongoing matching and evaluation of information about the biological self to information outside that self—to the outside reality. PC is the basis for the emergence of higher-order consciousness (HOC), which is a conceptual memory of self and nonself linkages. HOC precedes the development of logical and verbalizable thoughts. According to Liotti:

> The working model of self and the attachment figure is an early aspect of the conceptual memory of self-not self. In order for the process of HOC to proceed properly, the matching of ongoing environmental information with a coherent (if not unitary) conceptual memory of self/not-self is necessary. If the conceptual schemata of the self/not-self distinction against which the ongoing environmental information is *at a given moment* matched, are multiple and incompatible, HOC will tend to collapse. It is likely that, *in that particular moment*, the subjective experience of the person will tend to be reduced to the PC. An altered state of consciousness will be experienced, inside which the non-conceptual, non-verbalizable aspects of the biological self (visceral and emotional information) will be confronted with stored and ongoing information concerning outside reality. If two or more of the incompatible conceptual models of self/not-self alternate rapidly during this altered state of consciousness, dissociated actions (each related to one of these incompatible models) such as those observed in D babies during the SS [strange situation] may make their appearance. If one among the competing conceptual models (let us label it CM1) is then selected for matching with ongoing environmental information, the altered state of consciousness will come to an end, and HOC will be resumed. An amnesia barrier, however, will separate the information pertaining to CM1 from that pertaining to other models (CM2, CM3, etc.) when they will be eventually called into operation by new configurations of environmental stimuli. Until the process of switching from one CM to another in matching environmental information is completed, an altered state of consciousness (that is, a lapse of HOC and a resurgence of PC) will be subjectively experienced. (p. 201; italics in original)

The Karpman "Drama" Triangle of Victim, Persecutor, and Rescuer

Along with Ross (1989) and Putnam (1989), Liotti found the Karpman *drama triangle* a helpful heuristic model for understanding the dissociated self-states of DID. The Karpman drama triangle (1968) includes the helpless suffering victim, the powerful abuser, and the powerful rescuer. Liotti linked the origin of the identities specified in the Karpman triangle to the infant's experience of frightening or frightened parents. As noted, the IWM of DA expresses multiple, segregated, and dramatically different expectations of the attachment figure (Liotti, 1999, 2004, 2006). In particular, the

child may display incompatible attitudes involving care-seeking, caregiving, and fight-flight, and display shifts between these. This kind of dramatic shifting from one attitude to another—from helplessness to hostility
to caregiving—is also characteristic of adults who report histories of abuse
and traumatic attachments. Referring to Main and Hesse's (1990) studies
of disorganized children who suffered fright without a solution with regard
to parents who tended to be frightening or frightened, Liotti suggested ways
that these identities of victim, persecutor, and rescuer may develop. In the
first case of the frightening parent, the children will have an IWM in which
they experience themselves as helpless victims of a persecutor. In the latter
case of the frightened parent, the children might erroneously see themselves
as the source of the parents' fright and construe themselves as persecutors.
Linked to this self-view, they may also see themselves as blameworthy. In
response to a parent's inversion of the attachment relationship, these children may also develop an additional role: They may see themselves as the
parent's rescuer and comforter. In addition, with reference to a frightened
as well as a frightening parent, inasmuch as their own attachment needs
for modulation of fear are not being met, the children may also experience
themselves as helpless victims.

These roles, developed early into identities in the infant's experiences
with the caregiver, function as substrates that underpin later identities and
roles that are variants of caregiving, perpetration, and victimization.

Disorganized Attachment Precedes
a Wide Array of Disorders

It is important to note that attachment disorganization has been linked not
only to dissociative disorders but also to a wide range of difficulties and
diagnoses. Sequelae of early DA include deficiencies in reflective, mentaliz-
ing capacity (Fonagy, 2001; Fonagy et al., 2002) include increased aggres-
siveness with peers (Lyons-Ruth, 1996) and general difficulties with affect
dysregulation (Liotti, 2006; Lyons-Ruth, 2003; Schore, 2003a, 2003b).
These deficits following DA make it a general risk factor for a number of
psychiatric diagnoses. Inasmuch as DA is essentially a dissociative process,
this would be true: Dissociation underlies many diagnoses and problems in
living, including neurotic, superego, and trauma-based difficulties (Howell,
1997a); personality disorders (Bromberg, 1993, 1995, 1998; Howell,
2002a, 2003); and psychoses (Liotti & Gumley, 2008; Moskowitz, 2008;
Read, Perry, Moskowitz, & Connolly, 2001). However, DA is most directly
and clearly linked to disorders characterized by splitting and dissociation,
such as borderline personality (Liotti, Cortina, & Farina, 2008; Lyons-
Ruth, 2001, 2006), narcissistic psychopathology (Lyons-Ruth, 2001), and
psychosis (Liotti & Gumley, 2008) in addition to dissociative disorders.

It should be noted that DID has frequently been misdiagnosed as border-line personality disorder (BPD). BPD is also often diagnosed as comorbid with DID. I have previously outlined why I believe that BPD is dissocia-tion based (Howell, 2002a). Howell and Blizard (2009) proposed a new diagnostic term of relational trauma disorder that would encompass BPD. In these last conceptualizations, BPD is not comorbid but is an aspect of dissociative psychopathology.

Sequelae to DA: Controlling Strategies

How do the later-developing aspects of DA manifest themselves? Often, as these disorganized babies and young children grow older, they develop an organizing strategy (Liotti, 2006; Lyons-Ruth, 2001, 2006). By 3 to 5 years old, many of these formerly disorganized infants and young children have reorganized their attachment strategies in such ways that they began to control their mothers and other people in particular ways: They became either compulsive caretakers of their parents or aggressively bossy and hos-tile. Lyons-Ruth (2001) concludes:

> The developmental transition from disorganized behaviors to controlling forms of attachment behaviors over the preschool period supports the notion that one "grows into" a borderline or narcissistic stance through a complex series of alternative developmental acquisitions.... The child in a disorganized attachment relationship appears to use emerging devel-opmental capacities to construct increasingly polarized coercive or role reversed "false-self" relations with the parent. (p. 45)

While Lyons-Ruth (2006) views this reorganization as due to the chil-dren having "given up turning to the parent to help regulate their security and stressful arousal, [instead becoming] immersed in maintaining the par-ents attention" (p. 608), Liotti (2006) suggests more specifically that these strategies inhibit the attachment system, substituting other motivational systems, such as an inverted caretaking behavioral system or a competitive, hierarchy-based behavioral system. Furthermore, these strategies work as a defense against "the unbearable feeling of disorientation and disorganiza-tion linked to fright without a solution" (p. 68). The problem is, however, that when the attachment system is activated in these now seemingly orga-nized older disorganized children, they lose their organization derived from the substituted behavioral system and become vulnerable. In testing situa-tions in which separation anxiety is invoked by such things as the presenta-tion of pictures of a child being left alone, these children suddenly become anxious and helpless, sometimes expressing catastrophic fantasies about what will happen to the pictured child who has been left alone (Liotti, 1999). In these instances, their organization falls apart: "Whenever mental pain activates the attachment system, the dissociative processes linked to the disorganized IWM emerge in consciousness, and disrupt the integrative powers of consciousness, as a consequence of the collapse or failure of the defensive controlling strategies" (Liotti, 2006, p. 68). As long as the attachment system is not activated, they are relatively anxiety free, but when the attachment system is activated, they become highly symptomatic. Clearly, people who have not had the opportunity to integrate conflicting and dissociated IWMs but who could only sidestep them by invoking other behavioral systems are poorly equipped to handle new trauma.

Defense

According to Liotti's (2006) conceptualization (with which I agree) in the above instances, the organizing controlling strategy, that is, the side-stepping of the attachment system and the engagement of an alternative behavioral system, is the defense. The underlying dissociative organization is not understood to function defensively. Rather, the emergence of the unresolved dissociative structure is the result of attachment dilemmas that could not be resolved and synthesized. *Because the underlying dissociative structure, which does not contain in itself an adequate psychic defense, has been exposed when the attachment system has been activated, the attachment-related anxieties and catastrophic fantasies emerge.* This is in contrast to saying that the dissociative structure is being used defensively in these instances. This is not to gainsay that dissociative processes once established may later be used defensively. However, it is fundamental to understand that, in contrast to the insecure styles of avoidant and resistant attachment, which integrate the discordant IWM into an overall defensive style, DA, with its segregated, incompatible IWM (and the corollary, dissociated self-states), is not a defensive style. The existence of these segregated IWMs should not be misinterpreted as defense, such as splitting. To the contrary, the emergence of the dissociated IWMs may result as a failure of defense. As Liotti (2006) noted, the extreme separation anxiety and catastrophic fantasies of these children whose attachment system was suddenly activated appears "as a consequence of the collapse or failure of the defensive controlling strategies rather than as a primary defense against mental pain" (p. 6).

People With Disorganized Attachment Are Poorly Equipped to Deal With Painful Attachment Dilemmas and Relational Trauma

The disorganized children who developed controlling strategies that side-stepped the attachment system become symptomatic when the attachment system is activated. The person with DID may switch between activation and deactivation of the attachment system, but the dissociation is a short-term solution, not a cure for the unresolved attachment traumas. When the attachment system is activated, separation issues can be extremely painful. The psychotherapy relationship is a key arena in which the attachment system is activated.

What does this have to do with our work clinically? What I have realized and what needs emphasizing here is that these disorganized children and later unresolved adults (the adult counterpart to DA) *can only regulate themselves by regulating others.* They are hyperalert to the mental states of others but less to their own. In contrast to the insecure attachment styles, in which there is a defensive, not entirely happy, but workable organizing strategy for regulating affect and for coping with the interpersonal situations that they have faced, in DA the child and later the adult has not been able to develop a coherent strategy for self-regulation. As a consequence, the only way to develop a unitary strategy is to control others. But, when this strategy fails, they become disorganized. And, when trauma strikes anew, they do not have a means to self-regulate, to recover, or to handle it.

This has several implications for clinical work. One is that it gives us, as clinicians, a better conceptual sense of how our patients feel when their attachment system is activated in psychotherapy, as it will be. For instance, our patients with DID (and those with an unresolved attachment style) may frequently make intrusive demands on us in the therapy (e.g., many and lengthy messages, many requests for callbacks, or other extra-session attention, or even, sometimes jokingly, the request to move in). If we keep in mind that this is how they are regulating themselves and that they have not learned other ways, we can mitigate problematic countertransferential responses. Then, there is the additional problem that rejection of these attachment bids is shaming. What are we to do? I suggest bearing in mind, or perhaps even saying, something like the following:

> I know that you may be hurt when I am unable to [return the phone call as quickly as you would like, or give you extra time, etc.]. And I know that you may be especially hurt because you don't know what else to do, and also because it is painful [shameful] to ask. But part of our job is to work on this problem from your childhood: that you were deprived of being able to develop good ways of self-regulation. We will work together on your learning how to do this. I hope that knowing this will help you not to be so hurt or to feel so abandoned when I am not able to do these things.

One might include things that are specific to the patient's situation, such as, "You can remember that I have told you that I will call you back when you call me," or "If you are just wanting contact, you can call and listen to my voice message. Leave a message if you wish, but be sure to tell me if you need me to call you back."

The Care-Taking Controlling Strategy May Also Preserve the Capacity to Love

I would like to offer a somewhat different perspective on the care-taking/ controlling strategies emanating from disorganized attachment on the basis of my experience with DID patients who have developed this strategy. I am not in disagreement with the general formulations provided by Liotti and Lyons-Ruth. What I would like to add (with recognition of Kernberg's [1975, 1984] similar stance with regard to the role of splitting in protecting the good from the bad) is that the caretaking strategy, in conjunction with the dissociation of rageful and terrified self-states, can facilitate the preservation of the capacity to love. Although this capacity to love may be infiltrated with other motivations such as need to please and primitive idealization, I believe that in many cases of DID, the preservation of this capacity is a kind of "digging-in-one's heels" insistence on the potential for a loving orientation to life. The opportunity for this insistence is provided by some aspect, no matter how small, of a loving relationship in the person's experience.

For example, recall the case of Janice presented in Chapter 1: Janice was a thoroughgoing caretaker to her mother, providing her mother with her own daily tea, massages, as well as providing family meals, sewing, and party clean-up. She was tuned in to her mother's chronic depression, and hoped to help heal her with her attentions. Even though Janice also had dissociated rageful self-states, in most other self-states she cared about her mother's comfort and well-being. Her dissociation, stemming from her disorganized attachment, allowed her a way to preserve her ability to love. Albeit, this is an extremely high price to pay, it is better than the possible alternatives of psychosis or psychopathy.

In another case, Violet, who was severely terrified, neglected, and abused as a child, clung to the task of rescuing and loving her mother into health, even as a young child. Her belief in her power to restructure her mother's psyche through her love provided a mainstay to her psychic equilibrium. In her household her father was unpredictably violent and aggressive in his behavior, corroborating his frequent verbal threats to murder his children and his wife. Violet's mother acquiesced to his domination, was highly self-absorbed, and was unable to defend her children. Not only was she unable to defend them, but it seems that she was envious of their potential to escape his domination. Violet's childhood was one of being constantly under siege, but with no respite, no comforting other presence, other than an older brother who was available to her some of the time, who could provide her with even temporary solace. She longed for her mother to be well and stronger than she was, really did care about her, tried hard to get through her mother's barrier to receive her help and to reach her, and was able to help her to some degree. While one could say that this was a controlling/caretaking behavior stemming from disorganized attachment, her fiercely held belief that she could help and transform her mother preserved her ability to believe in human goodness. Her ability to love and to truly care about certain others became expanded in her inner-oriented as well as her in outer-oriented psychic landscape. However, her entrenched belief in the power of her love operated defensively to take the focus off her own personal daily terror. This illusion that the power of her love could restructure her mother and her brother became an aspect of her identity. Today the prospect of giving up that illusion of power is a huge shift for her, and especially for one of her self-states. This is especially powerful because the Inner Violet believed that she was responsible for protecting the Outer Violet at age 3 from her father's abuse. Although such a shift is severely disequilibrating and brings on annhiliation anxiety, it does not mean the loss of her capacity to love.

Chapter 6

Some Neurobiological Correlates of the Structure and Psychodynamics of Dissociated Self-States

INTRODUCTION

The neurophysiology of self-states is a complex and fascinating subject that is in its infancy. Regardless, there is hope that an understanding of the physiologic basis of self-states, combined with our already existing more developed knowledge of psychodynamics, will eventually lead us to craft an even more powerful approach to treatment. In this chapter, I explore ways in which our increasing knowledge base of the neural processes related to dissociative experience can support our potential for healthy living and potentially improve the psychotherapy of the chronic complex trauma, posttraumatic stress disorder (PTSD), and the dissociative disorders. First, I focus on how a traumatic experience is processed in the brain. In the second part of this chapter, I focus more on the importance of depersonalization and hypoarousal and ways that different physiological organizations of self may develop, including DID.

TRAUMATIC EXPERIENCES ARE PROCESSED PIECEMEAL

Over a century ago, Pierre Janet (1907) described how "vehement emotions" evoked by trauma can prevent the integration of traumatic memories. Because they cannot be assimilated, aspects of these experiences became separated from ordinary consciousness. As subconscious fixed ideas, the residues of the traumatic experience continue to intrude into experience. Today, we know more of how traumatic experience is processed in the brain differently from nontraumatic experience. One way the processing differs is that traumatic experiences are often encoded in procedural repertoires and somatosensory modalities rather than in declarative memory, where nontraumatic memories are commonly encoded (Courtois, 1999; Levine, 1997; Scaer, 2001, 2005; Terr, 1990, 1994; Van der Kolk, 1996a, 1996c). By definition, traumatic experiences come with high levels of emotional arousal, and there is cause to believe that extremely high levels of emotional arousal cause a deficiency in declarative and narrative memory.

There are two basic memory systems: declarative, also known as explicit memory, and nondeclarative, which is also known as implicit memory or procedural memory. Declarative memory, which relates to facts and events, refers to the "what" of experiences (e.g., "What did I do? I know that I rode a bike; I know it was red"). Autobiographical or narrative memory is a form of declarative memory. Procedural memory, which has to do with motor skills, habits, conditioned emotional responses, and emotional memories, refers to the "how to" (e.g., "I know how to ride a bike—my body knows to remain balanced, my legs know how to alternate," etc.). There are many things that a person knows how to do procedurally—ways of moving, talking, responding to others—that are difficult to put into the language of facts.

Dissociated memories are evoked in procedural, sensorimotor, somatic formats that will emerge when the person enters the mental state in which the trauma was originally salient. For example, Bruce Perry (1999) wrote of a little boy he met in a residential treatment center who persistently refused to eat his hot dog unless it was cut up, a matter that caused escalating conflicts with the staff. Perry's inquiry revealed that the child had been forced to perform fellatio on his father and other men until he was 6 years old. The oropharyngeal patterns of stimulation of eating things like hot dogs evoked state memories of the abuse, involving terror and confusion. Until this discovery, no one knew why this child was being so "difficult" (and it is likely that the child would not have been able to explain his reaction). Survivors of sexual abuse often describe repeated vaginal and rectal pain; survivors of physical abuse often describe back pain that corresponds to the location of previous injuries, even though there is no current medical explanation for such continual experiences. The persistence of intrusive physical reactions linger long after actual traumatic injuries have physically healed is often termed *somatoform dissociation*. In many cases, the simplest explanation of somatoform dissociation could be that the trauma prevented the experience from being processed in a way that it could become narrative memory; instead, the "memory" remained an aspect of sensorimotor memory only. Indeed, common symptoms of hysterical shell shock among soldiers in World War I were paralysis, mutism, anesthesia of a limb, and other somatosensory functional losses. Amnesia for the event almost always accompanied these symptoms.

As Van der Kolk (1996a) eloquently noted: "The body keeps the score" (p. 214). Localized yet otherwise inexplicable body pain may be a reactivation of a traumatic memory reexperienced in a body part that was injured during the trauma. Terr (1990), writing of her work with children, demonstrated the effect of procedural, implicit, somatic nonverbal memories powerfully. She described the behavior of a 5-year-old patient who had intensely inappropriate fears of projectile objects and who was inordinately protective of her upper abdomen. As an even younger child, she had often pointed to this area. As a toddler, and unlike most other children this age, she had screamed while being diapered. This child drew age-inappropriate pictures of anatomically correct naked people. When she was 5 years old, photographs surfaced that showed the girl at 18 months of age being pinned down on the diaper table by a man's hard, erect penis, *exactly in the location of her upper abdomen.* Terr (1990) called this kind of an event "psychophysiologic reenactment" (p. 271) and noted that often the part of the body that was injured or hurt during the trauma manifests or "recalls" the pain.

What are the psychophysiological processes that bring about such events? According to Van der Kolk (1996c), extremely high levels of emotional arousal lead to inadequate evaluation of the sensory information in the hippocampus. Van der Kolk described a basic model for the processing of traumatic experience: Sensory information is partially processed by the thalamus, which then passes along raw sensory information to the amygdala (which is involved in evaluating emotion) and to the prefrontal cortex. From the amygdala, this emotionally evaluated information is passed on to areas in the brain stem that transform it into hormonal and emotional signals, as well as to the hippocampus (which is involved with the organization and integration of information). The strength of the hippocampal activation has an inverted U-shaped function: Up to a certain point, the stronger the significance conveyed by the amygdala, the stronger the memory consolidation into declarative memory will be. This may explain how we tend to remember significant events such as births and adventures more vividly and often with more narrative detail than the less emotionally charged day-to-day events. However, too much stimulation interferes with hippocampal function. The result of such interference with the integrative function of the hippocampus is that memories may be stored in nonintegrated sensorimotor modalities, affective states, visual images, and somatic sensations.

> The experience is laid down and later retrieved as isolated images, bodily sensations, smells, and sounds that feel alien and separate from other life experiences. Because the hippocampus has not played its usual role in helping to localize the incoming information in time and space, these fragments continue to lead an isolated existence. Traumatic memories are timeless and ego-alien. (Van der Kolk, 1996c, p. 295)

Van der Kolk noted that what is important about the processing of traumatic experience is that, because the sensory information from the thalamus reaches the amygdala first, "preparing" it for evaluation by later-arriving information from the cortex, the emotional evaluation of this information ends up occurring in advance of the conscious evaluation. The result is that stress hormones and the sympathetic nervous system (SNS) are activated before the person understands the cause for this activation.

Because traumatic memories have been incompletely processed (i.e., integrated) in the hippocampus, they are experienced as isolated somatic and sensorimotor experiences and can "make themselves known" piecemeal and often through strange and terrifying contents. When a memory emerges in a flashback, it is frequently expressed in a sensory way that then requires cognitive interpretation to understand because contextual pieces are missing. For example, Brenmer (2002) described a patient who was locked in a closet as a child. She recalled the smell of old clothes but had no visual memory of the closet or an affective memory of fear. Nijenhuis et al. (2001) found that somatoform dissociation was best predicted by physical abuse and threat to life by another person. In many cases it seems that the simplest explanation of somatoform dissociation could be that the trauma prevented the experience from being processed in a way that would have it become a narrative.

In response to stressful situations that require an effective emergency action, the body releases endogenous stress hormones: norepinephrine and cortisol. Norepinephrine (adrenaline) causes heightened alertness and focus, increases heart rate and blood pressure, and facilitates memory at lower levels by making the brain more efficient. However, norepinephrine levels that are too high cause the brain to shut down (lowering and hindering effective action). In stressful circumstances, the HPA (hypothalamic-pituitary-adrenal) axis also goes into action and regulates the response of the body to stress. The response to stressful circumstances activates a complicated circuit of reaction and feedback loops that involves the hypothalamus, the pituitary, and the adrenal glands, and that among other chemical reactions prompts the production of the hormone cortisol by the adrenals (Yehuda, 2000). Cortisol increases survival functions by shutting down systems that are not immediately necessary in time of danger: immune function, digestion, and pain perception. Although helpful in a sporadic emergency, long-term effects of high cortisol secretion are harmful to brain function and health. Indeed, PTSD has repeatedly been associated with HPA dysfunction, and early life stresses may have a long-term effect on its development and function (Bremner & Vermetten, 2007; Simeon & Abugel, 2006; Yehuda, 1998, 2000).

An additional problem related to incomplete processing by the hippocampus is that procedural memories of the threatening event continue to operate as if the danger is still present. A positive-feedback loop of stress reactions may ensue, so that sensitized neurons continue to resensitize each other, continually activating neuronal pathways independently of external cues for current danger. This can result in a automatic overactivation of a person's arousal system, which in turn leads to too frequent activation of the HPA axis, overproduction of cortisol, and even subsequent hippocampal damage (Scaer, 2005).

When the stress response is activated too often, the hippocampus may suffer damage and decrease in size (Bremner & Vermetten, 2007;

Nijenhuis, Vanderlinden, & Spinhoven, 1998; Perry, 1999; Van der Kolk, 1996b). A number of studies have found decreased hippocampal volume in adults with dissociative identity disorder (DID) and PTSD (Nijenhuis, 2003). Vermetten, Schmal, Linder, et al. (2006) found that women with DID had 19.2% less hippocampal volume and 31.6% less amygdalar volume than healthy controls. Ehling, Nijenhuis, and Kirkke (2003) found that patients with florid DID had 25% less hippocampal volume than controls, whereas patients with dissociative disorder not otherwise specified (DDNOS) had 13% less hippocampal volume compared to controls, suggesting a dose effect: Hippocampal volume may correlate with severity of posttraumatic stress and dissociation. Such reduction in size need not be permanent. In fact, after successful integrative treatment, patients with DID recovered considerable hippocampal volume (Nijenhuis, 2003). It should be noted that these effects on hippocampal and amygdalar size and volume are not specific to trauma and dissociation but occur in other disorders as well. Interestingly, administration of antidepressants has also been associated with restoration of hippocampal volume in traumatized persons (Bremner & Vermetten, 2007).

Until fairly recently PTSD has mostly been understood in terms of overarousal and anxiety—involving hyperactivation of the noradrenergic system, with symptoms of increased heart rate and blood pressure. However, it has been proposed more recently that there are two types of PTSD, one involving hyperarousal, and one involving hypoarousal (Bremner, et al., 1999; Perry, 1999; Frewin & Lanius, 2006a).

Bruce Perry (1999) has described these two PTSD patterns—posttraumatic neurodevelopmental processes of hyper- and hypoarousal, in traumatized children. The patterns become more pronounced with more severe, chronic, and early trauma. The hyperarousal pattern involves "fight or flight" reactions, including elevated heart rate, vigilance, behavioral irritability, increased locomotion, and increased startle response. The hypoarousal (dissociative) pattern involves symptoms such as numbing, analgesia, derealization, depersonalization, catatonia, and fainting, along with low heart rate, bradycardia. The hypoaroused children exhibited robotic compliance, glazed expressions, and passivity, a response more characteristic of infants, young children, and females. This pattern is adaptive to immobilization or inescapable pain. Although these patterns are interactive and most people suffering from such altered neurobiology use combinations of these two patterns, the boys' posttraumtic responses tended to be more hyperaroused and the girls' more hypoaroused. Perry speculated that these gender patterns were evolutionarily adaptive in that invading tribal warriors would be more likely to kill the men, but capture the women and young children. Thus, fight or flight would be the men's best defense, while being still and quiet would be the best survival behavior for women and young children.

This attention to hypoarousal is extremely important to our clinical work. When, for instance, the patient's eyes glaze over or it there appears to be a sudden bodily collapse, this likely heralds important material—either something internal from the past or perhaps something in the interpersonal interaction that is evoking it.

SECONDARY PTSD, HYPOAROUSAL, AND DEPERSONALIZATION

Clinical experience suggests that most patients with DID go through life much of the time in varying degrees of a chronic hypoarousal and depersonalized state. This has also been described as secondary dissociative PTSD. The depersonalization response is initially adaptive because it blunts the terror response that the person would otherwise feel and thereby allows the person to continue attending to the functions of daily living. There is increasing evidence to indicate that such a depersonalization response may be involved in the creation of the distinct identity states of DID. Thus, while in the past clinical attention leaned toward noting hyperarousal in patients, now there is an understanding of the need also to check for hypoarousal as part of what is being reenacted. Similarly, there is the need to look for underlying fear states whenever the patient talks about depersonalization (i.e., if there was a need to depersonalize, then there likely was fear as well).

The following is a brief vignette of a patient indicating this line of thought:

JANICE: I wonder who I am. That person who came out and taught that wonderful class—she did it, it was great! Everyone loved what she did. But then she went away. Is she real? Is she me? I don't know. It is so weird. I want to be able to wake up in the morning and know who I am. But I don't.

ME: What you say makes me think that the one who taught the great class—yes, she is you. She is real. It is just as if you took a medication, propanolol—which some people take to alleviate performance anxiety—to teach the class. Propanolol blocks the effect of norepinephrine, a hormone that is released in response to stress. Norepinephrine makes the brain hyperalert, but sometimes it causes too much anxiety. So, by blocking the effect of the norepinephrine, the propanolol helps the person perform without anxiety. The brain can do something similar to alleviate terror.

JANICE: Okay. It's as if I took a propanolol, but I don't know where she went. I imagine most people have a reservoir of who they are. I would like to have a reservoir of me.... I always lived in terror. I was always terrified that I would get in trouble. I was afraid to be me.

I responded as I did to Janice (uncharacteristically lecturing because I was preparing this chapter) as a way to normalize her feelings—and suggested an integration with normal life by linking her nonstressed teacher identity to an analogous physiological response of secondary dissociative PTSD and depersonalization. That is, the nonstressed teacher may have been nonstressed as a result of being emotionally blocked and depersonalized—simply unaware of any emotional turmoil. The teacher part might have appeared to be a more evolved and healthy aspect of self, but she was in fact a part of the self that was able to teach without terror because the turmoil was kept out of awareness. Following my "tutorial," my patient correctly reminded me that I had not explained the dissociation: Where did the teacher part come from, and where did she go? The comparison to propanolol only goes so far—in reality, the evolutionarily adaptive depersonalization/dissociation response plays for higher stakes and has a much longer-lasting effect than the several hours of a propanolol-induced response. That said, the analogy did launch an investigation of strategies for relinking mental states as well as a discussion about depersonalization as a way to go on functioning in the face of constant terror. What are the physiological circuit breakers that operate in the background and contribute to Janice's experience? If we could understand this mechanism better, perhaps we could speak to it psychodynamically or influence the process in some other useful manner.

Another important question concerns why Janice does not have a reservoir of experience. How do we understand this lack of integrative experience neurophysiologically, and how can we use our understanding to foster more of an experience of personal "reservoir" for people who have DID?

The following section describes some of the neuroscience relevant to the problems of posttraumatic and dissociative disorders, in particular the importance of depersonalization and hypoarousal and the ways that different physiological organizations of self manifest and may come about.

Two responses to traumatic stress have traditionally been noted in the literature (Frewin & Lanius, 2006a, 2006b; Nijenhuis & Der Boer, 2007; Simeon & Abugel, 2006; Van der Kolk, 1996b, 1996c). One is the better-known PTSD reaction of hyperarousal, characterized by heightened anxiety, elevated heart rate, increased electrical skin conductance, along with intrusions, such as flashbacks. This reaction, which characterized about 70% of individuals diagnosed with PTSD in the studies of Frewen and Lanius (2006b), has been called "primary dissociation" by Van der Kolk (1996b). The other response, known as peritraumatic dissociation, is a depersonalized, numb reaction in which anxiety, heart rate, and electric skin response do not rise, and the person becomes "detached," observing events as if from a distance from the self, often feeling separated from the body. Van der Kolk (1996b) called this "secondary dissociation." These last symptoms are also prominent in depersonalization disorder (Simeon

& Abugel, 2006). The hyperarousal aspect of PTSD has been overemphasized in the psychophysiological and mental health literature, somewhat to the detriment of recognizing the importance of hypoarousal (Neijenhuis & Den Boer, 2009; Porges, 2003; Schore, 2009); which is linked to experiences of both depersonalization and shame and is a significant problem for many with dissociative disorders.

The psychological distancing of depersonalization protects against the heightened arousal of the trauma and has an anesthetizing effect. It is an invaluable bodily resource in times of extreme danger and emergency, allowing the person to manage attending to the tasks that are necessary to continuing life and to function through the traumatic event without the derailing and disabling neurological messages of terror. However, if relied on chronically, this process results in the person living much of his or her life in a depersonalized state.

Depersonalization relegates overwhelming traumatic experience to the realm of "Not-Me" (Sullivan, 1953). For example, during an EMDR (Eye Movement Desensitization Reprocessing) session a highly dissociative patient was describing an assault by her father when she was a young adolescent in which he cut the flesh near her eye with his fingernails, endangering her vision. The patient recalls at first saying to herself, "Oh, No!" However, as soon as the actual physical attack toward her started, both in the EMDR session and in her memory of the event, she suddenly went into a peaceful state, feeling nothing and could not visualize anything anymore. This is a kind of depersonalization response. It is a type of response that is part and parcel of the hypnoid state described by Breuer and Freud (1893–1895a,b), by Pierre Janet (1907, 1925) and by 19th-century French psychological writers. Given our increased understanding of neurophysiological processes, can we now better understand the biological patterns of such provocative experiences, and will this understanding help us better define how to work with depersonalization in psychotherapy?

Taken together, various positron emission tomographic (PET) scan and functional magnetic resonance imaging (fMRI) studies indicate that in secondary dissociative PTSD and in depersonalization disorder, certain parts of the brain that are involved in emotional response are inhibited by several other higher cortical areas. Frewin and Lanius (2006b) reported that fMRI studies of people with secondary dissociation responses to trauma-script imagery showed increased activity in the ACC (anterior cingulate cortex) and mPFC (medial prefrontal cortex), compared with nonpsychiatric controls. These areas, the ACC and mPFC, are involved in cognitive processing, modulating emotional response, and inhibition of the activation of the limbic system (the "emotional brain"). The authors noted that the increased activity in these two cortical areas indicates "a possible enhanced suppression of limbic emotion circuits in secondary dissociation" (p. 117). Most of the same brain regions that are involved in secondary dissociation are also implicated in depersonalization disorder (Nijenhuis & Der Boer, 2007).

Philips, Medford, Senior, Bullmore, Suckling, Brammer, et al. (2001) used fMRI to track changes in brain activity to neutral and aversive-disgusting pictures in patients with depersonalization disorder in comparison with controls. While in response to the aversive pictures, the controls had greater activity in emotion-sensitive areas, such as the insula (a limbic area involved with disgust perception), and these areas were not activated in the depersonalized patients. Only in response to the neutral stimulus did the depersonalized patients show activation in the insula. At the same time, the depersonalized patients did have heightened activity in the prefrontal cortex in response to aversive stimuli: "Only in the depersonalized patients, however, did activation in the right ventral prefrontal cortex occur in the absence of activation in the insula response to these scenes" (p. 157). The depersonalized patients *understood* that the aversive pictures were *supposed to* evoke disgust, but they did not *experience* this emotion. In fact, they did not differentiate neutral and aversive pictures in their ratings of their own responses. In summary, these authors stated, "Our findings indicate that a core phenomenon of depersonalization—absent subjective experience of emotion—is associated with reduced neural responses in emotion-sensitive regions, and increased responses in regions associated with emotion regulation" (p. 145). Consistent with these findings, Simeon et al. (2001) found that in people with depersonalization disorder, the amount of norepinephrine in urine was inversely related to the severity of depersonalization disorder. (This is also consistent with the vignette at the beginning of this section in which I compared the action of depersonalization to the effect of taking a drug that blocks norepinephrine.) Simeon and Abugel (2006) noted that the Phillips et al. fMRI research on aversive versus neutral images suggests that:

> Depersonalized individuals hypo-activate limbic regions, the emotional regions that are important for processing emotions, and conversely, that they hyper-activate higher cortical areas. Ultimately, this suggests a brain mechanism that may underlie the emotional inhibition, numbness, and sense of unfamiliarity experienced by chronically depersonalized people. (p. 116)

The Body Anchors States of Mind

In secondary dissociative PTSD and in depersonalization, one feels separated from one's body. It appears that the areas of the brain that are responsible for an integrated body schema are the ones that have functional abnormalities in depersonalization disorder (Nijenhuis & Den Boer, 2007; Simeon & Abugel, 2006). Noting that the secondary dissociative response, like depersonalization, entails an experiential separation of mind from body, Frewin and Lanius (2006a) emphasized the role of altered body perception in secondary dissociative PTSD. For that, they pointed to the association of depersonalization disorder with somatoform dissociation as observed by Nijenhuis et al. (1999). Somatoform symptoms have been significantly correlated with peritraumatic dissociation (Nijenhuis, 2000; Nijenhuis, Van Engen, Kusters, & Van der Hart, 2001).

Noting the possible role of altered body perception in secondary PTSD, Frewin and Lanius (2006b) suggested that "disconnection of neural pathways normally linking self-awareness with emotional body-state perception could occasion the development of dissociative identities in traumatized children" (p. 113). Continuing this line of thinking about the linkage of secondary dissociative PTSD and depersonalization with the creation of the dissociative identities in DID, they also emphasize alexithymia (no words for emotion).

> We believe deficits in the conscious awareness of bodily states are integral to the alexithymia construct because the substance that is felt during an emotional feeling seems inherently to be a particular body state. *Associations between trait alexithymia and secondary dissociative states may develop over the course of chronic childhood physical and sexual abuse. Specifically with increased repetition and automatization of secondary dissociative processes during situations of long-standing abuse, the priming of the dissociative state may become sensitized and increasingly automatic and unconscious. In addition, repetitious entry into secondary dissociative states may produce progressively more marked departures from external reality and consciousness for self.* As dissociative individuals become increasingly less aware of and connected with their identity, feelings, body, and surroundings, they may become alexithymic and thereby deficient in how much they are able to cognitively understand their emotional experiences. In addition, with little cognitive insight about their emotional feelings, dissociative-alexithymic individuals are correspondingly unable to regulate their affective responses...in an adaptive coping manner. (pp. 120–121, emphasis added)

Secondary Dissociative PTSD and Depersonalization in Terms of the Structural Theory of Dissociation

Van der Hart et al. (2006) and Nijenhuis et al. (2004) (see summary of the structural theory of the dissociation of the personality in Chapter 3) described the effects of primary and secondary dissociative response to PTSD in terms of the structural dissociation of the personality. The apparently normal part (ANP) of the personality is focused on performing functions of daily life, and the emotional part (EP) of the personality is focused on response to physical defense to threat. The ANP may be described as chronically depersonalized: "Patients in their ANPs indeed report low body awareness and feel generally more or less detached from their body" (Nijenhuis & Den Boer, 2007, p. 228).

These ANPs and EPs have at least a rudimentary sense of self that is accompanied by distinct differences in psychobiological function: "Traumatized individuals tend to alternate between re-experiencing traumatic events and being more or less detached from these painful memories on account of not integrating such experiences into their personality. Moreover, the survivor's sense of self typically changes with these alternations" (Nijenhuis & Den Boer, 2007, p. 219). In fact, it was found that EP and ANP responses differed markedly in heart rate and facial expression when exposed to a small object that was moved in the direction of the face (Nijenhuis & Den Boer, 2007).

In people who have been subjected to early chronic stress or have been abused early in life, we might expect to see the appearance of separate phenomenological-physiological self-states as evoked by differing contexts. Two ingenious studies by Reinders et al. (2003, 2006), summarized in the following discussion, demonstrate this.

One Brain, Two Selves

Dennett (1991) commented that having 2, 3, or 17 selves per body is really "not more metaphysically extravagant than one self per body" (p. 419). In DID, different identity states are characterized by different memories, affects, behaviors, sensations, perceptions, postures, and so on. In particular, patients with DID often have amnesia for traumatic memories when in the nontraumatized identity state, which is also the one often in executive control and is generally an ANP. In the first of two fascinating studies, titled "One Brain, Two Selves," Reinders et al. (2003) documented the cerebral correlates of two autobiographical selves. Using functional neuroimaging (PET scan), the authors demonstrated particular changes in localized brain activity—two different cerebral blood flow patterns—that occurred in accordance with the presence of a traumatic personality state (also known as an EP) versus a neutral personality state (also known as an ANP). The research participants in both the first and second study were 11 persons with DID who had the ability to switch at will between a traumatic state and a neutral one. These participants were asked to listen to an autobiographical trauma script and an autobiographical neutral script while in both personality states. Among the four conditions, the trauma script elicited blood flow changes only in the traumatic personality state. In the neutral personality state, the participants did not recognize the trauma script as a personally relevant narrative and responded to it in a way that was similar to the way they responded to the neutral script. Likewise, no significant differences were found between the two personality states in response to the neutral script.

The EPs (or TPs, traumatized personality) states presented data that supported the presence of a network of deactivated brain areas; including the mPFC, which is involved in conscious processing of experience. In contrast, patterns in the ANP states (neutral personality states, NPS) showed disturbances in the parietal and occipital blood flow and were indicative of an inability to integrate visual and somatosensory information. The results of the 2003 study suggest that when patients with DID are in neutral personality states there is a "blocking" of trauma-related information that

> prevents further emotional processing, which reflects the defense system, as applied by DID patients, to enable them to function in daily life (Nijenhuis, 2002). Thus, the NPS, as compared to TPS, shows disturbances of parietal and occipital blood flow, suggesting a relatively low level of somatosensory awareness and integration (Simeon et al., 2000), by suppression of the (re-)activation of these areas. These results match the clinical depersonalised features of NPS (Nijenhuis et al., 2002) as well as their subjective responses in the current experiment. (pp. 2122–2123)

In the 2006 study, Reinders et al. found that in response to listening to a trauma script, the EPs, but not the ANPs, showed increased heart rates and blood pressure, as well as reported strong emotions and sensory reminders of the traumatic event. In response to the neutral script, neither EP nor ANP displayed elevated heart rate or blood pressure. The EPs (or traumatized identity states) showed more activity in the amygdala and other areas relevant to defensive motor activity, as well as reduced activity in prefrontal areas. In comparison, the ANPs (or the neutral identity states) showed more activity in the ACC, which is involved in inhibitions of emotional responses, as well as more activity in other frontal areas involved in self-awareness and planning. In sum, Reinders et al. (2003) stated:

> We have shown that these patients have state-dependent access to autobiographical affective memories and thus different autobiographical selves.... Our results indicate the possibility of one human brain to generate at least two distinct states of self-awareness, each with its own access to autobiographical trauma-related memory, with explicit roles for the mPFC and the posterior associative cortices in the representation of these different states of consciousness. (p. 2124)

The Polyvagal Theory

As noted, PTSD presentations are not uniform: As a case in point, Frewin and Lanius (2006b) described highly differing PTSD responses in a husband and wife who had been in a car accident. The husband presented with the more typical pattern of elevated heart rate, anxiety, and posttraumatic intrusions. The wife, however, described herself as "frozen" and did not have an elevated heart rate. We may be able to understand more of this "frozen" hypoarousal response—as well as learn more about the possible pathways to the one brain/two selves phenomenon by turning to Porges's polyvagal theory.

Porges (2001, 2003) advanced the polyvagal theory of the phylogenetic substrates of the social nervous system. According to this theory, there have been three primary adaptations and changes in the neural regulation of the autonomic nervous system (ANS) that in humans are arranged in a hierarchical organization of response patterns. The first of these response patterns is characteristic of reptiles, fosters digestion, and responds to threats by depression of metabolic activity, thus conserving oxygen and energy. The associated behavior of this response is immobilization. Porges called this the dorsal vagal complex, the DVC. The second stage of response is characterized by the sympathetic nervous system, the SNS, which can increase metabolic output, thus enabling "fight or flight." The third stage, which is unique to mammals, is characterized by the ability to regulate as well as increase metabolic output. This is the ventral vagal complex, the VVC, and involves a social engagement system, including social signaling systems for motion, emotion, and communication as well as self-soothing. This last stage includes what Porges called a "vagal brake" that inhibits the SNS, regulating the heart. Porges stated: "As the autonomic nervous system changed through the process of evolution, so did the interplay between the autonomic nervous system and other physiological systems that respond to stress, including the cortex, the hypothalamic-pituitary-adrenal axis, the neuropeptides of oxytocin and vasopressin, and the immune system" (p. 123). Although the polyvagal theory has some similarities to the triune brain proposed by McLean (1990), it emphasizes the phylogenetic changes in structure and function. This theory presents an evolutionarily progressive design, a design in which, when the more advanced strategies fail, the organism falls back on the next most recently phylogenetically developed organization.

> The polyvagal theory proposes that during danger or threat, the older, less social systems are recruited. The older systems, although functional in the short term may result in damage to the mammalian nervous system when expressed for prolonged periods. Thus, the stress and coping neurophysiological strategies that are adaptive for reptiles (e.g., apnea, bradycardia, immobilization), may be lethal for mammals. (p. 130)

Porges (2001) emphasized that for over a century researchers have operated according to an arousal theory involving sympathetic activation. (This coincides with the overemphasis on the hyperarousal aspect of PTSD.) He noted that the arousal theory overlooked the importance of the dorsal ventral complex and described an experiment by Richter (1957) that was meant to demonstrate the arousal theory. The experiment tested how long rats would be able to continue to swim before they drowned. It had been supposed that they would die from overactivation of the SNS, leading to increasingly rapid heartbeat and death in systole. Instead, the opposite happened. The rats died a vagus death resulting from overactivation of the parasympathetic nervous system and overengorged hearts. The rats reverted to the most primitive system, of immobilization, designed to conserve resources. The most stressed of the rats, in accordance with DVC activation, simply dove to the bottom of the tank, instead of trying to swim, and died most rapidly.

One of the important implications of the polyvagal theory is that in situations of extreme terror humans also can revert to dorsal vagal activation. Nijenhuis and Den Boer (2007) suggested that the woman in Frewin and Lanius's (2006b) husband-and-wife case may have been immobilized and paralyzed in a dorsal vagal response. This dorsal vagal response appears to be related to the secondary dissociative PTSD as well as to the hypoaroused "dissociative" response described by Schore (2002a, 2002b, 2003, 2009) and Perry (1999, 2001); "tonic immobility" (TI; Marx, Forsyth, Gallup, Fusé, & Lexington, 2008; Moskowitz, 2004); and the "total submission" response described by Van der Hart et al. (2004).

Animal Defense States Responsive to Predation: Fight/Flight, Freeze, and Tonic Immobility or Total Submission

A number of writers have addressed the correspondence between the more general animal defense states responsive to predation and the human posttraumatic and dissociative responses (Marx et al., 2008; Moskowitz, 2004; Nijenhuis, Vanderlinden, & Spinhoven, 1998, 2004; Perry, 1999, 2001; Sapolsky, 2004; Schore, 2002, 2003a, 2003b, 2009). Nijenhuis et al. (2004) and Van der Hart et al., in their landmark book *The Haunted Self* (2006), noted the similarity between human behavior following exposure to terror and various animal states, including fight/flight, freezing/analgesic, and hypoaroused states that they called "total submission." Humans may have inherited a repertoire of discrete behavioral states that have been adaptive to conditions of predation. For instance, bodily symptoms such as stiffness, analgesia, and high muscle tension may all represent a human freezing response. Total submission involves anesthesia and low muscle tension. These animal defense states may also underlie different dissociative parts of the personality (Nijenhuis, Spinhoven, Vanderlinden, Van Dyck, & Van der Hart, 1998).

In many species, freezing is the dominant response after a predator is encountered. Because flight might be dangerous at that moment, the animal "freezes" on the spot, becoming almost completely motionless. Freezing is adaptive in the sense that it increases the chances of survival by eliminating the motion cues that allow the predator to detect the animal and activate the strike response of the predator (Nijenhuis, Spinhoven, et al., 1998; Nijenhuis, Vanderlinden, & Spinhoven, 1998; Van der Hart et al., 2006). It may also create the impression that the prey is dead and therefore less desirable meat (Scaer, 2001).

Although freezing is characterized by stilled movement with motor actions inhibited, it involves increased rapid heartbeat, rapid breathing, high muscle tone, high blood pressure, and analgesia, all of which ready the animal for an explosion into the actions of fight or flight. The autonomic patterns of the freeze response are complicated. Freezing involves activation of the SNS and appears to be mediated by the loss of the ventral vagal parasympathetic brake on the SNS (Van der Hart et al., 2004).

Van der Hart et al. (2000) link forced helpless immobility and a concomitant freeze response, with somatoform dissociation. The helpless immobility of situations of terror appears to be prominently linked to the development of PTSD. These authors note that there was an especially high incidence of shell shock among World War I veterans as a result of fighting in the trenches, a situation in which the soldiers were simultaneously immobilized and terrified for long stretches of time. The authors suggest that the "high rate of somatoform dissociative symptoms in World War I combat soldiers was, at least in part, due to forced immobility in the face of threat to bodily integrity, thereby evoking chronic animal defensive states, in particular, freezing, with concomitant somatoform manifestations" (Van der Hart et al., 2000, p. 53).

Similarly, Scaer (2001) notes that whiplash patients of auto accidents, in contrast to racecar drivers and football players who are frequently subject to impacts of much greater force and velocity, were relatively helpless and immobilized at the time of the accident. The incidence of "whiplash syndrome" is much higher than would be expected on the basis of organic injury. He views "whiplash syndrome" as a prototype for somatoform dissociation and PTSD, as a "model of traumatization with long-standing and at times permanent neurophysiological and neurochemical changes in the brain that are experience-based rather than injury-based" (p. 33). This is based on the hypothesis that many whiplash patients may have entered a freeze state and dissociated the frightening experience at the moment of the accident.[1]

Another defensive response to predation is what Van der Hart et al. (2006) called "total submission," similar to tonic immobility (TI). This involves a different kind of physiological activation—including that of the parasympathetic nervous system—in which the animal in effect "plays possum." In this response, heart rate drops, including at times syncope (fainting); there is low heart rate variability, loss of muscle tone, emotional and bodily anesthesia, eye aversion from threat cues, and defocusing. This appears to be mediated by the dorsal vagal branch of the parasympathetic nervous system (Van der Hart et al., 2004). Total submission involves body paralysis, or at least low muscle tension, and can also involve being out of the body. People often report being paralyzed, unable to move or to think, in the face of extremely terrifying circumstances, such as a robbery, rape, or a reminder of such an event.

Tonic Immobility

Marx et al. (2008) have linked the literature on TI as an evolved response to predation to the hypoarousal states often reported by sexual assault survivors. Some of the evolutionary advantages of TI involve its potential to inhibit aggression of predators due to decreased visibility and possibly lessening the bleeding that occurs when injured. TI has been found in many animals: from insects and fish to primates (Marx et al., 2008). (It is interesting to note that some predators, such as orca whales against sharks, have reportedly found ways to use the TI reflex of the prey to their advantage.) Marx et al. (2008) compare TI to "rape-induced paralysis," in which sexual assault victims lose the ability to move or to call out during the assault. They refer to a study by Heidt, Marx, and Forsyth (2005), in which 52% of the participants reported TI in response to child sexual abuse, and note that the conditions for TI of fear and restraint are the same ones that have been found to be risk factors for PTSD following sexual assault. Fear in and of itself is insufficient, they say, but must be coupled with circumstances that prevent an escape. Similarly, Moskowitz (2004) notes that in TI "it is the perception of entrapment, with or without physical restraint, that is most important" (p. 986). The authors state that depersonalization may be a byproduct or component of TI, including a sense of "self" detachment.

Marx et al. (2008) describe the stages that lead up to TI. The first stage is the *preencounter stage* in which the predator has not yet been encountered. The next stage is the *encounter stage* in which a predator has been detected:

> The immediate response is for the prey animal to cease all movement (freeze). Additional responses during this stage include focused attention, sustained cardiac deceleration, defensive analgesia, and potentiated startle. These responses orient the animal toward potential threat and prepare it for action.
>
> Continued approach by the predator sets in motion a sequence of active defensive postures (e.g., flight or fight) that characterize the postencounter, or circa strike, stage. Here, most prey will first attempt to

escape. When escape is not possible or thwarted (as indicated by tac-
tile contact with a predator), a prey animal will subsequently fight or
resist. Clear evidence that the organism has changed to a defensive posture is first seen in the startle reflex response, a response that is often
potentiated during this stage, coupled with rapid acceleration in heart
rate and electrodermal activity. These behavioral action tendencies are
associated with the multicomponent emotional response known as fear
(LeDoux, 2000).

Unsuccessful escape or resistance typically results in the prey entering a state of TI. The most obvious feature of TI is profound but revers-
ible physical immobility and muscular rigidity. This immobilized state
includes a sustained and largely involuntary pattern of neuromuscu-
lar activity (i.e., cataleptic-catatonic) and sympathetic and parasympathetic responses. Additional characteristics of the response include
intermittent periods of eye closure, fixed, unfocused gaze or stare,
Parkinsonian-like tremors in the extremities, suppressed vocal behavior, analgesia, and waxy flexibility. (p. 75)

The authors (Marx et al., 2008) emphasized that TI needs to be distinguished from freezing behavior, the latter of which is characterized by alertness, responsivity to stimuli, and the capacity for voluntary action. In contrast,
TI involves unresponsiveness and catatonic-like motionlessness. They also
distinguished it from learned helplessness, which is a learned response during
which the animal can move.

Both Moskowitz (2004) and Marx et al. (2008) linked catatonia to TI.
The activation of the DVC and the SNS may be one reason that rape victims
were unable to move or to cry out. Writing of catatonia, which he characterized as "scared stiff," Moskowitz (2004) explained:

Engagement of the SNS in catatonic excitement or stupor may also
affect the type of communicative behavior available to an individual.
According to Porges's polyvagal theory of emotion and defensive
behavior (so-called because he believes mammals have evolved two
dissociable vagal systems; Porges, 1995, 1997, 2001), sympathetic activation results in an inhibition of the ventral vagal complex (VVC), a
parasympathetic component of the autonomic nervous system unique
to mammals that allows for rapid and subtle cardiac modulation in
situations perceived as safe and innervates the muscles of the face and
vocal system. Thus, inhibition of the VVC results in a decreased capacity to use sophisticated forms of communication with words and gestures—the first line of defense in situations of conflict. The loss of such
capacity would be consistent with the mutism frequently seen in catatonia as well as symptoms such as negativism, automatic obedience, or
echolalia and echopraxia. In addition, several of these behaviors (waxy

flexibility, automatic obedience) appear submissive, which would also be consistent with a defense reaction. (p. 994)

Allan Schore, Dissociation, and the Developing Brain, Especially the "Right Brain"

Allan Schore has synthesized a great store of knowledge about the types of posttraumatic responses and their interactions, making it easier for the nonmedical clinician to grasp the significance of these neurophysiological processes for clinical work. He explains the relational unconscious, which involves communication between the interacting unconscious minds, in terms of right brain implicit processes. Noting that "Studies show that 60% of human communication is non-verbal" (2008, p. 24), Schore has grounded the increasing awareness in the mental health field of the centrality of affect and the importance of affect regulation in the language of the brain—especially the right brain. This neurophysiological knowledge of right brain processes works interactively with our psychodynamic knowledge, complementing the relational trend in our field and the greater emphasis on intersubjective communication. As we become more aware of the nonverbal, relational unconscious, we are more cognizant of the effects that we have on our patients, and they on us.

Schore's work on the influence of the early environment on brain development has been especially important for alerting clinicians and researchers to the effects of the early social environment and relational trauma on the developing brain structures of the infant and young child. Contextualizing the dorsal vagal response described by Porges within a vast body of new research, he brought its meaning into more clinical specificity.

Schore (2009) describes the infant's two psychophysiological responses to trauma—hyperarousal and dissociation—but he emphasized that the two responses are interrelated: "Hyperarousal is the infant's first reaction to stress. Dissociation is a later reaction to trauma, wherein the child disengages from the stimuli of the external world" (p. 111). In the first phase, the infant's alarm activates the right hemisphere, which activates the SNS, which releases stress hormones and increases heart rate, respiration, and blood pressure. Following this phase of mounting distress and overarousal is dissociation, in which the child disengages from stimuli. "The child's dissociation in the midst of terror involves numbing, avoidance, compliance and restricted affect (the same pattern as adult PTSD)" (p. 111). Schore notes that in the dissociation response infants seem to be staring off into space with a "glazed look." This is a parasympathetic mechanism of conservation. However, Schore (2002a) elaborates, if this

> primary metabolic shutdown becomes a chronic condition, it will have devastating effects on the morphogenesis of limbic structures.

> Dissociation and conservation-withdrawal, functional expressions of heightened dorsal vagal activity, induce an extreme alteration of the bioenergetics of the developing brain. . . . An infant brain that is chronically shifting into hypometabolic survival modes has little energy available for growth.
>
> Despite the drawbacks, "this intensified parasympathetic arousal allows the infant to maintain homeostasis in the face of the internal state of sympathetic hyperarousal." (p. 452)

As we have seen in Chapter 5, abuse, severe neglect, massive misattunement, and lack of regulation of the child's affective distress on the part of caregivers may result in attachment trauma—and disorganized attachment. Attachment trauma, if chronic, may lead to "characterological use of primitive autoregulation—that is, pathological dissociation, during subsequent states of development" (2009, p. 114). This defense is maladaptive not only because it becomes chronically used, even in low-stress circumstances, but also because it is difficult

> to exit this state of conservation-withdrawal. During these episodes, the person is impermeable to attachment communications and interactive regulation. This deprives the person of input that is vital to emotional development . . . [and] social intimacy is habitually deemed to be dangerous. (p. 115)

Schore (2009) cited a number of studies that together indicate that, especially in the right hemisphere, the prefrontal cortex and limbic areas are central to dissociative response. Schore noted that the right brain is more involved with nonverbal and emotional communication and processing of experience that is not always conscious, while the left brain is more dedicated to verbal and logical processing of conscious experience. He pointed out that the right brain is also involved in implicit information processing, and that this is linked to the right lateralized amygdala. This is relevant to the fact that while PTSD research has previously focused more on deficits to declarative memory associated with hippocampal function, this research is now "shifting from the hippocampus to the amygdala, from explicit memory of places to implicit memory of faces" (p. 124). Emphasizing how crucially the right hemisphere is involved in these dissociative responses, he even stated, *The symptomatology of dissociation reflects a structural impairment of a right brain regulatory system and its accompanying deficiencies of affect regulation*" (p. 126, emphasis in original).

Schore (2009) noted that the right brain of the infant and young child matures earlier than does the left, and that it is more deeply interconnected with the limbic system, which myelinates in the first year and a half. As a result, early attachment experiences, including relational trauma, especially have an impact on the right brain and limbic system. In particular, traumatic attachment experiences are "burned into" the "limbic-autonomic circuits of the cortical and subcortical components of the right brain during its critical period of growth" (p. 130).

Schore (2009) further suggested that the dissociative response, as a kind of primitive form of affect regulation, is "best understood as a loss of vertical connectivity between cortical and subcortical limbic areas within the right hemisphere" (p. 117). Dissociation appears before the myelination of the cerebral cortex or the development of functionality of corpus callosum connectivity. This contributes to the disconnection of higher cortical function from subcortical function and negatively affects the ANS/CNS (central nervous system) links, which are more extensive in the right hemisphere.

Schore's (2009) work helps to explain how early abuse leads to disorganized attachment—that abuse and severe neglect are associated with deficiencies in brain development, notably that the capacity for affect regulation is impaired. (As we know, disorganized attachment and the accompanying affect dysregulation and risk for psychiatric disorders carries over into adolescence and adulthood.) In particular, there is an "impairment of higher corticolimbic modulation of the vagal circuit of emotion regulation on the right side of the brain that generates the psychobiological state of dissociation" (p. 130).

Schore (2009) said the foregoing most simply:

> From a developmental neuroscience viewpoint, early abuse and neglect have immediate impact on the developing right brain during a critical growth period; this produces an immature right brain that has limited ability to regulate intense affective states. (p. 130)

The good news, according to Schore (2009), is that psychotherapy heals in the context of the mind-to-right brain connection, and that it can

> positively alter the developmental trajectory of the deep right brain and facilitate the *integration* between cortical and subcortical rightbrain systems. This enhanced interconnectivity allows for an increased complexity of defenses of the emotional right brain—coping strategies for regulating stressful affect that are more flexible and adaptive than pathological dissociation. (p. 140)

So how does the clinician help with this? Schore (2009) explains, quoting from his 2003b work,

> "the psychobiologically attuned therapist acts as an interactive affect regulator of the patient's dysregulated state. The model clearly suggests that the therapist's role is much more than interpreting to the developmentally disordered patient either distortions of the transference,

or unintegrated early attachment experiences that occur in incoherent moments of the patient's narrative." Even more than the patient's late-acting rational, analytical and verbal left mind, the growth-facilitating psychotherapeutic relationship needs to directly access the deeper psychobiological strata of the implicit regulatory structures of both the patient's and the clinician's right minds. (p. 25)

The Orbitofrontal Cortex

Schore emphasized the importance of the maturation of the orbitofrontal cortex, which acts as executor of the right cortex and is influenced by dyadic interactions between caregiver and child. The orbitofrontal cortex, located between cortical and subcortical structures, is connected to the hypothalamus, the amygdala, and the brain stem, from which point it regulates the ANS. Schore (2002a) wrote:

> The highest level of the right brain that processes affective information, the orbitofrontal cortex.... The maturation of this prefrontal system overlaps and mediates... the developmental achievement of "the subjective self." This cortex functions to refine emotions in keeping with current sensory input, and allows for the adaptive switching of internal bodily states in response to changes in the external environment that are appraised to be personally meaningful.... The orbitofrontal system thus acts as a recovery mechanism that efficiently monitors and auto-regulates the duration, frequency, and intensity of not only positive but negative affect states. (p. 447)

Drawing on Schore as well as many others, Kelly Forrest (2001) has contributed a brilliant, synthetic integration of neuroscience and attachment literature, outlining a neurodevelopmental approach to the etiology of DID. Forrest emphasized the role of the orbitofrontal cortex in the inhibitory control of information. In her "orbitofrontal model," she proposed the following:

> The experience-dependent maturation of the orbitalfrontal cortex in early abusive environments, characterized by discontinuity in dyadic socioaffective interactions between the infant and the caregiver, may be responsible for a pattern of lateral inhibition between conflicting subsets of self-representations which are normally integrated into a unified self. The basic idea is that the discontinuity in the early caretaking environment is manifested in the discontinuity in the organization of the developing child's self. (p. 259)

Forrest (2001) observed that in contrast to insecure attachment, in which there is an underlying pattern of responsiveness, albeit suboptimal, in disorganized attachment, there is no underlying pattern. The fact that there is a pattern in insecure attachment makes it possible for the child to build a Me-in-relation conceptual system for organizing behavior that is context independent. The orbitofrontal cortex then facilitates this in part by biasing toward sympathetic high arousal or parasympathetic hypoarousal. In contrast, disorganized children, who have less consistency in their dyadic interactions, have less-integrated conceptual systems. The subset of disorganized children who go on to develop DID has not been able to experience relationships and thus basic Me concepts as continuous. Because of this high degree of unpredictability, the orbitalfrontal cortex cannot

> organize a context-independent regulatory system which anticipates parental responsiveness, such as is organized in securely attached infants. The only remaining option for organizing behavior available to the orbitofrontal system in these circumstances is to organize state and later self-functioning according to the immediate context. My contention is that the orbitofrontal system resorts to regulating autonomic functioning based predominantly, if not solely, on the immediate context. (p. 280)

Forrest (2001) further postulated that

> The orbitalfrontal region, based on chronic experiences of extreme environmental discontinuity, idiosyncratically develops a pattern of increased lateral inhibition sufficient to create relative isolation between conflicting, context-driven subsets of Me concepts such that dissociated Me concepts emerge. (p. 282)

Forrest's work lends neurophysiological support to Kluft's (1988) recommendations that in the interests of promoting integration, the therapist maintain a basically consistent stance toward all of the alters; the therapist should avoid a "multiple therapist disorder."

NOTE

1. Levine (1997) Scaer (2001, 2005) and others have written about the importance of "discharge" of the freeze response. Despite being apparently motionless, the animal in "freeze" and with the massive amount of norepinephrine that has been released in the body, rapidly increasing heart rate and blood pressure, is physiologically ready to flee at the moment that it becomes safe or necessary. Indeed, when animals can finally flee, they may exhibit stereotyped

shaking patterns, so that they seem to be completing the action of the escape that had been in progress before it became necessary to freeze. Levine, who has studied the process of discharge from freeze states, concluded that in contrast to domesticated or zoo animals that did not have a freeze discharge, undomesticated animals that were allowed to exhibit the freeze discharge of shaking, running, and/or continuing to do what they were doing just before the freeze, showed no signs of future impairment.

Scaer (2005) cited the study by Ginsberg (1974) in which the length of time that groups of chicks could delay drowning was measured. In one group immobilized chicks were allowed to discharge the freeze; and in another they were prevented from doing so. Those chicks who had the advantage of the freeze discharge survived the longest.

Levine (1997) believed that posttraumatic responses are "fundamentally, incomplete physiological responses suspended in fear" (p. 34) and that humans, like other animals, need to feel and then to release the pent-up energy in their bodies in order to heal. It should be noted that this is another version of the old abreactive theory of Breuer & Freud (1893–95). In addition, there is a distinction between "freeze" in one-time traumas and the effects of multiple traumas that have not been resolved. While important, such release, in itself, is often not sufficient to process the trauma, possibly especially so in people whose traumas were early and chronic, resulting in reduced ability to utilize discharge effectively.

In humans, abreaction (discussed in Chapter 9) involves the expression of intense emotion, often using words, but frequently accompanied by expressive motoric behaviors. The important thing for humans is the ability to communicate this emotion in a way that is not re-traumatizing, such that the listening and empathetically connected other can help to de-traumatize the experience, allowing it to become part of narrative memory.

Chapter 7

Dissociated Self-States
Creation and Contextualization

> To put it as simply as possible, I argue that there is no such thing as an integrated self—a "real you." Self-expression and human relatedness will inevitably collide ... but health is not integration. Health is the ability to stand in the spaces between realities without losing any of them. This is what I believe *self-acceptance* means and what *creativity* is really all about—the capacity to feel like one self while being many.
>
> Bromberg (1993, p. 166, emphasis in original)

In the first book of his science fiction trilogy, *Out of the Silent Planet*, C. S. Lewis has his main character, Ransom, begin to refer to himself as "We" when he is feeling completely alone and overwhelmed by the demands of the horribly harsh extraterrestrial climate and his uncertain fate in it. Ultimately, he sees what he is doing and pulls himself together as "I" to complete his coming adventures on this forbidding planet. Similarly, a mildly troubled patient begins to speak of herself as We when, in the course of an affectively heated-up eye movement desensitization and reprocessing (EMDR) session, she encounters awareness of extremely painful attachment dilemmas that she has always had. In short, many people who are not technically "dissociative" do at times refer to themselves as We as a mild and temporary verbal multiplication of self in response to aloneness and stress. None of the aspects of the plurality are personified or differentiated. Somehow, though, the plural self is comforting, and I suspect that it has to do with the fact that another part of the self can, or is imagined to be able to, provide support in times of stress and isolation.

Kluft (1985a, 1985b), who has addressed the creation of alters in great depth, spoke to the issue of the creation of alters in dissociative identity disorder (DID) more specifically:

> Understood in terms of their *raison d'etre*, the alters may be understood as rather desperate efforts to disavow and mitigate the impact of overwhelming life events. They express the wish, the fantasy, of supplanting an intolerable reality with a more tolerable one. In fact, it

has been my experience that the core of DID is the establishment of a "multiple reality disorder"... for which the alters are an embodied and personified delivery system.... There is a need to disidentify with the unacceptable experience (although after the first dividedness, the disidentification may be with an attitude, a wish, or an affect, etc.), a repudiation of empathic connectedness with one's state of mind during the unacceptable experience, and the formation of a boundary that maintains the disconnections noted above.... Therefore, a fantasized personified adaptation that serves and maintains these adaptations is formed. (p. 267)

Kluft (2000) demonstrated how different alters exemplify different coping strategies of belief, such as, "I would be safe if I were a boy," hence a male alter, or "I wish someone would comfort me," leading to the creation of a protective alter named Angel (p. 267).

Similarly, Shusta-Hochberg (2004) described how "the creation of another self-state enables the core of the traumatized child to avoid experiencing the abuse." She continued:

Dissociation offers an immediate escape through the perception of having another self-state occupy the body, so that the other self-state—often referred to by clinicians as an alter—experiences the pain, suffering and terror of the trauma. This results in the core self-state—usually referred to as the host—subjectively perceiving the trauma as happening to the alter, and the host may even have amnesia for the event. From an external point of view, the child, in its alter self-state, may appear to observers to be conscious and even cooperative, and may be mistaken for the host, but will tend to be more restricted in emotions and personality traits, with limited access to abilities and memories.

Repeated traumas are likely to elicit repeated emergence of the alter state. The more this happens, the more of the child's autobiographical memory will be stored in the alter state and the greater will be the host's amnesia, leading to an inability to recall significant parts of the past, which is consistent with theories of state-dependent memory. When trauma is complex and repeated over an extended portion of the child's life, this process may recur repeatedly, resulting in numerous alter states, each containing certain autobiographical memories, skills, procedural and general knowledge, behavioral patterns, physical sensations, and emotions. These are the building blocks of DID. The host, and subsequent alters as a whole—if integrated—constitute a fully cognizant and functioning human being. The various parts taken separately have major deficits in self-awareness and functioning. (pp. 14–15)

Dissociated and segregated states of mind are also less likely to be linked because trauma causes a decrease in metacognitive and reflective ability. Things become concrete, and it is hard to think about thinking. It is also important to remember that the inception of disorganized attachment is likely characterized by a trance state (Liotti, 2006). In a trance state, things do not have to make the kind of sense that they usually must. This is no inductive logic. In normal logic, Dangerous Mommy is an upsetting contradiction to Nice Mommy. However, in trance logic Dangerous Mommy and Nice Mommy can exist together. There is no contradiction. Their coexistence does not have to make sense.

Children have considerably greater self-hypnotic abilities than do adults, especially during late childhood, peaking around age 12 (Maldonado & Spiegel, 1998; Bernstein & Putnam, 1986). High dissociative ability continues into adulthood only in situations of ongoing traumatic abuse (Kluft, 1984). Thus, people who encounter even extreme trauma in adulthood do not develop extreme, florid symptoms of DID (Chu, 1998) unless they were highly traumatized in childhood.

ORIGINS OF DISSOCIATIVE IDENTITIES: THE KARPMAN DRAMA TRIANGLE OF VICTIM, PERSECUTOR, RESCUER—REDUX

In Chapter 5, I described one of Liotti's views of how the child develops dissociative identities in terms of the Karpman triangle and the attachment relationship: The child becomes victim, persecutor, and rescuer in relationship with the parents and "knows" these roles implicitly as a result. From this point of view, each of these identities emerges from real interpersonal experience: The child is the victim of the frightening caregiver, the child is the rescuer and comforter of the frightened caregiver, and the child perceives himself to be the persecutor of the frightened, withdrawn, or preoccupied caregiver.

However, it is also the case that these identities come about in ways that are not direct replications of the roles and experience that the child actually enacted vis-à-vis the caretaker. For instance, when the parent is too frightening to be regarded as in need of comfort or does not seem frightened, the child may develop these identities in the context of trauma. In this case, although the internal working models containing the substrates for these identities must precede their creation and development, these identities are not created solely in the context of interactions with frightened caregivers.

The Karpman triangle is still aptly descriptive (although it certainly does not cover all the varieties of dissociative identities). Apart from the identity who manages to function in the world with at least a fair degree of depersonalization and with some degree of amnesia (usually the "host"), variants on these three characters populate the inside. Most often, people with DID have dissociated victim identities, usually inner children who continue to suffer from the abuse. In addition, internal persecutors, some of whom may function in some ways like an exceptionally harsh, archaic superego, are created by a procedural enactive "identification with the aggressor" that occurs in response to trauma. Finally, internal rescuers are created. Similar to rescuers are dissociative identities who in the child's mind would be safe from the abuse.

The Victim Identity

Let us begin with the victim identity. If the attachment figure is overwhelmingly frightening or abusive, and if there is a history of disorganized attachment, then the segregated systems of attachment are invoked. In peritraumatic dissociation, people experience themselves as detached and distant from the event. Emotion-processing parts of the brain are damped down (Frewin & Lanius, 2006a, 2006b), and the person may feel like a calm observer while going through a situation of extreme terror. A child who is being raped by her father, for instance, may go into a detached state and experience herself as rising to the ceiling. Given her state of mind, she may literally see the child below as another child. Thereby, this child who is being subjected to terrifying abuse at the hands of a caregiver may be calm, not feeling the fear, and have some analgesia to the pain. If this were a case of simple posttraumatic stress disorder (PTSD), then fragmented memories of the traumatic experience would not become part of the memory system of another identity but would later intrude into consciousness, probably in fragmented ways. But, if this happens again and again, especially if this is in the context of earlier disorganized attachment, the detachment may become chronic as a way of escaping unendurable experience that is incompatible with attachment.

DID generally represents a very high magnitude of traumatization. For example, it is well known that a single rape for an adult can be a very traumatic experience, requiring months or years of recovery. For this, even the word "recovery" may be a misnomer, considering that one is almost never the same afterwards. In DID, a speculative multiplication factor (Kluft, 1993c) applies: Imagine a child misused by a trusted, loved and/or needed adult 2 times a week for 10 years. This is more than 1000 times, and it is a child.

If there is a preceding disorganized attachment, then the child watching from above embodies one self-state of calm who may be able to engage in an attachment relationship, but there is another child, another self-state, who is utterly terrified. Since these systems of experiencing are separate and unlinked, only one has executive control of the body at a time, and the calm, depersonalized one does not know about the other states of mind.

The Persecutor

Now, let us consider the persecutor/aggressor identity in relation to the previously discussed situation of a daughter's rape by a father. In the traumatic moment, the child will often become highly absorbed in a trancelike state with the problem of the persecutor. Self-hypnotic dissociation is the "escape when there is no escape" (Putnam, 1992). But in this situation, the child is likely to intently focus on the matter of most relevance, which is the abuser. Trance logic prevails, and there is an unclear distinction between self and other. In addition, the child, as a result of being intensely focused on the abuser, is likely to automatically mimic the aggressor's behavior. Through a process of identification with the aggressor, a part of the child may begin to feel that she is the aggressor. Once created, this identity state may become increasingly utilized in the service of predicting the aggressor's behavior, consequently avoiding some harm and preempting the aggressor's perceived power and threat.

Mirroring, Imitative Behavior, and Procedural, Enactive Identification With the Aggressor

It has long been known that infants, even soon after birth, are capable of engaging in what appears to be mimicry (Meltzoff & Moore, 1977; Trevarthen, 2009). Gallese, Fadiga, Fogassi, and Rizzolatti (1996) have documented "mirror neurons" in monkeys, finding that the same premotor neurons fire when the monkey performs an action, such as eating a peanut, and observes another monkey performing the action. Gallese (2009) and his colleagues have also documented what they considered "the likely human homologue of these monkey areas in which mirror neurons were originally observed" (p. 522). Gallese further stated, "Watching someone grasping a cup of coffee, biting an apple, or kicking a football activates the same neurons of our brain that would fire if we were doing the same" (p. 522). Gallese, however, emphasized that these neurons function via integration with other parts of the brain, in particular via integration with the motor system. All of this underscores the social design of our brains.

Recently, the activity of specific mirror neurons in the human brain have been discovered. According to *ScienceDaily* (http://www.sciencedaily.com/releases/2010/04/100412162112.htm, April 13, 2010), the April 2010 edition of *Current Biology* reported that Dr. Itzak Fried and his colleagues have made a direct recording of mirror neurons in the human brain, showing that these neurons fired and were most active when both executing an action and observing it. "Piggybacking" on a situation in which patients were being treated for epilepsy, they recorded activity of 1,177 neurons in the 21 patients. The researchers recorded both single-cell and multiple-cell activity, but interestingly the location of the neurons they recorded were in the medial frontal cortex and the medial temporal cortex, where this activity had not been previously observed, even in monkeys.

Colwyn Trevarthen noted (2009) that although we do not fully understand it, the interaction of mother and infant somatic and visceral processes gives the infant a "means of expression and access to the other anticipatory 'motor-images' and 'feelings' and permits direct motive-to motive engagement with a companion" (p. 70). Trevarthen also highlighted another aspect of this mirroring and imitation: The baby not only imitates but also anticipates. He (2003) described how after watching the baby imitate a parent or the researcher, if the researcher waited, the baby would repeat the same sound and behaviors that had been imitated as an aspect of a dance of intentional elicitation of the same response from the adult. This is a "protoconversation." Emphasizing the role of expectation, Trevarthen (2003) wrote:

> The classical way of diagramming the human cerebral cortex indicates that it processes sensory information coming in at the back and sends it forward to the "pre-central" motor system. In fact, all information that is perceived is *expected* by the brain. There is a process seeking in the other direction, first setting up a motor plan, then looking for the sensory information needed. The motor or "executive" action is leading to the cognitive experience, so the initiative is actually frontal in origin. It has got to do with initiating voluntary activity and then the experience comes about. (p. 12; emphasis in original)

Given that humans not only imitate but also anticipate, as part of relational neurological design, we can think in more detail about the process of "identification with the aggressor" in the formation of abuser and persecutory self-states in the persons with DID. In the process that is often termed "identification with the aggressor" (e.g., Ferenczi, 1932/1949), abuser and victim self-states become partially or entirely dissociated. (See Chapter 11 for more description of identification with the aggressor.) As a result perhaps of mirror neurons as well as imitative/anticipatory procedural enactment, a part of the child may behave like the abuser or even experience the self as the abuser in the internal world of the "third reality." The omnipotence and devaluation with which the abuser has treated the victim is automatically enacted. In the traumatic moment of being terrified and abused, the child cannot assimilate the events into narrative memory and goes into a trancelike state. In this state, the child focuses intently on the source of the danger, the abuser, including the abuser's postures, motions, facial expressions, words, and feelings but does so in a depersonalized and derealized way. Thus, identification with the aggressor relies on processes that Lyons-Ruth (1999) described as "enactive procedural representations of how to do things with others" (p. 385). In contrast to relationships of mutuality in which there is much validating and mirroring of the other's experience, in traumatic procedural learning, there is no opportunity for interchange of perspectives. In this way, these aggressor-identified, grandiose, and dominating abuser self-states that often embody rage, contempt, and omnipotence may arise procedurally and imitatively.

If in a situation of interpersonal terror the child has a dissociative hypoarousal response as described by Schore, or a secondary dissociative PTSD response (as described by Frewin & Lanius, 2006b, and by the Reinders et al. articles, 2003, 2006), to protect the ability to survive and to function, then we can add the procedural process of identification with the aggressor to this. Another part of the self that is disconnected from this depersonalized, functioning apparently normal part may be automatically imitating and anticipating the abuser's behavior. I am suggesting that, along with mimicking of the aggressor, in the context of such a depersonalized state the situation is ripe for the creation of aggressor-identified alter. Recall Frewin and Lanius's (2006b) statement that "disconnection of neural pathways normally linking self-awareness with emotional body-state perception could occasion the development of dissociative identities in traumatized children" (p. 113). Also recall these additional words:

> Specifically with increased repetition and automatization of secondary dissociative processes during situations of long-standing abuse, the priming of the dissociative state may become sensitized and increasingly automatic and unconscious. In addition, repetitious entry into secondary dissociative states may produce progressively more marked departures from external reality and consciousness for self. (pp. 120–121)

Although the human brain and nervous system are designed to be social, procedural enactments are not always happy affairs.

The Rescuer

Finally, also, in a hypnotic state traumatized children can create protectors, as noted. In his phrase "dissociative multiplicity," O'Neil (2009) emphasized that people with DID do not just dissociate but also creatively multiply themselves. Grotstein (2000), speaking of Fairbairn's schizoid position and the "phantasmal accommodations for survival" that the infant must make in situations of danger, observed "thus, in withdrawing, the infant becomes his own imaginary parent" (p. 138). Under conditions of abuse and neglect, an inordinate degree of self-sufficiency is required of the young child. Because this is generally more than can be managed, the child may invent an omnipotent protector, helper, or inner caretaker (Beahrs, 1982; Bliss, 1986). For example, Julie, a person with DID who had been brutally sexually abused, isolated, and periodically subjected to severe neglect and terror as a young child, described how she would make friends and protectors of the rocks and bushes, convincing herself that they would care for her. Since inner protectors are experienced as real, frightened parts may become highly attached to them. Thus, the attachment system characterizes the inner world as well as the outer one, and this sets the stage for what Kluft (2000) called "the third reality," the internal world of trance logic and multiple personifications.

The Third Reality

The third reality is in some ways like an interior dream world that has its own structure and consistent cast of characters. There is much playful creativity in this world. However, the third reality to some extent relies on a psychic system that is relatively closed. The closed system is contrasted to an open system that allows interaction with the outside and transformation of the individual through interactive interchange with others. This closed system makes for problems in living, and to the extent that this system is closed, it cannot grow.

The Self-Care System

Related to the third reality is what Donald Kalsched (1996) called "the self-care system." As we have seen, the attachment system can be understood as a psychological system for combating stress and modulating stressful arousal (Lyons-Ruth, 2001). It fails to work adequately in traumatic attachments, in which the attachment figure is dangerous or fails to provide a protective shield against the dangers of the environment. The effects of the failure of the attachment system, then, are profound. Kalsched (1996) described how the "self-care system," which operates by using dissociative defenses, such as psychic numbing, trance states, and self-hypnosis, defends the self against traumatic attachments and supplements the scarce supplies available in the interpersonal environment. However, the self-care system also results in the closed system:

> The self-care system is self-protective and compensatory rather than relational. As such, it cannot gain understanding from experience (Kalsched, 1996). Because it functions protectively to prevent retraumatization, the self-care system strenuously resists transformation. The illusions of the self-care system are only temporarily helpful and must be continuously replenished. Without a benign-enough connection to the interpersonal world, hope cannot last. (Howell, 2005, p. 221)

CONNECTING DISSOCIATED SELF-STATES: CONTEXTUALIZATION

Kelly Forrest's (2001) attachment-centered, neuroscience analysis of the processes probably involved in the origin of the dissociated identity states of DID emphasized how these states become and remain context bound. Following from her analysis, part of the healing process will involve promoting intercontextualization among these dissociated self-states. Forrest referred to Putnam (1997), whose discrete behavioral states (DBS) model of the personality emphasizes that rather than starting out as a unity, the human personality must become integrated over time. Originally, discrete behavioral and mental states are the building blocks of human behavior and consciousness. As the linkages between them become more complex, the child gains greater control and the ability to self-regulate. One of the important effects of trauma and neglect is that the expected linking of associative pathways among states is impeded. In this way, self-states stay bound to the original context.

As self-states become more aware of their contextual interrelatedness to each other, the increasing aggregates become more context independent. An example of being bound by context would be: A child part who remembers being beaten by a tall man may feel all the old terror when tall men are seen in reality. Such an occasion of seeing a tall man could re-evoke the old terror and be experienced as flashbacks, or it could be marked by a switch in which this terrified part appears. When they are context bound in this sense the separate parts are too responsive to the pulls, associations, and contextual elements of events and circumstances that were too overwhelming to assimilate in the past. As the alters are each separately working on how to avoid land mines—or stepping on them, they are less available to coconsciously empathize or be supportive to each other.

As self-states become more aware and accepting of their contextual interrelatedness to each other, the increasing aggregate of self becomes more context independent, with respect to vulnerability to being triggered by outside context. As this happens, the dissociative barriers diminish. For example, Little Denny, a terrified child part of Dennis (introduced in Chapter 1) lives in terror. When a sudden threat of abandonment evoked his terror, Little Denny became uncontrollably rageful and verbally destructive with a person that the host loved. Following this, Little Denny's guilt and despair permeated the whole aggregate personality, contributing to extreme instability that the host then tried to manage. This could be comparable to a less dissociative person experiencing an almost unmanageable rage, and perhaps expressing it, and then feeling shaken. An important difference is that the less dissociated person can recover more easily from being shaken—because other aspects of memory and more stable and confident self-states are contextually available. Likewise, Little Denny becomes less upset when he can receive some support from another alter who has more experience and comfort with rage. And he is also less upset when he can feel more empowered by being less alone, experiencing himself as standing next to the host, who can comfort and protect him.

Intercontextualization is also promoted in the relationship with the therapist. Inviting the parts into interaction with the therapist and to share their third reality with the therapist is integrative in the sense of binding together. The therapist operates as a relational bridge (Bromberg, 1998) for self-states to share more aspects of their segregated experience with each other.

Mitchell's (1993) statement about working with dissociated self-states in people who do not necessarily have DID applies to DID as well:

> Is the degree of discontinuity among different versions of the self a measure of the degree of psychopathology? Does the analysand end treatment with a more unified, homogeneous self? Certainly psychopathology might well be measured by degrees of dissociation of important versions of self. Yet it seems mistaken to assume that a digestion and blending of different versions of self is preferable to the capacity to contain shifting and conflictual versions of self. (p. 105)

Similarly, Watkins (1992) states:

> Integration means making the barriers between various alters more permeable, increasing communication and cooperation, then returning the various subpersonalities to the status of "covert" ego-states which cannot be contacted except under hypnosis. We feel it is unnecessary to fuse them into a unity since this is not a part of the "normal" personality. (cited in Phillips & Frederick, 1995, p. 166)

However, integration is a tricky concept. Of course, integration, along with less fragmentation, is usually a general goal in psychotherapy, including for people who do not have dissociative disorders. In a general sense, integration may be a lessening of separateness and an increase of permeability of internal boundaries between self-states, distinguishing this from the idea of the person becoming one seamless unit. Rivera (1996) suggests a continuum on which the robust multiplicity is at the healthy end of the continuum, and a fragile self, which can be characterized by either pathological dissociation or pathological association is at the other end: "Defensive association pretends to simple unity to hide fragmentation, suppression, and complex humanity in all its contradictory manifestations. Defensive dissociation acknowledges the depth and complexity of the human condition through the interplay of a multitude of self-states, but denies it utterly at the same time through disconnection" (p. 34). Similarly, Gold (2004) states that "'normal' people maintain a sense of integration and continuity ... by systematically and routinely invoking processes that enable them to ignore the glaring gaps, inconsistencies, and lack of continuity in their experiences and behavior."

People with DID frequently express fears of integration because their alters are afraid that they will die or be eliminated. While they do not die, what the parts do lose is their redundancy: There are often too many parts who are doing the same things, without the knowledge of the others who are also doing the same things. They are unaware of how many feelings and thoughts they actually share. As a result, there is much time wasted, and it is inconvenient, destabilizing, and sometimes disastrous to not know what one said or did. In addition, the dissociative separation of self-states and affect schemas, which resulted from unbearable affect, also impairs current affect regulation.

One of the problems is the word, *integration*, and the concept behind it. According to Wikipedia, the word, *integer*, from the Latin means untouched, hence, whole. The implication is of a unit or a unity. In this way, integration is also a one-person concept. However, the organization of self-states can differ in different relationships and interactions. There is not only the contextualization of self-states within the individual personality, but also the contextualization of each person's self-states within the dyad.

The concept of contextual interdependence avoids the problems in the often implied opposition between dissociation versus unity. And, it explicitly allows for intersubjectivity of parts in the internal world. As the different subjectivities can increasingly recognize that they can utilize their connectedness to each other, they are in a better position to bear their overwhelming affects.

Rather than a monolithic integration, a better ideal might be not only harmonious interaction among the multiple self-states but also an appreciation of contextual interdependence. I agree with Bromberg's (1993) statement at the beginning of this chapter: "To put it as simply as possible, I argue that there is no such thing as an integrated self—a 'real you'" (p. 166). Integration can mean different things. For me, an ideal integration would allow the different "voices" of different self-states to retain their own tenor although increasingly less dissociated, and in harmony or in conscious conflict, as the case may be. In other words, integration need not cover over multiplicity or even the capacity for dissociation.

I propose that contextualization might be a more fruitful way of thinking about our psychotherapeutic goal. Subselves within the context of the whole aggregate, when separate but not highly dissociated, add perspective and internalized multiple viewpoints. However, if viewed in three-dimensional space as Putnam (1997) did in his DBS model, each self-state looks different from the particular vantage point of the others. But, most important, as one self-state or group of self-states takes on different functions, such as executive or experiential functions, the relationships to other states change. This reorganization of internal relationships and points of view has the potential to release logjams. When these changes become more available to thought, through interaction with another person or another part of the self, therapeutic action has occurred. However, this is movement not only toward integration but also toward greater contextualization. That is, the different self-states become increasingly aware of how they are contextually related to each other. In so doing, they become, as a group or as groups, more independent of specific contexts and thus less vulnerable to being triggered by specific contexts.

While the contextualized self is one that can, in Bromberg's (2003) wonderful phrasing, "stand in the spaces between realities without losing any of them" (p. 166), it also encompasses an awareness of all of the parts together. From this perspective, we can take a different view of the concept of unity. Bromberg (2003) described his view of how the continuity of "I" must depend on human relatedness:

> "Unity" is a shorthand term for the experience of feeling fully in life, and "life" is the experience of our connection with the rest of humanity. That is, unity is the connection to mankind and other people. In analytic treatment...when the therapist...is able to relate to each aspect of the patient's self through its own subjectivity, each part of the self becomes increasingly able to coexist with the rest, and in that sense is linked to the others. It is an experience of coherence, cohesiveness, and continuity, that comes about through human relatedness. (p. 704)

Part 2

Treating Dissociative Identity Disorder

Chapter 8

Assessment and Diagnosis of DID

> Diagnosis has great meaning to our patients. While diagnosis should inform treatment, for the patient, it may be the first time they have "stopped to notice" that they have a mind that does not work like other people's minds.
>
> Chefetz (2005a, p. 661)

This chapter describes basic assessment methods to identify the presence of dissociative identity disorder (DID) and dissociative disorder not otherwise specified (DDNOS). These methods include diagnostic face-to-face interviews, screening instruments, and assessment instruments. Most patients with DID have spent years in the mental health system with incorrect primary diagnoses, such as schizophrenia, bipolar disorder, and anxiety disorders, before being correctly diagnosed. The primary reason for this is that most clinicians have not been adequately trained in graduate school or medical school to recognize dissociative disorders, if they have been trained for this at all. Frequently, the training they have received has included a bias against recognition of the existence of DID; furthermore, those who are willing to consider DID as a diagnosis have often been taught that the presentation of DID is florid, with switching that is easy to spot. To the contrary, "only 6% make their DID obvious on an ongoing basis" (Kluft, 2009, p. 600). Also, the result of poor clinical training, but much less frequent, is false-positive diagnoses. Clinicians who have not been adequately trained in differential diagnosis (including dissociative disorders) are more likely to make mistakes in either direction.

Because of this general lack in training, as well as because of the amnesia and hiddenness that so often characterize DID and DDNOS, I recommend that all incoming patients be assessed for dissociative disorders.

AMNESIA FOR AMNESIA: DID IS A DISORDER OF HIDDENNESS

There are important differences in the presentation of those with DID and DDNOS from other groups of psychotherapy patients. Whereas people who suffer primarily from anxiety or depression can tell you straightforwardly the nature of their problem, patients with undiagnosed DID usually cannot tell you that their primary problem is that they switch, have frequent intrusions into their experience, and have amnesia for large segments of their lives. In essence, they have amnesia for amnesia. Although prospective new patients who turn out to be highly dissociative will occasionally tell their clinicians that they have been previously diagnosed with a dissociative disorder or that they themselves suspect it, it is much more common that patients enter psychotherapy for some other concern, such as anxiety, depression, addictions, posttraumatic stress, or relationship problems. These multiple symptoms often accompany dissociative disorders and may themselves, in large measure, be the result of the unseen trauma-driven dissociation that governs the patients' lives. As Luxenberg et al. (2001) noted: "Yet trauma-related disorders, including dissociative disorders, continue to be grossly underdiagnosed. This underrecognition can be best understood in light of the multiplicity of symptoms with which these patients present that may not be readily recognized as being related to their traumatic experiences" (p. 377).

People with DID often do not know about their dissociative identities. Or, they may "sort of" know: They have an inkling, but they do not have the conceptual or emotional language yet to spell it out to themselves. Sometimes, if they do know, even sort of know, they may assume that everyone else is similar. Living in such a haze, people with DID often find it difficult even to think about, much less communicate about, their dissociative problems. Moreover, even when they know they have dissociative problems, they are often, for good reason, loath to reveal it: They fear being regarded as "crazy" and of being "put away." They also fear they *are* crazy. As a result, the assessment must be conducted with great care and sensitivity.

DIAGNOSTIC CONSTRUCTS

Another contribution to the difficulties of accurate diagnosis has to do with our diagnostic constructs. There are two primary constructs: switching and intrusions/withdrawals of experience. However, both the current *Diagnostic and Statistical Manual of Mental Disorders, Fourth Edition, Text Revision* (*DSM-IV-TR*; American Psychiatric Association [APA], 2000) and the proposed criteria for the fifth edition (DSM5; with a proposed publication date by APA in 2012) place the emphasis on the switching aspect of DID as well as DDNOS.

Switching

The *DSM-IV-TR* (APA, 2000) provides the following diagnostic criteria for DID (300.14):

A. The presence of two or more distinct identities or personality states (each with its own relatively enduring pattern of perceiving, relating to, and thinking about the environment and self).
B. At least two of these identities or personality states recurrently take control of the person's behavior.
C. Inability to recall important personal information that is too extensive to be explained by ordinary forgetfulness.
D. The disturbance is not due to the direct physiological effects of a substance (e.g., blackouts or chaotic behavior during Alcohol Intoxication) or a general medical condition (e.g., complex partial seizures). Note: In children, the symptoms are not attributable to imaginary playmates or other fantasy play. (p. 529)

Notice that Criteria A and B are vague about whether the clinician must witness the switches in identity states or whether the patient's self-report is adequate.

The reader may find the new proposed diagnostic criteria for DSM5 (expected publication date is 2012) at http://www.dsm5.org/ProposedRevisions/Pages/proposedrevision.aspx?rid=57. An important difference is that the new criterion A specifies that the client's self-report with respect to disruption of identity states is considered adequate: It is clear that the clinician need not witness such disruption. Another important difference is that in the new DSM5 criteria somatic symptoms are given diagnostic importance. The amnesia requirement that is specified in *DSM-IV-TR* continues in DSM5.

Dissociative Disorder Not Otherwise Specified

DDNOS (APA, 2000, 300.15) is used when there are predominant dissociative symptoms that do not meet the full criteria for DID or for any other *DSM* dissociative disorder. It is a frequently used category because many highly dissociative patients are "almost DID," in accordance with Example 1 of the DDNOS criteria. Example 1 of DDNOS refers to "Clinical presentations similar to Dissociative Identity Disorder that fail to meet the full criteria for this disorder. These include presentations in which there are not two or more distinct personality states, or amnesia for important personal information does not occur" (APA, 2000, p. 242). Thus, those severely dissociative patients who do not have amnesia between identity states should be diagnosed, according to the current and the proposed future criteria, as having DDNOS. This is despite the fact that they may have dissociated identity states; that these identity states function as autonomous, personified, separate subselves; and that they benefit from treatment designed for DID.

Some clinicians use the DDNOS category when the patient has not displayed obvious switching to the diagnosing clinician, although the patient may have reported it. Because of the ambiguity of Criterion B in the *DSM-IV-TR* (APA, 2000) regarding whether the clinician must have been in communication with alternate identities, many clinicians will take a more conservative approach and use the DDNOS designation for those severely dissociative patients they have not personally witnessed switching. However, if the proposed (2012) *DSM-V* goes into effect, this will no longer be an issue: These patients will be diagnosed with DID.

Additional examples for DDNOS given in *DSM-IV-TR* (APA, 2000) also include derealization without depersonalization, dissociative states due to brainwashing, dissociative trance disorder, loss of consciousness not attributable to medical disorder, and Ganser's syndrome. The most common reason, however, for the diagnosis of DDNOS is for reasons similar to Example 1 (International Society for the Study of Trauma and Dissociation [ISST-D], in press).

Other categories of dissociative disorders listed in *DSM-IV-TR* (APA, 2000) are dissociative amnesia (300.12) in which "the predominant experience is one or more episodes of inability to recall important personal information, usually or a traumatic or stressful nature, that is too extensive to be explained by ordinary forgetfulness" (p. 239); dissociative fugue (300.13), in which the "predominant symptom is sudden or unexpected travel away from home or one's customary place of work, with inability to recall one's past" (p. 240); and depersonalization disorder (300.6), which is characterized by persistent or recurrent "experiences of feeling detached from, and as if one is an outside observer of, one's mental processes or body (e.g., feeling like one is in a dream)," and in which "reality testing remains intact" (p. 241).

Intrusions and Withdrawals, Partial Dissociation

Although important, the phenomenon of switching occurs with relatively less frequency and may be less characteristic of DID (Dell, 2001, 2006a, 2006b, 2009a, 2009d) than the phenomenon of intrusion of other identity states into current experience. Examples are flashbacks, intrusive thoughts, intrusive emotions, and "made" behaviors. The importance of these intrusions for DID was first identified by Kluft (1987a). In his landmark study, Kluft found that patients with DID endorsed 8 of the 11 Schneiderian (Schneider, 1959, as cited in Kluft, 1987a) first-rank symptoms that had been considered indicative of schizophrenia. These symptoms were voices arguing, voices commenting on one's action, influences playing on the body, thought withdrawal, thought insertion, made impulses, made feelings, and made volitional acts. Kluft observed that while it is no longer generally accepted that these first-rank symptoms are diagnostic of schizophrenia, they are in fact characteristic of DID. He further specified that the hallucinated voices and the made actions were due to the activities of an alternate identity. Following Ross (1989) and Putnam (1997), who also observed that dissociative disturbances have often been misunderstood for schizophrenia, Dell (2001, 2009a, 2009d) described in depth how the preponderance of dissociative symptoms reported by patients with diagnosed dissociative disorders are these subjectively experienced made thoughts, emotions, or behaviors. He distinguished between full dissociation, which is characterized by amnesia, and partial dissociation, which includes such symptoms as flashbacks, hearing voices in the head, passive influence symptoms, and intrusions of dissociated experience. In partial dissociation, Dell (2001, 2009a, 2009d) noted that there is either subjectively experienced or objectively observable discontinuity in thought, affect, or behavior, without amnesia for behavior or identity. He incorporated these symptoms of partial dissociation in his Multidimensional Inventory of Dissociation (MID; Dell, 2006a) diagnostic questionnaire.

In practice, assessment questions and instruments incorporate both models: Many of the questions that are asked in the following assessment methods, which include diagnostic interviews as well as formal assessment instruments, rely on both switching and intrusions/withdrawals from dissociative identities.

ASSESSMENT INTERVIEWS

An important proviso for any of these approaches to assessment is that if severe cognitive or memory problems seem to be present or if the presentation does not seem to make sense, neuropsychological testing may be indicated (Brand, Armstrong, & Lowenstein, 1996). In addition, severe somatoform problems should also be addressed with a physical examination to rule out or assess medical contributions.

An additional proviso is that although this chapter covers the screening and assessment tools I use most frequently in private practice, it is not an extensive review of all of the relevant instruments. Selection of the best screening and assessment instruments will vary with treatment setting and the purpose of assessment. For more information on assessment, see the *ISST-D Guidelines* (ISST-D, in press), the work of Bethany Brand and her colleagues, and that of other clinicians in the field of dissociative disorders who are expert in assessment.[1]

Face-to-Face Interview: Basic Diagnostic Indicators

Although the inexperienced DID clinician is unlikely to detect overt switching in the first interviews, be alert to some basics. These include large gaps in autobiographical memory, logical inconsistencies in narrative, history of abuse, experiences of depersonalization and derealization, affective dysregulation, and somatoform dissociation. Large gaps in autobiographical memory and history of abuse are red flags. Experiences of depersonalization and derealization are important to inquire about as many patients with DID live a good portion of their lives in such states. One may ask something like, "Does it ever seem to you that things are not real?" or "Do you sometimes feel that you are not in your body?" Dissociative patients will often answer in the affirmative. They may think that this is normal, and as result, they do not notice this as something meaningful about themselves. Furthermore, they may rely on these ways of experiencing as a way to decontextualize experience and to continually damp down affect. Does intense affect bring on subjective shifts? One might also ask about thoughts and ways of thinking that come into the mind and do not seem like one's own. Chefetz (2000b) described the result of an instance when he asked his patient if she had ever noticed other, competing streams of thought in her mind: "She looked confused again. Suddenly she brightened, 'Oh, you mean my People! Sure, they've been there as long as I can remember! How did you know about that? Nobody ever asked'" (p. 308).

Topics for Inquiry

The following discussion conveys a brief description of important topics for inquiry during the clinical interview. For more comprehensive information, refer to an excellent, highly informative, and classic article by Richard Loewenstein (1991) on assessment via an office mental status examination. This thorough examination inquires after many of the symptoms of DID and is organized according to categories of evidence of (a) alternate identities, (b) amnesia, (c) autohypnotic phenomena, (d) posttraumatic stress disorder (PTSD), (e) somatoform symptoms, and (f) affective symptoms.

In addition to the standard questions of an initial interview, patients should be asked about memory and amnesia and experiences of depersonalization, derealization, identity confusion, and identity alteration (Steinberg, Cicchetti, Buchanan, Hall, & Rounsaville, 1993); somatoform experiences (Nijenhuis, 1999); intrusions/withdrawals into conscious experiences, such as passive influence symptoms (Dell, 2009a; Kluft, 1987a); and other continuities and discontinuities in their experiences and behavior.

Inquiry regarding child abuse has not always been included in standard initial interviews. Because early traumatization is usually a part of the history of those with DID, and because the rate of child trauma is higher for DID than any other diagnostic group (ISST-D Guidelines, in press), if I hear about prolonged severe abuse in childhood, my antennae are up for the possibility of a dissociative disorder. However, asking questions about abuse requires a great deal of care. If the person seems upset at all by the question, I generally indicate that we do not have to talk about that now. Premature detailed investigation could trigger an overwhelming and retraumatizing flood of memories and bring on decompensation.

With regard to memory, inquiries should address the continuity of childhood memories after the age of 3 or 4. Because the hippocampus, which categorizes and processes memories, does not come online until around the age of 3, narrative memory is generally lacking before this age. Large gaps, such as not remembering the seventh grade or not remembering anything until the age of 9, for example, signal cause for further investigation. Memory gaps in the present or recent past are also important. Does the person lose time, (that is) seemingly "coming to" and not knowing what she did for the last few hours or days? Does the person remember what she did last night or yesterday morning? Is there evidence of fugues, in which she finds herself in unexpected places and does not know how she got there?

I often ask patients if they remember anything about our last session. If they do not remember, does prompting bring the memory back? Many patients who are not highly dissociative may not remember the last session, but the memory usually begins to emerge with prompting. Ever since I began routinely asking this question, I have been surprised at how often highly dissociative people do not remember the last session and at how often prompting fails to bring back the memory—indicating that different dissociative parts of the person have been "out." I also check for memory in the session: Is the person aware of what we were discussing earlier?

The quality of memories is important as well. Perhaps most important is whether the memory is episodic (concerning personally remembered autobiographical episodes). For instance, a dissociative patient of mine told me, "I know that I graduated high school, because I was told I did, but I don't remember being there." Such an answer suggests the strong possibility that a different part of the person than the one currently speaking attended the graduation.

It is especially important to inquire about somatoform symptoms as these may represent bodily sensations related to past trauma (Nijenhuis, 1999). For instance, my patient Anna sometimes feels intense pain on the top of her shoulders, the point from which she as a young adolescent was forced down onto her knees, despite her resistance, to perform fellatio on her abusers. This is an aspect of dissociated memory from past trauma.

The clinician should be alert to changes in appearance or behavior. For instance, does a person's dress style change from session to session? Sometimes, a unisex hairstyle and clothing style on a woman may indicate that she has found a more comfortable way to switch to differently gendered identities. Does a person's voice change markedly in the session? Are taste preferences consistent? For instance, Dennis, introduced in Chapter 1, brought a cup of coffee into the session, opened the lid, and exclaimed in disgust, "Ugh! I hate black coffee! Sophia must have bought this." With regard to the body, the clinician should inquire about handedness, eyesight, allergies, and reactions to medications. People with DID may be right-handed in one self-state and left-handed or ambidextrous in others. Many highly dissociative persons will have parts whose visual acuity is quite different from others, or they will have different allergies and highly differing reactions to medications.

Does the person report having had the experience of meeting people she does not know but who seem to know her, perhaps by a different name? Often, those with DID are thought by others to be lying because different parts will say different things of which the host has no knowledge. Does the person appear to be going in and out of trance, report autohypnotic experiences or out-of-body experiences? How does the person handle emotions? Generally, the host will not express intense anger. I have often been surprised when inquiry about affects yields responses like, "I feel nothing." Painful as it is for their therapists to hear, many, if not most, highly dissociative people go through life feeling depersonalized and with highly damped down affect a great deal of the time.

Does the person hear voices? If so, are they perceived as originating from inside the mind or from outside the head? This may help to differentiate a psychotic disturbance from a dissociative one: Kluft (1999a) noted that in 80% of those with DID, voices are heard from inside the head, while in 80% of psychotic disorders voices are heard from outside the head. However, making this discrimination is not foolproof for highly dissociative persons also hear voices from outside their heads (Moskowitz, 2008). Useful distinctions include whether the communications are bizarre and whether the person can hold the tension of knowing that voices are being heard in her head without attributing additional meanings to this.

Consider language: Does the person refer to herself or himself as "we"? Is the patient's spouse ever referred to as "her husband" or "his wife"? Are parents or other significant people referred to as "the parents," "her parents," "his friend," and so on? Are body parts ever deprived of the possessive pronoun, for example, "the hand hurts"?

What about PTSD symptoms such as visual, auditory, or somatic flashbacks or intrusions of intense affect or memories? Does the person have passive influence symptoms such as made experiences, thoughts, emotions, or behaviors (Dell, 2001; Kluft, 1987)? For example, the person might say, "It felt like the hand picked it up; I didn't."

I have one more diagnostic indicator. Even though it is not in my office for the purpose of assessment, I have a dollhouse visible on my bookcase. On more than several occasions, a person has revealed dissociativity by asking to see the dollhouse. Inevitably, as soon as the dollhouse is taken down, the patient has switched into a child part as she begins playing with the dollhouse.

FORMAL SCREENING AND ASSESSMENT INSTRUMENTS

Before assessing for dissociative disorder, it is often helpful to gently introduce the patient to the subject of investigation and to normalize dissociation as a trait and a defense, as something that everyone does to some extent (Nijenhuis, Spinhoven, Van Dyck, Van der Hart, & Vanderlinden, 1996). For instance, the Dissociative Experiences Scale (DES) has its title written at the top, as does the Somatoform Dissociation Questionnaire (SDQ).

I discuss four screening tools first: the DES, developed by Bernstein and Putnam (1986) and updated by Carlson and Putnam (1993); the Adolescent Dissociative Experiences Scale (A-DES; Armstrong, Putnam, Carlson, Libero, & Smith, 1997); the Child Dissociative Checklist (CDC) developed by Putnam (1997); and the SDQ-5. Following this, I discuss several assessment instruments: the SDQ-20 (Nijenhuis, Spinhoven, Van Dyck, Van der Hart, & Vanderlinden, 1997); the MID (Dell, 2006a); the Structured Clinical Interview for *DSM-IV* Dissociative Disorders–Revised (SCID-D-R) developed by Steinberg (1994a, 1994b, 1995); and the Dissociative Disorder Interview Schedule (DDIS) provided by Ross (1997). More detailed information about screening and assessment instruments can be found on the ISST-D Web site under the heading "Professionals" and the subheading "Education and Treatment" (http://www.isst-d.org/).

Screening Instruments

Frequently used screening instruments include the DES, the A-DES, the CDC, and the SDQ-5. The DES, the A-DES, and the CDC are available in the public domain and are available at http://www.isst-d.org.

The Dissociative Experiences Scale

The most widely used standard screening tool is the DES, a self-report measure developed by Bernstein and Putnam (1986) and further developed by Carlson and Putnam (1993) as the DES-II. In addition to clinical screening, the DES is an extremely popular measurement instrument in research. Usually the first diagnostic instrument to be used, this 28-item questionnaire asks about the extent of the presence of dissociative symptoms. It can usually be filled out in 20 minutes or less. It is scored by adding the total scores and dividing by 28 (Carlson & Putnam, 1993). Scores above 30 indicate the high possibility of DID and that further inquiry about this possibility should be conducted (Carlson & Putnam, 1993).

The DES correlated .78 with the SCID-D-R (Boon & Draijer, 1993), which is considered the "gold standard" of assessment instruments. However, it is important to remember that the DES is a screening tool, not an assessment instrument. Low scores do not rule out the presence of a dissociative disorder, and high scores (especially for people who may have a reason to want the diagnosis) do not indicate its presence. In fact, caution is advised, especially in research, for using the DES score as a cutoff that precludes further assessment for dissociative disorders. In their study of the prevalence of DID in psychiatric outpatients, Foote et al. (2006) noted that had they used the DES score as a cutoff, they would have missed a number of patients who were identified as having DID by formal, but more time-consuming, assessment measures.

Regardless of whether scores are high or low, taking the DES may bring up thoughts or associations the patient would like to discuss. These may become a meaningful part of both the diagnostic interview and the psychotherapy.

The DES-T

A shorter version of the DES is the DES-Taxon (DES-T). The DES taps into several dimensions of experience, including ordinary ones such as absorption, as well as the more clearly dissociative experiences such as amnesia, switching, depersonalization, and derealization. In addition, it is based on the concept of a continuum of dissociation. In contrast to the continuum model, Putnam (1997) found that a relatively small subgroup of subjects whose abuse was earlier, more chronic, and severe fit into a taxon or personality classification. Eight of the DES items, taken together, are taxonic for DID (Putnam, 1997; Waller, Putnam & Carlson, 1996). This group of eight specific items—3, 5, 7, 8, 12, 13, 22, 27—comprise the DES-T. The scoring program for the DES-T is available on the ISST-D Web site under the heading "Professionals," subheading "Education and Treatment" (http://www.isst-d.org/). As with the DES, a cutoff score of 30 indicates the high possibility of DID (ISST-D, in press).

Advantages for use of the DES-T are that it can be completed more quickly than can the DES, and especially in research studies, it is used with the hope that it will be more accurate. However, the view that the DES-T is more accurate has become controversial. More current research (Dalenberg, 2004) indicated that absorption is just as highly correlated with physical, sexual, and emotional abuse, as well as depersonalization, as are the taxonic criteria themselves. Several aspects of dissociative abilities and tendencies, such as absorption and detachment, appear to be functionally interlinked as well as highly intercorrelated. Thus, the conceptual and practical divide between normal and pathological dissociation is often left blurry.

The Adolescent Dissociative Experiences Scale

Although the DES and the DES-T are designed for people over 18, the A-DES (Armstrong et al., 1997), a 30-item self-report instrument, is designed for people aged 11 to 18. Adolescents with DID typically score between 4 and 7. A score of 4 or higher generally warrants further evaluation.

The Child Dissociative Checklist

The CDC, designed by Putnam (1997), is a 20-item checklist. It is scored by summing the item scores. Scores can range from 0 to 40; a cutoff score of 12 or more may tentatively indicate sustained pathological dissociation, indicating that further evaluation should be conducted.

The Somatoform Dissociation Questionnaire

The SDQ-5 (Nijenhuis et al., 1997) was developed as a self-report screening instrument for *DSM-IV* (APA, 2000) dissociative disorders. It addresses several somatic experiences, such as urinary pain, paralysis, and body stiffness. Having only five questions, it can be completed rapidly. It is scored on 5-point Likert scale, with possible scores of 5 to 25, which are obtained by summing the scores. A score greater than 7 indicates the high possibility of a dissociative disorder, which should then be addressed by formal assessment instruments. The SDQ-5 correlates well with the SDQ-20.

Nijenhuis, Spinhoven, Vanderlinden, Van Dyck, et al. (1998) have observed that somatic dissociation is commonly experienced by people with dissociative disorders, but that there has been a problem with diagnostic concepts. According to the *DSM-IV-TR* (APA, 2000), the "essential feature of Dissociative Disorders is a disruption of the usually integrated functions of consciousness, memory, identity, or perception" (p. 477). However, if the traumatic experience has been too intensely overwhelming to be assimilated into ordinary consciousness, it may be encoded in somatosensory modalities rather than as narrative memory. According to Nijenhuis (2000) and Van der Hart et al. (2006), our diagnostic system repeats the ages-old Cartesian dualism, in the form of a mind–body controversy with respect to the "location" of dissociation: Although the *DSM-IV-TR* (APA, 2000) categorizes the cognitive and affective aspects of dissociation as dissociative disorders, somatically experienced dissociative processes, such as motor control and sensation, are classified as somatoform. The only *DSM-IV-TR* dissociative disorder that even remotely refers to bodily symptoms is depersonalization disorder, in which the person feels detached from or outside the body. Nijenhuis, Spinhoven, et al. (1998) observed that major somatoform dissociative symptoms bear much similarity to animal defensive reactions to threat, including, notably, freezing and anesthesia/analgesia. (For additional discussion of this topic, see Chapter 6.)

More information on both the SDQ-5 and the SDQ-20 can be found in Nijenhuis's (2004) book, *Somatoform Dissociation: Phenomena, Measurement, and Theoretical Issues.*

Self-Report Assessment Instruments

The Somatoform Dissociation Questionnaire

The SDQ-20 (Nijenhuis et al., 1996), which includes the five SDQ-5 questions, is a measure of the severity of somatoform dissociation. It addresses such issues as tunnel vision, pseudoseizures, and psychogenic blindness. The SDQ-20 correlation is .85 with the DES (Nijenhuis et al., 1996, 1999) and .75 with the MID (Dell, 2006a, 2006b). Also scored on a 5-point Likert scale, it has possible scores from 20 to 100, which are obtained by summing the scores. The cutoff score of greater than 28 indicates the presence of somatoform dissociation, and scores increase with the severity of the dissociative disorder diagnostic category, such that those with DID may have scores over 50 (Nijenhuis, 2009).

The Multidimensional Inventory for Dissociation

The MID, developed by Dell (2006a, 2006b), is a sophisticated, comprehensive, 218-item self-report assessment instrument. With its 23 dissociation scales, the MID provides a multiscale measure of pathological dissociation. The premise of the MID is an important one: Having tested hundreds of patients with dissociative symptoms, Dell (2001) came to understand the intrusions of dissociated self-states into ordinary consciousness as more characteristic of DID than the more dramatic switching that is the primary phenomenon on which the *DSM* criteria are based. He also distinguished between full dissociation, characterized by amnesia, and partial dissociation, which includes such symptoms as flashbacks, hearing voices in the head, passive influence symptoms, and intrusions of dissociated experience. Administration of the MID usually takes about 1 hour. The MID has high correlations with other measures of dissociation: Its correlations are .90 with the DES, .75 with the SDQ-20, and .78 with the SCID-D-R (ISST-D, in press). It is the only measure of the dissociative disorder screening or assessment instruments discussed here that has a validity scale and screens for defensiveness, rare symptoms, attention-seeking behavior, factitious behavior, and neurotic suffering. The test also yields information about the prominence of certain kinds of identities, such as persecutor identities or child identities. I have found this a useful measurement, especially when I needed to provide documentation of a diagnosis on such things as patients' disability applications.

One caution, however, about the use of the MID, as well as any other questionnaire that refers to traumatic experiences, is that in my experience, it can be triggering to fragile patients.

Structured Interviews

Structured Clinical Interview for DSM-IV Dissociative Disorders-Revised

The SCID-D-R, developed by Marlene Steinberg (1994a, 1994b, 1995), is considered the diagnostic gold standard for DID. This is a 277-item interview that assesses five symptoms of dissociation: amnesia, depersonalization, derealization, identity confusion, and identity alteration. The SCID-D-R diagnoses the four *DSM-IV-TR* (APA, 2000) dissociative disorders and DDNOS. It usually takes between 45 minutes to 3 hours to administer. However, proper administration of this scale requires considerable familiarity with dissociative symptoms, and it generally requires specific training in its use.

The Dissociative Disorder Interview Schedule

Another excellent structured interview, the DDIS, was developed by Ross (1997). It has the advantages of easy access and requiring less training, and it takes less time to administer (usually between 30 and 45 minutes) than the SCID-D-R (it can be downloaded at http://www.rossinst.com). It is a 132-item structured interview that also assesses the symptoms of the five *DSM-IV-TR* (APA, 2000) dissociative disorders. In addition, it assesses somatization disorder, borderline personality disorder (BPD), major depressive disorder, and substance abuse. Ross (1997) reported a sensitivity of .95 for the diagnosis of DID using the DDIS.

The Minnesota Multiphasic Personality Inventory 2

Many people ask about the use of the Minnesota Multiphasic Personality Inventory 2 (MMPI-2) in diagnosing dissociation. This, along with other instruments such as the Rorschach (Brand, Lowenstein, Armstrong, & McNary, 2009), can yield useful information when properly understood. Often, patients with DID have elevated F (validity scale, indicating exaggeration of symptoms) and *Sc* (schizophrenia) scales due, in part, to trauma and dissociation-linked questions. Without the advantage of knowledge of dissociative disorders, these scores can indicate a different degree of and type of disturbance than is the case (Brand, Armstrong, & Lowenstein, 2006).

Factitious and Malingered DID

A factitious disorder involves a person's intention to take on a sick role; a malingered disorder, on the other hand, requires motivation by an external goal, such as getting disability payments or staying out of prison. For both of these reasons, there are some people who would like to falsely appear to have DID. I have met several such patients who seemed to have a desperate need for the diagnosis to give them license to behave aggressively, erratically, or selfishly as a way to justify a pathological relationship or as a way to claim entitlement. The diagnosis may also be sought as part of applying for disability, avoiding pending legal charges, or staying out of jail (Coons, 1991; Coons & Milstein, 1994; Draijer & Boon, 1999; Thomas, 2001). Especially if there is an issue of homicide, a false-positive diagnosis can be dangerous (Coons & Milstein, 1994).

While careful psychological testing is a requirement for making any official determination, there are some notable red flags in factious and malingering persons' presentations in the interview. Examples of red flags include (a) the person's open broadcast of the diagnosis (people who have DID tend to try to hide it rather than to flaunt it); (b) continuity of memory, in particular, being able to narrate a chronological life story without gaps; (c) affect tolerance, in particular, being able to express strong negative affect (people with DID are unlikely to move easily in affective range without dissociating; especially in the host presentation, it is unusual for people with DID to display intense anger); (d) telling of abuse without shame (people with DID are ashamed of their abuse and are generally loathe to tell about it); (e) reporting abuse that is inconsistent with medical history; (f) reporting dissociative symptoms but not having PTSD symptoms; (g) bringing "proof" of the diagnosis to the interview; and (h) dramatic and exaggerated presentation of symptoms (Coons, 1991; Coons & Milstein, 1994; Thomas, 2001). (For an especially informative discussion of this topic, see Thomas, 2001.) Although such red flags are helpful, it is important to be aware that given increased Internet information and dissemination of knowledge, people are becoming more and more sophisticated in their ability to dissemble.

The fact that these people are not as highly dissociative as they claim does not mean that they do not have serious emotional problems. For a more comprehensive evaluation of malingered or factitious DID, the use of the measures of dissociation discussed here, as well as measures of malingering and other standard psychological tests, are recommended.

DIFFERENTIAL DIAGNOSIS, MISDIAGNOSIS, AND COMORBIDITY WITH AN EMPHASIS ON PSYCHOSIS, BORDERLINE PERSONALITY DISORDER

As previously noted, the possibility for misdiagnosis works both ways. Other disorders can be misdiagnosed as DID, as well as the reverse. This is in part because dissociative symptoms are found in a number of disorders, for example, PTSD, eating disorders, and even schizophrenia.

Psychosis

Dissociative disorders have historically been conceptualized as, and confused with, schizophrenia (Kluft, 1987a; Moskowitz, 2008; Moskowitz et al., 2009; Putnam, 1989; Ross, 1989, 1997). In 1939, Schneider (1939/1959) described a set of symptoms, including audible thoughts, somatic passivity, "made" feelings, impulses, and behaviors, thought withdrawal, and thought insertion, as pathognomonic of schizophrenia. Kluft (1987a) observed that it is no longer generally accepted that these first-rank symptoms are diagnostic of schizophrenia; they are in fact characteristic of DID. To wit: Although some of these symptoms are often classified by the observing clinicians as psychotic, they may simply be posttraumatic intrusions attesting to an earlier real-life occurrence. What might appear to an outside observer to be psychotically hallucinatory or delusional may in fact be a reliving of an unassimilated aspect of traumatic experience that has an ever-present, vivid, and terrifying reality to the patient when it occurs. Many dissociative patients are subject to terrifying flashbacks, which may be visual, auditory, or somatic. If the patient can hold the tension between the posttraumatic "hallucination" as well as the awareness of present experience—basically maintaining a foot in both worlds simultaneously, with the ability to stay interpersonally connected, despite the terror—would we call this psychotic? Is this psychosis in the eye of the observer, or is it "in" the patient?

Seemingly psychotic symptoms and behaviors often accompany the presentation of highly dissociative patients. One of the reasons stems from the dissociation of memory itself. When a dissociated experience is triggered, the patient may be aware of only body sensations, sounds, sights, or vehement emotions such as terror or rage. If a patient begins writhing on the floor, flailing arms and legs, a dissociative part of the patient, for example, may be reliving the experience of trying to fight off a rapist. Without the wherewithal to make an inquiry about what the experience represents, a clinician may view such a patient as simply psychotic. Often, dissociated experiences do not manifest themselves as one whole experience but are instead revealed as sensory fragments, in accordance with the way they were stored. If the experience was too overwhelming to be processed by the hippocampus, where the experience may be synthesized with its auditory, visual, haptic, and other sensory components (and thus be too overwhelming to become part of narrative memory), only isolated aspects of the experience may intrude into the patient's consciousness. Yet, because the context is unknown, the patient may appear to be psychotic.

Hearing voices is for many clinicians, right away, an indication of psychosis, and the *DSM* specifies this. In fact, a patient who hears voices in conversation meets a criterion for schizophrenia. However, many people with DID hear voices a great deal of the time inside their heads. These are the voices of other parts, who comment on the patient's behavior or want their thoughts to be heard. A differentiation may be made by asking the patient if the voices are heard inside or outside the head. However, many dissociative patients also hear voices outside the head (Moskowitz, 2008). Useful distinctions are as follows:

- The degree to which the messages of the voices are, as a pattern, bizarre. With respect to the Schneiderian symptoms, those indicative of schizophrenia are more bizarre.
- Whether the patient has the ability to think about his or her psychotic thinking. For instance, if someone with the delusion that his or her body is disintegrating or that he or she is dead, unbeknownst to others, can say that he or she knows this is not true but cannot help feeling this way—that is, psychotic thinking in the context of dissociative thinking—does this merit a diagnosis of unqualified psychosis? It may of course be indicative of the need for hospitalization.
- Dissociative patients may have parts who are truly psychotic. When such a part appears, it is important to understand that this is a part, not necessarily a breakdown or regression of the whole person.

A study by Brand, Loewenstein, Armstrong, and McNary (2009) of personality differences between patients with DID, psychosis (PSD), and BPD as shown on the Rorschach found that that patients with DID had both a higher level of traumatic associations and more logical reasoning than did the psychotic patients.

Taken together with the results for BPD, this Brand, Loewenstein, et al. (2009) study found the following:

> Individuals with DID showed greater capacity to be self-reflective, to modulate affect, and to see others as potentially helpful. These abilities may contribute to some individuals with DID being able to more easily develop a working alliance than some patients with BPD and PSD. The patients with DID were able to think relatively clearly compared with the other patients, despite having high levels of traumatic flooding. These personality characteristics may contribute to patients with DID being able to engage in, and benefit from, insight-oriented therapy. (p. 203)

Borderline Personality Disorder

Frank Putnam's (1997) review of studies showed that 30 to 70% of those diagnosed with DID also met criteria for BPD. Sar et al. (2003) found that 64% of subjects with BPD had a dissociative disorder. A nationwide random sample study found that 53% of patients treated for BPD also had diagnoses of a dissociative disorder, 11% of these DID (Zittel Conklin &

Westin, 2005, cited in Brand, Classen, Lanius, et al., 2009). Is this comorbidity, or does it indicate a diagnostic sharing of a common dissociative spectrum (Howell, 2002a; Howell & Blizard, 2009)?

Misdiagnosis and Comorbidity

The issue of comorbidity is a complicated one. If BPD and DID/DDNOS are understood as both existing on the dissociative spectrum, they would not necessarily be comorbid. Or, is this dissociative spectrum concept potentially misleading, obscuring ways that the two disorders are distinguishable (Brand et al., 2009)? In addition, patients with dissociative disorders have often been misdiagnosed as having BPD because the clinician does not know how to make sense of the patient's dissociative symptoms, behavior, and reported experience.

The issue of psychosis just discussed bleeds into that of BPD even though the two are two different diagnostic categories (see Howell, 2008, which addresses dissociation, BPD, and psychosis). BPD was originally conceived of as a kind of "borderland" or a disorder lying on the borderline between neurosis and psychosis. Initially, this made sense in that there were a number of patients who presented as neurotic, but under stress or in situations of intimacy would appear to become psychotic. And, they did not improve in the psychoanalytic therapies that neurotic patients did. Replacing such earlier terms as *pseudoneurotic schizophrenia*, *ambulatory schizophrenia*, and *psychotic character*, the term *borderline personality disorder* became for a while a kind of wastebasket category (Millon, 1981). In time, BPD was understood as both a personality disorder and a separate category (borderline personality organization [BPO]; Kernberg, 1975) in developmental diagnosis. It was characterized by the person's reliance on the defense of splitting, and other lower-level defenses associated with it, such as projective identification, denial, primitive idealization, devaluation, and omnipotence, rather than on repression and its associated higher-level defenses, such as reaction formation, projection, and negation (Kernberg, 1975).

It is not uncommon for patients with DID to be misdiagnosed as having BPD on the basis of their clinicians' misunderstanding of dissociative presentations. For example, a clinician unfamiliar with switching may misunderstand this phenomenon as borderline splitting. Or, when different identity states convey contradictory information and then have amnesia for what the other identity states said, the patient may be thought to be lying. This can appear to be characterological mendacity when it is not. Poor affect regulation characterizes both BPD (Linehan, 1993) and DID (Chefetz, 2000a, 2010). Likewise, disorganized attachment, corresponding to the *unresolved attachment* category in the adult attachment scale, is often understood to precede both BPD and DID (Blizard, 2003; Fonagy, 2000; Liotti, 1999, 2006; Liotti et al., 2008). Finally, the symptoms of

BPD are more and more understood as being trauma based (Allen, 2001; Gunderson & Sabo, 1993a, 1993b; Herman, 1992) and as dissociation based. The last criterion for BPD refers to dissociation directly, and all of the *DSM* criteria can be understood as stemming from underlying dissociation (Howell, 2002a).

An additional problem with the diagnosis of BPD is that so many different presentations and organizations of symptoms can receive the same diagnosis. The terms complex PTSD and DESNOS (disorders of extreme stress not otherwise specified), proposed by Herman (1992), Van der Kolk (1996b), Courtois (1999, 2004), and Courtois, Ford, and Cloitre (2009), include both DID and BPD. A partial remedy to the overlap of BPD and DID diagnoses and the overapplication of BPD is the proposed diagnosis of *relational trauma disorder* (Howell & Blizard, 2009). In contrast to borderline personality, the term *relational trauma disorder* is less pejorative, more accurate, and more experience-near for those who manifest the trauma symptoms consistent with the diagnosis of BPD.

What I suggest (Howell, 2008) is that BPD and DID are both based in dissociation, but often, what we call BPD (preferably *chronic relational disorder*), in contrast to DID, results from a more massive and less intricately compartmentalized avoidance system for terrifying and overwhelming affects, emotions, and memories. Because the splitting is more massive, there is less of the self or ego—what Fairbairn called the *central ego*—available for reflection, resulting in the wild affective swings we often see (see Celani, 2001). In essence, it is sometimes more difficult to treat this particular dissociative pattern than it is to treat DID. Interestingly, the study by Brand, Loewenstein, et al. (2009) of personality differences shown on the Rorschach found that patients with DID had a greater capacity for self-reflection, greater social interest, greater capacity for accurate perception, and more logical thinking than those diagnosed as borderline.

Bipolar Disorder, Obsessive Compulsive Disorder, Eating Disorders, and Substance Abuse Disorders

Another disorder that is often misdiagnosed when the patient has DID is bipolar disorder. DID is not uncommonly misdiagnosed as bipolar disorder. On the other hand, mood changes that are part of bipolar disorder may be misunderstood as dissociative symptoms. Careful diagnostic assessment with a knowledge of dissociative disorders is crucial. Of course, a number of disorders, such as bipolar disorder, as well as eating disorders and substance abuse disorders, are all often comorbid with dissociative disorders as well.

In particular, rapid mood swings in DID patients are often diagnosed as rapid-cycling or Bipolar II. These rapid mood swings may be due to posttraumatic intrusions or a switch of identity. Bipolar disorder has not been found to be more common among patients with DID than in the general population (ISST-D Guidelines, in press). Patients who have complex PTSD, of which DID is one variant, have problems with affect regulation; and chronic depression, as well as mood swings, is likely to be part of the symptom picture. Because of the substantial traumas that could not be assimilated and accompanying enormous emotional pain that could not be alleviated, substance abuse is not an uncommon outcome. Substance abuse may indeed mask the dissociative disorder, until abstinence or control has been achieved or the disorder has otherwise been diagnosed. Those with complex PTSD are also likely to have substantial body image problems, including somatoform dissociation. Eating disorders, including binge eating, bulimia, and anorexia are frequently comorbid with dissociative disorders. Furthermore, it appears that along with body dissatisfaction, the somatic symptoms of dissociation contribute to defects in body-based awareness, as manifested in binge eating (Fuller-Tyszkiewicz & Mussap, 2009). Obsessive-compulsive spectrum disorders have also been linked to dissociative disorders (McNevin & Rivera, 2001; Shusta, 2001). Shusta (2001) has reported on a case in which her patient's obsessive-compulsive symptoms that had been previously resistant to therapy were actually the result of intrusions of an alter; only following the correct diagnosis (DID) was treatment able to resolve these symptoms.

Diagnosing dissociative disorders can be a daunting task. Many clinicians have not been trained to diagnose dissociative disorders and are thus prone to misdiagnosing DID or DDNOS as something else or to misdiagnosing other disorders as DID. When this happens, it is regrettable for the patient is not receiving the correct treatment and may be harmed by incorrect medications and treatments. There are notable points of similarity—and difference—between DID and psychosis and between DID and BPD, as well as other disorders. These should be understood so that a correct diagnosis can be made.

NOTE

1. See Armstrong and Lowenstein (1990); Bernstein and Putnam (1986), Berstein and Putnam (1993); Brand, Armstrong, and Loewenstein (2006); Brand, Armstrong, Loewenstein, and McNary (2009); Brand, Classen, Lanius, Loewenstein, McNary, Pain, and Putnam (2009); Brand, Classen, Zaveri, and McNary (2009); Brand, McNary, Loewenstein, Kolos, and Barr (2006); Boon and Draijer (1993); Courtois (2004); Courtois et al. (2009); Dell (2006a, 2006b, 2009a, 2009c, 2009d); Ellason and Ross (1997); Foote et al. (2006); Foote and Park (2008); Loewenstein (1991); Nijenhuis (1999); Nijenhuis, Spinhoven, Van Dyck, Van der Hart, and Vanderlinden (1996, 1997); Putnam (1989, 1991, 1997); Ross (1997, 2007); Ross, Heber, et al. (1989); Ross and Keyes (2004); Ross et al. (1992); Steinberg (1994a, 1994b, 1995); Thomas (2001); and Waller and Ross (1997).

Chapter 9

Phase-Oriented Treatment

> The core experiences of trauma are disempowerment and disconnection
> from others. Recovery, therefore, is based on the empowerment of the
> survivor and the creation of new connections.
>
> Herman (1992, p. 133)

The phase-oriented treatment model requires that careful stabilization
and ego building precede any work with traumatic memories. Originally
formulated by Pierre Janet (1919/1976) in the early 1900s, phase-oriented
treatment has become increasingly advocated by clinicians in the field of
dissociative disorders. It is now considered the standard of care in the
treatment of complex posttraumatic stress disorder (PTSD) and dissociative disorders (Brand, 2001; Chu, 1998; International Society for the Study
of Trauma and Dissociation [ISST-D], in press; Steele, Van der Hart, &
Nijenhuis, 2005).

The phase-oriented model is especially important because of the dangers
of opening up traumatic memories before a patient is ready. Exposure to
dissociated memories and affects that is too rapid or poorly handled can be
retraumatizing. For example, following the successful use of exposure techniques with traumatized Vietnam veterans in the 1980s and 1990s, some
trauma therapists used the same treatment models with patients with complex PTSD and dissociative disorders. Too often, the unfortunate result was
that, rather than being helped, many of these patients were retraumatized or
required hospitalization. Unlike the Vietnam veterans who had suffered their
trauma as adults and were more likely to have an underlying solid and fairly
integrated personality structure, those traumatized in childhood may not be
able to endure the destabilizing effect of reencounters with dissociated traumatic memories in the initial phase of treatment. As Chu (1998) explained:

> The pervasive myth that aggressive abreactive work will lead to rapid
> improvement in most patients has its origin in treatment models devel-
> oped for combat-related posttraumatic stress disorder (PTSD) (Foa,
> Steketee, & Rothbaum, 1989; Keane, Fairbank, Caddel, & Zinering,

1989). These models emphasize flooding patients with stimuli that trigger reexperiences of the traumatic events that are then abreacted in the context of highly interpersonal support. The applicability of these techniques early in the treatment of those patients with severe childhood traumatization and complex posttraumatic and dissociative disorders is limited. (pp. 76–77)

Janet's (1919, 1925) early model of phase-oriented treatment outlined three basic stages: (a) stabilization and symptom reduction, (b) treatment of traumatic memories, and (c) personality integration and rehabilitation (Van der Hart et al., 2006). Following Janet, writers such as Putnam (1989) and Herman (1992) have modified some specific emphases and language but have retained the three basic stages. I find Herman's articulation of the stages of recovery especially useful:

- establishing safety
- remembrance and mourning
- reconnection with ordinary life

Subsequently, over the past decade or so, a number of writers in the field, including Chu (1998); Courtois (1999, 2004); Courtois and Ford (2009); Kluft (1999a); Steele et al. (2005); Van der Hart, Van der Kolk, and Boon (1998); Van der Hart et al. (2006); and others, have further elaborated on the use of these phases in the treatment of chronically traumatized people, some with expanded phases and different emphases but with basically the same format. The ISST-D guidelines (in press) also outlines three phases:

- establishing safety, stabilization, and symptom reduction
- working directly and in depth with traumatic memories
- promoting identity integration and rehabilitation

I also adhere to these three phases in this chapter. However, I believe, along with Herman (1992), that Phase 2, working with traumatic memories, implicitly requires much mourning.

The phases of treatment are a basic model, not a rigid timetable. Although theoretically described in a linear way as proceeding from one phase to the next, in practice there is always a backward-and-forward progression, as is the case in standard psychodynamic psychotherapy. Some have compared this back-and-forth movement stabilization and trauma processing to an upward moving spiral that continually revisits old issues but with increasing levels of complexity (Courtois, 1999; Steele et al., 2005; Wheeler, 2007). Safety issues, which are characteristic of the first phase, are likely to come up from time to time in the second or even third phase. In addition, flashbacks, disturbing memories, or abreactions may well erupt in the first phase

(Chefetz, 1997a), but here the task is to help the patient contain and modulate the intensity of the affect rather than to explore the memories (ISST-D, in press). The pace and intensity of the treatment must be in tune with the patient's current vulnerabilities and resilience. With patients with dissociative identity disorder (DID), it is important to remember that different self-states are likely to be in different phases of the treatment simultaneously. Some, such as more apparently adaptive parts, may appear to be moving toward Phase 3, while other parts may still be in Phase 1 and in need of stabilization. It is hard to know the extent to which reports of oscillating stages represent this kind of isolated and staggered self-state growth.

Kluft (1994a) has distinguished between high-functioning, middle-functioning, and low-functioning DID patients. There are some patients who have been so damaged and who have so few resources with respect to social support, mobility, financial resources, and intelligence as well as a paucity of early positive experiences to draw on that moving to the second phase of treatment is not realistic or helpful. These patients will continue to need primarily supportive work to help them to manage their lives. Although this may seem sad, these patients benefit enormously from this support because it enables their lives to be more stable. Also, sometimes after years of what looks like a low-level treatment, a person may graduate, so to speak, and begin to do trauma work, with the accompanying gains in life satisfaction.

PHASE 1: ESTABLISHING SAFETY

The focus of the first phase is the establishment of safety, stabilization, and reduction of symptoms. Before I begin this section, I want to insert the proviso that much of what follows is an ideal. A good number of patients with DID enter treatment by hitting the ground running. They do not necessarily know or tell you that they have DID. They do not necessarily want to—or are able to—deal with their trauma slowly. They may enter with florid PTSD. Once they discover that they have parts, they may want to get to know them all at once. Or, a traumatic transference may begin right off the bat. Therefore, the clinician's job in this initial phase is usually no paint-by-the-numbers affair. We do our best to contain, explain, and promote as much trust as possible.

Kluft (1993b) noted that his research indicates that "those patients who accept and endorse the approaches that are designed to slow and pace the treatment make more rapid progress and have many fewer crises than those who do not; i.e., 'the slower you go, the faster you get there'" (p. 146). Chu (1998) has proposed the mnemonic SAFER (self-care and symptom control, acknowledgment, functioning, expression, and relationships) as a summary of the Stage 1 tasks. More specifically, this means that responsibility of self-care and symptom control, acknowledgment of the reality of the abuse and the fact that it was not the patient's fault, continued functioning in the context of treatment, support for the expression of feelings, and the establishment of models of relationships that are collaborative and mutual are all emphasized.

People with complex PTSD and DID have developed their dissociative structure for good reasons. Many, such as Janice, Dennis, and Margaret, who were introduced in Chapter 1, have been severely and chronically traumatized in childhood. Often, the self-view of people with complex PTSD and DID is suffused with shame and a conviction of defectiveness. As a result of early abuse or severe neglect, they have considerable difficulties with affect regulation, self-soothing, and trust. Because the external world was often dangerous and frightening in the past, they (or many parts of them) expect the present to be dangerous as well. Because their internal world often reenacts the earlier external one, it is likely that they may have been or are currently enmeshed in abusive or violent relationships. They often lack effective skills to help themselves confront and deal with their problems. As Forgash and Knipe (2008) commented, "Many of our clients describe trying to function in adult life without the blueprints" (p. 36).

To help with their chronic terror, sense of deficiency, and poor affect regulation, people with complex PTSD and DID have often developed eating disorders, substance abuse, sex addictions, or severe masochistic problems, manifesting as self-punishment or in harmful relationships (Howell, 1996). In the latter case, they may have flown into the arms of someone from whom they sought love and protection only to come under the influence of an abusive relationship. These solutions only work in the very short term; in the long term, they decrease a person's ability to negotiate life's problems. As a result, the person is left with not only the original problems unsolved but also additional ones.

The intense distress of all of these situations coupled with poor affect management may lead to frequent dangerous and self-destructive behaviors, such as unsafe sex, reckless driving, and medical self-neglect, as well as self-mutilation and suicidality. In addition to self-mutilation, for which Brand (2001) cited an incidence of 34 to 48% for DID, there is the danger of suicidality, which has an incidence of 61 to 72% for attempted suicide; in addition, 1 to 2.1% of patients with DID have completed suicide.

Brand (2001) identified five reasons that severe trauma survivors are especially likely to be self-destructive:

> *First*, ambivalence about self-care is to be expected in patients who came to believe they were worthless due to chronic childhood abuse and who have no concept of self-care, much less methods for healthfully caring for themselves (Herman, 1992; Chu, 1998). *Second*, there is frequently an element of reenacting abuse dynamics through self-destructiveness. These reenactments may feel "normal" to the client

because they mirror their early experiences. *Third*, the self-destructive behaviors may have developed because the person had no support group, no words, or other holding environment in which to express distress. Self-destructiveness may be a primary form of communication for those who do not yet have ways to tame their excruciating inner conflicts and feelings and who cannot yet turn to others for support (Chu, 1998). *Fourth*, there may be a physiological basis associated with early abuse and poor attachment which contributes to acting on affect rather than verbalizing it (Van der Kolk et al., 1991; Van der Kolk, 1996). *Fifth*, the process of therapy may challenge defenses that have served to distract the traumatized patient from painful feelings and memories. The weakening of outmoded defenses can result in an increase in attention to exceptionally painful childhood experiences. Thus, some patients become self-destructive when they attempt to process memories of trauma, especially if the timing of trauma work is not carefully planned (Courtois, 1999). (p. 138, emphasis added)

I would like to elaborate on Brand's (2001) second reason as it pertains specifically to DID. Persecutor or abuser parts often torture or punish other parts for various things, such as telling about the abuse, which the abuser had required kept secret, or for other activities that were forbidden during childhood. For example, one of my patients, Rosemary, has on several occasions been punished by an internal persecutor with self-injury for telling me of her abuse. Similarly, Anna was forbidden to eat by an internal persecutor as punishment for eating good food in her current home. This was in accordance with the fact that her abusers forbade her to eat anything other than peanut butter sandwiches when she was growing up and brutally beat her if they caught her doing so.

The Development of Trust and Establishment of the Treatment Alliance

One of the most important tasks of the first phase is the establishment of trust—something not to be taken for granted with chronically traumatized people. Kluft (1993b) noted that genuine trust in early treatment is rare, and that the early appearance of trust in DID

> is usually a leap of faith, a wish, an enactment of a fantasy, an expression of hope, or telling a potential aggressor, the therapist, what the patient thinks he or she want to hear.... A more operational definition of what appears to be early trust is enough hope, curiosity, or desperation to return for the next session. (p. 149)

It is especially true of traumatized patients that trust cannot be taken for granted and must be earned. Persons with DID have often had the experience of their boundaries being violated early in life, situations in which they have been powerless before someone else's demands or desires. Chu (1998) described this as chronic disempowerment. At least some of the patient's dissociated identities expect to be violated again. Not only do parts of the patient expect to be violated again, but also violations may not be viewed as unacceptable, and the very topic of boundary violation is often unexamined in the patient's mind. Therefore, the establishment of proper boundaries at the outset and throughout the treatment is of utmost importance. Such things as beginning and ending on time, returning phone calls in a timely manner, announcing vacations and absences with adequate warning, and a clear cancellation policy are all reassuring. Looseness of these technical boundaries may be interpreted as a sign of potential boundary crossings or violations from the patient's perspective. It is also important for the therapist to protect his or her boundaries, including the setting of appropriate limits. This also reassures the patient that she will not be able to easily harm the therapist. It is also good modeling for the patient. As in any psychotherapy, the therapist must be trustworthy. People who have been betrayed throughout their lives are sensitive to issues of honesty and dishonesty. Thus, with chronically traumatized patients, Ben Franklin's aphorism, "Honesty is the best policy" (i.e., it is better not to lie to the patient), is generally appropriate. The importance of admitting a mistake is crucial—even if it hurts the therapist's self-esteem to admit a mistake or a failing.

Complex and difficult-to-manage transference and countertransference patterns constantly emerge (Davies & Frawley, 1994; Loewenstein, 1993; Pearlman & Saakvitne, 1995). Traumatic transferences, in which the patient experiences the therapist as the abuser, are common (Herman, 1992; Loewenstein, 1993; Spiegel, 1986). It is important to be aware that traumatic transferences may be hidden. While the therapist may be in overt communication with a trusting host (the part who is usually in executive control), who is trusting, beneath the surface some parts of the person who have not made themselves known expect to be betrayed and abused. For example, in the case of a recent new patient, following a pleasant and reassuring discussion with the part usually in executive control, suddenly a child alter emerged and asked if I intended to abuse her. The result was that we then talked about her fears. It turned out that she, like many chronically traumatized patients, had in the past been abused by one of her therapists. (See Kluft, 1990, for a description of the "sitting duck syndrome.")

It is often useful to ally with the patient's distrust. As Kluft (1993b) said:

> Rather than confront, explain, or reassure in response to the patient's mistrust, I encourage my patients to value mistrust as an important warning sign. I indicate that since the patient has been hurt quite deeply,

the development of apprehension, suspicion, and misgiving are natural and essential protections against further traumatization. (p. 149)

The language one uses is important; for instance, using words like "parts," or "different ways of being you," instead of "alters" is helpful. Chefetz's (2005a) felicitous phrase, "different ways of being you" (p. 661), is both nonchallenging and inviting. It is also an integrative metaphor that allows for the individuality of parts in the context of the whole person.

The Establishment of the Treatment Alliance With Multiple Different Dissociated Self-States

An important aspect of the development of trust in Phase 1 work is the establishment of the treatment alliance, which when working with DID can be quite complicated. One should be prepared for such events as a new patient telling you one day about horrifying parental abuse, only to tell you in the following session or sessions that her parents were wonderful, and she was a very bad child. This then becomes an opportunity for the therapist to explore whether "different parts of you may feel differently about that."

It is ideal to establish an alliance with as many parts as possible in the beginning stages of treatment. However, one must also be sensitive to the strong possibility that the diagnosis has not yet been accepted. Therefore, the therapist should be careful not to put pressure on dissociative parts who are not ready to come forward. Speaking to dissociative parts should be done in a way that does not feel over-exposing or shaming to the patient. One way of doing this, unless otherwise indicated, is to address comments to the system as a whole. This avoids putting any particular part on the spot and may soften the patients' reluctance to expose their multiplicity.

Safety Agreements

Because patients with complex PTSD and dissociative disorders are especially vulnerable to suicidality and dangerous behaviors, safety agreements are helpful for maintaining safety in DID trauma treatment. Often, safety agreements will include a series of constructive alternatives to self-harm to be taken if the patient begins to feel endangered. The agreement may spell out a hierarchy of actions, such as reaching out to supportive others, various forms of self-soothing such as relaxing activities, relaxation exercises, or exercise itself—all of which are to be implemented before calling the therapist or going to the emergency room. This supports patient self-responsibility and avoids putting the therapist in the position of rescuer (Courtois, 1999). Safety agreements also usually include calling the therapist and being in voice contact with the therapist before any action is taken. The topic of safety agreements is discussed in more detail in Chapter 14.

Psychoeducation

Psychoeducation contributes to the development of the treatment alliance, but it is often useful throughout the treatment. For starters, the patient needs to be informed about how treatment is expected to progress, including that treatment is likely to bring about emotional pain in its course, and that the patient and parts of the patient may become intensely angry or disappointed with the therapist at some points in the work. Psychoeducation may include information regarding what trauma is and how it has an impact on the personality, how dissociation works, and why the person has developed dissociative problems. Patients with complex trauma may at times develop extreme reactions to something the therapist has said or not said, done or not done. It is often wise to anticipate this in advance, and perhaps to note this anticipation in initial communications with the patient. For example, one may say something like, "It is likely in our work together, there will be a time or times when you will feel angry with me, disappointed with me, or that I have failed you. We should expect this and not be surprised if and when it happens, which it probably will." It is also vital to emphasize to the patient that despite the diagnosis and experience of dividedness, the whole person is responsible and will be held responsible for the acts of any part.

Other aspects of psychoeducation include relaxation and breathing techniques, grounding techniques, and methods of self-soothing. Breathing exercises often facilitate a mood of calm and focus. Because unmodified instructions to do deep breathing can induce hyperventilation, I prefer breathing exercises that require mental focus and discipline as the person performs and notes inhalations and exhalations. One exercise that I like is taking a breath in to the count of 4, holding for 4 counts, breathing out for 6, holding for 2, and repeating a number of times. Often, patients may indicate that just breathing makes them feel silly, and they doubt it will do any good. In such cases, I may volunteer to do the breathing with them or just ask them to try it. In one case, I invited a new patient, who had had multiple hospitalizations and was currently on many medications, to try a simple breathing technique. Initially, she pooh-poohed it, saying, "I am someone who has taken very heavy medication. A breathing technique will not touch the problems I have." To my great pleasure and surprise, the next day she called and left a message for me, saying that she was amazed that the breathing techniques worked, and she felt much less anxious. Conscious breathing is also grounding as it creates contact with the body and the senses. In addition, the buildup of carbon dioxide in the bloodstream, along with inadequate oxygen that occurs with shallow breathing, potentiates anxiety, which is relieved by the deeper breathing.

Because chronically traumatized patients may lose touch with their surroundings when anxiety is evoked, methods of grounding are helpful. In addition to breathing, these may include turning on the lights, stamping one's feet, touching one's face, or intently looking around the room to mentally describe the objects in it. Steven Gold's book, *Not Trauma Alone: Therapy for Child Abuse Survivors in Family and Social Context* (2000), is an excellent resource, as is Chu's *Rebuilding Shattered Lives: The Responsible Treatment of Complex Posttraumatic and Dissociative Disorders* (1998). In addition, see Boon, Steele, and Van der Hart's *Coping With Trauma-Related Dissociation: Skills Training for Clients and Therapists* (2011).

Getting to Know Alters and Working to Improve Internal Communication

Another important aspect of the initial phase is getting to know the dissociative parts of the person and their internal structuring (i.e., their relationships and interactions with each other on the inside). However, this should be done without undue anamnesis. As Kluft (2000) stated: "It is neither necessary nor advisable to bring all parts into co-consciousness all the time early in treatment. There is considerable virtue in allowing permissive amnesia for traumatic material until given personalities are able to tolerate the material under discussion" (p. 272). This is not always easy to do. For example, early in treatment, Janice, introduced in Chapter 1, began to become acquainted with some of her parts. Despite the fact that some of this information had emerged in her hospitalization, she was amazed at the result of our work with her parts in therapy and became enthusiastic, especially as her seemingly always known phrase for herself, "the We of Me," now made sense. However, as more parts emerged, they shared their intense sadness and grief with Janice. Since she had built so much of her public, as well as her subjective, life around being cheerful, we had to quickly slow this process of meeting new parts as the experience was becoming upsetting and almost overwhelming to her.

Other ways of becoming acquainted with the parts in the initial phase are mapping of the system and journaling, by which parts make entries that are then available to other parts to read. Mapping is discussed in greater detail in Chapter 10.

PHASE 2: WORKING WITH TRAUMATIC MEMORIES AND ENABLING TRAUMATIC MEMORIES TO BECOME NARRATIVE MEMORIES

The second phase of treatment involves working directly and in depth with traumatic memories (ISST-D, in press). Herman (1992) stressed how trauma deprives the survivor of a sense of control over her life and of connectedness with others: "Recovery, therefore, is based on the empowerment of the survivor and the creation of new connections" (p. 133). The purpose of Phase 2 memory work in mitigating the trauma, then, is to bring more control over one's life and increased connection with other parts of the self and other people. This is best accomplished by reducing dissociative barriers between parts so that traumatic memory may become continuous narrative memory. As the traumatic memories become more resolved and integrated, they are less likely to derail the person via sudden intrusions or switching.

Contraindications to initiating this second phase of trauma work include severe limitations of the patient's capacity for reflection and self-control, pervasive psychosis, malignant regression, extremely unstable lifestyle, ongoing abuse, and uncontrollable rapid switching (Van der Hart et al., 2006). For those patients who have the skills and the resilience to tolerate work on memories, an important proviso remains that it is retraumatizing, rather than helpful, to the patient simply to relive a traumatic memory. Any reexperiencing is best done in a protective context that links the past terrors with current safety and that therefore indicates the past horrors are, in reality, over. The patient's communication must be in the context of safety and acceptance: The other listening person is a secure base and a safe place. In this way, safety is connected with the traumatic event.

This section has three parts: specific ways of working with traumatic memories; reconceptualizing abreaction; and understanding the central conflict. While they are interrelated, I deal with them separately.

Approaches to Working With Traumatic Memories

Phase 2 work involves working with traumatic memories. How this work is understood depends on one's theoretical model. Core aspects of this work have been described in different terms, ranging from "abreaction," to "guided synthesis," and "realization of traumatic memories" (Van der Hart et al., 2006, p. 322). Kluft (1993a), Fine (1993), and others emphasize abreaction. Herman (1992) emphasizes remembrance and mourning. Van der Hart et al. (2006) emphasizes synthesis and calls this phase "overcoming the phobia of traumatic memories" (p. 319).

Although traumatic memories will emerge spontaneously in the treatment as a result of organic forces within the system, work with these memories is often carefully planned by the therapist in collaboration with the patient. The purpose of planned work with traumatic memories is to avoid uncontrolled eruptions of triggered affect and behavior that may be damaging and unnecessarily painful to the patient. However, it is important to be aware that we cannot always plan for work on traumatic memories in an ordered and systematic way, for intense affect will emerge spontaneously. As Chefetz (1997a) maintained: "The abreaction of intense affect is not a goal of psychotherapy; it is an inevitable concomitant experience in the history of persons with posttraumatic histories, physical and/or sexual abuse, neglect, and related intense experiences" (p. 209). The primary issue is that the therapist know how to handle it when it does emerge or erupt (Chefetz, 1997a).

Planned approaches that reduce the dangers of triggered affect from becoming overwhelming often involve working with memories in a systematic fashion, explicitly implementing certain titration strategies to keep the affect about the memories manageable (Fine, 1993; Kluft, 1994, 1998, 1999b; Putnam, 1989; Ross, 1989; Van der Hart et al., 2006). This may include use of fractionated abreactions (Fine, 1993), which involves deliberately dividing the memories into sections so that only pieces of the entire memory are experienced at one time as a way of protecting the patient from becoming overwhelmed.

In addition to fractionating techniques, muting techniques are useful for a therapist to know as a way to help with the patient's frightening memories that emerge. Muting techniques include such things as suggesting to the patient that she imagine she has a remote and is watching the memories on a television screen. With the remote, he can turn the sound down, slow the action, drain the picture of brightness, or make the images smaller so that they seem farther away; and he can also turn the television off. Although the image of the remote is visual, the same concept can be applied to a virtual affect dial or rheostat, perhaps with a dimmer switch. The patient may use this to lower or even turn off affect that is too intense. Sometimes, therapists will ask the patient to imagine a picture in a picture, or split screen, in which a frightening memory is playing on one screen while on another screen is a calming scene (Twombly, 2000). The calming screen can be a resource when the frightening memories feel too painful to bear in their full intensity. These help to give the patient a sense of control. Incompletely processed disturbing memories and feelings that were worked on in the session may be left in a virtual locked vault in the office until the next session (Kluft, 1989). These metaphors are generally compelling to patients with DID because of the pervasiveness of the trance logic. Finally, in addition to the above, to decrease the danger of retraumatization as well as fear of it, it may be suggested to the patient that intense traumatic affect may be shared across dissociative boundaries slowly over time (Kluft, 1989). For example, one of Kluft's metaphors is "the slow leak" (1988).

The Relational Perspective: Reconceptualizing Abreaction

Abreaction is both a pivotal and a highly controversial concept with respect to Phase 2 work. As indicated at the beginning of this chapter, phase-oriented treatment is so important because patients with complex trauma and dissociative disorders are highly vulnerable to triggering and to spontaneous abreactions, which may carry a risk of retraumatization. Furthermore, as indicated, in some of the mental health literature from early psychoanalysis to new age therapy, including primal scream therapy literature (Janov, 1970/1999), there has been much emphasis on the expected healing benefits of abreactions. The idea behind abreaction is that emotional discharge of affects connected with traumatic memories is healing. But, is it so? Or, if it is so, how do we understand it? What does abreaction mean, anyway?

In their well-known and relied-on dictionary of psychoanalytic terms, Laplanche and Pontalis (1973) defined abreaction as follows:

> An emotional discharge whereby the subject liberates himself from the affect attached to the memory of a traumatic event in such way that this affect is not able to become (or to remain) pathogenic. Abreaction may be provoked in the course of psychotherapy, especially under hypnosis, and produce a cathartic effect. It may also come about spontaneously, either a short or a long interval after the original trauma. (p. 1)

The terms *abreaction* and *catharsis* have often been used interchangeably. They are distinguished only in that abreaction refers to mental reliving, whereas catharsis refers to bodily physical expression (Cameron & Rychlak, 1985). My primary disagreement with the definition provided by Laplanche and Pontalis (1973) has to do the idea of discharge, which derives from a one-person psychology as well as from quasi-neurological (Van der Hart & Brown, 1992) 19th-century models of psychics and neurology. Importantly, these models of mind do not encompass a two-person psychology or a multiple-self perspective.

This idea of discharge or release, with all of the ambiguities in language and conceptual interpretation, is a source of confusion that continues to plague us. Understandably, patients and therapists may often endorse the wish to "get it all out," as if that will simply make the problematic feelings go away. Understandably, the dissociative parts who hold these terrible memories are shunned by the rest of the system because they are protecting the rest of the system from memories that have been unbearable. Thus, the part who is usually in executive control, and other parts who have been shielded from these affects and memories, may often wish they would just go away. But then, one might ask, where would those affects go? It is an illusion to think that these affects are actually disposed of. To the contrary, they can only be redissociated. The therapeutic goal is for the affects and memories to be shared across dissociative barriers, so that, in this way, they become narrative memories—that is, memories that are accepted markers of past experience, that are recalled as part of a continuous narrative, and that can be tolerated and mourned. If the affects were simply gotten rid of, the memories could not be mourned, which is a core part of healing.

In contrast to older, solely cathartic concepts of abreaction, I suggest that it is not the discharge of tension, the getting it out, that is helpful, but the communication of emotion and memory to another person (i.e., a two-person psychology)—and other parts of the self—that is healing. In the most literal sense, tension refers to bodily tension. The body tension relief aspect of abreaction is not unimportant, but it is intertwined with the emotional, including intrapersonal and interpersonal, meaning of the situation and occurs in large measure as a result of these.

As opposed to the idea that one unified person just gets rid of all the bad stuff, I propose that the therapeutic action of abreaction derives from the trusting and sharing of affect and knowledge among parts of the self and with another person. Here, the therapist's compassion and sensitivity to the patient's pain serves as a model for the kind of response that alters can learn to give to each other. Even without specific reference to DID, I find that this multiple-self perspective is the most promising for trauma work. A two-person psychology applies not only to the genesis of intrapsychic difficulties but also to their resolution. A multiple-self perspective is compatible with the idea that, in a general sense, integration, or synthesis, is a goal in the healing of trauma, as in psychotherapy in general.[1]

Chefetz (1997) observed that affect is the centerpiece of experience. By this, he meant that affect is the most potent contextualizer of experience, and that without knowing the emotional dimension of experience, personal narrative may remain incoherent or bereft of meaning. The sharing of dissociated affect between parts of the self and between persons may feel like a release or discharge because it is no longer being kept locked down and hidden from the part usually in executive control, from some other parts of the self, and from other people. However, in my view, it is more properly understood as a kind of sharing that is intersystemic and interpersonal. The expressed affect does not go anywhere but becomes part of a person's accepted and conscious repertoire of experience. The formerly unbearable affect is now tolerable as an aspect of narrative memory. Chefetz (1997) provided a more precise definition of abreaction: "the verbal or non-verbal expression of intense affect, which when associated with a coherent narrative of experience, may provide relief of chronic anxiety states" (p. 203).

Abreactive experiences can be powerful and healing. The therapist should bear in mind that intense affect may be expressed, and unusual behavior may be enacted. People may scrunch their bodies, flail about, roll into a ball, roll on the floor, and so on. The healing effect of abreactions derives from strangulated affects (Breuer & Freud, 1893–1895a) becoming expressible and from previously untellable experiences being brought to the light of day in the context of an interpersonal environment that allows these to feel real. In all phases, but especially in Phase 2, the affective communication is often intense in abreactions, and it may be painful for the therapist to hear and witness.

The Central Conflict: Silencing Versus the Eagerness to Be Known

When working with traumatic memories, it is useful to bear in mind what I call the central conflict. An advantage for using the concept of the central conflict for doing memory work is that it is not mired in a one-person psychology. A key problem with solely cathartic techniques (i.e., "getting it out") is that they do not take into account the complexities of the intrapersonal and the interpersonal systems.

As the integrative work of sharing painful memories and affect across more parts of the system occurs, a central conflict often emerges: The parts who hold the unbearable painful affect are often desperate to share and express their pain and to be known. And, they want to do it now. Other parts are equally desperate to keep them silent. This means that some parts feel that they cannot wait. Moreover, not having formulated that this is how they feel, they cannot easily examine their impulses to make everyone, including the part usually in executive control, other parts of the system, and the therapist, acquainted with it immediately. This may occur in the form of flashbacks, terrifying emotions, and the like. At the same time, other parts, also not having had a chance to formulate their feelings and thoughts, impulsively say, "Never!" The gradual resolution of this conflict enables mourning for the recognition of terrible traumatization as well as mourning for the losses of previously needed psychic illusions. (I must note that this model of the central conflict is oversimplified. For example, parts holding painful memories often feel that it is their job to contain them.)

It is important to be alert and to become informed regarding what knowledge may be too much for the usually presenting part or other dissociative parts to handle. Often, dissociative parts will tell me spontaneously if they think the usually presenting part can or cannot handle certain knowledge. Out of respect to the likelihood that they may be correct as well as out of safety concerns that might arise from a part feeling betrayed, I will often ask a dissociative part who has shared information with me if it is all right if I share this with the usually presenting part. However, such matters should always be handled judiciously. Safety concerns can work both ways. Sometimes, the usually presenting part needs to know of imminent threats and unresolved difficulties that may have been communicated by another part who does not want the usually presenting part to know about them (Van der Hart et al., 2006). In such a case, one may request that the dissociative part share the information with the usually presenting part of the person. It is important for the clinician to strive to avoid becoming part of a reenactment of a neglectful, unseeing parent who stands idly by (Davies & Frawley, 1994) and allows the child to be harmed. Such issues can be complicated. For example, there may be sexual reenactments by adolescent parts who want to keep these behaviors hidden from adult parts in the system. In the interests of general safety, the part who is usually in executive control must know. However, such information may need to be sequestered from some child parts. Thus, negotiating this conflict about sharing information and affect, in which, in simplified form, some parts are desperate to share and express their pain while others are equally desperate to keep them silent, requires careful clinical judgment.

Emotional safety is a pertinent matter: The parts need to feel safe enough to share, knowing that their concerns about other parts knowing are respected. However, it is not always easy for the therapist to keep so much in mind. On one occasion, a tough, protective female part, who always clenched her fists, had told me about the patient's brutal abuse by an uncle when she was a little girl. The host did not know about this abuse, and this part had told me the host did not and should not know yet. Shortly thereafter, I was speaking to an adolescent part who had some coconsciousness with the host and forgot myself, making reference to the abuse. Suddenly, the tough, protective female part who had originally informed me of the abuse appeared before me, fists clenched and clearly annoyed with me for exposing the adolescent to information prematurely. The switch happened so suddenly that the adolescent part did not hear what I had said.

In the approach, I describe, the traumatic memories and affects are revealed and shared in dialogue between separate dissociative identities and the therapist—and among each other. This involves not only a two-person psychology but also a multiple self or multipart dissociative psychology. It includes collaborating with the system to work on memories in an organic way. This is further complicated and aided by the multiple self-states of the therapist. As Bromberg (1998) noted: "Therapeutic action depends on the freedom of the analyst to make optimal use of dissociation as an interpersonal process that includes the analyst's dissociative experience as well as the patient's" (p. 288).

Often, dissociative parts will let me know, sometimes in oblique ways, when the patient is ready. In the work that Janice and I have done together, there was a time that the parts had alluded to some extremely horrifying, demeaning, and sadistic abuse the patient had suffered as a child at the hands of some boys, in what she referred to as the Torture Room. They also alluded to a mute, ugly little girl called The Little Girl in the Torn Dirty Slip, who had been locked up and was not allowed to speak. When I asked why she was forbidden to speak, I was told that it was because the knowledge of her story would be too much for the part who is usually in executive control to handle. These allusions had gone on for a long time, and I kept getting reports that The Little Girl in the Torn Dirty Slip would not be allowed to come out, despite my requests and statements of concern for her: She was "locked up" and forbidden to speak. As the sessions progressed, however, it became clear that parts who were out in the session were telling a hidden part to "shut up." The following is part of a session in which this previously off-limits aspect of her unspoken memories begins to be revealed; here, one of the dissociative parts (DP), rather than the part who is usually in executive control, is speaking:

DP: [*Turning her head to the right as if speaking to someone.*] Shut up!

ME: Why are you telling someone to shut up? Who are you telling to shut up?

DP: The Little Girl in the Dirty Slip. She is supposed to be locked up.

ME: What does she want?

DP: She wants to come out and tell you all about it. But if she knows what's good for her, she'll stay where she is and keep her mouth shut. Nobody else wants to know about her pain.

ME: Why does she need to keep her mouth shut and stay put?

DP: Because that's where she belongs, and it is our job to keep her there. There are others, the soldiers. I don't know what they'll do if we let her out.

ME: How do you feel about keeping her locked up?

DP: Actually, I feel sorry for her. She's not a bad kid. Sometimes she cries, and I wish I could help her, but it is my job to keep her where she is.

ME: So you actually have sympathy for her?

DP: Yeah, I gotta go now.

ME: [*It was time to stop this conversation because the session will soon come to an end.*] I just want to say before we stop that I am thinking about how The Little Girl in the Torn Dirty Slip feels, even though she can't talk, and I will be thinking about her. I am aware of her pain and how awful this is for her.

In a later session, The Little Girl in the Torn Dirty Slip did come out and speak to me. She told me a horrifying story. This story also enabled us to locate the traumatic events in time and place, and it gave us more information about what was going on and not going on with the parents that this was allowed to happen. The part usually in executive control was informed and became coconscious about the event. Nobody crumbled. But, the system had time to get used to the idea that this part wanted and needed to share her story. The alters whose job it was to keep her locked up had some time to think about whether this was really necessary and whether it was what they really wanted.

This vignette illustrates a way of working with the central conflict and of achieving a successful integration of memories.

PHASE 3: RECONNECTION WITH EVERYDAY LIFE: IDENTITY INTEGRATION AND MOURNING

As Van der Hart et al. (2006) noted: "There is ... the persistent myth that merely integrating traumatic experiences is sufficient for overcoming traumatization. In fact, Phase 3 may contain some of the most difficult work yet" (p. 337). In addition, third-phase work may reopen second- and first-phase issues. As a result, vigilance for suicidality should be maintained, even in Phase 3.

The third phase of treatment resembles in many ways work with less-traumatized and less-dissociative persons. This makes sense because by the third phase, the patient has gotten better and is less dissociative and less prone to react to triggers of past trauma. However, there are important differences. Because the dissociative personality organization has entailed avoidance of many life issues, the healing of dissociation can leave the patient with many previously unconfronted but daunting issues. As patients shift their focus from their traumatic pasts to their current lives, many core beliefs emerge and need to be reexamined. These may include such things as continuing to feel and believe that one is worthless, continuing to believe that comfortable intimacy is not possible, facing existing unhappy relationships and work problems, as well as learning some of the "blueprints" for adult life for the first time. Perhaps even more painfully, these core issues also include facing the narcissistic personality structure that is often the residue of the dissociative personality structure (Howell, 2003; Schwartz, 1994, 2000). As Kluft has frequently said, following work on the problems posed by DID, patients increasingly must deal with the everyday problems of "unitary personality disorder."

Conflicts about getting better are also likely to surface in the third phase of work. These conflicts may include fears of becoming independent and losing the therapist or having to become completely self-reliant (Van der Hart et al., 2006).

The profound mourning that comes with assimilating painful memories in Phase 2 continues in Phase 3, but with more finality. The quality of grief work continues to mature. Rage about the recognition that life is not fair and that one has suffered many extreme injustices may eventually become mature acceptance. Gradually, patients begin to relinquish the role of the victim. Chu (1998) recounted an anecdote one of his patients told to him:

> I once read a story about a man who had been a political prisoner. For years he was kept in a cell that was 5 feet wide and 9 feet long, separated from anyone else. His routine was the same each day—he got up at 6 each morning, ate twice a day, and was allowed to bathe once a week. The rest of the time he spent walking up and down the 9 feet of his cell, back and forth, back and forth. As an old man, after almost 30 years, he was released and went to live with relatives. For the rest of his life, he got up at 6 each day, ate twice a day, bathed once a week, and spent his time walking back and forth in his bedroom—up 9 feet, and back 9 feet. I realize that's what I've done most of my life—living in captivity although I'm no longer a captive. I now know I don't have

to stay in my cell. My life has been ruled by fear, but I finally feel as though I can escape and be free. (p. 89)

NOTE

1. As I indicated at the beginning of this chapter, in some of the mental health literature from early psychoanalysis to new age therapy literature, there has been much emphasis on the expected healing benefits of abreactions. For instance, "primal scream" (Janov, 1970/1999) therapy was popular in the 1970s. This idea was extended to interpersonal relationships. Soon, however, it was noticed that indiscriminantly venting one's feelings toward other people was often destructive rather than helpful to relationships and therefore ultimately destructive to the person venting.

   In an evaluation of abreactive techniques used in World War II, Horowitz (1976/1986) wrote the following:

   > Abreaction led to more abreaction, to seemingly endless accounts.... Abreaction may relieve anxiety, but this effect can be non-specific and transient. To obtain durable improvement, it seems necessary to understand the individual patient, the meaning of the experience... and to revise discrepancies in self-object representations and other organizing constructs. (p. 119)

   I have suggested that the reason that "abreaction led to more abreaction, to seemingly endless accounts" is that the expected benefit was misunderstood as "getting rid of it" as opposed to integration.

   Some aspects of the problematic attitudes regarding the indiscriminant use of cathartic and exposure techniques in inappropriate circumstances trace back to Breuer and Freud, whose writings contained the germ of the controversy: In *Studies in Hysteria*, "Preliminary Communication," Breuer and Freud (1893–1895a) linked psychological trauma and dissociation. The basic strategy described by Breuer and Freud can be understood within the dissociative framework.

   In this treatise, Breuer and Freud (1893–1895a) compared the memory of the trauma to a "foreign body which long after its entry must continue to be regarded as an agent that is still at work" (p. 6). The reason that the traumatic memory acts as a foreign body is that it has been isolated from the person's other memories. Noting that hysterical reactions corresponded to traumatic memories, they said, "It may therefore be said that the ideas which have become pathological have persisted with such freshness and affective strength because they have been denied the normal wearing-away processes by means of abreaction and reproduction in states of uninhibited association" (Breuer & Freud, 1893–1895a, p. 11). Breuer and Freud further noted that when the isolated "strangulated affect... can find its way out through speech" (p. 17), it becomes associated with normal consciousness, and the symptom recedes. Breuer and Freud stated that while they had not found the etiology of hysteria, their new discoveries had yielded the mechanism of hysterical symptoms—and their cure. The cure was remembrance and abreaction. In short, they found that symptoms disappeared when the memory and its affect could be discharged (abreacted), expressed in words, or both.

With regard to this, Freud emphasized the discharge of affect, while Breuer emphasized the verbally communicative aspect (Van der Hart & Brown, 1992). Dell (2009d) noted that the "Preliminary Communication" reads between the lines like an argumentative dialogue between Freud and Breuer. According to Hirschmuller (1978, as cited in Van der Hart & Brown, 1992), who was Breuer's biographer (and importantly, his biographer with respect to the famous case of the highly dissociative Anna O.), the "talking cure" did not require Anna O. to discharge affect. Citing Hirschmuller, Van der Hart and Brown (1992) observed that in his initial descriptive notes Breuer did not stress emotional expression. According to these authors, Breuer emphasized verbal, more than emotional, expression of feelings, and Freud added emotional expression in 1895 in *Studies on Hysteria*.

The problem, according to Van der Hart and Brown (1992), arose with Freud's introduction of the constancy principle, according to which

> the nervous system endeavors to keep constant something in its functional condition that may be described as the "sum of excitation." It seeks to establish this necessary precondition of health by dealing with every sensible increase of excitation along associative lines or by discharging it by an appropriate motor reaction. Starting from this theorem, with its far-reaching implications, we find that the psychical experiences forming the content of hysterical attacks have a common characteristic. They are all of them impressions that have failed to find an adequate discharge. (p. 130)

The idea of catharsis ("getting it out") in abreactive treatment followed from this "quasi-neurological model" based on the constancy principle. The implications of this model are different from the implications of "working over" and sharing between parts. While these two models of treatment are different, they are not always distinguished. According to Van der Hart and Brown (1992), the "key problem here is to relate the latter abreaction-catharsis model based on the discharge of excitation and the principle of constancy with the association-reintegration therapeutic model based on the concept of dissociation" (p. 131).

In contrast to the quasi-neurological concepts of abreaction, Van der Hart and Brown (1992) emphasized the importance of integration, or resynthesis, in the healing of trauma. Van der Hart and Brown were emphatic that "since Janet, it has been repeatedly demonstrated that in most cases of posttraumatic stress, particularly chronic disorders, treating the traumatic memories alone (whether by abreaction or by any other approach) is insufficient" (p. 136). Integration of memories, followed by their acceptance and mourning, is needed.

Chapter 10

Facilitating Coconsciousness and Coparticipation in the Treatment

> Paradoxically, the more one is prepared to see the DID patient as an aggregation of alters that is capable of coordination and cooperation, the more effectively one can approach the DID patient as a single individual. Far from reifying the alters, it usually erodes their separateness quite aggressively.
>
> Kluft (2000, p. 264)

Coconsciousness refers to two or more alters sharing the same mental, affective and/or perceptual space at the same time. Each may be aware of the other's presence and have ongoing memory of the situation. This does not mean, however, that they are behaving as one. Generally, one part is in executive control, while one or more others are watching, listening, and thinking about what is happening. The achievement of coconsciousness is a necessary step toward greater harmony and cooperation in the system, as well as toward integration.

By coparticipation in the treatment, I mean participation in treatment on a level of not only one person but also multiple subjectivities. While not all of the alters necessarily see themselves as participants in treatment, the goal is to enlist them in the process. Encouraging the different parts to participate together furthers the treatment in many ways:

- More information essential to healing and enhanced functioning is shared among dissociative parts.
- Dissociative barriers are lessened.
- The different parts feel less isolated, exiled, or unwanted as they engage more in communication with each other and with the therapist.
- Functioning is more effective when relevant information and affect are available to the one in executive control.
- Switching is exhausting and derailing.

Achieving coparticipation is a formidable task for the patient, and fostering it can be formidable for the therapist as well. The stability of the system, unwieldy though it may be, depends on the dissociative structure that developed to protect the person's survival and sanity. This means that many parts may enter treatment with a substantial commitment to the status quo in the system. The psychodynamics of this status quo are intricate and usually difficult to decipher completely. Multifarious issues involve (a) commitment to hiddenness, (b) complicated but often minimally successful efforts at affect regulation, and (c) variations on aspects of self-punishment. Parts who have been hidden want to remain hidden because so much shame, terror, and realistic circumspection have been associated with the multiplicity being found out.

Often, there are parts who torture the host or others on the inside because they believe this is necessary for the person's safety and protection. In the original family environment, often it was not safe for the patient to express feelings of dissatisfaction or anger. In fact, in environments in which potentially deadly parental rage could easily be set off, the expression of true affect had to be extremely curtailed. As a result, the system has depended for its safety on the inhibition of expression or the exclusion from consciousness of powerful overwhelming affects, such as terror and rage.

The system works in a certain way to contain affects and thoughts that feel unbearable and that were at one time unexpressable. When the person is no longer in an abusive environment, this dissociative organization is no longer necessary or efficient. Information and affects that may be relevant to a given situation are often unavailable to the part of the personality in executive control. It would be so much more efficient if this part could, for instance, instead of dissociating, access anger and the ability to say "no," when the patient is being abused. For instance, when Janine's husband was verbally abusive to her, she was unable to access appropriate feelings of anger and self-defense. The anger was held by another part who had seldom seen the light of day because it would have shattered her belief in her parents' goodness as well as having gotten her into a great deal of trouble as a child. As a result, Janine maintained the dissociative barriers, with the result that current abuse caused her to switch into a helpless child state. To say the least, this did not help her to resolve this situation; indeed, it only rewarded the sadism of the abusive husband.

For coparticipation of parts to occur, the therapist must be willing to acknowledge the subjective existence of all of the dissociative parts, that is, the alters. As Richard Kluft (Kluft & Fine, 2009) noted, not to acknowledge their presence is simply rude. Since alters are already present with their own experiencing and acting subjectivities, there is no danger of the iatrogenic creation of these alters via acknowledgment of what the patient has already presented.

One must be aware in the therapy session that other parts who are behind the surface and not currently out can be and often are listening. When one sees the evidence of an alter coming through, it is often, although not always, helpful to acknowledge this. When patients become comfortable with the idea that they have dissociative parts, it is helpful to encourage the participation of other parts who are listening to share their observations and concerns. However, all interventions must be done with extreme care. It is generally helpful to ask the host and the parts if it is safe or if it is all right with them to ask for information or to speak to a part who has been hiding. Parts who are beneath the surface may be encouraged to share their thoughts with the part who is out.

On a practical basis, the dissociative parts, as an aggregate, know much more than the therapist knows, and they know more than the host knows. It is important to develop an attitude of "We're all in this together" (Itzkowitz, 2010). One important caveat: There are no "good" and "bad" alters. The therapist must never play favorites. There is an important psychic reason for the existence of each alter. They are all of equal importance.

In this chapter, I discuss some ways, by no means exhaustive, of interacting with the dissociative parts to (a) facilitate coconsciousness and coparticipation, (b) increase empathy among the parts, and (c) increase knowledge across the system. This includes engaging directly with parts, talking through, and asking inside. I also cover negotiating the time that parts have out in the session, helping the parts to differentiate themselves so that they are not so enmeshed in maladaptive patterns with each other, the integrative benefits of paying attention to perceptions of the body, and specific visualization techniques. The approaches I describe are not exhaustive. I refer the reader to the *Journal of Trauma & Dissociation* for a wealth of articles on this topic. What I consider most important is the principle behind the "technique."

Many therapists, including myself, who work with highly dissociative patients find hypnosis and eye movement desensitization and reprocessing (EMDR) invaluable tools in the work. In many of the vignettes that follow, the operation of hypnotic processes is assumed. For more discussion of hypnosis and EMDR, see the end of this chapter.

INTERACTING WITH DISSOCIATIVE PARTS OF THE PERSON

There are several ways of interacting with dissociative parts of the person: asking to speak with them directly, talking through, and asking the host to ask inside.

Working Directly With Dissociative Parts

It can be helpful to engage with the different alters directly to find out how they are feeling, what they need, and what problems they are experiencing in the system and in life. Not only is this helpful to them individually in feeling understood and in facilitating better adaptation to life circumstances both inside and out, but also it enlists their support in what must be a joint effort for the patient to get better. Most of the time, they will simply appear naturalistically when they have something to communicate or when they are triggered by something that has occurred in the session or in the inner world. However, they are also often shy, reluctant, or afraid to come forward. If it is relevant to the clinical work—for instance, a hostile alter causing trouble or an alter behaving unsafely—the clinician may choose to invite such an alter to come forward. If a dissociative part is having trouble emerging, the clinician might ask the host to "step back" and to allow the designated part to "step forward." Sometimes, especially if it is the first time, hypnosis helps parts who are otherwise unable to come forward to do so. Generally, however, hypnosis is not required.

Sometimes, clinicians will schedule "roll calls" and call out the known alters to see who is present (ISST-D Guidelines, in press). However, the clinician should be respectful of the patient's energy and the alters' subjectivities and should not call them forth without clinical reasons.

Talking Through

Because switching takes energy and working with parts separately takes up session time, it is often most effective to interact with the alters as an aggregate or without a switch of executive control. One method of doing this is talking through (Putnam, 1989). Talking through is a way of speaking to parts who are more withdrawn and beneath the surface. The therapist in effect talks past or through the host to those who are beneath the surface, sharing thoughts, or giving important information. This is especially useful when alters do not come forward or when there is limited time. For example, if the therapist is going on vacation, the therapist may say, "Please, everyone listen. I want to remind you that I will be away next week, and I want to make sure every one of you who might be responsible for getting here is aware of this. If any one of you has feelings about this, I really want to know." Often, there will be a part who will speak up with feelings of abandonment. Or with a safety contract, the therapist talks through to all of the alters after a contract has been negotiated with the host, saying something like, "This is what has been agreed on. I am assuming that all parts are in agreement with this unless you speak up now."

Talking through is particularly useful when the dissociated self-states are so locked down that they are unable to come forth (or the host may feel unable to let them do so). For example, Anna's parts are resistant to coming forward. Rather than direct interaction, the best approach with her has been talking through. She exhibits distinct changes in animation, facial expression, voice tone, and body posture when I am talking through to different parts of her. For example, there is a part who calls himself Lucifer and often engages in self-injury. While Lucifer has never come out directly to talk to me, there have been times when I have made contact with Lucifer by talking through, with good results. On one occasion when I was talking through to Lucifer, suddenly Anna's face changed dramatically, and she looked furious. Then, just as suddenly, she switched back. The next day, she called and left a message that she was completely without self-injury and felt wonderful—like she had not felt for many years. She added that she hoped it would continue. Because she almost always feels terrible, this was quite a change.

In one particular session with Anna, a child alter naively and delusionally wanted to go to the ocean to be carried away by the waves to go back to her mother, from whom she had been separated as a child, not realizing that such an act would drown her. I talked through to her in the following way:

> ME: [*Talking to little girl.*] You have been through unimaginable horrible things. Of course, you wanted to find a way to get home. That was very active thinking—to be wanting to get out. But you know of course that you can't really get home that way. And you know that your mother is dead, and the rest of your family is now here in the United States. Your mother isn't there anymore. The ocean can't take you to your mother because she isn't there. It is proactive to be thinking of how to get home, though. You have been through so much, and you are thinking so hard. But we can't solve that problem in Chicago now. We will work on it. Right now, you need to take a rest. Is that okay?
>
> ANNA: [*Her face shows much emotion. Talking to the little girl inside is bringing up a great deal of emotion. Informed by the child self-state that had clearly been touched, she, Anna says*] I am so angry with myself.
>
> ME: For what?
>
> ANNA: I should have figured out a way to get home.

Here, the result of talking through is like what Greenson (1967) has described as the result of a good interpretation: It brings up more information and more important material for the work of therapy. The seemingly suicidal alter (who mostly just wanted to go home) was engaged, oriented to the present, and then presented with her self-blame, which was another problem to be handled, but it was far better than suicidality.

Asking the Host to Ask Inside

Another way of encouraging coparticipation is to encourage the host to listen inwardly and to ask inside. Encouraging the host to help the parts to become more coconscious and mutually participative on the inside helps the host to do so on a regular basis on his or her own, continually breaking down dissociative barriers. Asking inside and listening inwardly may become necessary when the alters do not want to come forth, but there is clear evidence of their presence through some crisis. For example, sometimes in cases of self-injury, when the host seems not to be aware of any precipitant and no other parts are volunteering any information, asking the host to ask inside does have fruitful results, with either an alter offering information to the host or with a switch in which the alter comes forth directly to discuss the situation.

Sometimes, asking the patient to ask inside brings forth images, words, or fleeting thoughts. In the following report of part of a session, I asked Janice, introduced in Chapter 1, to ask inside because it was a telephone session. I use this example to show how asking inside can effectively bring forth much inside information. However, please be aware that the session may sound a little confusing because there were many parts contributing to the conversation. In addition, while the alter who is speaking is not the usual host, she is functioning as host. The usual host did not speak during this session. Many other parts of Janice did speak. Rather than arriving in person, Janice called on the telephone to say she did not feel stable enough to drive:

> ME: How are you? What is going on?
>
> JANICE: I'm just doing what has to be done. The Girl in the Torn Dirty Slip still has a hold right now. She is very powerful. She doesn't speak. She is in their head. . . . I was so frozen. I felt like the person I had been before is just gone. [*In other words, the presence of The Girl in the Torn Dirty Slip was intensely felt by other parts.*]
>
> ME: What happened?
>
> JANICE: My husband was horribly yelling at me for about an hour. And then he felt better, and said "Isn't it wonderful being married to me?" I have been in a fetal position. Someone said, "We have taken her to a place where it doesn't hurt." Can you explain what has been happening to me?
>
> ME: I don't know. But let's try this. This is on the phone. So, it is not the same as in person, but can you ask inside of The Little Girl in the Torn Dirty Slip what is going on now?
>
> JANICE: I think she wants—I keep hearing, "total power and control"—like she does another's bidding, although she feels the pain. I just had images of being tied up—maybe in the torture room. I roll myself into a ball. All I want to do is sleep. [*The Girl in the TDS feels the pain of intolerable situations, and memories of the torture room are brought forth.*]
>
> ME: Can you ask her what she is feeling?
>
> JANICE: Rage. She can't scream. That's why they took her mouth away—because she screamed so much.

ME: When?

JANICE: A long time ago. That's when she learned to be quiet and invisible. She is who they bring out to take it when I can't take it anymore.... She says the slip act is getting old. She wants to make an appearance in something else. She is sick of the brown dirty slip.

ME: What would she like to appear in?

JANICE: Something fresh. Whoa! She just said a lot. She is a combination of things— scared and power—changing her clothes, a new dress.

In this session, The Girl in the Torn Dirty Slip was accessed and able to speak through the part in executive control. In a later session, because of the work in this phone session of asking inside, The Little Girl in the Torn Dirty Slip, who had always been locked away, did finally come out in session to share her story, a story that was horrifying, a story that most people would not want to know if they had endured it. The result of her coming out in many later sessions was that her suffering was much diminished; she became aware that these events were in the past, that it was not her fault, and that she is not bad, unworthy, or unlovable because of what was done to her. This leads into another important issue, that of encouraging empathy among dissociated parts of the self.

Helping Dissociated Parts of the Person Have Empathy for Each Other

In the example just discussed, The Little Girl in the Torn Dirty Slip had been kept in lockup because other parts feared that her telling her story would fill them with dread and horror. They were afraid to feel what she feels and to know what she knows. And, they have come to rely on this system of defense, fearing that everything will fall apart if they do not. The other parts who keep their distance from The Little Girl in the Torn Dirty Slip, excluding and denigrating her, also rely on her denigration for some of their self-esteem.

As one of the parts said in the phone session just described (the following vignette is a continuation of the session just described but illustrative of a different topic):

JANICE: [Her voice deepens considerably as she switches.] That girl with the slip! She is such a pain!—a downer! I am here to speak for myself.

ME: I understand you feel she is a pain.

JANICE: When she was little, she crawled into the slip. Really gross! Gotta go now.

ME: Glad to talk to you.

JANICE: [Voice higher.] I'm back now. That was too funny! That is exactly what I did when as a little girl Janette [Janette is both a child alter and what Janice was *called as a little girl.*] had her "tired spells," you know, when she couldn't move? I just could not go on anymore—could not do anymore.

ME: I have a suggestion. She said she wanted something fresh. Could you get her something fresh?

JANICE: That would really be self-care! I don't know. I order from catalogues for everyone else. I got a beautiful sweater for L, and etc. for others.

ME: And have you gotten anything for yourself? You could in those catalogues get something for her and for yourself.

JANICE: That would be in the same category. Self-care. I don't think we can do that. The whole structure is built a certain way. Best not mess with it! No. She is the indentured servant. We all need a bottom of the heap, and she's ours. She has to stay there. None of us are [sic] going to go down there. I have to stop talking now. . . . [*Janice switches back to the part who had called.*] There are a lot of soldiers here. [*Sympathetically.*] She has been locked up her whole life. That is sad for her. She is happy being not locked up now. It is sad, though. We are going to have to rebuild the structure again. This is tiring for all of us.

In this example, by the parts talking with me, they were increasing coconsciousness. As a result of clearly stating the reasons for the rejection of The Little Girl in the Torn Dirty Slip, the parts who had rejected her began to see that this was an unacceptable way to behave. By being free to express their hostility and their fears, they became less hostile and less fearful. The Little Girl in the Torn Dirty Slip is okay now, and she helps others inside who have been exiled and denigrated.

Helping People With DID to Remember: Asking Inside

Another important function of asking inside is to restore memory. Dennis, introduced in Chapter 1, came into his session distraught and disoriented. He had just made a deadline for his job despite the fact that his computer had broken (his work required a computer). He had purchased a new computer, but he did not know how he had done this. Some part of him had done the work required for the job task, but he knew that he had not, and he did not know who had. He was filled with feelings of terror and confusion about the whole thing.

In this case, the immediate benefit of remembering was that he would feel less confused and less disoriented. And, he was in great distress. First, I inquired about the situation in general terms. What had happened? What was at stake? What did he remember? His first response was that all he could remember was that he had a deadline of Sunday night, and his computer had frozen on Friday night. Our current meeting was on a Thursday night, following the Sunday. He was anxious beyond measure, and it was hard for him to be able to talk about it at all.

The most important thing for me as a therapist for dissociative identity disorder (DID) was to be aware of the fact that Dennis had many different parts who were working together, despite their narcissistic disharmony, to help him to stay alive and financially solvent.

When I asked about the status of his job, the first thing Dennis told me was that he was supporting his mother who has had debilitating rheumatoid arthritis and cannot work at all now and who lived in a separate city, several hundred miles away. He loves his mother very much. She was the only parent who had raised him. And, she had raised him alone, emotionally and financially. Neither her family nor her deceased husband's family had been available to help. As noted previously, there was often little money, and there were many times Dennis and his mother were completely without food. It is these kinds of experiences that would intrude on Dennis's mind when he thought about the terrors of not being able to keep his own job.

Thus, I knew how intensely important it was for Dennis to be able to keep his job—if he lost his job, this whole house of cards would fall apart. His mother, basically helpless, would be without resources and in danger of receiving zero or, at best, inadequate, medical care and starving as well. Living in a different city, Dennis was of course in similar danger, but he was younger and stronger. Most important, he was impaired in his own ability to tell past from present: Yes, if he loses his job, it is a problem, a big problem, but it is not exactly the same as his mother losing hers when he was a child.

The next thing I asked was an open-ended inquiry into who it was that saved the day. Who bought the new computer? Who did the final work that resolved the situation? I wondered if it might have been Sophia, a maternal figure who Dennis states is often much better with numbers than he is and would have been in a better position to resolve the situation. At first, he did not remember. Then, I specifically requested that he ask inside who had bought the new computer and where. First, he told me that he had checked, and there were no credit card records of any transaction. It must have been in cash. There were some cash stashes unknown to Dennis but known to some of the other parts. So, I persisted with the question and the request that he ask inside—specifically of Sophia. Finally, he told me that the computer had been bought on Saturday at a particular store in Manhattan, and that Sophia had indeed finished the work. I asked why she had not put it on the credit card. His answer was that Sophia had known that he would "freak out" with the knowledge of such an expense. It was a very good (and comparatively expensive) computer, and although he needed it for his job, it was something of an anathema for him to have purchased it: Could he really be that important? Implicitly, "No." Thus, Sophia, along with others, kept the information from him so that the project could be finished and so that he, Dennis (but truly, all of them), could keep his job.

As the two of us addressed the intensity of his emotions about this situation, he volunteered that if he had been in a different, but at present unimaginable, state of mind, he might have been able to tell his boss that his computer had broken, and that he needed more time. He said this in the mode of self-criticism. I echoed the same sentiment with more support, considering all of his fears, many of which had never been publicly expressed: A reasonable boss would understand the situation, and as a result, he would not have had to feel so terrified.

One striking and notable thing about this incident was the revelation of how lovingly interconnected his parts can be. Because they did not want him to be too distraught to be able to finish the project, together they found a way to buy him a new computer with stashed cash, and they kept the information from him so that the project could be finished.

At the end of the session, Dennis felt much better. He had reclaimed this aspect of his memory thanks to the collaboration of Sophia and other parts, who, in the protective framework of the therapy session, felt that it was safe to let him know what had happened. He then said, "I would feel so lonely without them.... In such a desolate world, they keep me company."

Negotiating the Time Specific Parts Have in the Session and Getting Parts Who Have Come Out in the Session to Go Back Inside

Generally, it is not difficult to get dissociative parts who have come out in the session to go back inside. Usually, they are cooperative and understand that the session must end at a specified time, or if they are young, that they are too young to drive or to take care of themselves outside without the copresence of a more grown-up part. However, especially if these parts have not been out before or have only rarely been so, it may be difficult. They enjoy being out and interacting with a human being who is interested in them, and they may not want to go when it is time for them to go. I often reassure them, especially if they are child alters, that I will look forward to meeting with them again in the future. If they indicate that they have not had enough time, I may promise to make time for them in another session.

While I do not want a child part leaving the office for reasons of safety, and the parts know this, sometimes they like to feel grown up and try to trick me. When I catch them and say, "You are not so-and-so," I get a sheepish look and an agreement to go back inside. This may have to be repeated again, but usually they go back, even if grudgingly.

However, reluctance or inability of an alter to leave can sometimes be a serious matter. Sometimes, an emergency extension of a session may be required. This is difficult when sessions are scheduled back to back. There have been occasions when I have had to call for a spouse to come and get the patient. In the case of my patient Anna, whose alters are generally rigidly locked inside, communication with alters has at times resulted in extreme disorganization. Sometimes, when parts have emerged in her session, she has become wobbly on her feet, and I have to walk her down to the lobby.

On one occasion, when I was trying to talk to an aggressor part, a child part was thrown out instead. After some conversation with the child part, I asked her to leave so that the Anna could return. Unfortunately, Anna did not return. Half an hour later, with no success, I called her husband to explain to him that Anna was in a child state and asked him to take her home. I phoned her in the evening, and when she got on the phone, she said in a child's voice, "Who are these people? What a nice house! Can I stay here?" I asked her husband to watch her vigilantly, especially to make sure that she did not leave the house. Fortunately, by the following day, the host had returned.

Asking One Part to Step Aside

This approach of asking a part to step aside for the betterment of the system of the overall person derives from the work of Richard Schwartz (1995). Schwartz was a family therapist who became involved in the treatment of eating disorders. As a good family therapist would, he began to notice that the index patient (the eating-disordered patient) was often forced by the family dynamics to be compliant with the most powerful forces in the family system, and that the most powerful players were motivated to block the improvement of the patient. Following from this observation, he learned to ask the person who was most dominating and interfering to step outside so that he could learn what the interpersonal dynamics would be between the remaining parties without that person present. For example, Schwartz might notice that a father would intervene in a negative way every time a mother and daughter would try to resolve something between themselves. The father would make it impossible for the mother to be heard by her daughter. When Schwartz realized that all of these family dynamics had been internalized, he developed the internal family systems approach. The internal family systems approach encompasses work with all levels of dissociative problems, from ego state dissociation to DID.

As have DID therapists, Schwartz (1995) noticed that often there are parts who are punishing, criticizing, or dominating the part who is in executive control most of the time. It is not necessarily that these parts enjoy the activity, but that they have just always done it this way because it has worked in the past as a means of maintaining system stability and keeping the patient out of trouble—or so they believe.

One of Margaret's sessions may illustrate: Margaret, introduced in Chapter 1, always had to be the "Good Girl" to survive. In the family of her upbringing, there was no room for her to have any feelings about how she was treated. She was repeatedly raped by her father since she was a girl and sadistically and repeatedly raped by her stepfather when she was an adolescent. Her father, who was often full of booze and drugs, tried to drown her when she was 8. When Margaret was 12, he shot at her with a rifle, missing her head only because of the intervention of her stepmother, who moved his hand. On another occasion, after knocking out her front tooth in a beating, he tried to strangle her. Had she been anything other than the Good Girl, her tenuous safety in the family would have been extremely endangered. Not surprisingly, she is a hard-working and conscientious employee, spouse, and mother. Her lessons in being the Good Girl were hard-learned, and in many cases, they illustrated the principle of one-time learning.

Having always played the Good Girl, she quickly takes the other person's point of view. The problem is that she has no validated stance from which to care about herself and take her own point of view.

In this session, Margaret reported that she was feeling depressed, frustrated, and stuck. She was feeling exploited by a coworker, and while she acknowledged feeling angry, she also felt helpless. She experienced somatic symptoms in which she felt that her throat was closing, and she could not breathe. In addition, her heart was hurting her, another symptom that she develops at times when she is under extreme stress. Inquiry into her somatic symptoms yielded the fear that she would be strangled if she failed at her task, one in which she (a) was being taken advantage of, (b) was put in the position of taking the blame for someone else's mistakes, and then (c) was being forced to do extra work because of this other person's mistakes. She said that she was feeling extremely frustrated and hated having to be the Good Girl. I then asked her more of how she was feeling:

ME: How are you feeling toward the Good Girl?

MARGARET: I am feeling murderous toward the Good Girl. I am also feeling frustrated with being stuck and with only having her to work with.

ME: She'll get strangled if she fails at being good?

MARGARET: Yes.

ME: The Good Girl was so important to you when you were younger. She did keep you safe to the extent that that was in your control when you were younger. I shudder to imagine what would have happened if you would have indicated outrage at the way you were treated. The Good Girl enabled survival.

Would it be all right for The Good Girl to step aside so that I could talk to the one who was frustrated and angry with her?

MARGARET: [Her response is unexpected; initially, she did not want the Good Girl to step aside.] It is terrifying to the rest of me. I did not expect this. But I am completely terrified. I don't know if I want this, or if I am ready for her to step aside.

ME: Even if it is only for a minute? Could she step aside just for a minute, and then could she step back?

MARGARET: This is absolutely terrifying. But, OK, if it is only for a minute.

MARGARET: [*Continues.*] I am enraged at the people who won't take the responsibility. I am angry that they won't take responsibility and fix their mistakes. I feel that I have to fix everything.

ME: What would you like to say?

MARGARET: Look, Winston, we have all the coding done! Everything is set to go into production. Someone in your department made a big mistake in coding, and now production will be slowed down. You are causing us to lose sales. You need to fix this problem.

ME: That sounds like a strong place to be standing in.

MARGARET: It does not sound like a crazy person, and it does not sound out of bounds.

ME: Maybe the Good Girl can have a friend from you in this?

MARGARET: [*Correcting me.*] Maybe I can be the grown-up that the little (good) girl never had.

ME: The Good Girl was great to be willing to step aside. I see that she has been very powerful and in many ways dominant in the system.

MARGARET: She is bossy! She has been the boss of me! I feel so liberated. I could only do this if she weren't around!

ME: She's around. It is wonderful that she could concede your having more space.

But how did this feel to you?

MARGARET: I have had strong images. There is a way that I felt—on top of a mountain. The air is clear and feels good. I have a cape.

ME: A cape?

MARGARET: Like Superman's cape.

A week later in her next session, Margaret reported that the changes in her mood and her feelings of competency had remained, and while she did not necessarily feel like Superman, she continued to feel powerful and good.

Working With Dissociative Parts' Experience of the Body

It is often integrative to help patients with DID connect to their bodies and, specifically, to help parts to notice the body. Child parts, for instance, often do not realize that they are in a grown-up body. Specifically noticing the body often helps them to gain coconsciousness and to accept that they share the body with other parts. The therapist may ask them to notice such things as how tall they are, what their body looks like to them, and so on. This might include asking child alters to do such things as to stand up and note their height against the size of the room, against the furniture, or in comparison to the therapist's height. I have often found it helpful to ask the part who is out to look at the hands. Whose hands do they see?

The following vignette is a section from a session with Shirley, who had just been triggered and frightened by an event at work that reminded her of her childhood trauma. When she came into the session, she was still agitated and upset about it. I began by asking her who was upset and in a general sense what was going on inside her.

ME: Who is upset?

SHIRLEY: Sam [*a protective male alter*] is very upset. He could have hurt somebody. He was so upset he might have punched somebody—or worse. I had to physically stay away from the situation in order to control him.

ME: [*Realizing that Sam is starting to speak.*] How old are you?

SAM: I'm 8. I have to protect Shirley. I have to watch all the time.

[*Sam has to watch because the danger to Shirley as a child was almost constant from perpetrating family members and from perpetrators in the environment.*]

ME: That's a big job. That must be so lonely.

[*Sam nods.*]

ME: I bet Shirley appreciates how you have protected her.

SAM: No, she runs away. She is only 5. She is not there enough to know what I do. I don't need any appreciation.

ME: Oh, the little Shirley runs away. And you, you just do your job? You don't need appreciation.

[*Sam nods.*]

SHIRLEY: [*Intercedes.*] Things are not dangerous now like they once were. Sam is contemptuous of the little one.

ME: Yes, I can understand that he would be. It has been all up to him to protect the body. You are right though that the constant danger is past. Sam does not need to be so vigilant and on edge all the time. The traumas of the past are over.

SHIRLEY: Maybe he will let me sleep tonight! That would be wonderful!

ME: Yes, it would. How does that feel to Sam?

SHIRLEY: [*Visibly becoming very anxious.*] Something is wrong. He is so separate. I can feel him, but he is so disconnected. I see things through his eyes, but it is disconnected from me. Help me. Something is not working. This is very upsetting.

ME: Sam, through your eyes, please look at the hands.

[*Sam looks at the hands.*]

ME: What do you see?

SAM: [*At first, I am not sure whether it was Sam or Shirley speaking.*] I see two hands.

ME: What do they look like?

SAM: One is old, and one is a hand. They are very unconnected. [*Sam is upset.*]

ME: How old is the hand that is not old? Is it a child's or a grown-up's hand?

SAM: It is a child's.

ME: I would like to ask you to put your hands together and twist your arms together at the same time, like this. [*I demonstrate.*]

[*Sam does this. Suddenly, there is a switch to Shirley, who now feels and understands Sam, and she is very moved. She stays with her arms entwined for several minutes.*]

SHIRLEY: Oh, it is connecting. They are connecting. This is amazing. Sam is not so separate. He understands that he does not have to be constantly on the defense. He is more connected.

SHIRLEY: Sam likes you.

ME: I like Sam, too.

Shirley contacted me the next day to tell me what a powerful session it had been for her.

Sheldon Itzkowitz (personal communication, 2010) has described a technique that a patient of his devised to help her in sharing memories between dissociative parts. The patient discovered that while imagining that each of her hands was a different dissociative part, one of them the host, she could put her fingers together and enable the host, who had been amnestic of memories to be given those dissociated memories. The host then confronted a significant and painful task of mourning, but at least she now knew more of the life that she had actually led.

MAPPING THE ORGANIZATION OF DISSOCIATIVE IDENTITIES

Mapping "can be understood as an introduction to the personalities on the patient's own terms. . . . Therefore, the therapist is empowering the patient and respectfully supporting the patient's involvement in the therapy process" (Fine, 1993, p. 142). The creation of a map of the patient's internal world often helps therapists in learning their way around the system. The map represents the patient's current understanding of their dissociative system, indicating the identity of the parts, their relationships with one another, their ages, their genders, often their appearances and personal styles, when they came into being, and their particular function. Maps can also provide the clinician with clues regarding hidden influences and potential danger from the inside. Maps are often worked on throughout the first phase of treatment as more parts are identified and more information about the ones already identified is revealed. An initial map may function as a baseline against which subsequent ones can be compared (Fine, 1993).

Mapping the patient's organization of self-states can take many different forms. Fine (1993) described a user-friendly format for mapping that requires no drawing skills. The patient is invited to place the name of the part in usual executive control, which is generally the name the patient goes by, in the center of a large piece of paper and then to meaningfully indicate the position of each dissociative part in this representation of psychic space to indicate how similar or dissimilar the parts are to each other. The map may reveal ways that certain parts are clustered together or separated and in this way may help to elucidate the relationships and the conflicts that the parts have with each other.

Sometimes, a patient simply makes a list of dissociative parts and provides descriptions. Often, the patient may prefer to draw some form of visual diagram of the different parts and their functions and interrelationships. Some patients have used pie charts. One of my patients mapped her alters onto a picture of the brain. Others may visualize houses with individual and special rooms for everyone. Sometimes, people visualize tree houses, with separate places for the different parts. There may be landscapes, castles, moats, and so on. Those with some drawing skills may spontaneously draw pictures of the cast of characters on a piece or pieces of paper.

Maps can be telling in terms of what they leave out as well as what they include. Maps reveal an organization of affects, as well as the way parts are interrelated and work together. For example, one person's map had significant parts arranged around an empty center, where often the part who is most frequently in executive control is placed. In this case, the part who bore the patient's given name not only was not in the center but also was not listed at all. Here the part who acknowledged depressive affect was left out, revealing a clue to one particular way that the system was organized defensively to avoid depressive affect.

Figure 10.1 is a map that Dennis drew of his system. This map is a structure hanging in space, called the Onyx House. Dennis is in the center. He has a two-way, often reciprocating, interaction with a part he grew up with as a child, who is now an adult, Sophia. This is a strong connection. Sophia is connected to a child Little Sophia. Part of Sophia grew up, and part of her did not. There is a partial amnesia between these two parts. A male child part, named Denny, is the counterpart to Little Sophia. Denny holds an enormous amount of pain and longing for nurturance from Dennis. He can also be impulsive. Dennis holds him close to his heart and loves him, even though he often also is annoyed by his behavior—and even though

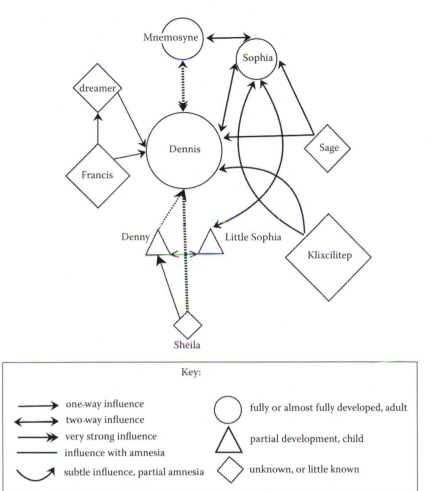

Figure 10.1 Dennis's map.

he often cannot hear him because of the amnesia barrier. Denny and Little Sophia are in communication with each other, as two main child parts of the system. Then, there is Mnemosyne, who is pictured as above Dennis, as a highly developed part, who has a strong influence, even though it is an influence with a good deal of amnesia, on Dennis. Mnemosyne is brutal and cruel and contains pure rage—hot, bloody, bone-crunching rage. She enjoys her fury, and this gives energy to Dennis. Mnemosyne is the personification of memory in Greek mythology. She is the daughter of Gaius and Uranus and, as consort to Zeus, the mother of the nine muses. At the very bottom of the structure is a sentry, defined mostly by her function, named Sheila. Dennis says, "Sheila feels cold and lonely when I touch her. She feels unrelated to us. I suspect she holds something more terrible than any of us, but she won't talk to me or let me see." On the right-hand side of the map is Sage, a somewhat less-known part, who will at times impart valuable wisdom to Dennis. His responsibility is to tell the truth when any of the parts ask. Then there is Klixcilitep, who is a nonhuman part and is more like a machine that sits deep under the roots of the pylon on which the Onyx House sits. According to Dennis:

> Klixcilitep's purpose is to keep the Onyx House stable and organized. It acts as a medium for memory and experience and has access to every memory and every thought of everyone in the Onyx House, except for Sheila. It has no personality of its own and doesn't talk or listen, but its presence is felt everywhere in the house, almost as if the entire thing is of Klixcilitep's own design.

Mapping often occurs naturalistically as alters come out and indicate their concerns and relationship to others in the system. The map may consist only of the patient's verbal communications of how they visualize the organization of the dissociative parts of the system. For example, one patient had a tree house that she described. If the patient does not explicitly communicate it, the map may have to be constructed in the therapist's mind. The main point is that the therapist should be getting to know the cast of characters and their interrelationships. Just as technique should not be privileged over purpose, creating a map of the different parts should not take precedence over sensitivity in the clinical work. For example, parts should not be called out for the sake of a map (International Society for the Study of Trauma and Dissociation, in press).

THE USE OF VISUALIZATION AND METAPHOR TO INCREASE COCONSCIOUSNESS: VISUALIZING OTHER PARTS

Most patients with DID have a good ability to visualize aspects of their inner world as well as the appearance of other parts on the inside. People with DID often visually imagine houses and other lodging places, which are divided in particular ways to accommodate the occupancy of different parts. They may visually imagine special rooms, landscapes, even seascapes. They also visualize each other's physical appearance. This ability enables them to utilize visual metaphors and guided imagery therapeutically. Therapists often devise metaphors and images that are custom made for their particular patients. However, some that have broad utility I mention here. Kluft (1989, 1993b, 1999b, 2009) has suggested a number of visualizing and metaphoric techniques, such as suggesting that parts impart information to each other through means of a slow leak or a dripping faucet. This allows for the information to be imparted by one part to another but in a way that is not overwhelming. Another of his metaphors is of irrigation ditches from a river-fed lake that may overflow.

George Fraser (1991, 2003) has offered the dissociative table technique, a guided imagery or, more specifically, inner-guided imagery technique. The dissociative table technique generally utilizes an image of a table surrounded by empty chairs in a safe room. Parts are then invited to enter the room and to sit in the chairs around the table and share their concerns. However, other images, such as sitting around a rock at a beach, may be utilized just as well. After important preliminary work, the therapist may say something like the following:

> "I want you to imagine yourself in a safe room. In this room is a table. Around this table are chairs. One chair is for you, the other chairs are for those others who play a role in your internal life," or if the internal parts are better known, "The chairs are for you and those you are aware of who are inside." (2003, p. 13)

It is emphasized that it is a safe room in which no one gets hurt, and that the purpose is for the parts to get to know each other better. The dissociative parts are then invited to speak with each other or through the host. To aid in the process, Fraser (2003) suggested use of a virtual spotlight or microphone to help individual parts to speak. Next, he suggested saying something like, "OK, now I want you all to listen when someone else speaks so you can all be aware of what is said in therapy" (p. 16). As this is a powerful technique that may tap into hypnotic phenomena, Frazier recommended that those using the table technique should either have formal training in hypnosis or have supervision for their first few cases in which it is used.

Shielagh Shusta-Hochberg (2004) has proposed the window-blind technique, which also involves visualization of other parts. First, the person visualizes a window with the blinds drawn closed and is told that other parts of the system are on the other side. When ready, the patient is invited to slightly and slowly twist the virtual wand of the blind and describe what she sees. Shusta-Hochberg offered the following vignette:

> A patient with persistent adult-specific denial of the existence of other parts continued to take issue with the assessment that she suffered from DID. Review of her high DES [Dissociative Experiences Scale] score and some of her answers failed to convince her. I would again and again relate to her what I observed in session to support the diagnosis, including childlike behaviors, affective tone, vocabulary and vocal tone and pitch. I also reported to her that she would gather up stuffed

toys and interact with them very much as a child would. My reports of these observations seemed to do little to satisfy her that my diagnosis was correct. Eventually we tried the window-blind technique using guided imagery. I started by addressing the issue with her child parts. One of her childlike parts looked through the window and saw adult alters "moping," appearing depressed, with shoulders stooped and heads hanging down, defeated, hopeless, and alone. Tears rolled down her face as she said, "It's so sad." Then, one of her adult parts looked through the partially opened blinds and glimpsed a group of little girls playing a colorful children's board game, having fun down on the floor. Seeing them, she suddenly grasped the concept of not knowing as being part of the disconnection of dissociation. Following this exercise, she found tears on her cheeks and wondered why. She was told that one of the child parts had seen her and felt compassion for her pain. She was amazed. This was a very difficult but invaluable turning point in this treatment. The technique was used several subsequent times with this patient to help her view her dissociation more objectively. This seems to accomplish in part what videotaping can do, without presenting the dilemmas videotaping can entail. (p. 18)

OTHER APPROACHES TO FACILITATING COCONSCIOUSNESS

Many people with DID have successfully used written venues as ways for parts to share information with each other. One of these is a group journal in which parts make entries that are then available to other parts to read. This is an invaluable tool for achieving coconsciousness. Some people will use an actual journal; others will use a computer. Putnam (1989) has described a specific form of this: a bulletin board on which dissociative parts may post notices to each other and to the system. The general principle is to offer suggestions and support for the parts to share experiences and be in communication with each other.

Throughout each session, Kluft's (1993a) "rule of thirds" is important to bear in mind: Uncovering or intensely emotional work should be completed by the time 2/3 of the session is up, allowing the remaining 1/3 to wrap up and restore equilibrium.

Hypnosis and EMDR

Both hypnosis and EMDR are adjunctive modalities in DID therapy, not treatments in themselves. Clinicians who use these modalities in work with highly dissociative patients should have received, not only the appropriate training to use these modalities, but also the specialized training requisite for use with highly dissociative patients. In addition, patients should be carefully informed about the possible risks as well as the benefits they may expect. Therapists should receive from the patient the appropriate informed consent for use of these modalities.

Hypnosis

With regard to the usefulness of hypnosis in DID treatment, there is no substitute for reading the works of Richard Kluft. He has written prolifically on this topic and has formulated a great number of hypnotic interventions. To learn more about these interventions and to understand how he uses hypnosis, I refer the reader to his many edited books and widely placed articles. Fortunately a number of his articles may be found in the journal, *Dissociation*, electronically retrievable at https://scholarsbank.uoregon.edu.

Kluft (1982, 1991, 1994b) noted that hypnosis has been a controversial issue in the treatment of DID. Arguments that have been made against the use of hypnosis include the claim that DID may be iatrogenically induced, and the claim that hypnosis can be harmful. With regard to the first argument, he observed that "personalities" created under experimental hypnosis are highly limited, do not have a center of subjectivity, initiative, and personal history, and they don't last. In addition, in DID treatment, the number of alters usually decreases. If the therapist were creating alters, their number should increase. With regard to the second argument, Kluft noted that there is little firm evidence that hypnosis in itself is damaging. As with many interventions, the problem arises from a therapist's lack of skill, rather than from the use of the intervention. Finally, people with DID tend to be highly hypnotizable (Bliss, 1984; Frischholz, Lipman, Braun, & Sachs, 1992). Trauma, especially repeated trauma may spontaneously induce self-hypnosis. Trauma victims have often unwittingly learned autohypnosis as a way to avoid or buffer the full impact of traumatic experiences. As a result, the patients' developed autohypnotic techniques may permit much hypnotic work to be done without the induction of a formal trance. Thus, it is likely that the treatment is suffused with hypnotic phenomena even if the therapist does not believe that he or she is employing hypnosis (Kluft, 1994b).

Hypnosis has many uses in psychotherapy with highly dissociative patients: relaxation, grounding, self-soothing, enhanced coping skills, increased sense of self-efficacy, creating safe places, and help with the reduction of emotional pain, to name a few. It is an excellent way to contact alters who have otherwise been reluctant to appear. While Kluft has described numerous hypnotic techniques, a few that are illustrative include the provision of sanctuary, bypassing time, distancing maneuvers, bypassing affect, and alter substitution (Kluft, 1994b). The provision of sanctuary involves the creation of a safe place for alters whose affect has become unmanageable. Safe place work is used in other modalities of therapy, such as EMDR. However, in DID treatment a safe place must be created for every known alter: Different alters are unlikely to have the same perspective on safety. Bypassing time may be achieved in at least two ways: (1) hypnotically helping overwhelmed alters to go their safe place or to go to sleep until the next session; (2) hypnosis may be used to assuage a patient's terror that may be evoked by certain dates, such as Halloween, or an abusive parent's birthday. In this second technique of bypassing time, Kluft suggests to the patient that he or she is currently looking backward in time and is feeling good about how well he or she had handled it. An example of a distancing maneuver is the library technique, in which the patient envisions a trip to a library where there are fascinating volumes, "some of which we will study together and close whenever we have read as much as we can absorb" (1989, p. 95). This method allows the exploration of memories in a setting that is safe and circumscribed, and provides a distance from potentially overwhelming memories. Bypassing affect may be achieved by suggesting that the patient put the overwhelming affect in a time-locked vault that will only open a few minutes before the session. Another technique is alter substitution—used when a key alter who has usually shouldered the major responsibility for managing daily life becomes exhausted and overwhelmed. Rather than let this situation devolve into retraumatization and the patient's experience of failure, the overwhelmed alter will be replaced by another alter who is not exhausted, with the consent of the patient. Such hypnotic methods teach skills of affect management, alleviate suffering, and give the patient a greater sense of self-efficacy—highly relevant because helplessness is generally at the root of DID.

Hypnosis may also be used for retrieval of memories (Kluft, 1994b; Maldonado & Spiegel, 1998), but Kluft teaches that great care must be used: "I avoid asking leading questions or dropping hints that I anticipate finding an abuse history...I treat any technique, including hypnosis, as having potential for both desirable and undesirable outcomes and so inform the patient. I encourage the patient to regard all recovered material as tentative, and deserving consideration in depth and at length before action might be taken on its basis" (1994b, p. 210).

EMDR

Eye Movement Desensitization Reprocessing (EMDR) is also often used adjunctively in DID treatment. EMDR helps to heal trauma and dissociation, restoring associative pathways within neural networks. However, because EMDR intensifies painful affect in the process of resolving it, it should be used with great care in DID treatment. Generally, the sets should be shorter than those used with less dissociative patients, and there should be heightened vigilance for the possibility that affect may become unmanageable. There is a vast literature on EMDR, starting with Francine Shapiro's (1995) *Eye Movement*

Desensitization and Reprocessing (EMDR): Basic Principles, Protocols, and Procedures. However, there is less literature on the application of EMDR with highly dissociative patients. Catherine Fine is notable for her work in this area. One particularly excellent article, authored by Fine and Berkowitz (2001), describes a Wreathing Protocol for the imbricated use of EMDR and hypnosis in the treatment of highly dissociative patients. The authors noted that premature abreactive work can promote regression and decompensation, which, when it occurs, gives "the message to the DID patient . . . that past experiences contained within parts of the mind remain overwhelming and unmanageable, and that they should continue to be avoided at all cost. Therefore, because of the easy affective destabilization of the DID patient . . . great caution should be exercised in the use of EMDR because it is such a powerful methodology" (p. 277). In the Wreathing Protocol, hypnosis renders the heightened affect more manageable, but the benefits of EMDR, which works faster than hypnosis does, are retained.

Chapter 11

Working With Persecutory Alters and Identification With the Aggressor

Persecutor parts function as trauma shields (Putnam, 1989) to protect the person from horrifying memories and defending against feelings of helplessness. Having persecutory and abuser identity states is like having an internal Al Qaeda or Taliban that punishes you for the slightest infraction of bizarre and arcane rules. It involves being emotionally attached to inner and perhaps outer persecutors, even though you were tortured by them. It is in part this relational configuration that gives the persecutor parts their power.

Abusive parts often engage in self-harm and self-sabotage, and they may be aggressive and frightening toward other people and destructive of property. These parts may also do such things as cut or burn the body, hit the face or other parts of the body, put the person in physical danger, and behave homicidally toward other parts in the system. They may instruct the part who is in executive control to commit suicide, engineer falls down stairs or on the pavement, or cause a person to fall out of bed. They may call the part in executive control denigrating names, tell that part that he or she is worthless, and so on. Although abuse of other people is less frequent, these parts may also behave in threatening and dangerous manners toward the therapist and other people. Abusive and persecutory alters are common in people with dissociative identity disorder (DID). Ross, Norton, et al. (1989) found 84% of a sample of 236 cases of DID had such parts.

Why do these persecutor and abuser parts behave as they do? In the most general sense, they are usually modeled after a caretaker who was abusive. However, their psychology is complex. The parts who punish, hurt, and torture the host or others on the inside often do so because they believe this is necessary for the person's safety and protection. In the original family environment, it was often not safe for the patient to express feelings of dissatisfaction or anger. In fact, in environments in which potentially deadly parental rage can easily be set off, the expression of true feeling must be extremely curtailed. As a result, the system depends, for its safety, on the inhibition of expression or the exclusion from consciousness of powerful overwhelming affects, such as terror and rage. For example, Margaret's (Chapter 1) father was an unpredictable alcoholic who knocked out her front tooth because his football team lost. After his team lost, he found a quarter in the carpet that he claimed she had let fall out of her pocket. He said to her, "I told you not to let any money fall into the carpet!" and then began beating her. It eventually involved her teeth being knocked out, her bedroom dresser being knocked on top of her, and her entire face being bloodied. It would not have been safe for Margaret to express any feelings about the way she was being treated—especially when her mother's only concerns were that she would not be able to get the blood out of the shirt and that she would now have to take Margaret to the dentist. Thus, the development of a part who oversees and preemptively curtails thought and behavior by intuiting and predicting the frightening parents' behaviors is a great asset to the child in this environment. In a way, it is like a preemptive strike; this part's control of the person's behavior often mimics that of the original aggressor.

The purpose and activity of abuser parts has much in common with what Bromberg (1996) called an *early warning system*, a fail-safe security system that is always hypervigilant for trauma. Although the part of the self that functions as the early warning system is also motivated in people without DID, in people with DID this part is personified with its own sense of purpose and subjectivity. This dissociative vigilance of being on alert, which I believe is part of the underlying reason for the reliability and speed with which abuser parts can appear, is highly protective of sanity. As Bromberg (1996) stressed, this dissociative vigilance "doesn't prevent a harmful event from occurring and, in fact, may often increase its likelihood. It prevents it from occurring unexpectedly" (p. 230). In this sense, it safeguards an ongoing sense of subjectivity and protects against emotional deregulation and annihilation anxiety. Thus, the vigilant intention to avoid current and future trauma ends up as a continual internal reenactment of the past traumatic situations.

In addition to preserving safety and sanity, the persecutor part has the job of protecting the child's attachment to the abusive caretaker. Attachment serves survival (Bowlby, 1969/1983) and buffers fear (Lyons-Ruth, 2001). Because proximity to an attachment figure provides protection to the infant against predators, separation from the attachment figure signals danger (Bowlby, 1969/1983). What happens when survival is predicated on attachment to a caretaker who is also a predator? When the person from whom protection is sought is the same one against whom protection is needed? In such situations, the child's ability to maintain attachment will depend on the dissociative compartmentalization of parts of the self containing contradictory memories and affects. By containing the child's enraged and angry feelings, the abuser part helps the part most frequently interfacing with the world to maintain an idealized attachment relationship with the needed abuser. In DID, as in less-severe problems in living, this *betrayal blindness* (Freyd, 1996), in which awareness of the malevolence of the caretaker is sequestered, allows an ongoing positive, or at least safer, relationship with that caretaker to be maintained.

Even when the original environment is no longer present, as long as the dissociative barriers are in place, this aggressor-identified part believes punishment, and threat to the part most frequently out, is the most reliable means to achieve and maintain survival of the person, the system, and the attachment to the abusive caretaker. Instead of the behavior of the perpetrator, the child comes to identify his or her own rageful feelings and potential behavior as the threat (Howell, 1997a). Of course, the affects of rage and anger forbidden to the host are exactly the ones these persecutor and abuser parts hold. In this way, they function in a way that has some commonality with the arcane and primitive superego (Howell, 1997b).

The fact that the perpetrator self-state feels like Not-Me also reflects the collusion of the part who is usually out. Sometimes, the memories of the experiences are so horror filled that the part of the person usually out front (the host) is so extremely sensitized that he or she refuses to know about them. Thus, the host may depend on the abuser part's parentlike function of providing safety and protection from memories (Beahrs, 1982; Goodman & Peters, 1995; Howell, 1996, 1997b). The attachment of the host to the abuser self-state takes the place of the capability for trust of a real protective other person. The fact that the host often desperately does not want to know about traumatic childhood experiences renders the host unappreciative of the intended-to-be-helpful activity of the abuser part. This, then, perpetuates and strengthens the dissociative barriers between self-states. It also feeds the grandiosity of the abuser part: By allying with the omnipotence of the persecutor, the host does not have to feel the terror and can be shielded from memories. Of course, this kind of internal bondage does not work in the long run for it increases the grandiosity of the persecutor part and does not, in the end, prevent the intrusion of terrible memories.

The persecutor part, the one who holds much of the fury for the system, often feels omnipotent. In addition, as domination feels good, it is self-reinforcing:

> For example, Sally is a patient with DID who has a grandiose dominating part called Devil. This part persecutes the helpless-host self-state with brutal self-injury, and will at times erupt into demonic-sounding laughter, sounding much like the original perpetrator. Devil boasts to Sally about how powerful he is, yet when the therapist tries to engage him and to encourage him to wield his power by defending Sally against domineering people, Devil disappears. He does not come forward to defend. To the contrary, the only real interpersonal defense comes from a precocious 9-year-old part within the intrapsychic system. Devil exerts tremendous power toward counterparts that are weak and helpless, and it is this relational configuration that affords Devil his feeling of power. In fact, Devil is only powerful internally. Because it apparently originated from Sally's childhood identification with the original

perpetrator, in reality, this part has only the power of a child. (Howell, 2003, pp. 61–62)

How did these parts develop? Often, these abuser parts function as *protector-persecutors* (Howell, 1997b). Although they start out as protectors (Spiegel, 1986), friends, or helpers in childhood, even as imaginary play-mates (Kluft, 1985a), they often become persecutors as the person grows older (Putnam, 1989). One reason for this is that there was more persecution than protection in the child's environment. Moreover, the scarcity of protection in the child's environment means that there was little protection for the child to model: An imitation cannot be better than what it imitates. As such, the protector becomes a persecutor because the protection existed primarily in fantasy.

Another important route for the development of abuser parts is by the process that occurs via a combination of traumatization and procedural learning called *identification with the aggressor*. In my view, identification with the aggressor is a two-part process. The first part is passive and automatic, and the second is defensive. In the traumatic moment of being terrified and abused, the child cannot assimilate the events into narrative memory. But, the child does what people often do when they are overwhelmed by danger: The child goes into a trancelike state in which the source of the danger, in this case, the abuser, is focused on intently but in a depersonalized and dere-alized way. Partly because the child is intensely attached to the abusive care-taker (generally much more so than if there had been no abuse), the abuser's facial expression, posture, and words are automatically mimicked. This is an aspect of procedural enactive learning in the attachment relationship.

Because the abusive events could not be assimilated, the experience could not be connected with other ongoing aspects of self. Thus, it is not like a positive identification in which a person's identity is augmented. Instead, it is as if the person has been "taken over from the outside" filled with the aggressor (Coates & Moore, 1995, 1997). However, even though behavioral enactments may appear to be like those of the original aggressor, and even though this part may identify so intently as even to feel that it *is* the original aggressor, it is important to remember that this part expresses its *own* aggression. (I expand on this discussion of the development of identification with the aggressor at the end of this chapter.)

IMPORTANCE OF ACCESSING, RELATING TO, AND EMPATHIZING WITH AGGRESSIVE, ABUSIVE, AND PERSECUTOR SELF-STATES

It is vitally important for the therapist to do what the host has been unable to do: connect with the abuser parts of the person. The therapist may invite these parts into the session and talk through to them. Although they can be dangerous and debilitating to the person as a whole, these abuser and persecutory parts contain a great deal of the energy and vitality of the system. Because they hold the feelings of anger, aggression, and fury, other parts, including those most often in executive control, are often depleted of energy. The goal is that abuser and persecutory parts ultimately become allies in the treatment so that the affects they have exclusively held become gradually shared across dissociative boundaries.

Persecutory and abuser parts most often erroneously believe that they are bad. In these cases, the therapeutic action involves increasing their appreciation of their own subjectivities, which almost always reveals a greater complexity of affect and thought than they were aware of previously. A frequent problem for these persecutory parts is that they have been pushed into a corner and see themselves as only having the job of keeping the patient in line by punishing the host. Thus, interactions with them emphasizing how helpful they have been, how hard they have worked, and how burdensome it may have been for them can help them to become aware of a broader and more complex array of emotions and thoughts than they thought they had. Often, they have not been at all happy about their pigeonholed position but have not been able to get out of it on their own. It is often hard for the part who is usually in executive control, who often likes to see himself as "good," to really "get" how rotten it feels to be considered "bad" and to understand that he or she gets to be good only because another part is holding the badness. Thus, it is actually unfair for the part usually out to be critical of the parts holding the badness because these parts are in a certain way doing the host a favor.

These parts may present themselves as scary, even calling themselves demons and names like Satan or Devil. Despite this, they are usually angry adolescents or even children in subjective identity. As Ross (1997) explained: "Usually one is dealing with a school playground bully who really wants to be contained and loved" (p. 336). Once a persecutory part emerges, it is often helpful to emphasize that there must be a good reason for the way he or she behaves. Here, depending on the circumstances, explanation of the development and purpose of these parts may be useful. I often say something like the following:

> You have done a very important job all these years, keeping so-and-so safe. You keep her from getting in trouble, and you may have even saved her life by keeping all this fury to yourself. You kept her from having to know about it and from getting punished because of it. You enabled her to continue to have a positive view of the parents, despite what they did to her, and this enabled her to carry on more safely. You should be thanked for what you have done for her and for the system. I think it must not have been easy for you to carry such a heavy load of feelings.

In addition, inquiry into the feelings and motivation for the behavior is helpful. For instance, why is the persecutory alter behaving in a way that is so onerous or injurious to the body and to the one who is usually out (e.g., arm slashing, vagina gouging, sending horrifying hallucinations, etc.)? Often, the answer may be something like, "She deserves it; she is such a wimp." Acknowledgment of the abuser's perspective, along with the statement that such acknowledgment does not mean the host deserves abuse, may invite more communication. Further inquiry may reveal that the view of the host as a wimp or something similar is an aspect of the persecutory alter's self-aggrandizement. This self-aggrandizement may be experienced as deserved because this persecutor part has had to be so tough and to contain terrible memories and emotions from which the host has been protected. At this point, observing that the host could really use some of that energy, while the persecutory part could be less burdened, can lead to a direct request that this strong part lend some of his or her strength.

Whereas the grandiose abuser part monitors and punishes the host's experience and expression of aggression, the reverse is not true. Without the overriding constraints of concern that are developed with adequate interpersonal guidance and empathy or that would be present with more integration of the self, it simply feels good (and therefore is reinforcing) to a persecutor part to be powerful and to punish other parts (Howell, 1997a). These parts often enjoy their power over other parts. Abuse toward the other parts can become cruel sport. When these parts emerge in the session and engage in such behaviors as striking the patient's face or scratching the patient's body, it can be extremely upsetting to the therapist. Unless or until the therapist, using words, can prevail on the abuser part to stop harming the body, the therapist is forced to watch helplessly or to intervene physically. The abuser parts must be told that this is not acceptable behavior. And, the part who is out most of the time must be encouraged to say "no."

It is almost always best for the therapist to avoid power struggles with abuser parts because you are unlikely to win (Ross, 1997). This does not mean, however, that the therapist should not maintain appropriate boundaries and self-defense. In one case noted by Wagner (Chu, Baker, O'Neil, & Wagner, 2001), a part emerged threatening to kill the therapist. The therapist responded, "Then you would no longer have a therapist." This remark was sufficiently realistic to halt the threat. In another case (M. Hainer, personal communication, 2010), an abuser part threatened to throw coffee in the therapist's face and was promptly told that if she felt like that she would have to leave immediately; she was also told that when she felt differently, she could come back. This part immediately calmed down. Although the clinician may encounter some abuser parts who, like psychopathic people, are apparently nonrehabilitatable, these are in the great minority.

Often, abuser parts are able to develop and grow into more complex self-states in the treatment. Itzkowitz (2010) presented a case in which an abuser/aggressive part tested him in the session with minor acts of aggression, with the result that the part learned that Itzkowitz would not retaliate as her abusive stepfather had. This part would throw things on the floor with a smiling half-smirk, as if to say, "What are you going to do about that?" She was taking a reflective stance toward her transference, if you will, thinking about her way of thinking about people and anticipating that it would be different with Dr. Itzkowitz. When the host was able to reaccess these emotions, she was learning to regulate a feeling that was *hers*. This is something hard for many patients with DID. Helping these parts to learn that they can use words rather than action to express their feelings is valuable. The acceptance of this part's feelings along with the setting of reasonable limits enabled the achievement of much greater integration in the system.

JANICE

The following discussion regards another excerpt from a session with Janice, who was introduced in Chapter 1. Janice is generally cheerful and optimistic, although at times she has been extremely depressed and suicidal. From her infancy until she was about 5 years old, she was sickly. In addition, her parents were so harsh and physically abusive to her that she felt at times that they did not want her to live. Janice soon learned to keep her mouth shut and put on a happy face. In accordance with, or in repetition of, the way she was treated in her nuclear family, she has had many close calls in her life and has indeed cheated death many times.

The following 75-minute session was about our 20th session. Having become increasingly amazed at the awareness of her alters, she said that she would like to let whoever wants to come out, come out—as it was her stated wish to have greater communication in this way. Out came one that expressed utter contempt and malicious hatred toward Janice, a hostile contemptuous alter.

> HOSTILE, CONTEMPTUOUS, PERSECUTORY ALTER (HCPA): She is such a Pollyanna—always helping others; it is disgusting. I want to kill her, and I am always setting traps to try to kill her, but she always slips through my fingers. I don't know how she escapes. She does not deserve to live. She should not be alive.
>
> ME: Why do you want to kill her?
>
> HCPA: Because she is so disgusting, and she was never supposed to live. It was always intended that she should die. [*Insists that she should be dead,*

and she intends to kill her, and that she is just helping things along to be the way they should be.]

ME: Because she is so sickly?

HCPA: My job is just to carry out things as they were supposed to be. I keep setting traps, and she keeps escaping. I don't know how she gets away.

ME: But if you kill her, you would die, too!

HCPA: [*Now identifying herself as Ereshkigal and screaming so loudly the room shakes and the sound carries beyond the office, and I am a bit shaken, too. The next day I received a complaint about the noise.*] I don't care! I know that, but I don't care! I am Ereshkigal, The Destroyer![1] I am all powerful, and I will get her, and I don't care if I die. She just shouldn't be alive. She begins slapping her face, hard and uncontrollably.

ME: [*I have a moment of panic, not knowing what to do.*] Please stop slapping your face. This is not okay. Please look at me. I need to talk to you right now.

[*Ereshkigal reengages with me, and the slapping stops.*]

ME: Who is Ereshkigal?

ERESHKIGAL: The Sumerian goddess of destruction. I am all-powerful! She is such a do-gooder. That's ridiculous! What is that happy mood she is so often in? Stupid! She's stupid!

ME: [*I am desperately trying to bond with this part.*] Well, yes, she is a bit of a do-gooder, and she does have a lot to learn from you. I bet you did a pretty good job keeping her out of trouble in the family—you with your power—you must have found ways to keep her quiet and out of trouble with those very difficult and scary parents.

ERESHKIGAL: [*After a while.*] Well, that I did.

ME: I bet you were very much able to make her behave perfectly in that family of hers. Janice should be very appreciative for all the help you gave her. I think she really needed your help in the family.

ERESHKIGAL: Yes. I was pretty good at that. But she is still just a piece of crap and deserved everything she got.

ME: [*I emphasize her power and how Janice has a lot to learn from her.*] It must feel good to be so powerful. That must be something for you to want to stick around for. I bet a lot of Janice's energy actually comes from you! I am very interested in the things you have to say and am glad to have met you, but I am going to have to ask for Janice to come back soon. Is there anything you especially want me to tell Janice of what you have said—or anything you feel concerned about?

ERESHKIGAL: I don't care what you tell her. No, there is nothing you need to hold back. Tell her whatever you want.

ME: Thank you. I am glad to have met you.

ERESHKIGAL: I'll bet you were glad to meet me! [*Sarcastically; she cackles.*]

[*Buzzer rings. Next patient is quite early.*]

ME: [*I get up.*] I guess I am going to have to get this rewired so I don't have to get up.

ERESHKIGAL: It's probably good for you to get up—you need the exercise.

ME: I was glad to meet with you and want to talk to you again. But, I would really like it if you would step back now and let Janice come forward.

ERESHKIGAL: I'm not going yet!

ME: I'm sorry. I really need to speak to Janice now.

[*Practically growling, she begins shaking again. And, Janice is back.*]

JANICE: Oh, my God. That was scary! Was I slapping my own face?

ME: Yes.

JANICE: She said she wanted to kill me!

ME: Yes, but I think she also helped you when you were growing up. I think she helped you deal with the destructiveness of your parents.

JANICE: That is really weird and scary. I had no idea.

Janice is visibly quite shaken. I ask her to sign a new safety contract, and I also ask her to call her husband and tell him what happened and when she will be home. At first, she does not want to call him because he is busy at work. When I insist that she call him, she does. We also talk about the need for her to drive home safely, but she is too shaken to leave. I tell her she can stay in the waiting room until I finish with the next session. My next patient, also a multiple, sees how shaken Janice is, asks her if she is a multiple, and tells her it gets better. She says she herself is so much better now, even though she went through some rough periods. She also mentions that she has been in therapy for 14 years.

After the following session, I return to the waiting room and invite Janice back into the office for a few minutes. She is better and says that she is going to get lunch and then drive home. Then, she tells me what my other patient told her, and says, "Oh, my God. I don't want to have to be in therapy for 14 years! I've been in so long already! It'll be almost my entire adult life." I ask her to call me when she gets home to let me know she is safe. She does.

Two days later, she comes back. She is feeling much better. She reports that she let Ereshkigal out for a bit with her husband. She became much more assertive than she usually is, but when Ereshkigal was getting out of hand, she took over again.

IDENTIFICATION WITH THE AGGRESSOR

As a term, *identification with the aggressor* is much used but frequently confusing and difficult to understand. What are the processes by which identification with the aggressor occurs? And, how is an explanation meaningful clinically?

In my view, identification with the aggressor can be understood as a two-stage process. The first stage is initiated by trauma, but the second stage is agentic and defensive. While identification with the aggressor begins as an automatic organismic process, with repeated activation and use, it becomes a defensive process. As a dissociative defense, it has two enacted relational parts, the part of the victim and the part of the aggressor. Here, when I use the phrase *identification with the aggressor,* I emphasize its intrapersonal aspects—how aggressor and victim self-states interrelate in the internal world.

Historically, the concept of identification with the aggressor was introduced by two writers, Sándor Ferenczi (1932/1949) and Anna Freud (1966), each with different meanings for it. Ferenczi introduced the term first in his famous "Confusion of Tongues Between the Child and the Adult" (1932/1949) article in which he described how the child who is being abused becomes transfixed and "robbed of his senses," as a result of which the child becomes subject to automatic mimicry of the abuser. In contrast, Anna Freud's better-known concept of identification with the aggressor (1966) described active identification with an authority or with the authority's aggression and power. It has a self-protective and agentic cast and can presage superego formation. The way I understand the process owes much more to Ferenczi's description. Ferenczi (1932/1949) wrote:

> These children feel physically and morally helpless . . . for the overpowering force and authority of the adult makes them dumb and can rob them of their senses. The same anxiety, however, if it reaches a certain maximum, compels them to subordinate themselves like automata to the will of the aggressor, to divine each one of his desires and to gratify these; completely oblivious of themselves they identify themselves with the aggressor. . . . The weak and undeveloped personality reacts to sudden unpleasure not by defense, but by anxiety-ridden identification and introjection of the menacing person or aggressor. . . . One part of their personalities, possibly the nucleus, got stuck in its development at a level where it was unable to use the *alloplastic* way of reaction but could only react in an *autoplastic* way by a kind of mimicry. (p. 228, emphasis added)

I read Ferenczi as saying that as a result of being overwhelmed, the child becomes hypnotically transfixed on the aggressor's wishes and behavior, automatically identifying by mimicry rather than by an agentic identification with the aggressors role. Ferenczi was not describing an identification that involves willful initiative or a healthy identification in which the process augments and expands the child's developing sense of identity—in which the identification is linked with the rest of the self.

The word *autoplastic* means changing the self. The child's sense of agency, identity, and integrity of self are diminished in the process of identification with the aggressor. The child, having experienced him- or herself as an object of use for the caretaker, rather than as a person of intrinsic value, may orient around the caretaker's needs and responses, as the center of self. In chaotic, neglectful, or abusive familial environments, this may involve an intent focus on the abuser's postures, motions, facial expressions, words, and feelings. In their description of the compulsive mimicry of their mothers by some traumatized boys with gender identity disorder (GID), Coates and Moore (1995, 1997) described this kind of experience as one of "being taken over from the outside" (1997, p. 301). This phrase describes well the assault on the self by trauma, something that has also been called *soul murder*. In his book *Soul Murder* (1989), Shengold revisited a scene in Orwell's *1984*, in which O'Brien, the boss, torturer, and brainwasher of Winston Smith, the hero, speaks to Winston. He said: "You will be hollow. We will squeeze you empty, and then we shall fill you with ourselves" (1949/2003, pp. 264–265).

As Ferenczi (1932/1949) also noted, the aggressor

> disappears as part of external reality and becomes intra- as opposed to extra-psychic; the intra-psychic is then subjected, in a dream-like state as is the traumatic trance, to the primary process. . . . In any case, the attack as a rigid external reality ceases to exist and in the traumatic trance the child succeeds in maintaining the previous situation of tenderness. (p. 228)

Thus, a positive attachment relationship with the abuser, a *situation of tenderness*, is preserved in consciousness, but this is illusory. In the traumatic trance, knowledge of malevolence that cannot be dealt with in the "real" physical world becomes a living terror in the inner world:

> Although the terror-filled relationship is dissociated, it frames the survivor's world view as an inescapable constant background definition. In this way, the "bad objects" never go away (Fairbairn, 1952). Many such individuals consciously abhor violent and abusive behavior and may have developed the lack of its expression as a personal ideal. Yet, try as they may, this maneuver often ends up being undertaken in the realm of illusion, for they cannot avoid being overtaken at times by the identity of the aggressor as a result of having so many times filled this person's shoes. (Howell, 2002a, p. 935)

With respect to this world of illusion, the problem of the child's own aggression is an important one in abusive circumstances. The experience of unfettered and unpunished aggression toward a loved one has often been absent in dissociative patients. Winnicott (1971) described how the child's experience and expression of aggression toward an object (the other person) who survives and does not retaliate can enable the other to become "real in the sense of being part of shared reality and not just a bundle of projections" (p. 88). This transformation involves an important psychological shift away from a relatively primitive form of interacting "that can be described in terms of the subject as an isolate" (p. 88) in which the object is experienced primarily in terms of projection and identification. The object becomes real by virtue of having been killed in fantasy, surviving, and not retaliating.

Considering this issue of "survival," Benjamin (1990), in common with Ferenczi, observed how unaccepted experience becomes exclusively intrapsychic:

> The flipside of Winnicott's analysis would be that when destruction is not countered with survival, when the other's reality does not come into view, a defensive process of internalization takes place.... What cannot be worked through and dissolved with the outside other is transposed into a drama of internal objects. It shifts from the domain of the intersubjective into the domain of the intrapsychic.... When the other does not survive and aggression is not dissipated, it becomes almost exclusively intrapsychic. (p. 41)

Traumatic Attachment

Like other attachments, traumatic attachments may involve mimicking of the attachment figure. For example, Van der Hart et al. (2000) described a soldier who had a posttraumatic twitch in his jaw that seemed to mimic the facial movements he saw on the face of his beloved comrade who was gasping for breath as he lay dying. The philosopher Michael Polanyi wrote of implicit knowing in his book, *The Tacit Dimension* (1967), and Emch (1944) wrote of how, in traumatized people, imitation may represent an attempt to master essential knowledge about significant others: "If I act like that person—become him—crawl into his skin, I shall know him and be able to predict what he will be and not be surprised—hurt—by him" (p. 14).

Current attachment theory provides ways of thinking about identification with the aggressor that rely on processes that Lyons-Ruth (1999) described as "enactive procedural representations of how to do things with others" (p. 385). Such unconscious enactive, procedural, relational knowing is the result of two-person interactions, and these procedural ways of being with another constitute the larger portion of our lives. In contrast to relationships of mutuality and interdependence in which there is much validating and mirroring of the other's experience, in traumatic procedural learning, there is no opportunity for interchange of perspectives. Inherent contradictions in behaviors and among implicit and explicit communications between caregiver and child cannot be examined. As a result, these procedural models of how to be with another do not get linked.

In sum, these aggressor-identified, grandiose, and dominating abuser self-states that often embody rage, contempt, and omnipotence may arise as procedural, imitative, dyadic enactments.

When the child learns the roles of both abuser and victim procedurally in conditions of traumatic attachment, the corresponding self-states are likely to be dissociated.

NOTE

1. Note on Ereshkigal: According to Merlin Stone, author of *Ancient Mirrors of Womanhood* (1979), Ereshkigal had been the all-powerful goddess of the dead who was forced into submission and marriage to the god of war, pestilence, and disease. Ereshkigal was a version of The Great Mother. An early prayer to her had been:

> I will praise the Queen of Humankind,
> I will praise Ereshkigal,
> Queen of Humankind,
> Among all the many deities,
> Ereshkigal is merciful.

Thus, it would appear that Janice's Ereshkigal has identified with only parts of the story—the powerful, omnipotent part (much as Freud did with the Oedipus story; see end note to Chapter 1)—omitting the more inclusive Great Mother identification and Ereshkigal's subjugation.

Chapter 12

The Therapeutic Relationship

Multiple Dimensions of Coconstruction

A DID patient calls me and leaves a message that he is canceling the next session and those in the near future because of money problems. He says that he will call me in the future when he has the situation under better control. I call him back to discuss this, and he answers, "What did I say?" Another patient calls in a suicidal crisis after having precipitously quit therapy. She does not remember the past 2 weeks.

What is a therapist to do? With patients with dissociative identity disorder (DID), the identity of the speaker may change unbeknownst to the hearer. It is imperative that the DID therapist be aware that the identity of the person he or she is speaking with now, may not be the same identity present a minute ago or last week. What Bromberg (2000) called the "ever shifting configuration of *multiple real relationships* in which dissociation has a role" (p. 568; emphasis in original) is especially the case with people with DID. The patient with DID will have multiple real relationships with the therapist and others, as well as multiple transferences. Of course, the therapist will also have multiple real relationships and multiple transferences and countertransferences.

TRAUMATIC TRANSFERENCES AND COUNTERTRANSFERENCES

Traumatic Transferences

The most basic transference paradigm for patients with DID is the traumatic transference (Herman, 1992; Loewenstein, 1993; Spiegel, 1986), although this may contain some versions of the erotic transference as well. The traumatic transference refers to the patient's expectation that he or she will be abused and exploitatively used as a narcissistic extension of the therapist. Some parts are consciously aware of this expectation. Others embody ways of coping with life that are designed to keep the expectation of exploitation out of awareness or to focus on other problems. Because most patients with

DID were traumatized in the family of origin and beginning at an early period in their lives, their expectations of abuse can be intense.

Not only multiple transferences develop with highly dissociative patients, but also multiple traumatic transferences. Traumatic transferences are often hidden: The therapist may be in communication with a trusting host, while beneath the surface are many who expect to be betrayed. Among the parts who are highly aware that they have been exploited and who expect that the therapist will behave in ways similar to their original abuser(s), some are sensitive and scared, fearing that if they trust the therapist, they will be hurt. Other parts may be easily ignited by a misplaced word or action. Yet other parts operate in denial of the trauma. In addition, it is not only individual parts who embody and express traumatic transferences but also the overall configuration of the interrelationships among the parts.

There is another important matter regarding traumatic transference. In certain important ways involving intersubjective attunement to another's unconscious, the suspicions and fears that some of the identities harbor may be correct. In contrast to the therapist's desire to be seen in a positive and benign light:

> The patient correctly perceives that within the therapist resides all those potentials for murderous rage, sadistic thought and action, collusive betrayal, and self-object devaluation which the patient knows too well from the past. The therapist's conscious or unconscious denial of these potentials is, in my experience, the most common source of impasse in the treatment of persons with posttraumatic disorders. (Chefetz, 1997b, p. 259)

Chefetz's observation is crucial. Therapists' blindspots for their own potentials for murderous rage, and so on, as Chefetz observes, may result in unresolved enactments. Enactments in therapy do not occur *on a level playing field*. Although the therapeutic dyad is coconstructed, this does not mean that it is equally so.

Dissociative patients are more vulnerable than nondissociative ones as a rule: They cannot always answer directly, but may disappear without engaging if their therapist becomes harsh or hostile with them. Or, an angry alter may appear. Although disappearance of the host or appearance of an angry alter may transferentially repeat the patient's early experience, such events should also be understood in terms of the real power relationship.

Traumatic Countertransferences

The complexities of multiple dissociated identities, who all have their own transferences, are likely to increase the therapist's countertransferential vulnerabilities. Traumatic transferences yielding behaviors that are aggressively angry, aggressively needy, passively needy, passively aggressive, and so on, especially if they are hidden, may elicit a traumatic countertransference before the therapist is ready—or knows that it is happening. At such times a therapist's ability to accept and "hold" the impact of the patient's horror-filled memories and feelings, without tuning out or reciprocally respond-ing, is crucial.

Patients' posttraumatic expectations can have quite startling effects on their therapists. Loewenstein (1993) described an occasion in which he become momentarily

> flooded with an insistent visual image and tactile hallucination of touching the patient in an intimate manner. Although I felt intensely disquieted and disoriented by this experience, I managed to inquire neutrally if "something had shifted" within her at that moment. She replied, "Yes, the sexy one is here now.... She's a child." (p. 67)

Loewenstein reported that as they were able to talk about this, his visual hallucinations disappeared.

Such experiences of intense, strange, upsetting nonverbal response to severely traumatized patients are common. Loewenstein (1993) noted that the patient that he described had "previously been overinvolved with sev-eral therapists" (p. 66). Kluft (1990) addressed this common countertrans-ferential problem that far too many therapists have enacted as "the sitting duck syndrome" for many vulnerable patients. The dissociative patient is a sitting duck for exploitation because the dissociation of parts of the self able to read danger cues having to do with malevolent attachment fig-ures was in the service of survival and attachment when she was growing up. Thus, the sexy ones may come out, enacting "a procedural way of being with others" that is familiar but potentially dangerous to them. They are too vulnerable to defend themselves—or sometimes even to know that they need defending.

Two kinds of traumatic countertransferences are the pull to be abusive and the feeling that one is being abused. In addition to the kind of pull to be exploitative that Loewenstein (1993) identified, DID therapists may also find themselves feeling exploited or emotionally maimed in the work and often angry, exasperated, burned, shamed, drained, anxious, and depressed as a result. Davies and Frawley's (1994) outlined four matrices of eight transference and countertransference positions that are typically in operation in trauma therapy. The matrices that they described involve the "uninvolved nonabusing parent and the neglected child"; the "sadistic abuser and the helpless, impotently enraged victim"; the "omnipotent res-cuer and the entitled child who demands to be rescued"; and the "seducer and the seduced." The therapist will most likely get to occupy all eight posi-tions. (However, from Ferenczi to Davies and Frawley, I think that *seduce* is usually too mild a word to describe the kind of behavior on the part of the original perpetrator that is actually meant. *Sexual exploitation* would often be more accurate.)

With highly dissociative patients, therapists may find themselves feeling a variety of other intense emotions, such as anger, fury, horror, terror, sleepiness, utter exhaustion, and parental-like caring, among others. The emergence of these emotions in the therapist may be due to a variety of factors, including processes often called "projective identification," enactment, dissociative attunement (Hopenwasser, 2008), as well as empathy (which may lead to vicarious traumatization). Of course, all of these processes occur in relationship, but as is also true for the patient, there will be many times when something in the therapist's own history, defense structure, and other vulnerability is the major source of the therapist's idiosyncratic response.

By the nature of the work, as well as their own humanity, trauma therapists are also vulnerable to vicarious traumatization. It can be exhausting to empathize with so much pain and to truly take in the extent of the capacity for evil of the perpetrators of some traumatized people. It is important for therapists to have their own support systems, including consultations and peer groups.

Erotic Transference and Countertransference

Especially with dissociative patients, erotic transferences have multiple meanings. Chefetz (1997) highlighted how the seeming erotic transference may express the patient's need to be special, and how apparent hypersexuality may cover all kinds of dissociated affects, including sadness, grief, terror, loss, and longings for intimacy, that the child could not express. A response on this level is a more accurate and helpful approach than responding to the "erotic" transference as an adult attempt to seduce. The erotic transference may express the traumatic transference in that a part of the patient may feel that she must please the therapist in this way. It may also be an attempt to preempt control of the therapeutic milieu to avoid dealing with painful and difficult issues. Erotic transference in a male with a female therapist may at times represent a way to claim masculinity and as an aspect of defense to avoid feeling like a helpless little boy. Chefetz (1997) sees erotic countertransference coming in part from the same sources as erotic transference: the need to feel special and to deny painful and "unacceptable" feelings: "The therapist unconsciously longs for repair of his or her wounds. The therapist privately wishes to be nurtured.... Hatred of the patient and his or her demands remains unconscious" (p. 258).

PROJECTIVE IDENTIFICATION: THE INTERPERSONAL
LANGUAGE OF DISSOCIATED SELF-STATES

The vignette described by Loewenstein (1993) could be called projective identification. In this case, a dissociative part of the patient, who was "out," was communicating by posture, facial expression, motion, and so on. She was sending cues to which the therapist was responding. This example illustrates how work with DID clarifies understanding of the dissociative communications (often also described as projective identification) of people who do not have DID. Usually, people who are communicating dissociatively are not able to help us to understand our unusual responses by saying something like "the sexy one is out." His patient's communication helped Loewenstein to formulate his experience (Stern, 1997). The presence of the dissociated self-state is most often felt in the interpersonal field without the benefit of its presence being identified. In DID, this involves the partial or temporary appearance of a part who had not been out (who had been on the inside), in the context of the behavior of the usual presenting self. The therapist may find him- or herself responding in a reciprocal way but not knowing why. In this formulation, DID is the template for understanding enactments in work with patients who do not have a formal dissociative disorder.

Projective identification is often used to refer to a person's attempt to disown his or her own experience by "putting it into" another person. The disowned affect or experience is then considered to be induced in the other person. However, in my view, projective identification is a term rife with multiple meanings and problems. Among the problems are the following:

- The assumption that something is "put into" Person B by Person A in a way that allows Person B to disown any sources of the experience (which is supposed to originate in and be disowned by A) in him- or herself and simply blames A for whatever B is thinking or feeling. For example, his patient was not "putting anything into" Loewenstein. His response was his own and came from his own cognitive and sensorimotor system. (This is not to say that he was not responding to the initially unidentified presence of The Sexy One.)
- The assumption of a unified self in the original definition of projective identification is problematic. The projector must somehow simultaneously know and not know about the projection. With reference to the hypothetical unified self, if the self does not somehow know the disavowed material, how would the person know what to expect to interact with in the receiver? On the other hand, if the unified self knows, the process would be conscious, and there would be no need for the projective identification.
- The assumption that the projector is trying to control the other person,

I think it is less problematic and more accurate to think in terms of the inter-personal language of dissociated self-states or, more simply put, enactments:

> Once a dissociated self-state is expressed (in whatever way), it enters the interpersonal field as a way of being with another. Here this way of being with another meets another person who also has ways of being with another. In this way of thinking, projective identification and enactment are two sides of the same coin. (Howell, 2005, p. 11)

Another way to say it might be that projective identification is one person's dissociated experience in communication with another person's disso-ciated experience. The language is interpersonal and coconstructed because the recipient's register for the experience is also comprised of dissociated self-states. Without dissociation in the recipient, there would be no sense of an induction of "out-of-the-blue" experience, only an empathic recogni-tion. Therefore, dissociation in both parties is required for the concept to be meaningful. It is far simpler just to speak of enactments.

As I see it, there are two primary ways to view this interpersonal lan-guage of dissociated self-states. One is in terms of dissociated reciprocal role relationships, and the other involves communication from right brain to right brain (Schore, 2003a, 2003b).

In Melanie Klein's original meaning, projective identification was a purely intrapsychic and unidirectional process. Laplanche and Pontalis (1973) defined projective identification as "a mechanism revealed in fantasies in which the subject inserts his self—in whole or in part—into the object, in order to harm, possess, or control it" (p. 356). Later, Bion, Ogden, and oth-ers expanded the meaning of the term to include interactions in the mother–infant dyad and in the transference–countertransference. Despite these more positive formulations that included the interpersonal nature of the process, articulations of this process often get repackaged in a one-person psychol-ogy devoid of shared responsibility for the experience. Sandler (1976), also assuming the interpersonal nature of the process, wrote that he does not find the concepts "projective identification" or "putting parts of oneself into the analyst" adequate to understand the dynamic interactions that "occur in transference and countertransference. It seems that a complicated sys-tem of unconscious cues, both given and received, is involved" (p. 46). As if in answer to Sandler, Anthony Ryle (1994, 1997a, 1997b) described how reciprocal role procedures, involving generalized procedural memories of dyadic interactions, are enacted. When dissociated, these dyadic reciprocal role patterns provide templates for rigid reenactments of old experience.

Because deprivation and abuse can interfere with integrative personal-ity organization, in traumatized patients there will be greater isolation, or dissociation, of reciprocal role patterns and greater personality fragmenta-tion. The internalization of self–other procedures implies the corresponding ability and need to elicit reciprocation from others: "In enacting a role there is always pressure on the other to relate and reciprocate in a particular way" (Ryle, 1994, p. 110). As they are less consciously contextualized within the structures of other dyadic role patterns, given dissociated role patterns will be narrower and have a more urgent need for reciprocation to obtain confirmation of the self. People whose reciprocal role patterns are more isolated (dissociated) and whose repertoire is more limited tend to interact more forcefully with others and to do so in search of a specific response to obtain confirmation of the self. Consequently, the other person in interaction is more likely to feel pressured. Because the demand from the "projector" is not conscious or formulated it forces people into reciprocating *implicit* modes of knowing another.

In Loewenstein's (1993) vignette, his patient's "sexy one" was an "isolated subjectivity" (Chefetz & Bromberg, 2004, p. 431) in the context of her overall self-structure. Because of her isolation, the stance and intention of the "sexy one" were not modulated by other aspects of her self, and she exerted a stronger pull than she might have if she had been less isolated. However, there is another aspect of what often falls under the rubric of projective identification; and that is communication from right brain to right brain (Schore, 2003a, 2003b).

Schore wrote of the power of intersubjective affective responsiveness via communication from right brain to right brain. These affects are communicated by body rhythms, somatic states, and facial expression, all in a right-brain-to-right-brain way. The processing of this information is so rapid that it is not consciously perceived. Inasmuch as dissociated traumatic memories are stored in implicit procedural memory, they are also communicated nonverbally, right brain to right brain.

> Thus, in the clinical context, although it appears to be an invisible, instantaneous, endogenous unidirectional phenomenon, the bidirectional process of projective identification is actually a very rapid sequence of reciprocal affective transactions within the intersubjective field that is coconstructed by the patient and the therapist. (Schore, 2003b, p. 73)

Whatever we call it, the interpersonal language of dissociated self-states affects various aspects of the treatment frame. Boundary management is often more complicated in the treatment of DID than when we are not thinking in a dissociative paradigm. When we are thinking of the patient as a unitary personality, we think of the whole person's motivations and actions. For instance, the patient intrudes into the therapist's life with many phone calls or requests for the expenditure of extra time. At least in theory, this is a simple matter of maintaining proper boundaries. For someone with DID, it is often a particular part who is making the calls or requests, and the activity of this part may or may not be known about by the part most frequently out.

For example, Maggie, a college student who is academically talented, suddenly wanted help with her homework and wanted it outside the session as well, including wanting me to read all of her papers to be turned in to the teacher. At the same time that she was making the request for homework help, I noticed that I was feeling as I did when nursing my own children when they were babies. Literally, I was feeling a somatic "wish" to feed her from my own body.

Immediately after that, Maggie informed me that her 8-year-old part was out. This particular part longs for mothering and feels frightened and vulnerable. (Maggie was extremely neglected by her mother and certainly never got any help with homework from her.) The 8-year-old then began to tell me in various ways how needy for loving life sustenance she is. (Maggie did not put anything "into" me because the way that I responded was already part of my experience. However, the way that I responded remained partially unformulated until Maggie gave me some context.) My awareness of how extremely vulnerable this part is then aided me in thinking about how to address the situation. Speaking to the child part, I told her that I understood that she feels insecure about her homework and that she longs for the feeling of having a strong, helpful, reliable relationship— of someone being there for her, as a buttress from which to proceed in her interactions with the outside world. I said that I would be willing to look over a small amount of the work that she wanted me to see and see how that feels to her, but that I could not do this routinely. Since we both know that she is in fact smart, I suggested that we could talk about what she is afraid of, what she wants, and what she feels she needs.

Finally, I asked if there are older, more grown-up parts who are academically more secure. There were. I then asked if they would be willing to stay with this 8-year-old when she is frightened about so much—about needing and about her papers. In addition to furthering integration, this approach to helping the child part is premised on her responsibility for herself and avoids the potentiation of an out-of-control enactment in which the treatment becomes about getting mothering and bypassing the painful work of mourning the fact that she got far too little mothering.

So far, I have been discussing the interpersonal language of dissociated self-states in the framework of enactments. But, there is another important aspect of dissociation that often goes unnoticed in the treatment: dissociative attunements.

DISSOCIATIVE ATTUNEMENTS: DANCING TO THE OTHER'S (AND HENCE, ONE'S OWN) UNRECOGNIZED MUSIC

We are drawn into attunements with the rhythms and moods of others often without knowing it or without knowing why. For example, therapists working with patients with dissociative disorders often report experiencing a fog at certain points in sessions; indeed, these experiences of the therapist may be diagnostic markers for the presence of dissociative disorders (Loewenstein, 1991). As part of being attuned to the patient, we may experience much more than simply our own cognitive and emotional reactions, including the horror of what has happened to someone that we register in the normal ways. When we are attuned, we are "in" it. We also experience the rhythm and the "music" of the patient's mood. Often, we do not know it. This is a matter completely aside from projective identification, counter-transference, and enactment: dissociative attunement.

I think that the concept of dissociative attunement, originally presented by Karen Hopenwasser (2008), may well become pivotal for much relational psychoanalytic thinking of the future. Drawing on chaos theory and the work of infant developmentalists, such as Colwyn Trevarthyn, Hopenwasser conceptualized dissociative attunements as "systematically self-emergent moments in which multiple self-states are shared by means other than projection" (p. 349). Further, she stated that "a mutually held state of attunement is neither a 'do to you' nor a 'do to me' experience. It is a synchronized, simultaneous awareness of knowing that is nonlinear and fully bidirectional" (p. 351). Dissociative attunement with respect to our psychotherapeutic work involves empathic attunement and affective resonance that are dissociated initially by both parties. What is required is that the therapist stay with the unwelcome experience, helping the patient to do the same. Eventually, both parties are able to mourn the pain and the loss that were too unbearable to enter conscious experience. The therapeutic dyad does this together. It has some similarity to Bion's (1957, 1959) and Ogden's (1983, 1986) descriptions of the mother and the therapist metabolizing unbearable material and then giving it back to the baby/patient, but unlike that concept of projective identification, this is a parallel process in which the therapist joins with the patient as they mourn and suffer together the jointly held painful affects and ugly intentions. One could liken it to modeling or witnessing, in that the therapist is respectively engaged in the same process and standing by, but in contrast to "showing from above" or "knowing from the side," this model is completely equalitarian.

Likening dissociative attunement to a dance, in an extension of the metaphor of the dissociative dance used by Baker (1997) to describe projective identification and enactments, Hopenwasser (2008) emphasized that this is a dissociative dance in which we as therapists willingly join. In this process, what matters most is what we and the patient do *with* each other. In this frame, what we do *to* each other becomes more or less a distraction. Hopenwasser described two cases, one who did not have DID and one who did. For the patient who did not have DID, both patient and therapist experienced a "meanness" within themselves that they expressed to each other, but that for both in the interaction felt like not-me. In describing the case, she asked why the events would not be describable as projective identification and answered that the patient was fully aware of her meanness. Why, then, was this not countertransference enactment? She answered as follows:

> But the repetition of these painful encounters suggested to me a shared process beyond countertransference yet still outside of our jointly held awareness. It felt like a jointly dissociated awareness that was actually a function of attunement, rather than misattunement. I was not missing the mark in my comments. I was hitting a bull's-eye over and over again in some kind of reckless precision that stunned us both. (p. 356)

Hopenwasser (2008) stated that she began to take on the quality in interaction with this patient that the patient had most complained about in herself: a tendency to be gratuitously mean. This was not a quality that Hopenwasser had experienced as an aspect of her normal self. But in interaction with this patient, try as she would not to be mean, "every now and then I would open my mouth, words would spill forth with only the best intentions, and wham—Marina would feel punched in the stomach" (p. 356).

Hopenwasser (2008) decided to work on the problem as her own:

> Over a period of many, many months I opted to work with my reiterated meanness the way one would work with internal perpetrator parts. I never blamed her for the provocation or attempted to help her understand this as a coconstructed catastrophe. Instead I struggled to sit with the urges to rid myself of shame and guilt. It became clear that an underlying attunement would allow her to sit with me, with my shame and guilt, with her shame and guilt, together in this whole miasma of relationally induced shame and guilt. Simultaneously I reflected on my own countertransference issues. (pp. 356–357)

The author (Hopenwasser, 2008) stated that for over a year she and her patient "sat in a state of dissociated internal perpetration that was finely attuned. This attunement held us like gravity to each other. We both suffered, we both struggled, but enough of the time we could both remember that neither of us was solely malevolent" (p. 357). Finally, they each learned, with great effort, to stop being mean with each other. They each learned better how to recover from attacks and to display caring, so that finally their connection did not have to include this torment. Hopenwasser stated that she believes "it was this dissociated attunement that allowed us to stay connected through a mutual inner experience of perpetration" (p. 357).

Hopenwasser (2008) ended by saying the following:

> When we bring our own rhythmic ability into the mourning experience we are facilitating healing in an implicit, embodied manner. When we

sit with our patients in a state of mutual grief and disappointment, we are utilizing dissociative attunement in its most therapeutic form. (p. 362)

Our conceptual history, including concepts of projective identification as well as transference and countertransference, has much emphasis on *done to*, such as descriptions of the experience of being invaded by the patient's psychic contents. There have been many descriptions in our work with traumatized and dissociative patients of the therapist being overtaken by sleepiness—an attunement to the sleepiness that the patient is experiencing, often as an aspect of a trance. While the therapist may assess this in the framework of an intrusion, I do not believe that it needs to be understood this way. The therapist has willfully joined with the patient on the path of sharing her experience. The therapist has made a choice to enter. When one opens new doors, what lies ahead is likely to be unexpected. We are attuning to the patient's experience, which is new to us. There is no intrusion. We are simply entering a new world. This is truly a dyadic engagement because both parties are there together. The model of projective identification is a "done to" model. While in its later, post-Kleinian forms, projective identification is a model of dyadic interaction, it involves each party with separate experience, intruding and receiving experiences each into and from the other. In the forms of role enactments (Ryle & Kerr, 2002) and countertransference matrices, both the patient and the therapist are split into experiential parts that are the reciprocal of the other. Hopenwasser's (2008) model builds on these earlier ones, but I think that her model of mutually synchronizing systems is a most therapeutically promising one.

I would like to describe a case vignette that illustrates some of these points. As opposed to Hopenwasser's (2008) example, this is a case of DID. The vignette illustrates attunement with multiple self-states in the patient at any given moment.

Linda switched to a 5-year-old self-state and described her torture as she was a captive in her home where her brothers and their friends would force her to perform fellatio on them. Her mother would not believe her reports but would instead beat her for suggesting such things. At times, she would go to the ceiling, watching the "other" 5-year-old Linda who was being beaten. As the 5-year-old part of Linda was describing this, I became aware of the distinct feeling that she was so sweet and vulnerable as she was beaten. For a moment, I became aware that I could hurt her. There was a feeling in me of potential sadism, potential brutal sadism. (At that moment, I was attuned also with her internal perpetrators, who were not "speaking" at that moment. These self-states understood the experience as sadistic, although the 5-year-old Linda did not.) Once the grown-up host had returned, I said to her, "You were treated with incredible sadism." Linda's response indicated that she felt exactly understood by my comment.

In our interaction, the 5-year-old part was able to reexperience her trauma, but with the added component that important parts of the nature of the experience had been articulated and formulated. She could also add to her experience the fact that talking about it with me had been safe, and that nothing had happened to her. It was a corrective emotional experience. All of these were part of the therapeutic action.

However, I would like to examine this experience from the standpoint of dissociative attunement. I was joining with Linda in the horrible music and brutal rhythm of a self-state of a 5-year-old abused child, who was both suffering abuse and anticipating abuse. She was not "putting any experience" into me, and I would not describe this as a "complementary" identification with her. I had stepped into her music and had joined her in her experience of being abused and anticipating being abused by another. She was not doing anything to me; I was not doing anything to her. I was sitting with her and experiencing with her the way she, both as parts and as a whole, was organizing her experience.

By means of attunement, including dissociative attunement, when we pay attention to our experience, even when we do not have the verbal means of labeling or categorizing it, in session with the patient, we may be given important clues about the patient's experience—about what the patient feels like, past and present.

States of mind shift in our patients and in ourselves. The analyst relies on his or her acquired knowledge, past experiences of similar instances and how they were resolved; at such times, we have little "objectivity." What we have is a finely honed subjectivity—our knowledge of ourselves, which we attempt to use as a "baseline." And, no longer is it adequate to think of our interactions with our clients in terms of simple transference and countertransference. As humans, we influence each other in many ways that we do not understand well beyond the fact that it happens. Nonconscious affective communication of the sort Schore (2003b) described and likely mirrors neurons (Gallese, 2009) as well influences our responses to others as we empathize, identify, and imitate more than we know. But, as part of this we also become entrained (Hopenwasser, 2008) in another person's way of being. This helps us to know another person, but we must be able to exit the entrainment, to know the difference. We are like resonating tuning forks, but our job is to let that happen without shutting down or turning away.

Colwyn Trevarthen's Work

As some background to Hopenwasser's work, I would like to briefly say something about Trevarthen's work, which is based on some of the same premises. Trevarthen studies babies and the interactions between babies and their caregivers. In a way that has some similarity to Schore's right-brain-to-right-brain procedural communication, Trevarthen (2009) emphasized the rhythm and the musicality of interactions: "All animal actions take the form of rhythmic or pulsating measured sequences of movement.... Brains are networks or dynamic systems all obedient to the rhythms that flow in unison" (p. 76).

Trevarthen is also known for his concept of *innate intersubjectivity*:

> The combined operation of visceral and somatic "mirror" reactions between mother and infant gives, in ways we do not fully understand, the infant means of expression and access to the other anticipatory "motor-images" and "feelings" and permits direct motive-to-motive engagement with a companion.... *Thus arises the psychological phenomenon of intersubjectivity, which couples human brains in joint affect and cognition, and mediates all cultural learning.* (p. 70; emphasis in original)

Trevarthen (2009) described how "protoconversations" with infants younger than 4 months show primary intersubjectivity. These protoconversations are followed by musical games. Trevarthen emphasized how the baby is constantly organizing, constantly anticipating, constantly synchronizing with the tenor of his or her interpersonal environment. In an earlier (Trevarthen, 2003) work, he described a 20-week-old blind baby conducting with her hand as her mother was singing to her—with high and low beats in space, that is, with motoric perfect pitch and perfect rhythm. What was most remarkable was that the baby's beats were several seconds ahead of the mother's. This meant that the baby not only was following along but also was anticipating her mother's song. I believe that this is what people do: We anticipate the other. And, as Trevarthyn said, we anticipate the other to interact with the other.

Chapter 13

Dreams in DID

> In analytic treatment or in dreamwork, when the therapist or dream-worker is able to relate to each aspect of the patient's self through its own subjectivity, each part of the self becomes increasingly able to coexist with the rest, and in that sense is linked to the others. It is an experience of coherence, cohesiveness, and continuity, that comes about through human relatedness.
>
> Bromberg (2003, p. 704)

Dreams are especially important to ask about in work with patients with dissociative identity disorder (DID) because they can easily fall between the cracks in the midst of the complicated and time-consuming work with the many different parts. Dream work may often reveal important information and feelings that were not brought forth in work with parts.

Dream work with DID patients is in many ways similar to dream work with patients who do not have DID; in many ways, it is quite different. In both cases, dream perceptions, thoughts, and reminiscences are often highly condensed, overlaid, one on top of the other, like a three-dimensional collage, in which the pieces blend into a structural whole. Dreams have their own profound and special language that renders experience with vividness, intensity, and in metaphor. Dreams telescope different times into a single dream event, symbolically substitute one dream element for another, condensing disparate people, places, and meanings into one image. Dreams may express wish fulfillment, state a message to the dreamer, or frame a point of view. While dreams can be intricately complicated, they can also sometimes be starkly simple and clear.

Nonetheless, often the dreams of patients with DID have characteristics that more ordinary dreams do not. To begin, unlike more ordinary dreams, posttraumatic dreams are often almost literally reenacted memories in the dreaming space. Among recurrent trauma dreams, some just tell the same story over and over; others modify the story somewhat from dream to dream. While some trauma dreams seem literal in the depictions, others may include all of the symbolism, displacement, and so on that are characteristic of more ordinary dreams. Even when they are symbolic, trauma dreams may often feel literal, partly because they convey raw emotion. For example, traumatized people often symbolize the decimation and burial of parts of themselves with dream images of fallen support beams that now trap and pin people, usually children, beneath them; of graveyards where children have been buried alive with horrific living memories; or of parts of the self that have been buried alive.

Dreams may express ways that the adult as a child attempted to regulate affect. For example, one patient who was traumatized as a child had recurrent dreams of rising to the ceiling, even over the trees. Yet, in the dreams this did not feel upsetting: Her ability to accomplish such "levitation," as she called it in her dreams, was a matter of pride. Strangely, in her dreams no one else ever saw her rise, and she often wished to share the joy of her accomplishment with others but was always unsuccessful. In our analytic work, it became apparent that these dreams probably did recall times that she experienced herself rising to the ceiling in response to trauma. But, they also reflected her pride in being able to dissociate as a defense, in being able to take care of herself by being able to regulate her affect in this way. Thus, the dream revealed not only that she had had early trauma that had sent her rising to the ceiling, and not only how she had learned to frequently "rise" in an anticipatory defensive way, but also how she had managed to deflect her experience of early terror, transforming her view of this defense into something of which she was proud.

When we move to the explicitly dissociative arena, dreams have a special language and more particular meanings. Although the basic structure and language are not limited to dissociative disorders, as they simply characterize the human mind, this language is especially important to be aware of in the case of dissociative disorders. While we all have dissociated self-states, dreams of people with DID illustrate with particular vividness how parts of the self take on a character and a voice, stating their perceptions, beliefs, fears, and desires.

Dreams may also sometimes even roughly adumbrate dissociated behavior that was enacted on the outer stage of reality (Barrett, 1994, 1996; Brenner, 2001). For example, in some of his earlier work, Fairbairn discussed personified parts of his patient's psyche—the "mischievous boy," the "critic," the "little girl," and the "martyr"—that regularly appeared in dreams as well as in waking life. Fairbairn (1931/1952b) stated that, for this patient, the "personifications seem best interpreted as functioning structural units which . . . attained a certain independence within the total personality, and it seems reasonable to suppose that the mental processes which give rise to multiple personality only represent a more extreme form" (p. 219).

Dreams may express relationships and conflicts between dissociated self-states. For example, a patient dreamt that she had a headache, and that she needed four aspirins—"two for both" of them. The same patient, a woman for whom aggression was very much dissociated, dreamt of two women who looked very much alike. One was trying to strangle the other. The problems of the dissociated self are especially apparent when self-states seek to dominate or annihilate each other, as in the dream just described. The correspondence to action on the stage of reality is that the annihilating parts often do not recognize that they share the same body.

THE SAME DREAM BUT FROM A DIFFERENT PERSPECTIVE

Another marked feature of the dreams of people with DID is that different self-states may have the same dream but from different perspectives. Different self-states may have different roles in the action of the same dream; they may literally "see" the action of the dream differently; they may notice different things; and aspects of the dream may be meaningful to some parts but not to others. Sometimes, the imagery of a dream recalled by one identity will influence the others; sometimes a dream may be specific to one identity but not to others. The confusion about such dreams can at times be extremely upsetting, much more so than a nightmare might be to a "singleton." As the therapist talks with different self-states about their experience of the dream, information may be gleaned that provides insight into the organization of the patient's self-states and system defenses.

The following dream of Dennis (introduced in Chapter 1) illustrates how different self-states may have the same dream and the importance of listening to the different things they know in the dream:

A few scientist friends were just arriving to a site in the woods. There were army barracks and a wall of woods behind. The day was autumn-like and overcast. The researchers wanted to study some fauna that lived only in the woods. These animals had been bred for the purpose of weaponizing. The scientists were told to stay on the path: "Don't get off the path! Because if you do, they can get to you!" There were leafless white trees that looked like they were made of bone, all around. They had branches coming to points. They were the fauna.

There was a family behind us, a mother and a father and a 4-year-old girl. I hear a clicky sound, like there was communication with each other from the tops of the branches. The trees were clattering. It was very loud. The little girl had momentarily stepped off, and three or four of the trees had skewered her through the chest, and murdered her. One of the trees very gingerly pulled a square film from her body—a filmy sheet that had a soft glow. The film was her essence. It was whatever makes that person distinctly them.

As they tore it apart, I heard this other scream—raw suffering—a scream that heralds the knowledge that you will no longer exist. Then everything was gone.

Dennis has had the same dream from the perspective of the little girl. She momentarily steps off the path, is skewered in the chest by the same trees, and is murdered in the same way. About this, Dennis said, "I thought that the little girl was a facet of me that had not been examined." Understandably, since she is murdered, her dream is not as complexly told as Dennis's. She holds the terror in the dream, a terror that came through to me as the listener quite starkly, a terror that Dennis lives with every day. It is understandable that Dennis, whose time spent as Dennis is so often depersonalized, *from the perspective of his dream as Dennis*, casts himself as a member of a group of scientists who are studying these cruel fauna, and he says of the little girl's plight, "I thought the dream was a warning; I had 60% curiosity and 40% empathy for the little girl." It is hard for him to fully take in, as Dennis, the horror the little girl's plight. He has the curiosity of a scientist, but he does also care about her a lot. It is not surprising that Dennis has a great many "zombie" dreams in which characters who are dead come back to life but without the physical or emotional vulnerabilities that they had previously had as humans.

When Dennis told me the part of the dream in which he described how "one of the trees very gingerly pulled a square film from her body—a filmy sheet that had a soft glow. The film was her essence. It was whatever makes that person distinctly them," I heard the word *film* as implying a visual record, as memory. It is one thing to suffer immense pain; it is another to have one's memory, essence, or soul stolen. Then, remembrance is not possible. Dennis, who is as the part, Dennis, and as a whole, a highly caring person, has ambivalently told revenge fantasies. However, the bloody, hot, bone-crunching fury is held by the part named Mnemosyne, who is the personification and goddess of memory in Greek mythology (see description of Dennis's map in Chapter 10). So, he does have memory. But, memory is mixed with rage. The dream also brings to my mind how psychopaths often wish to deprive their victims of the very thing of which they have been deprived—their humanity. With Dennis, they tried but did not succeed. In addition to his attachment to his mother, his dissociation saved him.

This dream also states in readily understandable symbolic terms how close to death Dennis often felt—in fact, that he did die subjectively at the hands of the human monsters who sexually and psychologically tortured him when he was 3, and then from 8 to 10 years old. This dream is not only about Dennis's experience, however. It is a dream that says it all about the nature of psychopathic human predators. In reflecting on the dream, Dennis added that the trees were not solely evil:

> They were surviving on the food they came by. The trees behaved according to their nature. I first felt sympathy toward the parents, who knew that the little

girl's primary essence was being devoured. It felt like a cold justness. It made me shiver profoundly that the world had something like them in it, that the world has something in it that is capable of that kind of destruction.

Hearing the dream also made me shiver.

THE MUTE GIRL

Jeannie, a lovely caring woman, has symbolized herself in her dreams as The Mute Girl. Interestingly, when Jeannie and I began our work together, 9 years ago, she was extremely disorganized in her speech, such that I often found it difficult to follow her—which I can generally do well, even when people go off on multiple tangents. One area where communication was clear, however, was in her dreams. Much of the integration that has occurred in our work together has been from her telling her dreams of her highly dissociated multiple internal characters.

She had many, many dreams about a mute girl. Sometimes, this girl had been buried by rubble and had to be rescued. Sometimes she was barely alive. There was also the beautiful boy for whom she longed. These were constant dream characters. Often, there were flocks of girls (or birds) together, with herself as the leader; when danger emerged, she would lead them away in flight. Sometimes, she was a bear who lives alone and keeps people away. In other dreams, she would be viewing the world through the eyes of another being, sometimes a cranky but loving gorilla.

The Mute Girl did not interact with anyone, but she was always part of a unit, often a twin. Although she was closed off to the world, she was watching and learning, and sometimes she was the dreamer. In one of the first and clearest mute girl dreams, she lived in a self-sufficient community of children, with a beautiful girl and beautiful boy as the leaders of several units within the community. The beautiful girl went missing. The Mute Girl was the only one who knew what happened to her. The Mute Girl also had a vision of a man in a cave who had his "kills" splayed out on the walls of his cave. It is unclear whether it was the beautiful girl who was killed, but it was a bloody scene. In this dream, Jeannie was The Mute Girl and heard murmurs of other voices, such as the other children's collective frustrations, fear, and sadness about the lost beautiful girl and that they did not know how to reach her, The Mute Girl, to get the information they needed to find the beautiful girl. Her dream poignantly describes the frustrations of parts who long for connectedness and communication, as well as the sense of her internal beauty having been killed or lost. But, it also points to the role of The Mute Girl as a closed-off source of information and the importance of her eventually becoming able to speak.

Telling her dreams and discussing what they meant to her has been healing for Jeannie. I did little interpreting, mostly asking questions. Sometimes, it has seemed to me that the Selves of her dreams were doing the talking to me just as much as Jeannie was. For example, as we have been discussing her tendency to avoid relationships in which romantic commitment is a possibility and how this may have something to do with early abuse, she began to dream of a little boy who had the job in the house of monitoring relationships. He lived in a house, in a special room where in a dedicated way he controlled the possibilities of romantic action and commitment. When, in the dream, he was questioned about his job, he avoided the questioning by flying deep into the basement. This little boy delighted in the formulas he had created to ensure distrust of men. Jeannie commented: "He could have been an enthusiastic and committed scientist were his task and skill not so limited."

When Jeannie began treatment with me about 9 years ago, she knew she had dissociative problems, but she had in the past been treated mostly for depression and suicidality rather than explicitly for dissociation. When we began work, she was chronically disoriented; for example, she could not remember left from right and had no regular sleep patterns. She protected herself in an extreme fashion against being impinged on by the environment. She worked only at night in a place where she had cocreated a benign, infantilizing environment, where a coworker called her Baby, and where she called that coworker Mommy. A good deal of her waking hours were spent fantasizing. She had primarily one friendship, which she described in a way that seemed hazy to me. She was deliberately isolated, even fearing the phone ringing. Jeannie commented:

> I still get jumpy with ringing phones. And I still relate to some people in an infantile manner. What's dramatically changed is my awareness of it and my ability to choose to be different or manage the circumstances. It looks like some of the dysfunctional behavior that was the result of a fragmented experience remains, but now it's part of a greater harmony which I can create more consciously.

A careful history revealed that when she was probably about 4 or 5 years old (she does not remember her age—like many events in her childhood), she was sexually abused, in a nonforcible rape, by an adolescent male babysitter. Her mother was a highly stressed and depressed hard-working parent who had to be away from home for long hours. In addition, the mother often dealt with her stress by beating Jeannie and her older brother, who then also beat Jeannie. In this context, perhaps the babysitter's attentions did not seem so bad. After this, Jeannie became a highly sexualized little girl who was often both attracted to and running away from men who wanted her to sit on their laps. Jeannie had many large memory gaps in her autobiographical memory. When she described graduation from junior high school, she said she knows she was there but does not remember it in an autobiographical way. Despite all these environmental difficulties, she was a smart, spunky, resourceful, energetic child. When her mother decided to take her brother and her to the river one day to drown them all, Jeannie averted this by calling on a neighbor. This story was told without the affect of terror. The parts of her that experienced the terror were dissociated. This kind of dissociation helps to explain how, even though she was generally exceptionally smart in school, sometimes she would suddenly forget much of what she knew.

Jeannie's "Happy Face"

Jeannie's mother and relatives knew that she was clever, but they did not value this *for her*. As a child, Jeanie often had to "put on a face," not only to cover up her misery but also to be clever for her relatives and her mother's friends—and at school. Her speech and her cleverness were exploited. She was talking because she had to, not because it was meaningful. About this, Jeannie said:

> I received a lot of attention because I was an engaging child but I felt isolated and was aware that all of me was not "seen." Over time, my temperamental friendliness became a happy face mask, and my interactions and words became meaningless. I was instinctively fearful people were only interested in the part of me that was entertaining, clever, infantile, attentive, or useful. They were not interested in any more interior part of me, so I stayed away from them, which in turn reinforced my isolation. The happy ways in which I related became increasingly meaningless because an important part of my experience and me was hidden. I wasn't all there for others to value, nor for me to value. The mute girl, or whatever wasn't expressed, wasn't accessible to anyone. What could have been genuinely connective interactions as a child and an adult where people were happy to be with me (my talents, skills, etc.) felt vacuous because there was no space for the "mute" or other sides of me.

She added:

> As I grew into a teenager, the feeling of being alone and not being seen turned inward into sadness and despair. I was more resentful as an adult, which now I see as a step toward growing into relationships—as an adult I had more expectations.

Jeannie grew up in a country where there was massive, extreme, endemic poverty. She moved to the United States when she was about 12. An intense, clear, flashbulb-type memory from her country of origin is the visceral reaction she had of seeing a nearly naked man walking by who had a huge bleeding gash in his side. This was right before her dance class, which she immediately quit afterward because she was viscerally disturbed by her relative privilege. In the beginning of our work together, she would frequently have dreams of large groups of traumatized people calling to her for emotional and physical relief from their pain. She reported that she had the same visceral reaction to these dreams as she did to the man with the gash. These dreams, which represent both herself and her connection to others' suffering, were extremely painful for her to remember and discuss. Today, she compares the silence about her abuse to the silence around the trauma of inescapable poverty. She attributes it to "collective helplessness." About this, she says,

> The friendly child developed a mute self who was stunned into silence due to trauma. The intense feelings of powerlessness and sadness merged with the trauma of living in a community where some suffered abject poverty, particularly children my age (or my height) for no apparent reason. Neither experience of violence was acknowledged in the prevalent form that I experienced it. To me, the threat of violence from men and poverty seemed to be everywhere and undermined the stability and meaning of the rest of life. How does a child start speaking about this? And what is there to say when everything unspoken clearly implied that the violence and silence is simply a feature of the world. These feelings are alive in me still, but obviously the big change is that I can speak about them. I can see that my mom's death and death itself evokes a mute-girl response. I am shocked, I avoid the feelings, I fear falling to pieces, I sob; eventually, it all passes.

The Mute Girl Learns to Speak

Finally, after many, many dreams about The Mute Girl, she learned to speak in Jeannie's dreams. Then, she came to life through Jeannie's speech.

Today, Jeannie's dreams are much more ordinary. Recently, she dreamt that "You were sitting on a couch looking annoyed. You were working. You weren't listening to me. I thought you were feeling impatient about my progress. I was worried that I was taking too long." She has moved from more exclusively exploring her internal relationships to exploring her interpersonal ones, notably her therapy relationship. But, the focus on her internal world, without my intrusion of myself into it, had to come first.

Through our work with dreams, The Mute Girl became a more integrated aspect of Jeannie, and Jeannie became clearer and more articulate. Jeannie got left and right together better. Her sleep schedule improved. Her life became more organized as she began to work partly in the daytime. Her social life expanded to include more real people with whom she had challenging and important relationships. She did not feel as internally confused.

In a dream that she had about 3 years ago, there were several needy children in front of her. In the dream, she was able to acknowledge them as part of herself, following which they all jumped inside of her. In a symbolic way, they integrated with her and became part of her. Now, she has much more ordinary problems—not that her dreams do not still spell out her problems in the language of dissociated self-states, but the conversations, inside and out, are much clearer and coherent.

The way that Jeannie had earlier structured her life exemplified a relatively closed system. Bromberg (1996) has noted that people who have been traumatized often develop an early warning system, reminding them that there is potential danger around every corner. This assumption guided the relatively closed structure that Jeannie had invented for herself. This relatively closed system helped to give her a sense of protection from the outside and kept her anxiety damped down.

Working with Jeannie's dreams was not only elucidating but also safe. It did not violate the protective structuring of her life in a way that a confrontational style of working with enactments in the treatment relationship might have—eliciting anxiety and a possible retrenchment of dissociative defenses. I was curious about her dreams—and interpretative in the sense of Aron's (1996) slant on the word *interpretation* as a personal way of making sense of something—as one would personally interpret a work of art. About this issue, Jeannie comments:

> This is so very very true! I can assure you I would have bolted if I detected the slightest hint of an agenda to heal me. I would have cast you as one of those people who cannot bear my living in uncertainty, depression, or despair or the unknown of what's making me depressed. I needed your sustained and caring attention to be based on trust that I, Mute Girl and all, want to be whole and know best how to get there and at what pace. With a confrontation of any sort, I would have been afraid you were trying to cast me into some mold of "healthy" that's not true to me and rush me as if I don't have enough motivation to resolve the conflicts. You created a safe space where not only The Mute Girl can emerge, but also validated other happier parts of me that I assumed were in conflict with The Mute Girl. I wonder if one way of understanding The Mute Girl's experience in therapy is that she came in not "breathing" or interacting in the real world, and as you listened, you made it safe to start breathing, so she came alive. Any confrontation would have only made her stay very very still to the point of stopping her—my—breath till the aggressors go away.

This approach allowed Jeannie as The Mute Girl to step out of her dreams, in an increasingly exploratory way, onto the adjoining stage of interpersonal reality.

Chapter 14

Suicidality in DID

There is a significant danger of suicidality in persons with dissociative identity disorder (DID). Studies show that 1 to 2.1% of patients with DID have completed suicide, with an incidence of 61 to 72% who have attempted suicide (Brand, 2001). Brand, who is a prominent expert in the field of dissociative disorders, believes this last figure is an underestimate given that therapists who have had patients who committed suicide may be less likely to fill out questionnaires, and that these numbers do not include dissociative patients who have been misdiagnosed or those not in treatment. Brand (2001) stressed that the rates for suicidality are comparable with—or in some cases higher than—suicidality rates for persons with severe depression, for which percentages are approximately 20% attempting and 3.9% completing suicide. Among persons with borderline personality disorder (BPD) the percentages are 75% attempting and 5 to 10% completing suicide; in schizophrenia, the percentages range from 30 to 40% attempting suicide and 10% completing it. In a recent study of psychiatric outpatients, Foote, Smolin, and Lipshitz (2008) found that a dissociative disorder diagnosis was more strongly associated with suicidality or self-harm than any other diagnosis—surprisingly, even more strongly than Major Depression or Borderline Personality Disorder. Furthermore, when dissociative disorder diagnosis and Borderline Personality Disorder diagnosis were entered simultaneously into a regression analysis, with suicidality as the outcome measure, the strong association between dissociative disorder diagnosis and suicidality remained, while the association between Borderline Personality Disorder and suicidality was no longer significant—suggesting that the dissociative disorder accounted for the suicidality of the BPD patients, and not vice-versa.

THE MEANING OF SUICIDE

Especially in DID, suicidality can have a great many meanings. Sometimes, it is an outgrowth of rageful fantasies and the vengeance of the powerless, as is more common in dangerous depressions. At other times, persons with DID have suicidal parts who hold the intention to put the person out of his or her misery when things get to be too unbearable. Dissociated emotions and thoughts are not limited to persons with DID. Even with severely depressed patients who do not appear to be dissociative, we may increase the clinical effectiveness of our treatment if we inquire about dissociation (e.g., about the part of the person who wants to live versus the part who wants to die).

Take for example the case with Ereshkigal, who is a persecutor part of Janice (Chapter 9). A persecutor part may act homicidally toward the host in a way that from the outside looks like suicidality. Even more so (although this was not the case with Ereshkigal), homicidal parts are often unaware that they share the same body with the parts they wish to punish or harm and therefore believe that they can murder another part while remaining unaffected themselves. When this illusion exists, one way the therapist can work to counter it is to do things such as ask the homicidal part to look at the hands or some other part of the body that would be recognized as belonging to another part—maybe to the part most usually out. If the hands are recognized as belonging to another part, how can the denying part insist that they do not share a body? Such cognitive dissonance aids in the dissolution of trance logic.

At other times, a homicidal part may say that he (or she, as all parts may be male or female) does not care if he also dies. At such moments, it can be helpful to engage that part in the treatment in a profoundly emotional way, for example, by emphasizing the valuable role that the part has played in survival, validating the toll it must have taken, and offering empathy for hardship they protected other parts from and endured themselves.

Often with DID, suicidality has represented a way out when life had become utterly unbearable. It may be a secret pact that was made internally; therefore, it is wise to ask directly about such secret pacts if one has reason to suspect that one exists. In one case, when I asked explicitly, the patient (a physician) revealed that he had kept a lethal supply of insulin ready for use for over 30 years in case continuing to live became too unbearable. This exploration resulted in his consenting to getting rid of the insulin and promising not to get more or anything else that would work as a substitute.

Often, this type of a secret way out is held by child parts who do not understand that the pain they are experiencing now is not interminable (although it may well have felt that way to the patient as a child). These parts are stuck in time and think that the terror and the pain they are experiencing will never end. For example, Janice, who had attempted to hang herself from the ceiling with her mother's stockings when she was 8 years old, has parts named The Suicides, actually child parts whose job it was to end life when they felt the pain was unendurable. Talking through to these parts involved saying things like the following:

I understand it feels to you like it will never end because that is the way it was for you and for Janice when she was young. It also felt like that was the only thing in your power to do. And, it may well have been true then, that was the only power you had at the time, other than to endure. But now, in this present time, Janice has many options in her power to make things better. Even though it may feel like it will never end, it will. Janice is a grown-up now. The horrible pain you feel will get better because Janice today is able to make things change.

Fantasies about suicide should be explored thoroughly. As noted, the secret way out may have been a calming salve for unbearable experience. As Chefetz (2005a) noted, "When the therapist engages in a detailed inquiry about these fantasies, the therapist then becomes part of the patient's associations 'in' the fantasy, and this has a stabilizing effect" (p. 664).

SAFETY AGREEMENTS

Safety agreements are often helpful for maintaining safety in DID treatment. Such safety agreements can include a series of constructive alternatives to self-harm to be taken if the patient begins to feel endangered. The agreement may spell out a hierarchy of actions, such as reaching out to supportive others or various forms of self-soothing (e.g., relaxing activities, relaxation exercises, or physical exercise), all of which are to be implemented before calling the therapist or going to the emergency room. Such lists and agreements support patient self-responsibility and avoid putting the therapist in the position of rescuer (Courtois, 1999). Safety agreements also usually include calling the therapist or being in voice contact with the therapist before any action is taken.

Safety agreements have several levels of utility. Not only are they concretely useful, but also, because dissociative patients often have ambivalence about safety, the negotiation of an agreement is likely to elucidate hidden issues. These include unformulated (Stern, 1997) meanings of being safe, such as ambivalence about personal safety and the meaning as well as the responsibility to oneself and others that this entails. Because so many patients with DID have experienced their parents as cruel, sadistic, or lethal, discussion of safety often brings up dominant transference beliefs concerning whether it is more desirable to be safe or endangered, well or sick, even alive or dead. Helping patients to understand their ambivalence eventually helps them to understand that they actually do have more control than they had previously thought.

Because dissociative parts often tend to think concretely (Putnam, 1989), a written agreement tends to be experienced as binding, helpful, and comforting. One such written agreement that is sometimes used is, "I will not hurt myself or kill myself, or anyone else internally or externally, accidentally or on purpose at any time" (Braun, 1986, p. 12). Here, the wording addresses potential loopholes in a safety agreement. It addresses dimensions of internal and external, delusions of separateness, and purposeful versus accidental behavior. If all parts are asked to subscribe to the agreement, it includes all the different "I" subjectivities. I often use some wording similar to this, as well as stress that it is the meaning, not the words themselves, that is important. I invite the patient to collaborate with me in drafting an agreement that feels right. One new patient and I spent an entire session on the safety agreement. After she had voiced many objections, she drafted her own promise (which she has subsequently kept), to which she attached the words: "It's the spirit of the thing that matters."

It is also often helpful to invite the patient to set a time frame during which the agreement applies. This gives the patient more control, and it also makes it more concrete. However, because of the concrete thinking, it is important for the therapist to be aware of the ending points of these time frames. Putnam (1989) described a serious crisis that emerged when a therapist, thinking that things were going well, became less vigilant and let a safety agreement lapse. As a result and no longer feeling bound and contained by the agreement, the patient became suicidal. When discussing safety agreements, I frequently tell the patient that my ability to work depends on my feeling safe about the therapy, and this includes my having basic security about the patient's safety. This works for me, and I feel that it also addresses some of the patients' concerns. Many patients are aware of how the litigious world works and are therefore suspicious that the agreement is only for my protection. My legitimizing my own need for safety by bringing it out into the open often dispels some such suspicion. It is important to remember that despite the benefits of an agreement, it is not literally binding. One should not underestimate the importance of careful exploration of the potential for suicide even if there is a safety agreement in place. (It is also important to note that such an agreement likely offers no legal protection.)

In contrast to the contract proposed by Braun (1986), I do not generally like to explicitly forbid minor self-injury in a safety agreement, although I make clear in discussion that self-harm is not a safe behavior regardless of the magnitude of the self-injurious effort. My reasoning is that I do not want the patient to break an agreement that is so stringent that even minor initial attempts to challenge the contract would cause a crisis. Even with an agreement in place, some suicidal behaviors may occur, as could other "infringements" of agreements. In addition to appropriate action by the therapist, such events speak to the need to learn more about what all parts of the patient are feeling and fearing and what they need for the safety of the body to be guaranteed. At such times, the spirit and the explicit content of the contract can be enlarged with the patient as coparticipant in the renegotiation. This is partially why I generally prefer to keep the contract as simple as possible, directed toward the essentials of preserving life and preventing serious injury. I make it clear that I do not want the patient to self-injure, but I do not include explicit language about all kinds of self-harm because this would just create a challenge for some patients to find something that is not listed in the agreement, hurt themselves, and say that they had abided by the agreement.

Safety agreements should be understood to apply to all dissociative parts of the person. Although some clinicians try to get as many as possible of the parts to sign an agreement, I more often say something like, "I am going to assume that all of the parts inside agree with this. If not, please speak up now."

Some patients with DID do not feel comfortable working with a written safety agreement but will make a verbal agreement for safety. Of course, neither a written nor a verbal agreement is a guarantee of safety. It is; however, often a great help in containment and in keeping all parties feeling safe. The therapist should consider the agreement in the context of the patient's life and should not substitute reliance on it for clinical judgment (International Society for the Study of Trauma and Dissociation, in press). The same premise that applies to the contract applies to its use: to keep the patient safe. Therefore, if the clinical situation suggests it, more stringent measures such as hospitalization should be explored and must sometimes be implemented.

As one negotiates and renegotiates safety agreements, it is advisable to continuously and thoroughly address the meaning of suicide for the patient and to keep in mind that it might not have the same meaning for all parts of the patient.

SUICIDAL BEHAVIOR IS NOT ALWAYS STRAIGHTFORWARD SUICIDALITY

The fact that suicidality in DID is not always straightforward suicidality is reason to be more, rather than less, alert for the danger of suicide. Different parts may have their own motivations for destructiveness toward other parts; and often the destructiveness is not necessarily intended to be suicidal or homicidal. This may be one of the reasons for Foote et al.'s (2008) finding that a dissociative disorder diagnosis was more strongly associated with suicidality than any other diagnosis.

Two case vignettes follow. Both illustrate behavior that appeared to be or was potentially suicidal but in fact had to do with a child part's lack of understanding about issues of lethality or death.

The Closed System

In this vignette, the problem was that a child part, though engaged in potentially lethal behavior, was not aware that the behavior was indeed potentially lethal. In addition, this child part was unaware of the irrevocability of death. This child part believed that she was simply making another child part go to sleep, but the result was what looked like an overdose as a suicide attempt.

Rosemary is a 45-year-old, married, professional woman who has no children. She came into treatment with me almost 8 years ago. At that time, she was on disability and suffering from almost overwhelming depression and anxiety on a daily basis. She was mostly nonfunctional, often losing time, frequently switching, and struggling to perform ordinary household chores. She had been hospitalized six or seven times in the preceding 7 years for extreme cutting, burning, and other self-injury. As background for these symptoms, what emerged over time was that as a child—from the age of 5 or younger and until she was about 13—Rosemary had been raped, night after night, by her father while her mother was asleep in bed, sedated in compliance with her doctor's and her husband's instructions. Rosemary's father had told her that if she told her mother about these events it would kill her mother—and since she did not want her mother to die, Rosemary did not tell. At some point, she did want to tell a teacher but had surmised, probably correctly, that no one would believe her. Later treatment work with me (e.g., through parts work and dream work) opened up memories of her suffering many untreated urinary tract infections as a child. Her pain was excruciatingly terrible and was suffered alone. (Anyone who suffered urinary tract infections as an adult can imagine what it would be like if one were a child with such unbearable pain that must be endured in silence, with no one in the world to tell about it or to ask for help.)

With respect to the father's abuse, it was only after more than 2 years of therapy that highly explicit memories of these experiences came to the surface, mostly through the narratives of child parts: "T," Michael, and Little Rosemary. At that time, Rosemary had not herself remembered most of these incidents, but certain child parts of her did. They remembered horrifying things, bloody underwear, terrible pain, and not being able to sit down. They remembered how she would stay in the bathtub, wet her pants, pretend to be asleep, and try all manner of strategies to deter her father's violations. These child parts were only able to tell of their pain bit by bit because what they had to say would have been too destabilizing and painful to bear in large doses to the overall system, including Rosemary herself, the adolescent parts, and other adult parts.

One of the child parts, "T, the Lifesaver, who has a hole in the middle," is a precocious child part who at times has taken a managerial role with respect to younger child parts. T was originally created to perform certain soothing and caretaking functions for younger child alters—as a life saver, as well as to hold memories of abuse. Her name (Lifesaver) also signifies her awareness of feeling that she has no "center," and that she functions in part as a transitional sugar salve. This followed from her mother's treatment of her; the mother, who was an excellent cook, would at times ply her daughter with sweet foods but would just as often deny them altogether. This connected sweet foods with both attachment and deprivation. Part of T's job was to care for Michael, her inner younger brother (Kluft's "third reality"), who held even more painful memories than she did. Michael was created as male to magically deflect her father's sexual violations.

These child parts had not finished telling about the details of their trauma when one morning Rosemary's husband called me to cancel her session for the day because she was in the hospital from what appeared to be a drug overdose. (Rosemary is still not clear about exactly what occurred or how it occurred.) The odd thing was that Rosemary had no memory of taking any pills and had always insisted that she was not suicidal. Later when we did meet, and in the process of Rosemary's and my discussion of the possible antecedents of this event, I asked to speak to T the Lifesaver. As it turned out, T the Lifesaver had gotten sick and tired of hearing the constant excruciating crying of a younger child part, Michael. T the Lifesaver knew that Michael was in terrible pain but did not know why he was crying so much more than usual. All T knew was that she could not bear to hear Michael's crying anymore and so decided to take matters into her own hands and to give him pills to shut him up and knock him out. As it happens, and because of the dissociative barriers, T did not know that the reason the younger part, Michael, was in so much grief was that Rosemary was about to take a trip back to the town where she grew up—Michael thought that the father (who in reality was dead) was still alive, still there, and still capable of raping him again.

T the Lifesaver, a child part who always had to fend for herself and had at the time needed to take too much responsibility for her young age, made a decision—unilaterally and without consulting anyone. It was a decision that she was too young to make but that did not seem so to a child part accustomed to taking on too much responsibility. When we were able to talk in session about the feelings and fears of Michael and T the Lifesaver, Michael was able to share why he was frightened and crying, and T the Lifesaver talked about hating to hear his crying. Following these interactions, T the Lifesaver knew why Michael was crying and understood that she was too young to give anyone pills. She has agreed, if ever in severe distress again, to call me rather than undertake any unilateral action. Rosemary also became aware of this intrapersonal conflict and knows how to get help to deal better with conflict (at least when she is able to recognize that a conflict is occurring). Work with Rosemary is still very much in progress.

If looked at only from the outside, the event appeared as a suicide attempt. However, not only did this make no sense to Rosemary (since she was aware of no suicidal ideation), but also the idea of suicidality did not make sense to T or to Michael. To put Rosemary's action as a whole into intelligible context, I needed to take her dissociation into account. In her case, I needed to be in contact with T the Lifesaver as well as with Michael, and when these parts were consulted, the emergent understanding of what was taking place was able to unfold: The action was more about attempting to silence another's unbearable crying and trying to deal with terrifying problems and events of long ago (via current action enacted by child parts) than about suicidality or homicidality. For the dissociative nature of this event in Rosemary's life to be understood and begin to be healed, I had to know T the Lifesaver and Michael, and I needed to be made aware of their own fears and desires. Rosemary also had to learn to know what I knew. While there is more healing work for Rosemary to do, this understanding was an important event in her history.

Promise Me You Won't Go to the Ocean

In this second vignette, the suicidal danger is specific to the way that this patient's dissociative structure adapted to and interpreted her life history. Anna had been separated from her beloved mother at age 9. She desperately desired to be reunited, and a child part wanted to find a way to go home to her beloved mother. The trance logic of this child part's thinking posed dangerous consequences that had the potential to result in a (dissociatively accidental) suicide.

Anna is a 43-year-old woman, married with four children, who has been in therapy with me for 7 years. Anna is highly intelligent and well spoken in spite of having had only minimal formal education and grammar that sometimes is poor in spots. After she escaped her sister's household when she was 15, on the basis of her intelligence, personability, and ability to work hard she managed to work her way up in the work world, eventually becoming a well-paid and well-respected midlevel executive. However, since her breakdown (which occurred when her oldest child reached the age that her own abuse began), she has been unable to work because of the constant posttraumatic intrusions and trance states that she experiences. She is a competent mother, certainly a caring one, and the usually presenting part is caring and responsible as a person. Although Anna spends most of her days in a zone of lost time, she comes to when it is time for her to go get the children at school and is an attentive, nurturing, caring, and vigilant mother. She supervises her children's homework and makes sure that they have top (A+) grades. She listens to her children's problems, has great empathy and concern for them, gives them advice, and is a strong disciplinarian. She defends her children at school and befriends and stands up to the teachers as appropriate.

Anna's plight began when, due to political instability in her country of origin, Anna's parents put her on a plane to go live with her sister in Chicago to help take care of her sister's children. She was 9 years old at the time. Unbeknownst to Anna's parents, she was made into a household slave by her sister and a sex slave by her brother-in-law. In terms of nutrition, she was forbidden to eat anything except peanut butter and bread. She slept in her jeans. She went to school only sporadically, and by the eighth grade even this ceased. She was forbidden to use the phone or leave the house and was threatened by her brother-in-law that he would tell her mother that she was a bad girl if she tried to leave. Anna imagined that this was the way it was supposed to be since everything was so completely different in this part of the world. For instance, snow was at first incomprehensible to her—she had never seen anything like it and had no idea what it was when she first saw it. On some vague level, Anna thought that everything that was happening must have been okay with her mother, and the last thing she wanted to do was displease her mother. So, she endured. Nevertheless, she accumulated a stash of lethal household cleaning agents that she planned to use if things got to be more than she could stand.

In many ways, Anna is currently low functioning: She spends most of the day in trance, often hallucinating, and is up many nights for much or all of the time, also in trance, doing such things as setting the table for unknown guests. There were times when she has needed my support to understand that her hallucinations are not real (e.g., she might see her living room filled with people, her different self-states, and feel that she literally cannot move in there because there is no room).

Anna has multiple physical problems that come and go. Sometimes, her feet swell (I have seen them). She reports that they want to "take off," both in a run and to the ceiling. At these times, she feels that she cannot keep herself on the ground but rises to the ceiling. She has been diagnosed with complex regional pain syndrome (CRPS), a condition in which she cannot move her right hand and in which the pain and paralysis also move to her shoulder. Her hand is swollen, and the skin has a different appearance on the right arm than on the left.[1] While CRPS is a medical diagnosis, it does tend to be cyclical and respond to weather changes, stress, cold/heat, and so on, with the result that symptoms can wax and wane in some patients. Like other of Anna's physical symptoms that would have been diagnosed as "hysterical" a century ago, it is hard to know the extent to which her CRPS symptoms may be somatoform, parts dependent, or entirely based in a medical disorder, which can be exacerbated by stress.

For a good part of the therapeutic relationship, Anna has been compulsively self-injurious to her vagina and her rectum, to the extent that she has had infections and much pain and might have done some damage to her vaginal wall. Interestingly, Anna reported that her hand "had to do it"; this self-harm did not feel like it was under her volition. In part due to the bleeding, but also because she experienced "sticky stuff" all over her, Anna reportedly felt that she had to shower four or more times a day. With the work in therapy, the somatic flashbacks, self-injury, and the constant showers have ceased in the last 3 years.

And yet, suicidal ideation has continued. From the beginning of our work and during many of our sessions until approximately the last 3 years, she would tell me that she wanted to kill herself. Generally, I could get her to promise to be safe until we met the next time, often by using slightly coercive psycho-education about how terrible it is for children whose parents have committed suicide and how it increases their own chances of suicide. Her complaints of suicidal impulses have greatly decreased over time but have not disappeared. It is most often terrible flashbacks about the abuse she suffered while in Chicago, as well as memories about that time, that have made her feel suicidal.

In the session excerpt that follows, Anna describes how a self-state modeled on her sister took her to get her hair cut. Then the memories of the abuse suffered in Chicago contributed to the emergence of a child part who desperately wanted to go home to her mother and thought she could get back to her mother by going over the ocean.

ME: You cut your hair. It looks nice.

ANNA: I got my hair cut in preparation for going to the ocean. My sister [*meaning the sister inside*] took me because I was too weak to go myself. *There was a very little girl in the chair.* [*She is describing her perception of herself in the hairdresser's chair.*] My sister walked me back. Then, I looked in the mirror at home. My face was all green. After that was when I saw the priest in the grocery store, who said I looked terrible and asked if I wanted to see him.

ME: You got your hair cut in preparation for going to the ocean? What about going to the ocean?

ANNA: I was going to the ocean because everything was so bad. That is the only way I could think of to get home. I would go to the ocean, lie on my back on the waves, and have the ocean take me home. I knew I came over the ocean, even though I came by plane.

ME: Yes, that is a little girl's imagining of a way of how to get home. She must have been desperate to get out and with desperate longing to go home.

ANNA: That is why I have been going to the ocean and sitting on the bench and wanting to go in. It is hard to keep myself from going there at night.

She and I discuss how she experiences a replay in her mind of events when she was in Chicago: getting her hair cut by her sister and getting her hair cut now, trying to figure out a way to escape from the home of her sister and brother-in-law and now from her own home. We explored why is this happening now.

ME: So, how long after you arrived in Chicago did your sister take you to get your hair cut?

ANNA: My sister took me and had my hair chopped off soon after I got there.

ME: That must have been a horrifying shock.

ANNA: My hair was down to my knees. That is the way girls wore their hair where I grew up. No one cut their hair.

ME: Why did your sister want your hair chopped off?

ANNA: She hated my hair. It's like what happened with a friend of my daughter's. My daughter has beautiful long hair, all the way down her back. This other little girl in her school was so mean to her all the time, until finally she grew her hair long, like my daughter's and now she is very nice to my daughter, and they are friends. It's like she couldn't stand my daughter having what she did not have.

ME: Yes, she was envious. She did not want your daughter to have what she couldn't just as your sister couldn't stand to see your beautiful long hair. So your sister—and also the sister inside—was upset with your beautiful hair. I would like to hear more about this.

She then remembers suddenly that her sister had told her that she had just eaten White Face. (White Face was her cow and pet when she was a little girl. White Face would come and stick her face in her bedroom window in the evening, and Anna would pet her face. She loved White Face and was comforted by her presence.)

ME: Your sister told you that you had just eaten White Face? [*She was not allowed to eat anything but peanut butter and bread, even though she cooked regular meals for her sister and brother-in-law.*]

ANNA: Yes; one day about a month after I had been there, my sister and brother-in-law said they were going to give me a treat. They gave me a hamburger, but I did not know what it was. I liked it. They were both watching me with interest and were gleeful. Then, my sister said after I finished it, "Did you like it?" I said "Yes." Then my sister and brother-in-law began laughing, and she said, "You just ate White Face!"

ME: How horrible! What a mean trick! You must have been devastated! And were you at the time observant of your upbringing dietary laws against eating beef?

ANNA: Yes. I would not eat beef. Cattle were sacred. We ate meat very rarely. Once or twice a year we would eat chicken or lamb. Of course, we ate fish all the time. All we had to do was go out and catch it.

As I try to explore how she felt about the incident, it is hard for her to stay with it, and she comes more into the present adult and says that her shoulder hurts. She holds her shoulder and says that she has not slept well, in great part because she is so preoccupied about going to the ocean and trying to prevent herself from going to the ocean. It seems that the memories of her sister's sadistic cruelty—both the haircut and the hamburger—while not something she could continue to think about, had been in part motivating the child part's desperate desire to go home to her mother via the ocean.

> ME: I am going to talk to that little girl now. Her suffering must be awful! That is so horrible, that trick about eating the hamburger, a terrible, terrible assault on your identity and beliefs. So sadistic. And, especially when you were hungry and so deprived of food.
>
> [*Talking to the little girl part.*] You have been through unimaginable horrible things. Of course, you wanted to find a way to get home. That was very active thinking—to be wanting to get out. But you know, of course, that you can't really get home that way. And you know that your mother is dead. Your mother isn't there anymore. The ocean can't take you to your mother because she isn't there. It is proactive to be thinking of how to get out, though. You have been through so much, and you are thinking so hard. But we can't solve that problem in Chicago now. We will work on it. Right now, you need to take a rest. Is that okay?

At this point, Anna is clearly becoming emotional. Talking to the little girl inside, even though she is not able to respond back to me in words, is bringing up a great deal of emotion.

> ANNA: I am so angry with myself!
> ME: For what?
> ANNA: I should have figured out a way to get home.
> ME: You were 9 years old.[2] The first thing that happened to you when you got there was that you were raped, you were deprived of food, deprived of sleep, your clothes were taken away, your sense of self and beliefs was systematically assaulted, and then your sister took you and had your beautiful long hair chopped off. You were in a state of shock. You couldn't get back by plane. You couldn't even get out of the apartment on your own. You didn't know the right elevator button to push. You were forbidden to use the phone, and you believed that somehow your mother thought this was best for you, and you did not want to disappoint your mother, whose health was so frail.

She seems satisfied, or at least does not continue saying she is angry with herself.

> ME: I'm sorry that we are going to have to stop soon. [*Talking to the little girl.*] You need to get some rest. Go inside and get some rest. Going to the ocean is proactive thinking given your situation, but it won't get you to your mother. We will come back to and talk about this awful situation more later. [*The little girl part goes inside.*]

We spend time in the session talking about how she, also, as an adult, needs to get some rest. She describes how she talked to the monsignor about her difficulties and how he was supportive. She also remembers how the nuns, whom she knows in the context of her children's religious training, had always been nice to her and how, when she was functional she would always bring cookies for them at Christmas because she had observed that people forget the nuns and only think of the priests. Then, she said that the nuns had offered that she could come stay with them.

She talks more of suicidality and of wanting to go to the ocean, saying as she has in the past that she would just like to get it all over with by sitting on a bench by the ocean in a bad neighborhood and hoping to get murdered. This is yet another (more present time) aspect of the wish to go to the ocean, which is in addition to the previously discussed child part's thought that she could go home to her mother by walking into the ocean. We explore other possible reasons for the reemergence of suicidal ideation now. In retrospect, I probably asked the little girl to go inside too soon or with inadequate reassurance that I wanted to hear more about her feelings. Perhaps some feeling of inadequate recognition was behind her response.

> ME: Do you think you should be hospitalized? That is an option. The number one priority is to keep you safe.
>
> ANNA: No. It would upset my children. They would be too upset and not be able to manage.
>
> ME: If you are not safe, then the most important thing is to protect you. Your kids would manage if you went to the hospital. If you think it would upset them for you to go to the hospital, remember that that upset would be miniscule compared to the effect on them if you died. It would be unbearably difficult for them if you died. It would be just horrible for them! Remember that children whose parents have suicided are much more likely to commit suicide themselves.
>
> ANNA: I will be all right. I just need to be by myself.
>
> ME: What about the nuns; they said you could stay with them if you needed.
>
> ANNA: I can't leave my kids.
>
> ME: So you don't want to go to the hospital or to the nuns? Can you, and can all your parts, promise that you will be safe, at least until our next meeting, and that you won't go to the ocean?
>
> ANNA: I promise.

NOTES

1. On the hunch that this may be somatic dissociation of parts of the body, I have asked her to twist her arms together and look at her hands and feel her arms against each other. This appears to have helped. (See also Feliu & Edwards, 2010.)

2. Age 9 is considered a late age for the onset of DID. However, the torture that she endured cannot be called anything else, and it was severe. Although she seems to have had a secure and loving attachment to her mother (which is the basis for her strong mothering and good relationships with her own children), there were some early separations from her mother on account of her mother's health that might have contributed to a disorganized attachment or perhaps to more severe fragmenting, and this might have provided a structural dissociative underpinning for the later dissociative solutions that may have saved her from suicide at that time or from psychosis.

Chapter 15

Comorbidity and Seeming Comorbidity

Problematic Outcomes of Severe and Rigid Dissociative Structuring of the Mind

This chapter addresses questions of comorbidity and seeming comorbidity. How do we understand and work with dissociation and dissociative disorders in the context of other categories of emotional difficulty and the diagnostic constructs of these? I discuss how symptoms of psychosis, personality disorder, and neurosis are manifest in dissociative disorders and how the underlying phenomenon of dissociation exists for many problems in living.

THE TRAUMA/DISSOCIATION MODEL

The trauma/dissociation model is edging its way into psychoanalytic and psychotherapy discourse as a good way of explaining many aspects of what is thought of as psychosis, personality disorder, and neurosis. We have a nosological system (the *Diagnostic and Statistical Manual of Mental Disorders* [*DSM*]) in which there are many overlapping categories that describe various problems in living. Our *DSM* is based on a medical model of disease, in which there is often a specific cause, such as a bacterium, that causes certain specifiable symptoms and that may or not be ameliorated by certain medicines and treatments that specifically target the cause. Because the *DSM* system does not exactly address problems in living, people who come to see us often have multiple diagnoses, such as anxiety disorder, depressive disorders, posttraumatic stress disorder (PTSD), sleep disorders, dissociative disorders, psychotic disorders, and so on. Does this mean that the anxiety, the depression, the sleep problems, the posttraumatic stress, the DID, and the psychotic symptoms all have different sources? It could, but on the other hand, at least some of them could be related to a common source. Often, a common source of these problems is relational trauma and consequent dissociation.

Sometimes, the issue of comorbidity is a complicated one to assess. For example, is it that someone has psychosis *and* PTSD, or that, unknown to the assessing clinician, the psychotic-seeming symptoms are actually intrusions of past trauma? In this case, the psychotic-seeming symptoms do not represent a loss of contact with reality because they are appropriate and understandable responses to a past situation that was real. The problem is that the clinician does not know about and understand their origin, and the patient may be automatically classified as psychotic. I am not suggesting that schizophrenia and certain other psychotic disorders are not separable from trauma/dissociation-based problems and may not often need a specific course of treatment. However, I am suggesting that the important process of diagnosis should include careful assessment of the source of the symptoms.

Similarly, personality disorders may well be trauma and dissociation based (Bromberg, 1998; Howell, 2002a). The correlations between borderline personality disorder (BPD) and dissociative disorders are high (Dell, 1998; Sar et al., 2003, 2006), they both have high histories of trauma (Dell, 1998; Putnam, 1997), and there are commonalities in assumed psychic structure (Howell, 2002a, 2003, 2008; Howell & Blizard, 2009). Sar et al. found in two studies (2003, 2006) that 64 and 72%, respectively, of the participants in the study who had BPD also had a dissociative disorder.

Finally, while the term *neurosis* is no longer in the *DSM* and is now infrequently used, the term is meaningful in psychodynamic diagnosis (McWilliams, 1994; PDM Task Force, 2006). Neurotic symptoms have been understood to be the result of psychic conflict between wish and defense, in which repression was the central defense. Hand in hand with neurosis was a punitive superego, which is understood both as the source of psychopathology and as a moral agency. Clinicians often work intuitively with superego as if it were a dissociated internal persecutory presence or self-state rather than as theoretically described in terms of the structural model and the Oedipus construct. Indeed, multiple personality disorder, now termed DID, was categorized as neurosis through the early 1900s. A harsh, punitive agency characterizes both severe superego and DID (Howell, 1997a). Thus, many people with DID have problems that could be explained by the superego construct; likewise, many people who might be called "normal" and "neurotic" can be understood to be suffering from problems of dissociated self-states.

I proceed first with a case illustrating manifestations of psychosis in a person with a dissociative disorder, followed by an examination of personality disorders (in particular BPD) in terms of dissociative processes, and finally present a case vignette demonstrating superego-type problems in a person with DID.

A Case of "Psychosis"

The following vignette describes how "psychotic" symptoms were resolved by addressing dissociative gaps in the person's experience, and how as a result of the work, the person felt she now "had a story." Margaret is a 35-year-old woman with DID who was introduced in Chapter 1. She is married with two children and is employed as a university literature professor. She is well groomed, attractive, and well put together.

Margaret came into my office and told me that she had again been feeling that she smelled; that is, she smelled a smell on her body with olfactory conviction. What she smelled was putrid, like a rotting dead person. She was awakened by the smell on Friday night, and since Saturday morning when she awoke, 3 days ago, she has been trying to scrub the smell away in the shower to no avail. Her husband has told her that she does not smell, but that has not been sufficient to keep her from trying repeatedly to shower it away.

About a year ago, Margaret presented with similar, but much more severe, symptoms. At that time, she stated her conviction that she was dead, and that others around her just did not seem to understand this. She had wondered how long she had been dead, and that they did not know. She could smell her body rotting as well. As in this more recent instance, the onset had been sudden. When it occurred last year, the appearance of psychosis, along with suicidality, necessitated hospitalization. Fortunately, on this more recent occasion, the conviction of being dead was not entrenched. It was still something we could talk about as a troubling set of thoughts and sensations.

I could have written this off as an emerging psychosis, arranged for a consult for antipsychotic medications, and begun inquiry into possible hospitalization. But, knowing that this person is highly dissociative and knowing that a crisis had not yet occurred, I worked from a different set of premises.

As one would normally, I first inquired about recent events. What might be the context that initiated this incident? In general, she had been thinking about her ex-husband and how he had both rescued her from her parents and had abandoned her. But, she was trying to make sense of some piece of this, some set of memories and beliefs and meanings. And in our session of the previous week, she had reported a dream in which he was walking around in her head. While she had had an intense headache following that dream, she did not feel dead or smell herself as dead. Although she was enveloped in the feeling of his earlier abandonment of her, along with the awareness of his great importance to her in the story of her life, she had e-mailed him to express her appreciation of the ways he had helped her earlier in their lives together. He did not respond. Other than these events, there was nothing notable about the context for these emerging olfactory symptoms.

Knowing that time was short, I asked if she would be willing to go into trance to further explore these symptoms. After deepening the trance, I described a pathway filled with her favorite flowers and leading to a library. I suggested that she would find a book with her name on it, and that I did not know where she would open it or whether she would see an image or print, that she would learn only as much as was safe for her to know, and that she could return the book to its place when she was done. I also suggested that the information could go to her mind without being conveyed to me at that time or that she could convey it to me, but that either way, she would only remember as much as felt safe.

While in the library and looking at her book, she began to tear up, and then she said, "I opened the book to page 28, and all there is on the page is blood. There is something about my hysterectomy and my mother's hysterectomy."

I asked her to tell me more about these hysterectomies. She said that she was 28 when she had her hysterectomy, and that she had been hemorrhaging profusely for months before, ever since her daughter was born. Then, she described her mother's hysterectomy, which occurred when her mother was 29 and had been occasioned by endometriosis. While in the hospital, her mother had complained that someone in the hospital had broken glass inside her uterus. When she returned home, she was screaming and crying and telling her children all how much she hated them, that they were nothing but trouble, and that she wished they had never been born. Understanding vaguely that her mother was psychotic and that this was ratcheting up her more normal hatefulness, Margaret had tried to comfort her.

I asked Margaret to tell me more about her own hysterectomy. She began to describe months of terrifying uncontrolled bleeding following a botched childbirth delivery. Her uterus had been so damaged that it did not return to its normal size following the birth but stayed huge, soft, and bleeding. For many months prior to the hysterectomy, she could not go places because of the profuse bleeding and her weakness. Because she was so weak, she stayed in bed with her baby. The blood had an intense, putrid, acrid smell, like something rotting. The smell was unremitting. No matter how many times she showered, it was always there. She could not get rid of it. She was alone. No family members could be called on or were willing to help her, and her husband had abandoned her prior to the childbirth. She felt lost and completely alone. Her baby was failing to thrive because, unbeknownst to Margaret, her baby was allergic to cow's milk. Margaret feared that her child was dying, and she feared that she would die. In fact, she was so certain that death was a real possibility that she filled her refrigerator and freezer with food just before her hysterectomy so that her other child would not starve if she died.

When I asked if that mental state of feeling near death, and being so helpless and alone, brought to mind any other time in her life, she reported that it did remind her of times in her early childhood when she had been left alone, tied up after being raped by her father. Referring to these times and to the months of hemorrhaging, she said, "I often wondered if anyone would notice if I were dead."

After we discussed all of this new material, Margaret said that she felt much better. One aspect of her feeling so relieved was that, "It's a story. I now have a story about it." Piecing these memories together had given narrative coherence to a certain set of overwhelmingly frightening and painful memories of her life. Now, they fit together, and she could situate herself in time. She did reexperience some of the pain as she talked about these times, but she was also in the present, feeling her sympathy for herself and my sympathy. In part because she was in two places at once, the telling was integrative rather overwhelming. She called me later in the day to tell me that she had no more symptoms of bad smells or of feeling dead, that she continued to feel relieved and was okay.

What Margaret was experiencing was the intrusion of olfactory flashbacks, originating from the time of the massive blood loss that resulted from the botched delivery of her child. The associated, but unformulated, memories, along with the threads of associations to these, concerned the anticipation that she was about to die—and perhaps the unformulated sense that she did die. What looked like psychosis was an intrusive flashback, probably evoked in this case initially by memories and feelings about her ex-husband and how she had been trying to pull together a narrative about that time in her life. But, an important part of that narrative was that her ex-husband had abandoned her in a situation in which she was helpless and alone, fearing death. This memory was associatively connected to earlier childhood memories in which her father had abused her and then left her tied up, helpless and alone. Because the flashback had no context in conscious memory, it could not be resolved on its own but expanded to the feeling that she was dying or dead. (As the trance was deepening, she heard me describe potted plants as "dead bodies.") The flashbacks of a putrid, rotting smell on her body that she could not rid herself of and the anticipation of her own death represented dissociated memories that were too overwhelming to be catalogued in narrative memory. As a result, they could not be placed in context with the present issues that were evoking them. As she said, following this work, she then had a story.

PERSONALITY DISORDERS/BORDERLINE PERSONALITY DISORDER

Philip Bromberg's (1995) "speculation" that personality disorders are dissociation based is one that I agree with wholeheartedly. He says:

> I have speculated...that the concept of personality "disorder" might usefully be defined as the characterological outcome of the inordinate use of dissociation, and that, independent of type (narcissistic, schizoid, borderline, paranoid, etc.), it constitutes a personality structure

organized as a proactive, defensive response to the potential repetition of childhood trauma....I am suggesting, in other words, that personality disorder represents ego-syntonic dissociation no matter what personality style it embodies.... A dissociative disorder proper (Dissociative Identity Disorder, Dissociative Amnesia, Dissociative Fugue, or Depersonalization Disorder) is from this vantage point a touchstone for understanding all other personality disorders even though, paradoxically, it is defined by symptomatology rather than by personality style. (pp. 200–202)

Bromberg's (1995) speculation was given partial support by Dell's (1998) findings that among DID outpatients, 53% were borderline, 68% self-defeating, 76% avoidant, and 45% passive-aggressive. In addition, many qualified for two or more personality disorders (Dell, 1998). As noted, Sar et al.'s studies (2003, 2006) found that 64–72% of those who had BPD also had a dissociative disorder.

I concentrate here on BPD because it is often the most problematic—as well as most frequently discussed—personality disorder. An estimated 2% of the general population, 10% of persons in outpatient clinics, and about 20% of admitted psychiatric inpatients are diagnosed as having BPD (APA, 2000, p. 708). As do people with DID, people with BPD frequently also have problems with anxiety, depression, substance abuse, eating disorders, and other manifestations of affect regulation. Because only five of the nine criteria are required to make the diagnosis of BPD, different combinations of these nine criteria yield strikingly different symptom and personality profiles.

Before the advent of the borderline category, the primary division in psychopathology had been that between neurosis (understood as manifestations of superego problems) and psychosis (loss of contact with reality). By the late 1800s, some patients were categorized as in a "borderland" between the two (Rosse, 1890, cited in McWilliams, 1994). By the mid-1900s the term *borderline* was introduced to demarcate this new domain of psychopathology (Stern, 1938).

Initially, borderline was understood in the context of schizophrenia. This categorization was supported by the tendency of this group of patients to have psychotic-like symptoms in situations of stress, intimacy, or projective testing. Following in this way of thinking, other diagnostic classifications that had been considered related to schizophrenia, such as "pseudoneurotic schizophrenia" (Hoch & Palatin, 1949), "psychotic character" (Frosch, 1964), ambulatory schizophrenia, and schizotypal personality, were recategorized as borderline (Kriesman & Straus, 1989). However, borderline became increasingly differentiated from schizophrenia as it was observed that borderline patients showed little evidence of thought disorder, that those psychotic symptoms seen in BPD were not typically schizophrenic

(Tarnopolosky, 1992), and that it almost never evolved into schizophrenia (Stone, 1992).

This view of borderline schizophrenia was supplanted by the view that borderline personality organization (BPO), which includes BPD, is a category of developmental diagnosis that is separate from psychosis or neurosis (Kernberg, 1975). Kernberg emphasized the problem of excess aggression and the defense of splitting, including five related defenses that characterized BPO (and BPD): projective identification, denial, primitive idealization, omnipotence, and devaluation.

High correlations between BPD and a history of trauma and neglect have been increasingly noted (Courtois & Ford, 2009; Golier, Yehuda, Bierer, et al., 2003; Gunderson & Chu, 1993; Gunderson & Sabo, 1993a, 1993b; Herman, 1992; Herman & Van der Kolk, 1987; Kroll, 1993; Perry & Herman, 1993; Putnam, 1997; Ryle, 1997a, 1997b; Yen, Shea, Battle, et al., 2002; Zanarini, 1997). Such high correlations have also been found for DID. Childhood abuse occurs in 50 to 81% of patients with BPD and 85 to 100% of patients with DID (Putnam, 1997).

At the same time, clinical literature was emerging that was in consonance with these studies. Judith Herman's landmark book, *Trauma and Recovery* (1992), with its focus on the traumatic sources of dysfunction, was informative and relieving to many people, both patients and therapists. Similarly, Christine Courtois's *Healing the Incest Wound* (1997) and her *Recollections of Sexual Abuse: Treatment Principles and Guidelines* (1999) have helped clinicians to formulate the trauma psychodynamics in their borderline patients.

Soon BPD, along with DID and DDNOS, was understood to be a form of "complex trauma" disorder, also described in the proposed diagnosis (Van der Kolk, 1996b) of disorders of extreme stress not otherwise specified (DESNOS). Howell and Blizard (2009) have also proposed the term *relational trauma disorder.* Difficulty with affect regulation, so characteristic of DID and PTSD, is an essential component of complex trauma and DESNOS, as well as relational trauma disorder. As Schore (2003b) stated: "It is well established that the loss of the ability to regulate the intensity of affect is the most far-reaching effect of early traumatic abuse and neglect" (p. 267).

Fonagy et al. (2002) noted that the abusive environment leads to deficits in reflective thinking, the capacity to think about mental states, processes, feelings, beliefs, and intentions of self and others. One of the reasons suggested by these authors is that maltreated children avoid thinking about the hateful intentions of their abusive caregivers toward them because understanding the implications of their maltreatment would make them more aware of the parents' malevolent views of them. In effect, they must dissociate knowledge of the parents' malevolence. This severely limits the development of reflective functioning (RF). Poor RF, then, inhibits the child's, and later the adult's, capacity to regulate affect. This in turn predisposes to dissociation and splitting.

What I would like to highlight is the particular dissociative organization that I think characterizes BPD and places it on the dissociative spectrum. As I see it, borderline splitting is similar to state switches in DID (Howell, 1999, 2002a, 2005). Splitting, in the sense of opposites, generally involves a dramatic switch or shift in affect state, including experiences of the self and expectations of the other. One difference between DID and BPD is that with BPD there is continuity of memory and acknowledgment of a dramatic shift in behavior and affect. To manage the experience, its meaning is disavowed. Since there is no amnesia for the switch in BPD, it is a partial, not a full, dissociation. Another difference is that personification of parts does not characterize BPD. Finally, in BPD there is the characteristic alternation between primarily two self-states (splitting).

With respect to splitting, it might be closer to experience and more specific to consider the alternating views of the other and the self in terms of victim and aggressor self-states. Splitting in this sense seems to involve a particular organization of alternating dissociated submissive/victim and rageful/aggressor self-states that reflect the impact of relational trauma on defense and psychophysiological processes (Howell, 2002a, 2005, 2008). These alternations reenact and embody the relational positions of the victim and aggressor. In the process that is often termed "identification with the aggressor" (e.g., Ferenczi, 1932/1949), these self-states become partially or entirely dissociated. (See Chapter 11 for more description of identification with the aggressor.) In the victim-identified position, the child may be passive, submissive, numbed out, helpless, robotic, and experience the self as attached to and dependent on the aggressor/caregiver. But, the child knows the abuser role well as a result of procedural identification.

Thus, the victimized child learns both roles: victim and abuser. Interestingly, some of the borderline defenses that Kernberg (1975) related to splitting can be understood specifically in terms of dissociated victim and aggressor states. For instance, primitive idealization is felt from, and only from, the victim state. Omnipotence and devaluation relate to the abuser's experience in relation to, and treatment of, the victim. This is evident in the aggressor state and may help to explain the isolated rage, contempt, and omnipotence often termed identification with the aggressor.

How, then, does this dissociative organization work in BPD?

> As long as the person oscillates between a hyper-attached self-state and an aggressive self-state in which attachment has been deactivated, terror is kept out of consciousness. Thus, splitting, like dissociative defenses in general, avoids the traumatic memories and impedes their assimilation and is thereby self-reinforcing and self-perpetuating. *While*

both of these states of mind avoid the terror-filled traumatic memories, the oscillation in tandem is even more rigidly avoidant, producing the "stable instability" of BPD....

This oscillation occurs because the rageful self-state can only be maintained briefly before fear of abandonment or annihilation triggers the idealizing self-state which, in turn, can only be maintained for a short while before fear of vulnerability triggers the rageful self-state (Howell, 1999). Perhaps it is the ability to switch to an alternating self-state, the splitting, that (like the dissociation in DID) affords some stability and organization that avoids full psychosis. In DID traumatized states and emotional parts of the personality are more fully encapsulated. This often allows more of what Fairbairn called central ego and the consistent ability to think reflectively. Because of the tendency of borderline persons to switch from victim to bully and back again, this domain of living is preoccupying, providing some sense of organization, purpose, and identity. (Howell, 2008, p. 111, italics added)

With the intent of showing how personality disorders can be understood as dissociation based, I have taken us through a brief diagnostic history— an etiology of an etiology, perhaps. What I want to emphasize is the specific way that I think this dissociative organization works in the prototypical personality disorder, BPD. I have accounted for the characteristic stable instability as an outcome of a procedural identification with the aggressor and oscillation of victim and aggressor self-states.

SUPEREGO-LIKE MANIFESTATIONS IN DID

The predominant defense in neurosis has been understood to be repression. For example, repression has been understood to be central in severe superego problems, hysteria, depression, and obsessions. However, it may be fitting to view the kinds of problems in living earlier understood as neuroses, as trauma and dissociation based. Clinicians often implicitly conceptualize and work with certain kinds of "superego problems" as one would conceptualize and work with dissociated, persecutory self-states. The following vignette is an example of superego-like problems in DID.

Archaic, Harsh Superego and DID

Shirley, an adult long in the workforce but returning to school, called to say that she had dissociated right before an exam. As a consequence, she had arrived 45 minutes late for a 3-hour exam. This was despite stringent, fail-safe measures that she had instituted to keep her focused and less vulnerable to dissociative intrusions, withdrawals, or overt switching. Because the exam was an hour earlier than regular class time, she had reoriented her internal time clock, setting the alarm an hour earlier every day for the entire previous week. She had set a timetable for last-minute studying and organizing the material in her mind in the morning before the exam. She had studied well and was prepared.

But, this well-prepared-for morning became disastrous when she decided that she had prepared so well that she had time to read her e-mail. She opened an e-mail (the possibility of danger from this source was one contingency for which she was unprepared) from a sister who had been physically abusive to her when she was a child. In the e-mail, the sister demanded that she call her and visit her mother, who lives in a distant city, for Christmas, and she chided her for not having done so. Her mother, who had already disowned her, had been highly unsupportive of her academic aspirations. In addition, intensely envious of Shirley's academic ability, her mother had actively undermined her academic pursuits on those rare occasions when she tried.

Despite her mother's extreme hostility and rampant neglect toward her, Shirley has some child alters who are intensely attached to her mother and who long for her mother's love. (As we know, in a way that seems contradictory, neglect and abuse often have the effect of intensifying attachment longings. In accordance with Bowlby's evolutionary theory about attachment, danger increases attachment to the caregiver in a young child in a way that is hardwired. Thus, even when the caregiver is the source of the danger, the child seeks the attachment bond all the more intensely because the danger is greater.)

Our work in session revealed that one of Shirley's child parts who denied her mother's abuse and who just wanted to be close to her had been triggered in a covert switch. This part only wanted to please and propitiate her mother. All this part knew was that it was up to her to ameliorate the situation—by messing up her exam. This part was out for about an hour. However, because this part was unfamiliar with all of the fail-safe measures that Shirley had instituted and had not been part of that decision, she did not know that the exam was an hour earlier. Just as she was going into class, Shirley switched again to the part of her who attends classes and realized that she was 45 minutes late. She was mystified about how this had happened.

This sort of psychodynamically motivated self-destructiveness is something we see all the time in so-called neurotic patients. The patient is bonded to the unsupportive or abusive parent and fails as a way to please the real parent and the parent introject. This particular example, however, illuminates the possibility that the dissociative process is universal and just as much a part of the human neurobiology as is attachment need. Furthermore, it suggests that the more familiar and usual way we have of conceptualizing psychodynamically motivated failures is not specific enough. In particular, there is a problem with conceptualizing these kinds of failures as behaviors of the whole person. This kind of behavior is a sign of lack of integration. If the motivation had been that of the whole, much more integrated person, in Shirley's case, the behavior most likely would not have occurred, for positions countervailing to the desire to please and propitiate mother would have been in mind along with that desire, and the overriding decision would have been something like, "I know this makes me anxious, but it is more important for Me to do well on this exam, even if Mother does not want me to."

More likely than motivation of this sort residing in the whole person, or even in "superego," the motivation is located in an isolated, dissociated self-state. The information about it is not available to other self-states. The traumatic bond, which for me (see Chapter 2) is by definition dissociative, is an operative motivational force. What this means is that "normal" psychodynamically motivated failures stem from the dissociated self-states that hold feelings that are not integrated with the rest of the personality.

In my view, many of the kinds of problems in living earlier understood as neuroses are highly trauma and dissociation based. Neurotic symptoms were understood to be the result of psychic conflict between wish and defense. Repression was considered central, and a unified self was assumed. Hand in hand with neurosis was a punitive superego, which is understood both as the source of psychopathology and as a moral agency. Superego was understood to arise from the threat of castration, eventually leading to the internalization of the parents' superegos. However, castration threat, which Freud (1925) felt made the boy's superego superior to the girl's, is potentially traumatic. Taken literally, castration threat as the threat of dismemberment and deprivation of masculinity can be understood as more potentiating of dissociation than of mature morality. Kohut (1984), viewing castration anxiety a pathological symptom of a disorder of the self, stated, "A boy who is exposed to the responses of psychologically healthy parents does not experience a significant degree of castration anxiety during the oedipal phase" (p. 14).

A crucial distinction may hinge on whether the structure called "superego" arises from the child's need to control uncivilized impulses, which would be moral; or from the child's attempt to deal with traumatic impingement from an uncivilized world....Harsh superego, arising from the threat of castration linked to the oedipal conflict, may better describe how the child becomes self-punishing than how the child achieves mature morality. Uncivilized wishes can be forgotten (repressed) in an overall sense of the continuity of personal history (Ogden, 1986; Bromberg, 1996) whereas overwhelming terror seems more likely to lead to a segmentation of self-experience (dissociation). [Howell, 1997a, p. 234]

Clinicians often work intuitively with superego as if it were a dissociated internal persecutory presence or self-state, rather than as theoretically described in terms of the structural model and the Oedipus construct. The superego is, of course, dissociated from the ego (Cameron & Rychlak, 1985). However, I believe that the psychodynamics involved are largely dissociation based, in addition to repression-based.

References

Ainsworth, M. D. S., Blehar, M. C., Waters, E., & Wall, S. (1978). *Patterns of attachment: A psychological study of the strange situation*. Hillsdale, NJ: Erlbaum.

Allen, J. G. (2001). *Traumatic relationships and serious mental disorders*. New York: Wiley.

Alvarado, C. S. (2002). Dissociation in Britain during the late nineteenth century: The Society for Psychical Research, 1892–1890. *Journal of Trauma and Dissociation, 3*(2), 9–34.

American Psychiatric Association. (1980). *Diagnostic and statistical manual of mental disorders* (3rd ed.). Washington, DC: Author.

American Psychiatric Association. (1994). *Diagnostic and statistical manual of mental disorders* (4th ed.). Washington, DC: Author.

American Psychiatric Association. (2000). *Diagnostic and statistical manual of mental disorders* (4th ed., text revision). Washington, DC: Author.

American Psychiatric Association. (2010). *Diagnostic and statistical manual of mental disorders* (5th ed.). Washington, DC: Author. Retrieved 1 September, 2010 from http://www.dsm5.org/ProposedRevisions/Pages/proposedrevision.aspx?rid=57

Amodeo, M., Griffin, M. L., Fassler, I. R., Clay, C. M., & Ellis, M. A. (2006). Childhood sexual abuse among Black women and White women from two-parent families. *Child Maltreatment, 11*, 237–246.

Anderson, C. L., & Alexander, P. C. (1996). The relationship between attachment and dissociation in adult survivors of incest. *Psychiatry: Interpersonal and Biological Processes, 59*(3), 240–254.

Armstrong, J. G., & Loewenstein, R. J. (1990). Characteristics of patients with multiple personality and dissociative disorders on psychological testing. *Journal of Nervous and Mental Disease, 178*, 448–454.

Armstrong, J., Putnam, F., Carlson, E., Libero, D., & Smith, S. (1997). Development and validation of a measure of adolescent dissociation: The adolescent dissociative experiences scale. *The Journal of Nervous and Mental Disease, 185*(8), 491–495.

Aron, L. (1996). *A meeting of minds: Mutuality in psychoanalysis*. Hillsdale, NJ: Analytic Press.

Aron, L., & Harris, A. (1993). Sándor Ferenczi: Discovery and rediscovery. In L. Aron & A. Harris (Eds.), *The legacy of Sándor Ferenczi* (pp. 1–35). Hillsdale, NJ: Analytic Press.

Baker, S. (1997). Dancing the dance with dissociatives: Some thoughts on countertransference, projective identification and enactments in the treatment of dissociative disorders. *Dissociation, 10*, 214–222.

Barrett, D. L. (1994). The dream character as a prototype for the multiple personality "alter." In S. J. Lynn & J. Rhue (Eds.), *Dissociation* (pp. 123–135). Washington, DC: American Psychological Association Press,

Barrett, D. L. (1996). Dreams in multiple personality disorder. In D. Barrett (Ed.), *Trauma and dreams* (pp. 68–81). Cambridge, MA: Harvard University Press,

Beahrs, J. O. (1982). *Unity and multiplicity.* New York: Brunner/Mazel.

Bem, S. L. (1983). Gender schema theory and its implications for child development: Raising gender-aschematic children in a gender-schematic society. *Signs, 8*, 367–389.

Benjamin, J. (1999). Recognition and destruction: An outline of intersubjectivity. In S. A. Mitchell & L. Aron (Eds.), *Relational psychoanalysis: The emergence of a tradition* (pp. 181–210). Hillsdale, NJ: The Analytic Press.

Bernstein, E. M., & Putnam, F. W. (1986). Development, reliability, and validity of a dissociation scale. *Journal of Nervous and Mental Disease, 174*, 727–734.

Bernstein Carlson, E., & Putnam, F. W. (1993). An update on the Dissociative Experiences Scale. *Dissociation, 6*(1), 16–27.

Betcher, R. W., & Pollack, W. S. (1993). *In a time of fallen heroes: The re-creation of masculinity.* New York: Guilford Press.

Bion, W. (1957). Differentiation of the psychotic from the non-psychotic personalities. In E. B. Spillius (Ed.), *Melanie Klein today: Developments in theory and practice, Vol. 1: Mainly theory* (pp. 61–78). New York: Routledge.

Bion, W. (1959). Attacks on linking: Differentiation of the psychotic from the non-psychotic personalities. In E. B. Spillius (Ed.), *Melanie Klein today: Developments in theory and practice, Vol. 1: Mainly theory* (pp. 87–101). New York: Routledge.

Bleuler, E. (1911/1950). *Dementia praecox or the group of schizophrenias* (J. Zinkin, Trans.). New York: International Universities Press.

Bliss, E. L. (1986). *Multiple personality, allied disorders, and hypnosis.* New York: Oxford University Press.

Blizard, R. A. (1997). The origins of dissociative identity disorder from an object-relations theory and attachment theory perspective. *Dissociation, 10*, 223–229.

Blizard, R. A. (2003). Disorganized attachment, development of dissociated self-states, and a relational approach to treatment. *Journal of Trauma and Dissociation, 4*(3), 27–50.

Boon, S., & Draijer, N. (1993). The differentiation of patients with MPD or DDNOS from patients with cluster B personality disorder. *Dissociation, 6*, 126–135.

Boon, S., Steele, K., & Van der Hart, O. (2011). *Coping with trauma-related dissociation: Skills training for clients and therapists.* New York: Norton.

Boulanger, G. (2007). *Wounded by reality: Understanding and treating adult onset trauma.* Hillsdale, NJ: Analytic Press.

Bower, T. (1971). The object in the world of the infant. *Scientific American, 225*, 30–38.

Bowlby, J. (1973). *Attachment and loss, Vol. 2: Separation.* New York: Basic Books.

Bowlby, J. (1980). *Attachment and loss, Vol. 3, Loss: Sadness and depression.* New York: Basic Books.

Bowlby, J. (1983). *Attachment and loss, Vol. 1: Attachment.* New York: Basic Books. (Original work published 1969)

Bowlby, J. (1984). Psychoanalysis as a natural science. *Psychoanalytic Psychology, 1*, 7–22.

Bowlby, J. (1988). *A secure base: Clinical applications of attachment theory.* London: Routledge.

Brand, B. L. (2001). Establishing safety with patients with dissociative identity disorder. *Journal of Trauma and Dissociation, 2*(4), 133–155.

Brand, B. L., Armstrong, J. G., & Lowenstein, R. J. (1996). Psychological assessment of patients with dissociative identity disorder. *Psychiatric Clinics of North America, 29*, 145–168.

Brand, B. L., Armstrong, J. G., & Loewenstein, R. J. (2006). Psychological assessment of patients with dissociative identity disorder. *Psychiatric Clinics of North America, 29*, 145–168.

Brand, B. L., Classen, C. C., Lanius, R., Loewenstein, R. J., McNary, S. W., Pain, C., et al. (2009). A naturalistic study of dissociative identity disorder and dissociative disorder not otherwise specified patients treated by community clinicians. *Psychological Trauma: Theory, Research, Practice, and Policy, 1*, 153–171.

Brand, B. L., Classen, C. C., McNary, S. W., & Zaveri, P. (2009). A review of dissociative disorders treatment studies. *Journal of Nervous and Mental Disease, 197*, 646–654.

Brand, B. L., Loewenstein, R. J., Armstrong, J. G., & McNary, S. W. (2009). Personality differences on the Rorschach of dissociative identity disorder, borderline personality disorder, and psychotic inpatients. *Psychological Trauma: Theory, Research, Practice, and Policy, 1*, 188–205.

Brand, B. L., McNary, S. W., Loewenstein, R. J., Kolos, A. C., & Barr, S. R. (2006). Assessment of genuine and simulated dissociative identity disorder on the Structured Interview of Reported Symptoms. *Journal of Trauma and Dissociation, 7*(1), 63–85.

Braude, S. E. (1995). *First person plural: Multiple personality and the philosophy of mind.* Lanham, MD: Rowman & Littlefield.

Braude, S. E. (2009). The conceptual unity of dissociation: A philosophical argument. In P. F. Dell & J. A. O'Neil (Eds.), *Dissociation and the dissociative disorders: DSM-V and beyond* (pp. 27–36). New York: Routledge.

Braun, B. G. (Ed.). (1986). *Treatment of multiple personality disorder.* Washington, DC: American Psychiatric Press.

Breger, L. (2000). *Freud: Darkness in the midst of vision.* New York: Wiley.

Bremner, J. D. (2002). *Does stress damage the brain? Understanding trauma-related disorders from a mind–body perspective.* New York: W. W. Norton.

Bremner, J. D. & Vermetten, E. (2007). Psychiatric approaches to dissociation: Integrating history, biology, and clinical assessment. In E. Vermetten, M. Dorahy, & D. Spiegel (Eds.), *Traumatic dissociation: Neurobiology and treatment* (pp. 239–258). Washington DC: American Psychiatric Publishing.

Bremner, J. D., Southwick, S., Brett, E., Fontana, A., Rosenheck, R., & Charney, D. S. (1992). Dissociation and posttraumatic stress disorder in Vietnam combat veterans. *American Journal of Psychiatry, 149,* 328–332.

Brenner, I. (2001). *Dissociation of trauma: Theory, phenomenology, and technique.* Madison, CT: International Universities Press.

Bretherton, I. (1992). Attachment and bonding: From ethological to representational and sociological perspectives. In V. B. Van Hasselt & M. Herson (Eds.), *Handbook of social development* (pp. 133–155). New York: Plenum.

Brett, E. A. (1996). The classification of posttraumatic stress disorder. In B. A. Van der Kolk, A. C. McFarlane, & L. Weisaeth (Eds.), *Traumatic stress* (pp. 117–128). New York: Guilford Press.

Breuer, J., & Freud, S. (1893–1895a). On the psychical mechanism of hysterical phenomena: Preliminary communication from studies on hysteria. In J. Strachey (Ed. & Trans.), *The standard edition of the complete psychological works of Sigmund Freud* (Vol. 4, pp. 1–17). London: Hogarth Press.

Breuer, J., & Freud, S. (1893–1895b). Studies in hysteria. In J. Strachey (Ed. & Trans.), *The standard edition of the complete psychological works of Sigmund Freud* (Vol. 2). London: Hogarth Press.

Briere, J., Scott, C., & Weathers, F. W. (2005). Peritraumatic and persistent dissociation in the presumed etiology of PTSD. *American Journal of Psychiatry, 162,* 2295–2301.

Bromberg, P. M. (1993). Shadow and substance: A relational perspective on clinical process. In P. M. Bromberg, *Standing in the spaces: Essays on clinical process, trauma, and dissociation* (pp. 165–187). Hillsdale, NJ: Analytic Press.

Bromberg, P. M. (1994). Speak! That I may see you: Some reflections of dissociation, reality, and psychoanalytic listening. *Psychoanalytic Dialogues, 4,* 517–547.

Bromberg, P. M. (1995). Psychoanalysis, dissociation, and personality organization: Reflections on Peter Goldberg's essay. *Psychoanalytic Dialogues, 5,* 511–528.

Bromberg, P. M. (1996). Hysteria, dissociation, and cure: Emmy von N revisited. *Psychoanalytic Dialogues, 6,* 55–71.

Bromberg, P. M. (1998). Staying the same while changing: Reflections on clinical judgment. In P. Bromberg, *Standing in the spaces: Essays on clinical process, trauma, and dissociation* (pp. 291–308). Hillsdale, NJ: Analytic Press.

Bromberg, P. M. (2003). On being one's dream: Some reflection on Robert Bosnak's "Embodied Imagination." *Contemporary Psychoanalysis, 39,* 697–710.

Bromberg, P. M. (2004). More than meets the eye: A professional autobiography. *Psychoanalytic Inquiry, 24,* 558–575.

Bromberg, P. M. (2006). *Awakening the dreamer: Clinical journeys.* Mahwah, NJ: Analytic Press.

Bromberg, P. M. (2009a). Multiple self-states, the relational mind, and dissociation: A psychoanalytic perspective. In P. F. Dell & J. A. O'Neil (Eds.), *Dissociation and the dissociative disorders: DSM-V and beyond* (pp. 637–652). New York: Routledge.

Bromberg, P. M. (2009b). Truth, human relatedness, and the analytic process: An interpersonal/relational perspective. *International Journal of Psychoanalysis, 90,* 347–361.

Bromberg, P. M. (2010). The nearness of you: Navigating selfhood, otherness, and uncertainty. In J. Petrucelli (Ed.), *Knowing, not-knowing, and sort-of knowing: Psychoanalysis and the experience of uncertainty* (pp. 23–44). London: Karnac.

Brothers, D. (1995). *Falling backwards: An exploration of trust and self-experience.* New York: Norton.

Brown, L. S. (1991). Not outside the range: One feminist perspective on psychic trauma. *American Imago, 48,* 119–133.

Bryant, D., Kessler, J., & Shirar, L. (1992). *The family inside: Working with the multiple.* New York: Norton.

Bryant, D., Kessler, J., & Shirar, L. (1995). *Beyond integration: One multiple's journey.* New York: Norton.

Bucci, W. (1997). *Psychoanalysis and cognitive science.* New York: Guilford Press.

Bucci, W. (2002). The referential process, consciousness, and the sense of self. *Psychoanalytic Inquiry, 22,* 766–793.

Bucci, W. (2003). Varieties of dissociative experiences: A multiple code account and a discussion of Bromberg's case of "William." *Psychoanalytic Psychoanalysis, 20,* 542–557.

Cameron, N., & Rychlak, J. F. (1985). *Personality development and psychopathology: A dynamic approach.* Boston: Houghton Mifflin.

Cardeña, E. (2001, December). *The domain of dissociation: A cross-cultural perspective.* Paper presented at the 18th International Fall Conference of the International Society for the Study of Dissociation, New Orleans, LA.

Carlson, E. A. (1998). A prospective longitudinal study of attachment disorganization/ disorientation. *Child Development, 69,* 1107–1128.

Carlson, E. B., & Putnam, F. W. (1993). An update on the Dissociative Experiences Scale. *Dissociation, 6,* 16–27.

Carlson, E. T. (1986). The history of dissociation until 1880. In J. Q. Quen (Ed.), *Split minds/split brains: Historical and current perspectives* (pp. 7–30). New York: New York University Press.

Carlson, V., Cicchetti, D., Barrett, D., & Brunewald, K. (1989). Disorganized/disoriented attachment relationships in maltreated infants. *Developmental Psychology, 25,* 525–531.

Celani, D. (2001). Working with Fairbairn's ego structures. *Contemporary Psychoanalysis, 37,* 391–416.

Chefetz, R. A. (1997a). Abreaction: Baby or bath water? *Dissociation, 10,* 203–213.

Chefetz, R. A. (1997b). Special case transference and countertransference in the treatment of dissociative identity disorder. *Dissociation, 10,* 255–265.

Chefetz, R. A. (2000a). Affect dysregulation as a way of life. *Journal of the American Academy of Psychoanalysis, 28,* 289–303.

Chefetz, R. A. (2000b). Disorder in the therapist's view of the self: Working with the person with dissociative identity disorder. *Psychoanalytic Inquiry, 20,* 305–329.

Chefetz, R. A. (2003). Healing haunted hearts: Toward a modeling for integrating subjectivity. Commentary on papers by Philip Bromberg and Gerald Stechler. *Psychoanalytic Dialogues, 13,* 727–742.

Chefetz, R. A. (2005a). A cognitive-psychoanalytic perspective on the treatment of complex dissociative disorders. *Psychiatric Annals, 35,* 657–665.

Chefetz, R. A. (Ed.). (2005b). Therapeutic advances in dissociative disorders [Special issue]. *Psychiatric Annals, 35*(8).

Chefetz, R. A. (2010). Life as performance art: Right and left brain function, implicit knowing and felt coherence. In J. Petrucelli (Ed.), *Knowing, not-knowing, and sort-of knowing: Psychoanalysis and the experience of uncertainty* (pp. 225–242). London: Karnac.

Chefetz, R. A., & Bromberg, P. M. (2004). Talking with "me" and "not-me": A dialogue. *Contemporary Psychoanalysis, 40,* 409–464.

Chu, J. A. (1998). *Rebuilding shattered lives: The responsible treatment of complex posttraumatic and dissociative disorders.* New York: Wiley.

Chu, J., Baker, S., O'Neil, J., & Wagner, A. (2001). Introduction to the diagnosis and treatment of complex dissociative disorders. Presented at the International Society for the Study of Dissociation 26th Annual Conference. New Orleans, LA, December 3, 2001.

Coates, S., & Moore, M. (1995). Boyhood gender identity: The interface of constitution and early experience. *Psychoanalytic Inquiry, 15,* 6–38.

Coates, S., & Moore, M. (1997). The complexity of early trauma: Representation and transformation. *Psychoanalytic Inquiry, 17,* 286–311.

Cody, D. (Creator), & Kaplow, D. (Producer). (2009). *The United States of Tara* [Television series]. United States: DreamWorks Television.

Coons, P. M. (1991). Iatrogenesis and malingering of multiple personality disorder in the forensic evaluation of homicide defendants. *Psychiatric Clinics of North America, 14,* 757–768.

Coons, P. M., & Milstein, V. (1994). Factitious or malingered multiple personality disorder: Eleven cases. *Dissociation, 7,* 81–85.

Coons, P. M., Bowman, E. S., & Milstein, V. (1988). Multiple personality disorder: A clinical investigation of 50 cases. *Journal of Nervous and Mental Disease, 17,* 519–527.

Cortina, M., & Liotti, G. (2010). The intersubjective and cooperative origins of consciousness: An evolutionary-developmental approach. *Journal of the American Academy of Psychoanalysis, 38,* 291–314.

Cortina, M., & Marrone, M. (2004). Reclaiming Bowlby's contribution to psychoanalysis. *International Forum of Psychoanalysis, 13,* 133–146.

Courtois, C. A. (1997). *Healing the incest wound: Adult survivors in therapy.* New York: Norton.

Courtois, C. A. (1999). *Recollections of sexual abuse: Treatment principles and guidelines.* New York: Norton.

Courtois, C. A. (2004). Complex trauma, complex reactions: Assessment and treatment. *Psychotherapy: Theory, Research, Practice, and Training, 41,* 412–425.

Courtois, C. A., & Ford, J. D. (2009). *Treating complex traumatic stress disorders: An evidence-based guide.* New York: Guilford Press.

Courtois, C., & Ford, J. D. (2009). Defining and understanding complex trauma and complex traumatic stress disorders. In C. A. Courtois & J. D. Ford (Eds.), *Treating complex traumatic stress disorders: An evidence-based guide* (pp. 13–30). New York: Guilford Press.

Courtois, C. A., Ford, J. D., & Cloitre, M. (2009). Best practices in psychotherapy for adults. In C. A. Courtois & J. D. Ford (Eds.), *Treating complex traumatic stress disorders: An evidence-based guide* (pp. 82–103). New York: Guilford Press.

Curtis, J. (1997, November). *Psychopathic alters in otherwise nonpsychopathic DID patients.* Paper presented at the 14th annual conference of the International Society for the Study of Dissociation, Montreal, Quebec, Canada.

Dalenberg, C. J. (2004, November). *What is normal about normal and pathological dissociation?* Paper presented at the 21st annual conference of the International Society for the Study of Dissociation, New Orleans, LA.

Davies, J. M., & Frawley, M. G. (1994). *Treating the adult survivor of childhood sexual abuse: A psychoanalytic perspective.* New York: Basic Books.

Dell, P. (1998). Axis II pathology in outpatients with dissociative identity disorder. *Journal of Nervous & Mental Disorders, 186,* 352–356.

Dell, P. F. (2001). Why the diagnostic criteria for dissociative identity disorder should be changed. *Journal of Trauma and Dissociation, 2*(1), 7–37.

Dell, P. F. (2002). Dissociative phenomenology of dissociative identity disorder. *Journal of Nervous and Mental Disease, 190,* 1–15.

Dell, P. F. (2006a). The Multidimensional Inventory of Dissociation (MID): A comprehensive measure of pathological dissociation. *Journal of Trauma and Dissociation, 7*(2), 77–106.

Dell, P. F. (2006b). A new model of dissociative identity disorder. *Psychiatric Clinics of North America, 29*(1), 1–26.

Dell, P. F. (2009a). The long struggle to diagnose multiple personality disorder: Multiple personality disorder. In P. F. Dell & J. A. O'Neil (Eds.), *Dissociation and the dissociative disorders: DSM-V and beyond* (pp. 383–402). New York: Routledge.

Dell, P. F. (2009b). The long struggle to diagnose multiple personality disorder: Partial MPD. In P. F. Dell & J. A. O'Neil (Eds.), *Dissociation and the dissociative disorders: DSM-V and beyond* (pp. 403–428). New York: Routledge.

Dell, P. F. (2009c). The phenomena of pathological dissociation. In P. F. Dell & J. A. O'Neil (Eds.), *Dissociation and the dissociative disorders: DSM-V and beyond* (pp. 225–238). New York: Routledge.

Dell, P. F. (2009d). Understanding dissociation. In P. F. Dell & J. A. O'Neil (Eds.), *Dissociation and the dissociative disorders: DSM-V and beyond* (pp. 709–825). New York: Routledge.

Dell, P. F., & O'Neil, J. A. (2009). Introduction. In P. F. Dell & J. A. O'Neil (Eds.), *Dissociation and the dissociative disorders: DSM–V and beyond* (pp. xxv–xxxiiii). New York: Routledge.

Dennett, D. C. (1991). *Consciousness explained.* Boston: Little Brown.

Devereux, G. (1953). Why Oedipus killed Laius: A note on the complementary Oedipus complex in Greek drama. *International Journal of Psychoanalysis, 32,* 132.

Draijer, N., & Boon, S. (1999). The imitation of dissociative identity disorder: Patients at risk, therapists at risk. *Journal of Psychiatry and Law, 27,* 423–458.

Dupont, J., Ed. (1988). *The clinical diary of Sándor Ferenczi.* Cambridge, MA: Harvard University Press.

Dutton, D. C., & Painter, S. L. (1981). Traumatic bonding: The development of emotional attachments in battered women and other relationships of intermittent abuse. *Victimology, 6,* 139–155.

Edelman, G. M. (1989). *The remembered present.* New York: Basic Books.

Edelman, G. M. (2004). *Wider than the sky: The phenomenal gift of consciousness.* New York: Basic Books.

Ehling, T., Nijenhuis, E. R. S., & Krikke, A. P. (2003). Volume of discrete brain structures in florid and recovered DID, DDNOS and healthy controls. Presented at the 20th Annual Conference of the International Society for the Study of Dissociation, Chicago, November 4.

Ellason, J. W., & Ross, C. A. (1997). Two-year follow-up of inpatients with dissociative identity disorders. *American Journal of Psychiatry, 154,* 832–839.

Ellenberger, H. (1970). *The discovery of the unconscious: The history and evolution of dynamic psychology.* New York: Basic Books.

Emch, M. (1944). On the "need to know" as related to identification and acting out. *International Journal of Psychoanalysis, 25,* 13–19.

Erdelyi, M. H. (1994). Dissociation, defense, and the unconscious. In D. Spiegel (Ed.), *Dissociation, culture, mind and body* (pp. 3–20). Washington, DC: American Psychiatric Press.

Fairbairn, R. (1952a). Endopsychic structure considered in terms of object-relationships. In *Psychoanalytic studies of the personality* (pp. 82–136). Boston: Routledge & Kegan Paul. (Original work published 1944)

Fairbairn, R. (1952b). Features in the analysis of a patient with a physical genital abnormality. In *Psychoanalytic studies of the personality* (pp. 197–222). Boston: Routledge & Kegan Paul. (Original work published 1931)

Fairbairn, R. (1952c). Schizoid factors in the personality. In *Psychoanalytic studies of the personality.* Boston: Routledge & Kegan Paul. (Original work published 1940)

Fairbairn, R. (1958). On the nature and aims of psycho-analytical treatment. In E. F. Birtles & D. E. Scharff (Eds.), *From instinct to self: Selected papers of W. R. D. Fairbairn* (Vol. 1, pp. 74–92). Northvale, NJ: Aronson.

Fairbairn, R. (1994). Child assault. In E. F. Birtles & D. E. Scharff (Eds.), *From instinct to self: Selected papers of W. R. D. Fairbairn* (Vol. 2, pp. 165–183). Northvale, NJ: Aronson. (Original work published 1935)

Feliu, M. H., & Edwards, C. W. (2010). Psychologic factors in the development of complex regional pain syndrome: History, myth, and evidence. *Clinical Journal of Pain, 26,* 258–263.

Ferenczi, S. (1949). Confusion of tongues between the adult and the child. *International Journal of Psychoanalysis, 30,* 225–231. (Original work published 1932)

Ferenczi, S. (1980). Notes and fragments: Relaxation and education. In M. Balint (Ed.) & E. Mosbacher (Trans.), *Final contributions to the problems and methods of psycho-analysis* (pp. 236–238). London: Karnac Books. (Original work published 1931)

Fine, C. G. (1993). A tactical integrationalist perspective on the treatment of multiple personality disorder. In R. P. Kluft & C. G. Fine (Eds.), *Clinical perspectives on multiple personality disorder* (pp. 135–153). Washington, DC: American Psychiatric Press.

Fine, C., & Berkowitz A. (2001). The wreathing protocol: The imbrication of hypnosis and EMDR in the treatment of dissociative identity disorder and other dissociative responses. *American Journal of Clinical Hypnosis, 43,* 3, 275–290.

Fonagy, P. (2000). Attachment and borderline personality disorder. *Journal of the American Psychoanalytical Association, 48,* 1129–1146.

Fonagy, P. (2001). *Attachment theory and psychoanalysis.* New York: Other Press.

Fonagy, P., Gergely, G., Jurist, E. L., & Target, M. (2002). Affect regulation, mentalization, and the development of the self. New York: Other Press.

Fonagy, P., Steele, M., Steele, H., Leigh, T., Kennedy, R., Mattoon, G., et al. (1995). Attachment, the reflective self, and borderline states: The predictive specificity of the Adult Attachment Interview and pathological emotional development. In S. Goldberg, R. Muir, & J. Kerr (Eds.), *Attachment theory: Social, developmental and clinical perspectives* (pp. 233–278). Hillsdale, NJ: Analytic Press.

Foote, B., & Park, J. (2008). Dissociative identity disorder and schizophrenia: Differential diagnosis and theoretical issues. *Current Psychiatry Reports, 1,* 217–222.

Foote, B., Smolin, Y., Kaplan, M., Legatt, M. E., & Lipschitz, D. (2006). Prevalence of dissociative disorders in psychiatric outpatients. *American Journal of Psychiatry, 163,* 623–629.

Foote, B., Smolin, Y., & Lipshitz, D. (2008). Dissociative disorders and suicidality in psychiatric outpatients. *Journal of Nervous and Mental Disorder, 196*(1), 29–36.

Forgash, C., & Knipe, J. (2008). Integrating EMDR and ego state treatment for clients with trauma disorders. In C. Forgash & M. Copeley (Eds.), *Healing the heart of trauma and dissociation with EMDR and ego state therapy* (pp. 1–60). New York: Springer.

Forrest, K. A. (2001). Toward an etiology of dissociative identity disorder: A neurodevelopmental approach. *Consciousness and Cognition, 10,* 259–293.

Frankel, A. S., & O'Hearn, T. C. (1996). Similarities in response to extreme and unremitting stress: Cultures of communities under siege. *Psychotherapy, 33,* 485–502.

Fraser, G. A. (1991). The dissociative table technique: A strategy for working with ego states in dissociative disorders and ego-state therapy. *Dissociation, 4*(1), 205–214.

Fraser, G. A. (2003). Fraser's "Dissociative Table Technique" revisited, revised: A strategy for working with ego states in dissociative disorders and ego-state therapy. *Journal of Trauma and Dissociation, 4*(4), 5–28.

Frawley-O'Dea, M. G. (1999). Society, politics, psychotherapy, and the search for "truth" in the memory debate. In M. Rivera (Ed.), *Fragment by fragment: Feminist perspectives on memory and child sexual abuse* (pp. 73–90). Charlottetown, Canada: Gynergy Books.

Frederick, C., & Phillips, M. (1995). *Healing the divided self: Clinical and Ericksonian hypnotherapy for post-traumatic and dissociative conditions.* New York: Norton.

Freud, A. (1966). *The ego and the mechanisms of defence* (Cecil Baines, Trans.). London: Hogarth Press. (Original work published 1937)

Freud, S. (1909/1955). Notes upon a case of obsessional neurosis. In J. Strachey (Ed. and Trans.), *The standard edition of the complete psychological works,* Vol. 10 (pp. 153–318). London: Hogarth Press.

Freud, S. (1925). Some psychical consequences of the anatomical distinction between the sexes. Standard Edition, Vol. 19 (pp. 243–258). London: Hogarth Press.

Freud, S. (1955). Group psychology and analysis of the ego. In J. Strachey (Ed., & Trans.), *The standard edition of the complete psychological works of Sigmund Freud* (Vol. 18, pp. 65–143). London: Hogarth Press. (Original work published 1921)

Freud, S. (1959a). Mourning and melancholia. In J. Strachey (Ed., & Trans.), *The standard edition of the complete psychological works of Sigmund Freud* (Vol. 14, pp. 239–260). London: Hogarth Press. (Original work published 1917)

Freud, S. (1959b). Repression. In J. Strachey (Ed., & Trans.), *The standard edition of the complete psychological works of Sigmund Freud* (Vol. 14, pp. 143–158). London: Hogarth Press. (Original work published 1915)

Freud, S. (1961a). The ego and the id. In J. Strachey (Ed., & Trans.), *The standard edition of the complete psychological works of Sigmund Freud* (Vol. 19, pp. 1–16). London: Hogarth Press. (Original work published 1923)

Freud, S. (1961b). The splitting of the ego in the process of defence. In J. Strachey (Ed., & Trans.), *The standard edition of the complete psychological works of Sigmund Freud* (Vol. 23, pp. 275–278). London: Hogarth Press. (Original work published 1938)

Freud, S. (1962). The aetiology of hysteria. In J. Strachey (Ed., &Trans.), *The standard edition of the complete psychological works of Sigmund Freud* (Vol. 3, pp. 187–221). London: Hogarth Press. (Original work published 1896)

Frewin, P., & Lanius, R. (2006a). Neurobiology of dissociation: Unity and disunity in mind-body-brain. *Psychiatric Clinics North America, 29*, 113–128.

Frewin, P., & Lanius, R. (2006b). Toward a psychobiology of posttraumatic self-dysregulation: Reexperiencing, hyperarousal, dissociation, and emotional numbing. *Annals of the New York Academy of Sciences, 1071*, 110–124.

Freyd, J. (1996). *Betrayal trauma: The logic of forgetting childhood abuse.* Cambridge, MA: Harvard University Press.

Fromm, E. (1980). *Greatness and limitations of Freud's thought.* New York: Signet.

Frosch, J. (1964/1986). The psychotic character: Clinical psychiatric considerations. In Stone, M. (Ed.), *Essential papers on borderline disorders: One hundred years at the border* (pp. 263–278). New York: NYU Press.

Fuller-Tyszkiewicz, M., & Mussap, A. J. (2008). The relationship between dissociation and binge eating. *Journal of Trauma & Dissociation, 9*(4), 445–462.

Gallese, V. (2009). Mirror neurons, embodied simulations, and the neural basis of social identifications. *Psychoanalytic Dialogues, 19,* 519–536.

Gallese, V., Fadiga, L., Fogassi, L., & Rizzolatti, G. (1996). Action recognition in the premotor cortex. *Brain, 119,* 593–609.

Gartner, R. (1999). *Betrayed as boys.* New York: Basic Books.

Gay, P. (1988). *Freud: A life for our time.* New York: Norton.

Gazzaniga, M. (1985). *The social brain.* New York: Basic Books.

Ginsberg, H. (1974). Controlled versus non-controlled termination of immobility in domestic fowl (*Gallus gallus*): Parallel with learned helplessness phenomenon. Unpublished manuscript, as quoted in Seligman, M. (1975) *Helplessness.* New York: W.H. Freeman & Co. (as listed in Scaer, 2005, p. 292).

Ginzburg, K., Butler, L. D., Saltzman, K., & Koopman, C. (2009). Dissociative reactions in PTSD. In P. F. Dell & J. A. O'Neil (Eds.), *Dissociation and the dissociative disorders: DSM-V and beyond* (pp. 457–469). New York: Routledge

Gold, S. (2000). *Not trauma alone: Therapy for child abuse survivors in family and social context*. Philadelphia: Brunner/Routledge.

Golier, J. A., Yehuda, R., Bierer, L. M. et al. (2003). The relationship of borderline personality disorder to posttraumatic stress disorder and traumatic events. *American Journal of Psychiatry, 160*, 2018–2024.

Goodman, L., & Peters, J. (1995). Persecutory alters and ego states: Protectors, friends, and allies. *Dissociation, 8*(2), 91–99.

Goodwin, J., & Attias, R. (1999). The self assumes animal form. In J. Goodwin & R. Attias (Eds.), *Splintered reflections: Images of the body in trauma* (pp. 257–280). New York: Basic Books.

Greenson, R. (1967). *The technique and practice of psychoanalysis* (Vol. 1). New York: International Universities Press.

Grotstein, J. S. (2000). Notes on Fairbairn's metapsychology. In J. S. Grotstein & D. B. Rinsley (Eds.), *Fairbairn and the origin of object relations* (pp. 112–148). New York: Other Press.

Gunderson, J. G., & Sabo, A. N. (1993a). The phenomenological and conceptual interface between borderline personality disorder and PTSD. *American Journal of Psychiatry, 150*, 19–27.

Gunderson, J. G., & Sabo, A. N. (1993b). Treatment of borderline personality disorder. A critical review. In J. Paris (Ed.), *Borderline personality disorder: Etiology and treatment* (pp. 385–406). Washington, DC: American Psychiatric Press.

Hébert, M., Tourigny, M., Cyr, M., McDuff, P., & Joly, J. (2009). Prevalence of childhood sexual abuse and timing of disclosure in a representative sample of adults from Quebec. *Canadian Journal of Psychiatry, 54*(9), 631–637.

Hegeman, E. (2010). Multiple personality disorder and spirit possession: Alike, yet not-alike. In J. Petrocelli (Ed.), *Knowing, not-knowing, and sort-of-knowing: Psychoanalysis and the experience of uncertainty* (pp. 99–114). London: Karnac.

Heidt, J. M., Marx, B. P., & Forsyth, J. P. (2005). Tonic immobility and childhood sexual abuse: Evaluating the sequela of rape-induced paralysis. *Behavior Research and Therapy, 43*, 1157–1171.

Hendriksen, K. M., McCartney, T., & Goodwin, J. M. (1990). Animal alters: Case reports. *Dissociation, 3*(4), 219–223.

Herman, J. L. (1992). *Trauma and recovery: The aftermath of violence from domestic abuse to political terror*. New York: Basic Books.

Herman, J. L. & van der Kolk, B. A. (1987). Traumatic antecedents of borderline personality disorder. In B. A. van der Kolk (Ed.), *Psychological trauma* (pp. 111–126). Washington, DC: American Psychiatric Press.

Hesse, E., & Main, M. (1999). Second-generation effects of unresolved trauma in nonmaltreating parents: Dissociated, frightened, and threatening behavior. *Psychoanalytic Inquiry, 19*, 481–540.

Hilgard, E. R. (1977). *Divided consciousness: Multiple controls in human thought and action*. New York: Wiley.

Hoch, P., & Polatin, P. (1949/1986). Pseudoneurotic forms of schizophrenia. In M. Stone (Ed.), *Essential papers on borderline disorders: One hundred years at the border* (pp. 119–147). New York: NYU Press.

Hopenwasser, K. (2008). Being in rhythm: Dissociative attunement in therapeutic process. *Journal of Trauma and Dissociation, 9*(3), 349–367.

Horowitz, M. J. (1976/1986). *Stress response syndromes*. Northvale, NJ: Aronson.

Howell, E. F. (1996). Dissociation in masochism and psychopathic sadism. *Contemporary Psychoanalysis, 32*(3), 427–453.

Howell, E. F. (1997a). Desperately seeking attachment: A psychoanalytic reframing of harsh superego. *Dissociation, 10*, 230–239.

Howell, E. F. (1997b). Masochism: A bridge to the other side of abuse. *Dissociation, 10*, 240–244.

Howell, E. F. (1999). Back to the states: Victim identity and abuser identification in borderline personality disorder. Presented at the Sixteenth Annual Conference of the International Society for the Study of Dissociation, Miami, November 12, 1999.

Howell, E. F. (2002a). Back to the "states": Victim and abuser states in borderline personality disorder. *Psychoanalytic Dialogues, 12*, 921–957.

Howell, E. F. (2002b). "Good girls," "sexy bad girls," and warriors: The role of trauma and dissociation in the creation and reproduction of gender. *Journal of Trauma and Dissociation, 3*(4), 5–32.

Howell, E. F. (2003). Narcissism: A relational aspect of dissociation. *Journal of Trauma and Dissociation, 4*(3), 51–71.

Howell, E. F. (2005). *The dissociative mind.* Hillsdale, NJ: Analytic Press.

Howell, E. F. (2008). Borderline personality disorder: Trauma, dissociation, splitting and psychosis: From hysteria to chronic relational trauma. In A. Moskowitz, I. Schafer, & M. Dorahy (Eds.), *Dissociation and psychosis: Emerging perspectives on severe psychopathology* (pp. 105–106). New York: Wiley.

Howell, E. F., & Blizard, R. A. (2009). Chronic relational trauma: A new diagnostic scheme for borderline personality and the spectrum of dissociative disorders. In P. F. Dell & J. A. O'Neil (Eds.), *Dissociation and the dissociative disorders: DSM-V and beyond* (pp. 599–624). New York: Routledge.

Hussey, J. M., Chang, J. J., & Kotch, J. B. (2006). Child maltreatment in the United States: Prevalence, risk factors, and adolescent consequences. *Pediatrics, 118*, 933–943.

International Society for the Study of Trauma and Dissociation. (in press). *Guidelines for treating dissociative identity disorders in adults.* McLean, VA: Author.

Itzkowitz, S. (2010, February 2). *We're all in this together.* Workshop at the W. A. White Institute, New York City.

Jacobvitz, D. (2000, November). *Disorganized mental processes in mothers, frightening caregiving, and disorganized and disoriented attachment behavior in infants.* Paper presented at the 17th International Fall Conference of the International Society for the Study of Dissociation, San Antonio, TX.

James, W. (1950). *Principles of psychology (Vol. 1).* New York: Dover. (Original work published 1890)

James, W. (1958). *Varieties of religious experience.* New York: New American Library. (Original work published 1902)

Janet, P. (1907). *The major symptoms of hysteria: Fifteen lectures given in the medical school of Harvard University.* New York: Macmillan.

Janet, P. (1919). *Les medications psychologiques* (3 vols.). Paris: Alcan.

Janet, P. (1925). *Psychological healing,* Vol. 1. New York: Macmillan. (Original work published 1919)

Janov, A. (1991). *Primal scream.* New York: Dell. (Original work published 1970)

Jung, C. G. (1960). The psychology of dementia praecox (R. F. C. Hull, Trans.). *The psychogenesis of mental disease* (pp. 3–151). London: Routledge & Kegan Paul. (Original work published 1907)

Kalsched, D. E. (1996). *The inner world of trauma: Archetypal defenses of the personal spirit.* New York: Routledge.

Karpman, S. (1968). Fairly tales and script drama analysis. *Transactional Analysis Bulletin, 7*(26), 39–43.

Kernberg, O. F. (1975). *Borderline conditions and pathological narcissism.* New York: Aronson.

Kihlstrom, J. F. (1984). Conscious, subconscious, unconscious: A cognitive perspective. In K. S. Bowers & D. Meichenbaum (Eds.), *The unconscious reconsidered* (pp. 149–211). New York: Wiley.

Kirmayer, L. J. (1994). Pacing the void: Social and cultural dimensions of dissociation. In D. Spiegel (Ed.), *Dissociation: Culture, mind and body* (pp. 91–122). Washington, DC: American Psychiatric Press.

Kluft, R. P. (1982). Varieties of hypnotic interventions in the treatment of multiple personality. *American Journal of Clinical Hypnosis, 24*(4), 230–240.

Kluft, R. P. (1984). Aspects of the treatment of multiple personality disorder. *Psychiatric Annals, 14,* 51–55.

Kluft, R. P. (1985a). Childhood multiple personality disorder: Predictors, clinical findings, and treatment results. In R. P. Kluft (Ed.), *Childhood antecedents of multiple personality disorder* (pp. 167–196). Washington, DC: American Psychiatric Press.

Kluft, R. P. (1985b). The natural history of multiple personality disorder. In R. P. Kluft (Ed.), *Childhood antecedents of multiple personality disorder* (pp. 197–238). Washington, DC: American Psychiatric Press.

Kluft, R. P. (1987). First rank symptoms as diagnostic indicators of multiple personality disorder. *American Journal of Psychiatry, 144,* 293–298.

Kluft, R. P. (1988). On treating the older patient with multiple personality disorder: "Race against time" or "make haste slowly?" *American Journal of Clinical Hypnosis, 30,* 257–266.

Kluft, R. P. (1989). Playing for time: Temporizing techniques in the treatment of multiple personality disorder. *American Journal of Clinical Hypnosis, 32,* 90–98.

Kluft, R. P. (1990). Incest and subsequent revictimization: The case of therapist–patient exploitation, with a description of the sitting duck syndrome. In R. Kluft (Ed.), *Incest-related syndromes of adult psychopathology* (pp. 263–284). Washington, DC: American Psychiatric Press.

Kluft, R. P. (1993a). Basic principles of conducting the psychotherapy of multiple personality disorder. In R. P. Kluft & C. G. Fine (Eds.), *Clinical perspectives on multiple personality disorder* (pp. 19–50). Washington, DC: American Psychiatric Press.

Kluft, R. P. (1993b). The initial stages of psychotherapy in the treatment of multiple personality disorder patients. *Dissociation, 6,* 145–161.

Kluft, R. P. (1993c). Treatment of dissociative disorder patients: An overview of discoveries, successes, and failures. *Dissociation, 6,* 87–101.

Kluft, R. P. (1994a). Treatment trajectories in multiple personality disorder. *Dissociation, 7,* 63–76.

Kluft, R. P. (1994b). Applications of hypnotic interventions. *Hypnos, XXI*(4), 205–214.

Kluft, R. P. (1998). Reflections on the traumatic memories of dissociative identity disorder patients. In S. J. Lynn & K. M. McConkey (Eds.), *Truth in memory* (pp. 304–322). New York: Guilford Press.

Kluft, R. P. (1999a). Current issues in dissociative identity disorder. *Journal of Practical Psychiatry and Behavioral Health, 5,* 3–19.

Kluft, R. P. (1999b). An overview of the psychotherapy of dissociative identity disorder. *American Journal of Psychotherapy, 53,* 289–319.

Kluft, R. P. (2000). The psychoanalytic psychotherapy of dissociative identity disorder in the context of trauma therapy. *Psychoanalytic Inquiry, 20,* 259–286.

Kluft, R. P. (2009). A clinician's understanding of dissociation: Fragments of an acquaintance. In P. F. Dell & J. A. O'Neil (Eds.), *Dissociation and the dissociative disorders: DSM-V and beyond* (pp. 599–624). New York: Routledge.

Kluft, R. P., & Fine, C. (1993). *Clinical perspectives on multiple personality disorder.* Washington DC: American Psychiatric Press.

Kluft, R. P., & Fine, C. (2009). Hypnosis in the treatment of DID: An advanced workshop. Presented at the International Society for the Study of Dissociation 26th Annual Conference. Washington DC, November 23, 2009.

Kohut, H. (1971). *The analysis of the self.* New York: International University Press.

Kohut, H. (1984). *How does analysis cure?* Chicago: University of Chicago Press.

Kroll, J. (1993). *PTSD/borderlines in therapy.* New York: W.W. Norton and Co.

Kupersmid, J. (1993). Freud's rationale for abandoning the seduction theory. *Psychoanalytic Psychology, 10,* 275–290.

Laplanche, J., & Pontalis, J. B. (1973). *The language of psycho-analysis* (D. Nicholson-Smith, Trans.). New York: Norton.

Laub, D., & Auerhahn, N. C. (1993). Knowing and not knowing massive psychic trauma: Forms of traumatic memory. *International Journal of Psychoanalysis, 74,* 287–302.

LeDoux, J. E. (2002). *The synaptic self: How our brains become who we are.* New York: Penguin.

Levine, P. A. (1997). *Waking the tiger: Healing trauma.* Berkeley, CA: North Atlantic Books.

Lewis, C. S. (1938). *Out of the silent planet.* New York: Scribner.

Lewis, H. B. (1981). *Freud and modern psychology, Vol. 1: The emotional basis of mental illness.* New York: Plenum Press.

Lewis-Fernandez, R. (1994). Culture and dissociation: A comparison of Ataque de Nervos among Puerto Ricans and possession syndrome in India. In D. Spiegel (Ed.), *Dissociation, culture, mind and body* (pp. 155–163). Washington, DC: American Psychiatric Press.

Lifton, R. J., & Markusen, E. (1990). *The genocidal mentality.* New York: Basic Books.

Linehan, M. (1993). *Cognitive-behavioral treatment of borderline personality disorder.* New York: Guilford Press.

Liotti, G. (1992). Disorganized/disoriented attachment in the etiology of the dissociative disorders. *Dissociation, 5,* 196–204.

Liotti, G. (1995). Disorganized/disoriented attachment in the psychotherapy of the dissociative disorders. In S. Goldberg, R. Moiré, & J. Kerr (Eds.), *Attachment theory: Social, developmental, and clinical perspectives* (pp. 343–363). Hillsdale, NJ: Analytic Press.

Liotti, G. (1999). Understanding the dissociative processes: The contribution of attachment theory. *Psychoanalytic Inquiry, 19,* 757–783.

Liotti, G. (2004). Trauma, dissociation, and disorganized attachment: Three strands of a single braid. *Psychotherapy: Theory, Research, Practice, Training, 41,* 472–486.

Liotti, G. (2006). A model of dissociation based on attachment theory and research. *Journal of Trauma and Dissociation, 7,* 55–74.

Liotti, G. (2011). Attachment disorganization and the clinical dialogue: Theme and variations. In J. Solomon & C. George (Eds.), *Disorganization of attachment and caregiving* (pp. 383–413). New York: Guilford.

Liotti, G., Cortina, M., & Farina, B. (2008). Attachment theory and multiple integrated treatments of borderline personality disorder. *Journal of the American Academy of Psychoanalysis and Dynamic Psychiatry, 36,* 295–315.

Liotti, G., & Gumley, A. (2008). An attachment perspective on schizophrenia: The role of disorganized attachment, dissociation and mentalization. In A. Moskowitz, I. Schafer, & M. J. Dorahy (Eds.), *Psychosis, trauma, and dissociation: Emerging perspectives on severe psychopathology* (pp. 117–133). London: Wiley.

Liotti, G., Intreccialagli, B., & Cecere, F. (1991). Esperienza di lutto della madre e predisposizione ai disturbi dissociativi nella prole: Uno studio caso-controllo [Losses in the mother's life and predisposition to the dissociative disorders in the offspring: A case-control study. *Rivista di Psichiatria, 26,* 283–291.

Loewenstein, R. J. (1990). Somatoform disorders in victims of incest and child abuse. In R. P. Kluft (Ed.), *Incest-related disorders of adult psychopathology* (pp. 75–113). Washington, DC: American Psychiatric Press.

Loewenstein, R. J. (1991). An office mental status examination for complex chronic dissociative symptoms and multiple personality disorder. *Psychiatric Clinics of North America, 14,* 567–604.

Loewenstein, R. J. (1993). Posttraumatic and dissociative aspects of transference and counter-transference in the treatment of multiple personality disorder. In R. P. Kluft & C. G. Fine (Eds.), *Clinical perspectives on multiple personality disorder* (pp. 51–85). Washington, DC: American Psychiatric Press.

Luxenberg, T., Spinazzola, J., & Van der Kolk, B. A. (2001). Complex trauma and disorders of extreme stress (DESNOS) diagnosis, Part 1: Assessment. *New Directions in Psychiatry, 21*(25), 373–394.

Lyons-Ruth, K. (1996). Attachment relationships among children with aggressive behavior problems: The role of disorganized early attachment patterns. *Journal of Consulting and Clinical Psychology, 64,* 64–73.

Lyons-Ruth, K. (1999). Two-person unconscious: Intersubjective dialogue, enactive relational representation, and the emergence of new forms of relational organization. *Psychoanalytic Inquiry, 19,* 576–617.

Lyons-Ruth, K. (2001). The two-person construction of defenses: Disorganized attachment strategies, unintegrated mental states, and hostile/helpless relational processes. *Psychologist Psychoanalyst, 21*(1), 40–45.

Lyons-Ruth, K. (2003). Dissociation and the parent–infant dialogue: A longitudinal perspective from attachment research. *Journal of the American Psychoanalytic Association, 51,* 883–911.

Lyons-Ruth, K. (2006). The interface between attachment and intersubjectivity: Perspective from the longitudinal study of disorganized attachment. *Psychoanalytic Inquiry, 26*, 595–616.

MacLean, P. D. (1990). *The triune brain in evolution.* New York: Plenum Press.

Main, M., & Hesse, E. (1990). Parents' unresolved traumatic experiences are related to infant disorganized attachment status: Is frightened and/or frightening parental behavior the linking mechanism? In M. T. Greenberg, D. Cicchetti, & E. M. Cummings (Eds.), *Attachment in the preschool years* (pp. 161–182). Chicago: Chicago University Press.

Main, M., & Morgan, H. (1996). Disorganization and disorientation in infant strange situation behavior: Phenotypic resemblance to dissociative states. In L. K. Michelson & W. J. Ray (Eds.), *Handbook of dissociation: Theoretical, empirical and clinical perspectives* (pp. 107–138). New York: Plenum Press.

Main, M., & Solomon, J. (1986). Discovery of a new, insecure-disorganized/disoriented attachment pattern. In M. Yogman & T. B. Brazelton (Eds.), *Affective development in infancy* (pp. 95–124). Norwood, NY: Ablex Press.

Main, M., & Solomon, J. (1990). Procedures for identifying infants as disorganized/ disoriented during the Ainsworth Strange Situation. In M. T. Greenberg, D. Cicchetti, & E. M. Cummings (Eds.), *Attachment in the preschool years* (pp. 121–160). Chicago: Chicago University Press.

Martínez-Taboas, A. (1991). Multiple personality in Puerto Rico: Analysis of fifteen cases. *Dissociation, 4*, 189–192.

Marx, B. P., Forsyth, J. P., Gallup, G. G., Fusé, T., & Lexington, J. M. (2008). Tonic immobility as an evolved predator defense: Implications for sexual assault survivors. *Clinical Psychology: Science and Practice, 15*, 74–90.

Masson, J. M. (1984). *The assault on truth.* New York: Signet.

Masson, J. M. (Ed.). (1985). *The complete letters of Sigmund Freud to Wilhelm Fliess.* Cambridge, MA: Harvard University Press.

McNevin, S. H., & Rivera, M. (2001). Obsessive compulsive spectrum disorders in individuals with dissociative disorders, *Journal of Trauma & Dissociation, 2*(4), 117–13.1

McShane, J. M., & Zirkel, S. (2008). Dissociation in the binge–purge cycle of bulimia nervosa, *Journal of Trauma & Dissociation, 9*(4), 463–479.

McWilliams, N. (1994). *Psychoanalytic diagnosis: Understanding personality structure in the clinical process.* New York: Guilford.

Meltzoff, A. N., & Moore M. K. (1977). Imitation of facial and manual gestures by human neonates. *Science, 198*, 75–78.

Middleton, W., & Butler, J. (1998). Dissociative identity disorder: An Australian series. *Australian and New Zealand Journal of Psychiatry, 32*, 794–804.

Middleton, W., Dorahy, M. J., & Moskowitz, A. (2008). Historical conceptions of dissociation and psychosis: Nineteenth and early twentieth century perspectives on psychopathology. In A. Moskowitz, I. Schafer, & M. J. Dorahy (Eds.), *Psychosis, trauma, and dissociation: Emerging perspectives on severe psychopathology* (pp. 9–20). London: Wiley.

Millon, T. (1981). *Disorders of personality, DSM-III, axis II.* New York: Wiley.

Mitchell, S. (1991). Contemporary perspectives on self: Toward an integration. *Psychoanalytic Dialogues, 1*, 121–147.

Mitchell, S. (1993). Hope and dread in psychoanalysis. New York: Basic Books.

Mitchell, S. (2000). *Relationality: From attachment to intersubjectivity*. Hillsdale, NJ: Analytic Press.

Moskowitz, A. (2004). Scared stiff: Catatonia as an evolutionary-based fear response. *Psychological Review, 111*, 984–1002.

Moskowitz, A. (2008). Association and dissociation in the historical concept of schizophrenia. In A. Moskowitz, I. Schafer, & M. J. Dorahy (Eds.), *Psychosis, trauma, and dissociation: Emerging perspectives on severe psychopathology* (pp. 35–50). London: Wiley.

Moskowitz, A., Read, J., Farrelly, S., Rudegeair, T., & Williams, O. (2009). Are psychotic symptoms traumatic in origin and dissociative in kind? In P. F. Dell & J. F. O'Neil (Eds.), *Dissociation and the dissociative disorders: DSM-V and beyond* (pp. 523–534). New York: Routledge.

Mukamel, R., Ekstrom, A.D., Kaplan, J., Iacoboni, M., & Fried, I. (2010) Single-neuron responses in humans during execution and observation of actions. *Current Biology*, DOI: 10.1016/j.cub.2010.02.045

Myers, C. S. (1940). *Shell shock in France 1914–1918*. Cambridge, MA: Cambridge University Press.

Myers, F. (1887). Automatic writing. *Proceedings of the Society for Psychical Research, 4*, 209–261.

Nijenhuis, E. R. S. (2000). Somatoform dissociation: Major symptoms of dissociative disorders. *Journal of Trauma & Dissociation, 1*(4), 7–32.

Nijenhuis, E. R. S. (2003). Looking into the brains of patients with dissociative disorders. *The International Society for the Study of Dissociation News, 21*(2), 6–9.

Nijenhuis, E. R. S. (2004). *Somatoform dissociation: Phenomena, measurement, and theoretical issues*. New York, NY: Norton.

Nijenhuis, E. R. S. (2009). Somatoform dissociation and somatoform dissociative disorders. In P. F. Dell & J. A. O'Neil (Eds.), *Dissociation and dissociative disorders: DSM-V and beyond* (pp. 259–272). New York: Routledge.

Nijenhuis, E. R. S. & den Boer, J. A. (2007). Psychobiology of traumatization and trauma-related structural dissociation of the personality. In E. Vermetten, M. Dorahy, & D. Spiegel (Eds.), *Traumatic dissociation: Neurobiology and treatment* (pp. 219–236). Washington DC: American Psychiatric Publishing.

Nijenhuis, E. R. S., & den Boer, J. A. (2009). Psychobiology of traumatization and trauma-related structural dissociation of the personality. In P. F. Dell & J. A. O'Neil (Eds.), *Dissociation and the dissociative disorders: DSM-V and beyond* (pp. 337–365). New York: Routledge.

Nijenhuis, E. R. S., Spinhoven, P., Vanderlinden, J., Van Dyck, R., & Van der Hart, O. (1998). Somatoform dissociative symptoms as related to animal defensive reactions to predatory imminence and injury. *Journal of Abnormal Psychology, 107*, 63–73.

Nijenhuis, E. R. S., Spinhoven, P., Van Dyck, R., Van der Hart, O., & Vanderlinden, J. (1996). The development and the psychometric characteristics of the Somatoform Dissociation Questionnaire (SDQ20). *Journal of Nervous and Mental Disease, 184*, 688–694.

Nijenhuis, E. R. S., Spinhoven, P., Van Dyck, R., Van der Hart, O., & Vanderlinden, J. (1997). The development of the Somatoform Dissociation Questionnaire (SDQ5) as a screening instrument for dissociative disorders. *Acta Psychiatrica Scandinavica, 96,* 311–318.

Nijenhuis, E. R. S., & Van der Hart, O. (1999). Forgetting and reexperiencing trauma. In J. M. Goodwin & R. Attias (Eds.), *Splintered reflections: Images of the body in trauma* (pp. 39–65). New York: Basic Books.

Nijenjuis, E. R. S., van Engen, A., Kusters, I., & Van der Hart, O. (2001). Peritraumatic somatoform and psychological dissociation in relation to recall of childhood sexual abuse. *Journal of Trauma & Dissociation, 2*(3), 49–68.

Nijenhuis, E. R. S., Van der Hart, O., Kruger, K., & Steele, K. (2004). Somatoform dissociation, trauma, and defense. *Australia & New Zealand Journal of Psychiatry, 38,* 678–686.

Nijenhuis, E. R. S., Vanderlinden, J., & Spinhoven, P. (1998). Animal defensive reactions as a model for trauma-induced dissociative reaction. *Journal of Traumatic Stress, 11*(2), 243–260.

Nijenhuis, E. R. S., Van Dyck, R., Spinhoven, P., Van der Hart, O., Chatrou, M., Vanderlinden, J., et al. (1999). Somatoform dissociation discriminates among diagnostic categories over and above general psychopathology. *Australia and New Zealand Journal of Psychiatry, 33*(4), 511–520.

Ogawa, J. R., Sroufe, L. A. Weinfeld, N. S., Carlson, E. A., & Egeland, B. (1997). Development and the fragmented self: Longitudinal study of dissociative symptomology in nonclinical sample. *Development and Psychopathy, 9,* 855–879.

Ogden, T. H. (1983). The concept of internal object relations. In J. S. Grotstein & D. B. Rinsley (Eds.), *Fairbairn and the origin of object relations* (pp. 88–111). New York: Other Press, 2000.

Ogden, T. H. (1986). *The matrix of the mind: Object relations in the psychoanalytic dialogue.* Northvale, NJ: Aronson.

O'Neil, J. (2009). Dissociative multiplicity and psychoanalysis. In P. F. Dell & J. F. O'Neil (Eds.), *Dissociation and the dissociative disorders:* DSM-V *and beyond* (pp. 287–325). New York: Routledge.

Orwell, G. (1949). *1984.* New York: Signet.

Oxnam, R. (2006). *A fractured mind.* New York: Hyperion.

Ozer, E. J., Best, S. R., Lipsey, T. L., & Weiss, D. S. (2003). Predictors of posttraumatic stress disorder and symptoms in adults: A meta-analysis. *Psychological Bulletin, 129,* 52–73.

Pearlman, L. A., & Saakvitne, K. W. (1995). Countertransference responses to dissociative processes in psychotherapy. In L. A. Pearlman & K. W. Saakvitne (Eds.), *Trauma and the therapist* (pp. 120–146). New York: Norton.

Perry, B. D. (1999). The memory of states: How the brain stores and retrieves traumatic experience. In J. Goodwin & R. Attias (Eds.), *Splintered reflections: Images of the body in treatment* (pp. 9–38). New York: Basic Books.

Perry, J. C. & Herman, J. L. (1993). Trauma and defense in the etiology of borderline personality disorder. In J. Paris (Ed.), *Borderline personality disorder: Etiology and treatment.* Washington DC: American Psychiatric Press.

Petrie, D. (Director), & Stern, S. (Teleplay). (1976). *Sybil* [Motion picture]. United States: Lorimar.

Philips, M. L., Medford, N., Senior, C., Bullmore, E. T., Suckling, J., Brammer, M. J., Andrew, C., Sierra, M., Williams, S.C.R., & David, A. S. (2001). Depersonalization disorder: Thinking without feeling. *Psychiatry Research: Neuroimaging Section, 108*, 145–160.

Pines, M. (1989). On history and psychoanalysis. *Psychoanalytic Psychology, 6*, 121–136.

Polanyi, M. (1967). *The tacit dimension.* New York: Anchor Books.

Porges, S. W. (2001). The polyvagal theory: Phylogenetic substrates of a social nervous system. *International Journal of Psychophysiology, 42*, 123–146.

Porges, S. W. (2003). The polyvagal theory: Phylogenetic contributions to social behavior. *Physiology of Behavior, 79*, 503–513.

Prince, M. (1969). *The dissociation of a personality.* New York: Greenwood Press. (Original work published 1906)

Putnam, F. W. (1989). *The diagnosis and treatment of multiple personality disorder.* New York: Guilford Press.

Putnam, F. W. (1991). Recent research on multiple personality disorder. *Psychiatric Clinics of North America, 14*, 489–517.

Putnam, F. W. (1992). Discussion: Are alter personalities fragments or figments? *Psychoanalytic Inquiry, 12*, 95–111.

Putnam, F. W. (1997). *Dissociation in children and adolescents: A developmental perspective.* New York: Guilford Press.

Putnam, F. W., Guroff, J. J., Silberman, E. K., Barban, L., & Post, R. (1986). The clinical phenomenology of multiple personality disorder: Review of 100 recent cases. *Journal of Clinical Psychiatry, 47*, 285–293.

Rachman, A. W. (1997). *Sándor Ferenczi: The psychotherapist of tenderness and passion.* Northvale, NJ: Aronson.

Raine, N. V. (1999). *After silence: Rape and my journey back.* New York: Crown.

Randal, P., Geekie, J., Lambrecht, I., & Taitimu, M. (2008). Dissociation, psychosis and spirituality: Whose voices are we hearing? In A. Moskowitz, I. Schafer, & M. Dorahy (Eds.), *Dissociation and psychosis: Emerging perspectives on severe psychopathology* (pp. 333–345). New York: Wiley.

Rauch, S. L., van der Kolk, B. A., Fisler, R. E., Alpert, N. M, Orr, S. P., Savage, C. R., Fishman, A. J., Jenike, N. A., & Pitman, R. K. (1996). A symptom provocation study of posttraumatic stress disorder using positron emission tomography and script-driven imagery. *Archives of General Psychiatry, 53*, 380–387.

Read, J., Perry, B. D., Moskowitz, A., & Connolly, J. (2001). The contribution of early traumatic events to schizophrenia in some patients: A traumagenic neurodevelopmental model. *Psychiatry, 64*, 319–340.

Reinders, A. A. T. S., Nijenhuis, E. R. S., Paans, A. M. J., Korf, J., Willemsen, A. T. M., & den Boer, J. A. (2003). One brain, two selves. *NeuroImage, 20*, 2119–2125.

Reinders, A. A. T. S., Nijenhuis, E. R. S., Quak, J., Korf, J., Paans, A. M. J., Haaksma, J., Willemsen, A. T. M., & den Boer, J. A. (2006). Psychobiological characteristics of dissociative identity disorder: A symptom provocation study. *Biological Psychiatry, 60*, 730–740.

Richter, C. P. (1957). On the phenomenon of sudden death in animals and man. *Psychosomatic Medicine, 19*, 191–198.

Rivera, M. (1991). Multiple personality disorder and the social system: 185 cases. *Dissociation, 4*, 79–82.

Rosenfeld, H. (1971). A psychoanalytic approach to the theory of the life and death instincts: An investigation into the aggressive aspects of narcissism. *International Journal of Psychoanalysis, 52*, 169–178.

Ross, C. A. (1989). *Multiple personality disorder*. New York: Wiley.

Ross, C. A. (1991). Epidemiology of multiple personality disorder and dissociation. *Psychiatric Clinics of North America, 14*, 503–517.

Ross, C. A. (1997). *Dissociative identity disorder: Diagnosis, clinical features, and treatment of multiple personality*. New York: Wiley.

Ross, C. A. (2007). Borderline personality disorder and dissociation. *Journal of Trauma and Dissociation, 8*, 71–20.

Ross, C. A. (2009, May). *Members' clinical corner: Expert commentary: How the dissociative structural model integrates DID and PTSD, plus a wide range of comorbidity*. McLean, VA: International Society for the Study of Trauma and Dissociation. Retrieved from http://www.isst-d.org/

Ross, C. A., Heber, S., Norton, G. R., Anderson, D., Anderson, G., & Barchet, P. (1989). The Dissociative Disorders Interview Schedule: A structured interview. *Dissociation, 2*(3), 169–189.

Ross, C. A., & Keyes, B. (2004). Dissociation and schizophrenia. *Journal of Trauma and Dissociation, 5*, 69–83.

Ross, C. A., Kronson, J., Doensgen, S., Barkman, K., Clark, P., & Rockman, G. (1992). Dissociative comorbidity in 100 chemically dependent patients. *Hospital and Community Psychiatry, 43*, 840–842.

Ross, C. A., Norton, G. R., & Wozney, K. (1989). Multiple personality disorder: An analysis of 236 cases. *Canadian Journal of Psychiatry, 34*, 413–418.

Ross, J. M. (1982). Oedipus revisited—Laius and the "Laius complex." *The Psychoanalytic Study of the Child, 37*, 169–174.

Russell, D. (1986). *The secret trauma: Incest in the lives of girls and women*. New York: Basic Books.

Ryle, A. (1994). Projective identification: A particular form of reciprocal role procedure. *British Journal of Medical Psychology, 76*, 107–114.

Ryle, A. (1997a). Cognitive analytic therapy and borderline personality disorder: The model and the method. New York: Wiley.

Ryle, A. (1997b). The structure and development of borderline personality disorder: A proposed model. *British Journal of Psychiatry, 170*, 82–87.

Ryle, A., & Kerr, I. A. (2002). *Introducing cognitive analytic therapy: Principles and practice*. New York: Wiley.

Salter, A. (2003). *Predators: Pedophiles, rapists and other sex offenders*. New York: Basic Books.

Sandler, J. (1976). Countertransference and role-responsiveness. *International Review of Psychoanalysis, 3*, 43–47.

Sar, V., Akyüz, G., & Dogan, O. (2006). Prevalence of dissociative disorders among women in the general population. *Psychiatry Research, 149*(1–3), 169–176.

Sar, V., Koyuncu, A., Ozturk, E., Yargic, L. I., Kundakci, T., Yazici, A. et al. (2007). Dissociative disorders in the psychiatric emergency ward. *General Hospital Psychiatry, 29*, 45–50.

Sar, V., Kundakci, T., Kiziltan, E., Yargic, I. L., Tutkun, H., Bakim, B., & Özdemir, O. (2003). The axis-I dissociative disorder comorbidity of borderline personality disorder among psychiatric outpatients. *Journal of Trauma and Dissociation, 4*(1), 119–136.

Scaer, R. C. (2001). *The body bears the burden: Trauma, dissociation, and disease.* Binghamton, NY: Haworth Medical Press.

Scaer, R. C. (2005). *The trauma spectrum: Hidden wounds and human resiliency.* New York: Norton.

Schneider, K. (1959). *Psychisher befund and psychiatrische diagnose* [Clinical psychopathology] (5th ed.). New York: Grune and Stratton. (Original work published 1939)

Schore, A. (2002a). Advances in neuropsychoanalysis, attachment theory, and trauma research: Implications for self psychology. *Psychoanalytic Inquiry, 22,* 433–484.

Schore, A. (2002b). Dysregulation of the right brain: A fundamental mechanism of traumatic attachment and the psychopathogenesis of posttraumatic stress disorder. *Australian and New Zealand Journal of Psychiatry, 36,* 9–30.

Schore, A. (2008). Paradigm shift: The right brain and the relational unconscious. *Psychologist–Psychoanalyst, 28*(3), 20–26.

Schore, A. N. (2003a). *Affect dysregulation and disorders of the self.* New York: Norton.

Schore, A. N. (2003b). *Affect regulation and the repair of the self.* New York: Norton.

Schore, A. N. (2009). Attachment trauma and the developing right brain: Origins of pathological dissociation. In: P. F. Dell & J. F. O'Neil (Eds.), *Dissociation and the dissociative disorders: DSM-V and beyond* (pp. 107–141). New York: Routledge.

Schwartz, H. L. (1994). From dissociation to negotiation: A relational psychoanalytic perspective on multiple personality disorder. *Psychoanalytic Psychology, 11,* 189–231.

Schwartz, H. L. (2000). *Dialogues with forgotten voices: Relational perspectives on child abuse trauma and treatment of dissociative disorders.* New York: Basic Books.

Schwartz, R. (1995). *Internal family systems therapy.* New York: Guilford Press.

Shapiro, F. (1995). *Eye movement desensitization and reprocessing: Basic principles, protocols and procedures.* New York: Guilford Press.

Shapiro, F. (2001). *Eye movement desensitization and reprocessing: Basic principles, protocols and procedures* (2nd ed.). New York: Guilford Press.

Shengold, L. (1989). *Soul murder.* New Haven, CT: Yale University Press.

Shusta, S. (1999), Successful treatment of refractory obsessive-compulsive disorder. *American Journal of Psychotherapy, 53,* 372–391.

Shusta-Hochberg, S. R. (2004). Therapeutic hazards of treating child alters as real children in dissociative identity disorder. *Journal of Trauma and Dissociation, 5*(1), 13–27.

Sidis, B. (1904). *Multiple personality: An experimental investigation into the nature of human individuality.* New York: Appleton.

Siegel, D. J. (1999). *The developing mind: Toward a neurobiology of interpersonal experience.* New York: Guilford Press.

Simeon, D., & Abugel, J. (2006). *Feeling unreal: Depersonalization disorder and the loss of the self.* New York: Oxford University Press.

Slavin, M. O., & Kreigman, D. (1992). *The adaptive design of the human psyche: Psychoanalysis, evolutionary biology, and the therapeutic process.* New York: Guilford Press.

Somer, E. (2004). Trance possession disorder in Judaism: Sixteenth-century dybbuks in the Near East. *Journal of Trauma and Dissociation, 5*(2), 131–146.

Spiegel, D. (1986). Dissociation, double binds, and posttraumatic stress in multiple personality disorder. In B. Braun (Ed.), *Treatment of multiple personality disorder* (pp. 63–77). Washington, DC: American Psychiatric Press.

Spiegel, D. (1990a). Hypnosis, dissociation, and trauma: Hidden and overt observers. In J. L. Singer (Ed.), *Repression and dissociation: Implications for personality theory, psychopathology, and health* (pp. 121–142). Chicago: University of Chicago Press.

Spiegel, D. (1990b). Trauma, dissociation, and hypnosis. In R. Kluft (Ed.), *Incest-related syndromes of adult psychopathology* (pp. 247–262). Washington, DC: American Psychiatric Press.

Spiegel, D. (1994). Introduction. In D. Spiegel (Ed.), *Dissociation, culture, mind and body* (pp. ix–xv). Washington, DC: American Psychiatric Press.

Spiegel, D. (2009, January). *Members' clinical corner: Expert commentary: Dissociation and ASD and PTSD—DSM-V considerations.* McLean, VA: International Society for the Study of Trauma and Dissociation. Retrieved from http://www.isst-d.org/

Steele, K., Van der Hart, O., & Nijenhuis, E. R. S. (2005). Phase-oriented treatment of structural dissociation in complex traumatization: Overcoming trauma-related phobias. *Journal of Trauma and Dissociation, 6*(3), 11–54.

Steinberg, M. (1994a). *Interviewer's guide to the Structured Clinical Interview for DSM-IV Dissociative Disorders—Revised (SCID-D-R)* (2nd ed.). Washington, DC: American Psychiatric Press.

Steinberg, M. (1994b). *Structured Clinical Interview for DSM-IV Dissociative Disorders, Revised (SCID-D-R)* (2nd ed.). Washington, DC: American Psychiatric Press.

Steinberg, M. (1995). *Handbook for the assessment of dissociation: A clinical guide.* Washington, DC: American Psychiatric Press.

Steinberg, M., Cicchetti, D., Buchanan, J., Hall, P., & Rounsaville, B. (1993). Clinical assessment of dissociative symptoms and disorders: The Structured Interview for *DSM-IV* Dissociative Disorders (SCID-D). *Dissociation: Progress in the Dissociative Disorders, 61*(1), 108–120.

Stern, A. (1938). Psychoanalytic investigation of and therapy in the borderline group of neuroses. *Psychoanalytic Quarterly, 7*, 467–489.

Stern, D. B. (1997). *Unformulated experience: From dissociation to imagination in psychoanalysis.* Hillsdale, NJ: Analytic Press.

Stern, D. N. (1985). *Interpersonal world of the infant.* New York: Basic Books.

Stolorow, R. D., & Atwood, G. E. (1979). *Faces in a cloud: Subjectivity in personality theory.* New York: Aronson.

Stone, M. (1979). *Ancient mirrors of womanhood.* Boston: Beacon Press.

Sullivan, H. S. (1953). *The interpersonal theory of psychiatry.* New York: Norton.

Tabin, J. (1993). Freud's shift from the seduction theory: Some overlooked reality factors. *Psychoanalytic Psychology, 10*, 291–298.

Tarnopolsky, A. (2003). The concept of dissociation in early psychoanalytic writers. *Journal of Trauma and Dissociation, 4*, 7–25.

Terr, L. (1990). *Too scared to cry: How trauma affects children and ultimately us all.* New York: Basic Books.

Terr, L. C. (1994). *Unchained memories: True stories of traumatic memories, lost and found.* New York: Basic Books.

Thomas, A. (2001). Factitious and malingered dissociative identity disorder: Clinical features observed in 18 cases. *Journal of Trauma and Dissociation, 2*(4), 59–77.

Trevarthen, C. (2003). Neuroscience and intrinsic psychodynamics: Current knowledge and potential for therapy. In J. Corrigall & H. Wilkinson (Eds.), *Revolutionary connections: Psychotherapy and neuroscience* (pp. 53–78). London: Karnac.

Trevarthen, C. (2009). The function of emotion in infancy: The regulation and communication of rhythm, sympathy, and meaning in human development. In D. Fosha, D. Siegel, & M. Soloman (Eds.), *The healing power of emotion: Affective neuroscience, development, and clinical process* (pp. 55–85). New York: Norton.

Trevarthen, C., & Aitken, K. J. (2001). Infant intersubjectivity: Research, theory and clinical applications. *Annual Research Review, Journal of Child Psychology and Psychiatry, 42*(1), 3–48.

Tronick, E. Z. (1989). Emotions and emotional communication in infants. *American Psychologist, 44*(2), 112–119.

Twombly, J. (2000). Incorporating EMDR and EMDR adaptations into the treatment of clients with dissociative identity disorder. *Journal of Trauma and Dissociation, 1*(2), 61–81.

University of California – Los Angeles (2010, April 13). First direct recording made of mirror neurons in human brain. *ScienceDaily.*

Van Derbur, M. (2003). *Miss America by day.* Denver, CO: Oak Hill Ridge Press.

Van der Hart, O. (2000, November). *Dissociation: Toward a resolution of 150 years of confusion.* Paper presented at the 17th International Fall Conference of the International Society of Dissociation, San Antonio, TX.

Van der Hart, O., & Brown, P. (1992). Abreaction re-evaluated. *Dissociation, 5*(3), 127–140.

Van der Hart, O., & Dorahy, M. J. (2009). History of the concept of dissociation. In P. Dell & J. O'Neil (Eds.), *Dissociation and dissociative disorders: DSM-IV and beyond* (pp. 3–26). New York: Routledge.

Van der Hart, O., & Friedman, B. (1989). A reader's guide to Pierre Janet on dissociation: A neglected intellectual heritage. *Dissociation, 2*, 3–15.

Van der Hart, O., Nijenhuis, E. R. S., & Steele, K. (2006). *The haunted self: Structural dissociation and the treatment of chronic traumatization.* New York: Norton.

Van der Hart, O., Nijenhuis, E. R. S., Steele, K., & Brown, D. (2004). Trauma-related dissociation: Conceptual clarity, lost and found. *Australia and New Zealand Journal of Psychiatry, 38*, 906–914.

Van der Hart, O., Van der Kolk, B. A., & Boon, S. (1998). Treatment of dissociative disorders. In J. D. Bremner & C. R. Marmar (Eds.), *Trauma, memory, and dissociation* (pp. 253–283). Washington, DC: American Psychiatric Press.

Van der Hart, O., Van Dijke, A., Van Son, M., & Steele, K. (2000). Somatoform dissociation in traumatized World War I combat soldiers: A neglected clinical heritage. *Journal of Trauma and Dissociation, 1*(4), 33–66.

Van der Kolk, B. A. (1996a). The body keeps the score: Approaches to the psychobiology of posttraumatic stress disorder. In B. A. Van der Kolk, A. C. McFarlane, & L. Weisaeth (Eds.), *Traumatic stress: The effects of overwhelming experience on mind, body and society* (pp. 214–241). New York: Guilford Press.

Van der Kolk, B. A. (1996b). The complexity of adaptation to trauma: Self-regulation, stimulus discrimination, and characterological development. In B. A. Van der Kolk, A. C. McFarlane, & L. Weisaeth (Eds.), *Traumatic stress: The effects of overwhelming experience on mind, body and society* (pp. 182–213). New York: Guilford Press.

Van der Kolk, B. A. (1996c). Trauma and memory. In B. A. Van der Kolk, A. C. McFarlane, & L. Weisaeth (Eds.), *Traumatic stress: The effects of overwhelming experience on mind, body and society* (pp. 279–302). New York: Guilford Press.

Van der Kolk, B. A. (2005). Developmental trauma disorder: A new rational diagnosis for children with complex trauma histories. *Psychiatric Annals, 35*(5), 390–398.

Van der Kolk, B. A., & Van der Hart, O. (1989). Pierre Janet and the breakdown of adaptation in psychological trauma. *American Journal of Psychiatry, 146*(12), 1530–1540.

Vermetten, E., Schmal, C., Lindner, S., Loewenstein, R. J., & Bremner, J. D. (2006). Hippocampal and amygdalar volumes in dissociative identity disorder. *American Journal of Psychiatry, 163*, 630–636.

Waelde, L. C., Silvern, L., Carlson, E., Fairbank, J. A., & Kletter, H. (2009). Dissociation in PTSD. In P. F. Dell & J. A. O'Neil (Eds.), *Dissociation and the dissociative disorders: DSM-V and beyond* (pp. 447–456). New York: Routledge.

Waller, N., Putnam, F. W., & Carlson, E. B. (1996). Types of dissociation and dissociative types: A taxometric analysis of dissociative experiences. *Psychological Methods, 1*(3), 300–321.

Waller, N. G., & Ross, C. A. (1997). The prevalence and biometric structure of pathological dissociation in the general population: Taxometric and behavioral genetic findings. *Journal of Abnormal Psychology, 106*, 499–510.

Wallin, D. J. (2007). *Attachment in psychotherapy.* New York: Guilford Press.

Wheeler, K. (2007). *Psychotherapy for the advanced practice psychiatric nurse.* New York: Mosby.

Winnicott, D. W. (1958). The capacity to be alone. *International Journal of Psychoanalysis, 39*, 416–420.

Winnicott, D. W. (1971). Use of the object and relating through identifications, *Playing and reality* (pp. 86–94). New York: Tavistock.

Yehuda, R. (1998). Neuroendocrinology of trauma and PTSD. In *Psychological Trauma: Annual review of psychiatry* (Vol. 17, pp. 97–125). Washington, DC: American Psychiatric Press.

Yehuda, R. (2000). Cortisol alterations in PTSD. In A. Y. Shalev, R. Yehuda, & A. C. McFarlane (Eds.), *International handbook of human response to trauma* (pp. 265–284). New York: Kluwer Academic/Plenum.

Yen, S., Shea, M. T., Battle, C. L. et al. (2002). Traumatic exposure and posttraumatic stress disorder in borderline, schizotypal, avoidant, and obsessive-compulsive personality disorders: Findings from the collaborative longitudinal personality disorders study. *Journal of Nervous and Mental Disease, 190*, 510–518.

Zanarini, M. C. (1997). Evolving perspectives on the etiology of borderline personality disorder. In M. C. Zanarini (Ed.), *The role of sexual abuse in the etiology of borderline personality disorder* (pp. 1–14). Washington, DC: American
Psychiatric Press.

Zittel Conklin, C., & Westen, D. (2005). Borderline personality disorder in clinical
practice. *American Journal of Psychiatry, 162*, 867–875.

Index

DATE DUE

DEC 0 3 2012	
NOV 1 0 2012	
JUN 1 0 2013	
OCT 0 9 2013	
NOV 1 5 2013	

DEMCO, INC. 38-2931